Beware the Evil Eye

BEWARE
THE EVIL EYE

The Evil Eye in the Bible and the Ancient World

—Volume 4—

Postbiblical Israel and Early Christianity through Late Antiquity

JOHN H. ELLIOTT

 CASCADE *Books* • Eugene, Oregon

BEWARE THE EVIL EYE
The Evil Eye in the Bible and the Ancient World
Volume 4: Postbiblical Israel and Early Christianity through Late Antiquity

Copyright © 2017 John H. Elliott. All rights reserved. Except for brief quotations in critical publications or reviews, no part of this book may be reproduced in any manner without prior written permission from the publisher. Write: Permissions, Wipf and Stock Publishers, 199 W. 8th Ave., Suite 3, Eugene, OR 97401.

Cascade Books
An Imprint of Wipf and Stock Publishers
199 W. 8th Ave., Suite 3
Eugene, OR 97401

www.wipfandstock.com

PAPERBACK ISBN 13: 978-1-4982-3072-8
HARDCOVER ISBN 13: 978-1-4982-3074-2
EBOOK ISBN: 978-1-4982-3073-5

Cataloguing-in-Publication data:

Names: Elliott, John Hall

Title: Beware the evil eye : the evil eye in the Bible and the ancient world / John H. Elliott.

Volume 4: Postbiblical Israel and Early Christianity through Late Antiquity.

Description: Eugene, OR: Cascade Books, 2017 | Includes bibliographical references and index.

Identifiers: ISBN: 978-1-4982-3072-8 (paperback) | ISBN: 978-1-4982-3074-2 (hardcover) | ISBN: 978-1-4982-3073-5 (ebook).

Subjects: LCSH: Evil eye—Biblical teaching. | Evil eye—Mediterranean region. | Envy.

Classification: GN475.6 E45 2017 (print) | GN475.6 (ebook).

Manufactured in the U.S.A.   03/31/17

Für
Herman C. Waetjen
spannenden Lehrer, profunden Exeget,
treuen Freund, echten Mensch

"Of one hundred persons, ninety-nine have died of the Evil Eye, and one of natural causes."

(Rav, b. Bava Metzi'a 107b)

"I am of the seed of Joseph, over whom the Evil Eye has no power."

(Rabbi Yohanan, b. Bava Metzi'a 84a)

"An Evil-Eyeing person is never without cause for grief and despondency."

(Basil the Great, Homily 11, Concerning Envy)

CONTENTS

Illustrations | ix
Preface | xiii
Acknowledgments | xv
Abbreviations | xvi

1 **Postbiblical Israel: The Literary and Material Evidence** | 1
   Introduction | 1
   The Literary Evidence | 4
     The Evil Eye as Moral Failure | 5
     References to the Evil Eye Detected in Biblical Texts | 7
     Harm Caused by the Evil Eye | 10
     Fascinators | 11
     Victims of the Evil Eye and Dangerous Situations | 15
     Joseph and Solomon—Protectors against the Evil Eye | 19
   Repelling an Evil Eye | 25
     Protective Words (Spoken or Written) | 25
     Protective Actions, Objects, and Gestures | 28
     Amulets and Other Apotropaic Objects and Images | 31
   Conclusion of Chapter 1 | 46

2 **Early Christianity (and Islam) through Late Antiquity** | 48
   Introduction | 48
   The Literary and Written (Epistolary) Evidence | 51
     The Apostolic Fathers | 51
     Further References to the Evil-Eyeing Demon and the Devil | 55
     Terminology: *Bask-* Word Family, *Ophthalmos Ponêros* | 59
     The Evil Eye in the Apocryphal Acts | 60
     Cyprian of Carthage on Envy | 62
     The Writings of the Fourth Century Church Fathers—
       Evil Eye, Envy, and the Devil | 65

    Christian Personal Letters—"Unharmed by the Evil Eye" | 98
    Christian Amulets and Other Apotropaics:
        The Material and Iconographic Evidence | 100
    The Speaking and Inscribing of Potent Words,
        Phrases, and Formulas | 107
    The Placing of Protective Formulas, Designs or Symbols
        for Safeguarding Homes and Sites | 122
    The Wearing of Personal Amulets and
        Use of Apotropaic Gestures and Objects | 129
Christian Liturgical and Ecclesiastical Apotropaic Practice | 150
Popular Remedies of Evil Eye Injuries | 151
Evil Eye Belief and Practice in Islam: A Brief Note | 152
Conclusion to Chapter Two | 155

3 Epilogue | 157

Bibliography 1 | 165
Bibliography 2: Works Concerning the Evil Eye Supplementing the Bibliographies of Volumes 1–3 | 195
Index | 205

ILLUSTRATIONS

Illus. 1.1: Jewish phylacteries (from *Jewish Encyclopedia* 1906 10:24, reproducing an engraved drawing from Bernard Picart, 1725) | 28

Illus. 1.2: Blue apotropaic tassels (*tzitzit*) on the four corners of the prayer shawl (*tallit*) worn by observant Jewish males during morning services | 29

Illus 1.3: Sketch of Byzantine bronze amulet (4th cent. CE) of Solomon (obverse) as cavalier spearing a prostrate demoness, and on reverse, an Evil Eye under attack from trident and various animals (from Seligmann 1910 2:314 and p. 445, fig. 231) | 36

Illus. 1.4: Jewish silver protective amulet: Hand of Miriam (*Hamesh*) with *Shaddai* ("God Almighty") in palm (from Seligmann 1910 2:193, fig. 162) | 38

Illus. 1.5: Image of the Islamic protective Hand of Fatimah (*Hamsa*) on façade of modern building, Spain (photo by John H. Elliott) | 39

Illus. 1.6: Metal amulet of protective hand with eye in palm, El Santuario de Chimayo, New Mexico (John H. Elliott collection) | 39

Illus. 1.7: Babylonian Incantation Bowl with Aramaic script, protecting owner and kin from all evil spirits and the Evil Eye (from Budge 1978/1930:289) | 40

Illus. 1.8: Dura Europus synagogue (245 CE): two ceiling tiles protecting against the Evil Eye. Line drawing by Dietlinde Elliott, after Hopkins 1979:141. p. 56 | 44

Illus. 1.9: Clay door plaque defending a home against the Evil Eye, from Syria Palestine, fifth century CE | 46

Illus. 2.1: Vignette of the angel Gabriel as cavalier spearing a prostrate demoness representing the Evil Eye (from Gollancz, *The Book of Protection* 1912:xl-xli, Codex A, §23, p. 34) | 115

x   *Illustrations*

Illus. 2.2: Vignette of Rabban Hurmizd as cavalier spearing a lion or mad dog (Illustration in Gollancz, *The Book of Protection* 1912:xlii) | 115

Illus. 2.3: Vignette of "Daniel the prophet as cavalier spearing a wolf (Illustration in Gollancz, *The Book of Protection* 1912:xlvi) | 116

Illus. 2.4: Vignette of Mar Thomas as cavalier spearing the spirit of lunacy (Illustration in Gollancz, *The Book of Protection* 1912: xxxii-xxxiii, Codex A, §12, p. 20) | 116

Illus. 2.5: Vignette of King Solomon as cavalier spearing the prostrate demon Asmodeus (from Perdrizet 1922:12, fig. 5; cf. Gollancz, *The Book of Protection* 1912, Codex A. p. 55) | 117

Illus. 2.6: Sketch of a Christian Byzantine silver/copper Seal of Solomon medallion amulet (Symyrna, Asia Minor) depicting Solomon as cavalier (obv., left) spearing a prostrate demoness and, on reverse (right), an Evil Eye (alias *phthonos*/envy) attacked by 3 daggers and beasts (from Seligmann 1910: 2:443, fig. 230, description in vol. 2:314–15) | 137

Illus. 2.7: Sketch of a Christian Byzantine bronze medallion amulet from Cyzikus, Phrygia, Asia Minor, depicting an Evil Eye attacked by a charging lion (obverse, left) and, on reverse (right), Solomon as cavalier spearing a prostrate demoness (from Seligmann 1910 2:449, fig. 233, description in vol. 2:314–15) | 139

Illus. 2.8: Sketch of a Christian Byzantine copper medallion amulet from Constantinople depicting on reverse (left) the three Magi and Virgin Mary with infant Jesus and on obverse (right), Solomon as cavalier on a lion attacking an Evil Eye (from Seligmann 1910 2:315 and p. 453, fig. 234) | 140

Illus. 2.9: Fresco at the monastery of St. Apollo, Bawait, Egypt (fourth-sixth century CE), St. Sisinnios the Parthian as cavalier spearing the demoness Alabasdria, and, above, an Evil Eye attacked (from Perdrizet 1922:14, fig. 6) | 141

Illus. 2.10: Scene on the Christian sarcophagus of Junius Bassus (d. 359 CE), front reliefs, top register, fifth panel from left: Pontius Pilate about to wash his hands, making the gesture of the *mano cornuta*. (Photo by Giovanni Dall'Orto, April 12 2008) | 145

Illus. 2.11: Sketch of the ceiling mosaic, Basilica of San Vitale, Ravenna (sixth century CE): Abel (left) and Melchizedek (right) making offerings at an altar. Extending from heaven above the altar, the right Hand of God in the gesture of a *mano cornuta* (from Seligmann 1910, 1:385, fig. 71; also 389, fig. 72; see also Elworthy 1895/1958:265, fig. 113) | 146

Illus. 2.12: Carthaginian Christian medallion amulet depicting an owl surrounded by six stars, with inscription from Rev 5:6 (from Perdrizet 1922:30, fig. 10) | 148

Illus. 2.13: Hand of Fatima (*hamsa*) as part of a lamp-holder with apotropaic bells, Morocco (from Seligmann 2:195, fig. 163) | 154

PREFACE

THIS FOUR VOLUME STUDY has traced evidence of Evil Eye belief and practice in the ancient world from Mesopotamia (c. 3000 BCE) to Late Roman Antiquity (c. 600 CE), with particular attention to the Bible and post-biblical traditions of Israel and early Christianity.

Belief in the Evil Eye is a long-standing and widespread folk concept that some persons are enabled by nature to injure others, cause illness and loss, and destroy any person, animal, or thing through a powerful noxious glance emanating from the eye. Also known as "fascination" (Greek: *baskania*; Latin: *fascinatio*), this belief holds that the eye is an active organ that emits destructive emanations charged by negative dispositions (especially malevolence, envy, miserliness, and withheld generosity). These emanations arise in the heart or soul, and are projected outward against both animate and inanimate objects. The full constellation of notions comprising the Evil Eye complex includes the expectation that various prophylactic words, gestures, images, and amulets have the power to counter and avert the damaging power of the Evil Eye.

From its likely origin in ancient Sumer (3000 BCE) and its early spread to Egypt and the Circum-Mediterranean region, to its later movement eastward to India and westward and northward to Europe, the belief eventually made its way from "old worlds" to "new." It now constitutes a cultural phenomenon with personal, social, and moral implications that has spanned the centuries and encircled the globe.

Our study has concentrated on the Evil Eye phenomenon in the ancient world, with new and extensive attention to mention of it in the Bible and the biblical communities of Israel and early Christianity. Volume One opened with an introductory overview of references to, and research on, the Evil Eye from the ancient past to the modern present (Chapter One). Chapter Two of Volume One examined Evil Eye belief and practice in ancient Mesopotamia and Egypt. Volume Two is devoted to evidence on the subject in ancient Greece and Rome. Within the geographical and cultural matrix detailed in these first two volumes, the evidence of Evil Eye belief and practice in the Bible was then examined (Volume Three). This present fourth and final volume considers Evil Eye belief and practice in Israel following the destruction of the Jerusalem temple in 70 CE (Chapter One) and in early Christianity (Chapter Two) down through Late Antiquity (500–600 CE). Numerous cross-references relate the subject matter of this volume to that of the previous three. A familiarity with the material presented in Volumes One to Three is presumed in the discussion of this final volume. A concluding Epilogue (Chapter Three) offers some final thoughts on this four-volume survey of Evil Eye belief and practice in antiquity and their role in conceptualizing and combatting the pernicious forces of daily life.

Beware the Evil Eye presents the first full-scale monograph on the Evil Eye in the Bible and the biblical communities (Volumes Three and Four). Its analysis of Evil Eye belief and practice in Mesopotamia, Egypt, Greece and Rome (Volumes One and Two) summarizes a century of research since the milestone two-volume study of Siegfried Seligmann, *Der böse Blick und Verwandtes* (1910), and describes the ecological, historical, social, and cultural contexts within which the biblical texts are best understood. Throughout this study we have treated the Evil Eye in antiquity not as an instance of vulgar superstition or deluded magic, but as a physiological, psychological and moral phenomenon whose operation was deemed explicable on rational grounds; for discussion see Volume 1, pp. 26–27.

ACKNOWLEDGMENTS

I AM HAPPY TO express once again my debt to colleagues and informants beyond number for all the material they have sent me or aided me in acquiring in my pursuit of this wide-ranging and century-spanning topic. Many have been named in the foregoing volumes. To the list I must add meinen alten Freund Peter Lampe of Heidelberg University, who, early in this project, introduced me to the marvelous computer resource, *Thesaurus Linguae Graece*, which afforded me a head-start on collecting all the appearances of Evil Eye terminology in the Greek literature of antiquity. As to this final volume, my special thanks go to my good friend and colleague Stephen Black of the University of San Francisco for his critical reading and advice on the text of Chapter Two.

K. C. Hanson, friend, adviser, and peerless editor, along with Ian Creeger, patient and expert typesetter, have guided this volume and the general project with their skill and sage counsel—my profound gratitude to both!

I dedicate this final volume to an early mentor and later colleague and collaborator who has avidly supported this research project from the beginning. Herzlichsten Dank und bleib *abaskantos*, lieber Herman!

ABBREVIATIONS

ANCIENT NEAR EASTERN SOURCES

KTU[2]   *The Cuneiform Alphabetic Texts from Ugarit, Ras Ibn Hani and Other Places.* Edited by M. Dietrich-O. Loretz-J. Sanmartin. 2nd, enlarged edition. Münster:Ugarit-Verlag, 1995

VAT   Museum siglum of the Staatliche Museen, Berlin, Vorderasiatische Abteilung, Tontafeln

OLD TESTAMENT (HEBREW, GREEK, LATIN)

Gen	Genesis
Exod	Exodus
Num	Numbers
Deut	Deuteronomy
1 Sam/1Kgdm	1 Samuel/1 Kingdoms
1 Kgs	1 Kings
2 Kgs	2 Kings
Prov	Proverbs
Job	
Ps	Psalms
Eccl	Ecclesiastes
Isa	Isaiah
Jer	Jeremiah
Ezek	Ezekiel
Zech	Zechariah

APOCRYPHA

2 Macc.	2 Maccabees
Sir/Ecclus	Sirach/Ecclesiasticus
Tob	Tobit
Wis	Wisdom

PSEUDEPIGRAPHA

| T. Sol. | Testament of Solomon |

NEW TESTAMENT

| Matt | Matthew |
| Gal | Galatians |

JOSEPHUS, FLAVIUS

| *Ant.* | *Antiquities of the Jews* |

RABBINIC WRITINGS

b.	Bavli (Babylonian Talmud)
m.	Mishnah
m. Avot	m. *Pirke Avot*
Pesiq. Rab Kah.	*Pesiqta de Rab Kahana*
y.	Yerushalmi (Jerusalem/Palestinian Talmud)

GREEK AND ROMAN WRITINGS

Aeschylus

| *Agam.* | *Agamemnon* |

Plutarch

Quaest. Conv.   *Quaestiones Convivales (Convivial Questions/ Symposium/Table Talk)*, Book 5, Question 7 (5.7.1–6), *Moralia* 680C–683B

Virgil

Aen.   *Aeneid*

INSCRIPTIONS, EPIGRAPHA

CIG   *Corpus inscriptionum graecarum*. Edited by A. Boeckh. 4 Vols. Berlin, 1825–1877

Gsell et al.   *Inscriptions latines de l'Algérie*. 1922, 1957. 2 vols. Edited by Stéphane Gsell, Xavier Dupuis and H.- G. Pflaum. Paris, É. Champion. Paris: Champion.

IG   *Inscriptiones Graecae*. Berlin, 1873–1903

IGLS   *Inscriptions grecques et latines de la Syrie*. 21 vols. Edited by L. Jalabert, R. Mouterde, et al. Paris: Geuthner, 1929–

ILCV   *Inscriptiones Latinae Christianae Veteres*. 3 vols. Edited by Ernst Diehl. Berlin: Weidmann, 1925–31. Vol. 4, Supplement, edited by Jacques Moreau und Henri Irénée Marrou. Berlin: Weidmann. 1967

I.Tyre   *Inscriptions grecques et latines découvertes dans les fouilles de Tyr (1963–1974). 1. Inscriptions de la nécropole*. By J.-P. Rey-Coquais. Bulletin du Musée de Beyrouth 29. Paris: Librairie d'Amérique et d'Orient A. Maisonnueve, 1977

Kaibel, Epig. Gr.   *Epigrammata graeca ex lapidibus conlecta*. Edited by Georg Kaibel. Berlin: Reimer, 1878

SB   Priesigke, Friedrich et al., eds. 1915–1993. *Sammelbuch griechischer Urkunden aus Ägypten*. 18 vols. Berlin: de Gruyter

SEG   *Supplementum Epigraphicum Graecum*. 1923–1971. 50 vols. Edited by H. W. Pleket and R. S. Stroud et al. Amsterdam: Gieben.

PAPYRI

P. Abinnaeus — *The Abbinaeus Archive: Papers of a Roman Officer in the Reign of Constantius II.* Edited by H. I. Bell et al. Oxford: Clarendon, 1962

PGM — *Papyri Graece Magicae. Die griechischen Zauberpapyri.* 2 vols. Edited by K. Preisendanz. Berlin: Teubner, 1928 (vol. 1), 1931 (vol. 2). Vol. 3 with index, edited by K. Preisendanz, with E. Diehl and S. Eitrem (1941/1942). 2nd revised edition by A. Heinrichs. Stuttgart: Teubner, 1973–1974. ET: *Greek Magical Papyri*, edited by Hans Dieter Betz. Chicago: University of Chicago Press, 1986

P.Mich. — University of Michigan Papyri. Various editors. 1931–

P.Oxy. — *The Oxyrhynchus Papyri.* Edited by B. P. Grenfell and A. S. Hunt etc. 72 vols. London: Egypt Exploration Society, 1898–

P.Ryl. — *Greek Papyri in the John Rylands Library, Manchester, I-IV.* Edited by A. Hunt et al. 1911–52

PSI — *Papiri greci e latini.* Pubblicazioni della Società italiana per la ricerca dei papyri greci e latini in Egítto. Florence: Arini, 1912–

P.Turner — *Papyri Greek and Egyptian Edited by Various Hands in Honour of E.G. Turner on the Occasion of his Seventieth Birthday.* London: Egypt Exploration Society, 1981

EARLY CHRISTIAN WRITINGS, SOURCES

Acts Thom.   Acts of Thomas

Ambrosiaster (Pseudo-Ambrosius)

Comm.   *Commentaria in xiii Epistolas beati Pauli*

Basil of Caesarea

Hom. 11   Homily 11, *Concerning Envy/Peri phthonou/De invidia* (PG 31.372–385)

BHG	*Bibliotheca hagiographica graeca*, 3rd ed., 3 vols. Edited by François Halkin, Subsidia Hagiographica 8a. Brussels: Société des Bollandistes, 1957, reprinted 1986
CCEL	Christian Classics Ethereal Library. Texts of Church Fathers
1 Clem.	*1 Clement*

Cyril of Jerusalem

Catech.	*Catechetical Lectures/Homilies*

Eusebius of Caesarea

Eccl. Hist.	*Ecclesiastical History*
GCS	*Die griechischen christlichen Schriftsteller der ersten Jahrhunderte.* Kirchenväter-Commission der Königl. Preussischen Akademie der Wissenschaften. Leipzig: Hinrichs, 1897–

Gregory of Nazianzus

Carm.	*Carmina*

Gregory of Nyssa

De beat.	*De beatitudinibus*

Ignatius of Antioch

Rom.	*To the Romans*

Irenaeus of Lyons

Adv. Haer.	*Adversus Haereses*

Jerome

Comm. Gal.	*Commentariorum in Epistulam ad Galatas*
Comm. Matt.	*Commentariorum in Matthaeum*
Exp. in ep. ad Gal	*Explicatio in epistulam ad Galatas*

John Chrysostom

Adv. Jud.	Adversos Judaeos
Catech. illum.	Catechesis ad illuminandos
Delic.	De futurae vitae deliciis
Hom. Act.	Homiliae in Acta Apostolorum
Hom. Col.	Homiliae in epistulam ad Colossenses
Hom. 1 Cor.	Homiliae in primum epistulam ad Corinthios
Hom. 2 Cor.	Homiliae in secundam epistulam ad Coninthios
Hom. Eph.	Homiliae in epistulam ad Ephesios
Hom Gal.	Homiliae in epistulam ad Galatas commentarius
Hom. Gen.	Homiliae in Genesim
Hom. Jo.	Homiliae in Joannem
Hom. Matt.	Homiliae in Matthaeum
Hom. Rom.	Homiliae in epistulam ad Romanos
Hom 1 Tim.	Homiliae in epistulam 1 ad Timotheum
Paralyt.	In paralyticum demissum per tectum
Serm. Gen.	Sermones in Genesim
Stat.	Ad populam Antiochenum de statuis

Justin Martyr

Dial.	Dialogue

PG	*Patrologia Graeca*. Patrologiae cursus completus. Series graeca. 176 vols. Edited by Jacques-Paul Migne. Cursus Completus. Paris, Garnier Freres, 1857–1876
PL	*Patrologia Latina*. Patrologiae cursus completus, Series latina. 221 vols. Edited by Jacques-Paul Migne. Paris: Garnier Freres, 1844–1864

Tertullian

Virg.	De virginibus velandis

ISLAM

Qur'an	The Holy Qur'an

ENCYCLOPEDIAS, LEXICA, SERIES, PERIODICALS

ABD	*The Anchor Bible Dictionary.* 6 vols. Edited by David Noel Freedman. New York: Doubleday, 1992
ArOr	Archiv Orientálni
BAH	Bibliothèque Archéologique et Historique. Paris
BAR	*Biblical Archaeological Review* 1975–
BCH	*Bulletin de correspondance hellénique.* Paris, 1877–
BE	*Bulletin épigraphique* (in *Revue des études grecques*) 1888– (replacing *Bull. Épig.*)
BHG	*Bibliotheca hagiographica graeca.* 3rd ed. 3 vols. Edited by François Halkin, Subsidia Hagiographica 8a. Brussels: Société des Bollandistes, 1957; reprinted 1986
CCL	Corpus Christianorum Latinorum 1953/54–
CCEL	Christian Classics Ethereal Library. Texts of Church Fathers online
CCSL	Corpus Christianorum Series Latina
CSEL	Corpus Scriptorum Ecclesiasticorum Latinorum. Vienna: Verlag der Österreichischen Akademie der Wissenschaften/Universität Salzburg, 1866–
DACL	*Dictionnaire d'archéologie chrétienne et de liturgie.* 15 vols. Edited by Fernand Cabrol and H. Leclercq. Paris: Letouzey & Ané, 1903–1953
Daremberg and Saglio	Charles Daremberg and Edmond Saglio, eds. *Dictionnaire des antiquités grecques et romaines.* 10 vols. (5 double vols.). Paris: Hachette, 1877–1919
GCS	*Die Griechischen Christlichen Schriftsteller.* Leipzig: Hinrichs, 1897–
HERE	*Encyclopaedia of Religion and Ethics.* 13 vols. Edited by James Hastings et al. 13 vols. Edinburgh: T. & T. Clark, 1908–1927. 4th ed. Reprinted, 1958
HTR	*Harvard Theological Review*
IDB	*The Interpreter's Dictionary of the Bible.* 4 vols. Edited by George Arthur Buttrick. Nashville: Abingdon, 1962
JAC	*Jarhrbuch für Antike und Christentum*
JAOS	*Journal of the American Oriental Society*
JBA	Jewish Babylonian Aramaic (Incantation bowls)

JE	*The Jewish Encyclopedia*
JPS	Jewish Publication Society
JQR	*Jewish Quarterly Review*
JSNTSup	Journal for the Study of the New Testament Supplements
LCL	Loeb Classical Library
NABU	Nouvelles Assyriologiques Bréves et Utilitaires. Paris, 1987–
New Docs	*New Documents Illustrating Early Christianity.* Edited by G. H. R. Horsley, S. Llewelyn et al. North Ryde, NSW: The Ancient History Research Centre, Macquarie University, 1981–
NIGTC	New International Greek Testament Commentary
NPNF	Nicene and Post-Nicene Fathers of the Christian Church
OTP	*The Old Testament Pseudepigrapha.* 2 vols. Edited by James H. Charlesworth. Garden City: Doubleday, 1983, 1985
PAES	Publications of the Princeton University Archaeological Expeditions to Syria. Princeton Archaeological Expeditions to Syria (PAES) 1904–1905 and 1909
PG	*Patrologia Graeca.* Patrologiae cursus completus. Series Graeca. Edited by J. P. Migne. 161 vols. Paris, 1857–1866
PGL	*A Patristic Greek Lexicon.* Edited by G. W. H. Lampe. Oxford: Clarendon, 1961–68
PGM	*Papyri Graece Magicae. Die griechischen Zauberpapyri.* 2 vols. Edited by K. Preisendanz. Berlin: Teubner, 1928 (vol. 1), 1931 (vol. 2). Vol. 3 with index, edited by K. Preisendanz, with E. Diehl and S. Eitrem (1941/1942. 2d revised edtion by A. Heinrichs. Stuttgart: Teubner, 1973–1974. ET: Greek Magical Papyri. Edited by Hans Dieter Betz, 1986
PL	*Patrologia Latina.* Patrologiae cursus completus. Series Latina. Edited by J. P. Migne. 221 vols. Paris, 1844–1880
PsVTG	Pseudepigrapha Veteris Testamenti Graece
RAC	*Reallexikon für Antike und Christentum.* 25+ vols. Edited by Theodore Klauser et al. Stuttgart: Hiersemann, 1950–
REB	*Revue des études Byzantines.* Succeeded *Échos d'Orient* (Paris, 1897–1942)
REG	*Revue des études grècques* 1888–1939

SBLDS	Society of Biblical Literature Dissertation Series
SC	Sources chrétiennes. Paris: Cerf, 1942–
Sophocles, *Greek Lexicon*	*Greek Lexicon of the Roman and Byzantine Periods*. 2 vols. Edited by E. A. Sophocles, Cambridge, MA, 1887
TLG	*Thesaurus Linguae Graece*. Leipzig: Teubner, 1900–
TLL	*Thesaurus Linguae Latinae*. 11 vols. Stuttgart and Leipzig: Teubner, 1900–1999; Verlag KG Saur, 2000–2006; Berlin: de Gruyter, 2007–
UJE	*The Universal Jewish Encyclopedia*. Edited by Isaac Landman. 10 vols. + Index vol. New York: Universal Jewish Encyclopedia, 1939–1943
VT	*Vetus Testamentum*
ZPE	*Zeitschrift für Papyrologie und Epigraphik*

OTHER ABBREVIATIONS AND SIGLA

a.k.a.	also known as
BCE, CE	Before the Common Era; Common Era (replacing BC/AD)
c.	circa ("about")
cent.	century
cf.	confer, see
chap.	chapter
codd.	codices
col.	column
cp.	compare, contrast
ET	English translation
fl.	floruit ("flourished," was active at a certain time)
fig.	figure
FS	Festschrift
gen.	genitive
HT	Hebrew Text, a.k.a. MT (Hebrew Massoretic Text)
Illus.	Illustration
inv. no.	inventory number
JHE	John H. Elliott (as translator)

l(l)	line(s)
lit.	literally
LXX	Septuagint (Greek text of Old Testament)
MT	Hebrew Massoretic Text a.k.a HT (Hebrew Text)
n.f.	neue Folge ("new series")
no(s)	number(s)
n.r.	neue Reihe ("new series")
NT	New Testament
OT	Old Testament
P.	Papyrus
Pl.	Plate
pl.	plural
p(p).	page(s)
Prol.	Prologus ("Prologue")
Ps.-	Pseudo- (inaccurately ascribed to)
Q	Qumran
SBL	Society of Biblical Literature
Vulg.	Vulgata (Jerome's Latin translation)
s.v.	sub voce ("under the [listed] word")
v.l.	varia lectio ("variant reading")
[ ]	Square brackets identify textual material supplied by the translator of the original source or by the present author (JHE)

I

POSTBIBLICAL ISRAEL
The Literary and Material Evidence

INTRODUCTION

THE ROMAN WORLD OF the Imperial period and through Late Antiquity (first century BCE–sixth century CE) experienced a continued, if not increased, anxiety concerning the Evil Eye. Fear of the Evil Eye and fascination with the noxious gaze continued unabated in Israel and the Christian communities, as with their Mediterranean contemporaries. In Volume 3 we identified and examined explicit and implicit references to the Evil Eye in the Old and New Testaments and related writings. These included fourteen text segments involving some twenty explicit references to the Evil Eye in the Old Testament (Deut 15:9; 28:54, 56; Prov 23:6; 28:22; Tob 4:7, 16; Sir 14:3, 6, 8, 9, 10; 18:18; 31:13; 37:11; Wis 4:12; 4 Macc 1:26; 2:15; Ep Jer 69/70), additional references in related writings of Second Temple Israel, and five explicit references to the Evil Eye in the New Testament (Matt 6:22–23/Luke 11:33–36; Matt 20:1–15/16; Mark 7:22; Gal 3:1) along with several possible implicit references. In this volume we trace evidence of Evil Eye belief and practice beyond the biblical period in both Jewish and Christian communities from the destruction of the Jerusalem temple (70 CE) through Late Antiquity (500–600 CE).

2 Beware the Evil Eye

The literary and material evidence is extensive, as is the research on this topic.[1]

The elaboration of Evil Eye belief in this period reflects the same worldview typical of antiquity as a whole, including belief in the existence of demons, witches, and of natural and supernatural forces capable of inflicting illness, injury and death, along with anxiety about human vulnerability to these potent forces.[2] Among these life-threatening forces, educated and commoners alike counted the malevolent and noxious Evil Eye. The rabbis maintained the biblical opposition to sorcery (Exod 22:17; Deut 18:10-11).

---

1. On Evil Eye belief and practice in Israel in this period, see Peringer von Lillieblad 1685 (Hebrew amulets) ; Grünbaum 1877; Hirsch 1892; Blau 1898:152-56, 1907a, 190b; Elworthy 1895/1958: 5-6:199, 233, 389-90, 425-26, 443-44; 1912; Blau 1898, 1907; Einszler 1899; Perdrizet 1903, 1922; Reitzenstein 1904; Kohler and Blau 1907; Brav 1908 (reprinted in Dundes 1992); Kennedy 1910; M. Gaster 1910; Dobschütz 1910: 424-25; Montgomery 1910-11:280-81; Seligmann 1910 1:16, 33, 71, 79, 86, 122, 160, 180, 181, 185, 193-94; 227, 248, 256, 278, 295, 314, 377; 2:1, 4, 8, 12, 19, 32, 72, 82, 96, 117, 170, 172, 176-77, 190, 215, 219-20, 222, 239, 247-48, 254, 260, 266, 280, 302, 328, 338-39, 358-59, 367, 370; Seligmann 1922; Seligmann 1927; Canaan 1914:28-32; Casanovicz 1917a, 1917b; Lilienthal 1924; Billerbeck 1926 1:833-35; Billerbeck 1928 4/1:527-35; Löwinger 1926; Peterson 1926:96-109; 1982; Gordon 1937/1961; Roback 1938; Friedenwald 1939; Trachtenberg 1939:47-48, 54-56, 133, 139-40, 158, 161-62; Levi 1941; 1947 1:28-34 & plates, esp. xl; vol. 2, plate IVa-c., see figs. 12-14; Contenau 1947:261, fig. 24 (Dura-Europos synagogue, ceiling Evil Eye panels); Bonner 1950; Meisen 1950; Goodenough 1953 vol. 1:163; vol. 2:153-207 ("Charms in Judaism"), 208-95 ("amulets"; 238-41 and figs. 1065, 1066 ["the much-suffering eye"]); vol. 3 (amulets), nos. 379-81 and passim in nos. 999-1209); vol. 4 (1954) 72, 79-81; vol. 7 (1958) 224-29 (Medusa); vol. 9 (1964) 54-55 (Dura-Europos synagogue and Evil Eye panels; vol. 11.3 (1964), fig. 352 is a photo of the Dura-Europus synagogue ceiling and its two eye panels; vol. 12 (1965) 58-63, 159-60 (Dura-Europus synagogue Evil Eye panels); Kötting 1954:474-76; Gordon 1937; Shrut 1960; Edwards 1971; Noy 1971; Kirschenblatt-Gimblett and Lenowitz 1973; Schrire 1973, 1982:6-9, 56-58, 102 and appendix (plates 2, 5, 12, 14, 16, 50) Brox 1974; Birnbaum 1975:462-63; Engemann 1975; Nador 1975; Maloney 1976; Moss and Cappanari 1976; Budge 1930:212-38 (Hebrew amulets); 366-79 and 390-405 (Kabbalah); Dunbabin and Dickie 1983; Patai 1983; Aschkenazi 1984; Lévy and Lévy Zumwalt 1987, 2002; Elliott 1988:55, 1991; 1994:64, 76; 2007, 2008; 2015a, 2015b; Naveh and Shaked 1987:5, 40-41, 44-45, 98-99, 102-3, 120, 133, 172-73; T. H. Gaster 1989; Ulmer 1991, 1992/1993, 1994, 1998, 2003; Walter 1989-90; Ross 1991; Yardeni 1991; Dundes 1992:41-43; 44-54; Kotansky 1994:145, 270-300; Davis and Frenkel 1995; Veltri 1996; Zumwalt 1996; Barkay et al. 2004; Teman 2008; Barkay 2009; Gregg 2000; Vukosavovic, ed. 2010; Kalmin 2012; Neis 2012, 2013:10, 31, 38, 40, 64, 149, 160, 163-65, 177, 189.

2. See Justin Martyr, *Dialogue with Trypho the Jew* 76, 85; M. Gaster 1910:452. On Jewish demonology see Billerbeck 4.1 (1928) 501-35; Canaan 1929; Langton 1949; T. H. Gaster 1962; Böcher 1970; J. Z. Smith 1978b; Ferguson 1984; Naveh and Shaked 1985; Stratton 2007:143-76; Bohak 2008. On witches in Israel see Bar-Ilan 1993; Stratton 2007:143-76.

But they, like their forebears, made no connection between the power and operation of sorcery and the natural human phenomenon of an Evil Eye.

The richly detailed examination of a fourteenth-century-BCE Ugaritic anti-Evil Eye incantation by James Nathan Ford (2000) has demonstrated through its comparison of ancient Mesopotamian texts with Jewish, Christian, Mandaic, and Arabic texts of later centuries the remarkable "thematic continuity" of concepts and motifs associated with the Evil Eye down through Late Antiquity.[3] In chapter 1 of this final volume we shall first review the *literary evidence of the Evil Eye belief in Israel's post-Second Temple rabbinic period* (Mishnah, Talmud, Midrashim, legends and folklore from the first through the sixth centuries CE). This will be followed by an examination of the *amuletic and iconographical evidence* from this same period. Rivka Kern Ulmer's 1994 study, *The Evil Eye in the Bible and in Rabbinic Literature*, provides a useful compilation of rabbinic references to the Evil Eye and warrants consultation. Our study locates this literature in a wider cultural context.[4]

The second chapter of this volume traces parallel developments of Evil Eye belief and practice in *early Christianity* during this same period, from the second to the sixth centuries CE.

---

3. On the themes and illustrative texts see especially Ford 2000:212 n.30; 215, 216, 223, 224 and n. 73, 232, 235–36 and n. 126; 249–50, 252, and 256–68. His extensive collection of evidence, however, is not accompanied by a theoretical explanation of the data. His distinction, moreover, between a putative "magical evil eye" and a "physiological" eye in antiquity (Ford 1998:230; 2000:713) is arbitrary and unconvincing. The terms are not explained and the basis of the distinction is not established. Consequently, his assessment of Deut 15:9 as part of a "clearly non-magical context" and hence not a reference to a "magical" Evil Eye (Ford 1998:230; 2000:713, contesting Elliott 1991:153, 156–58) is not persuasive. Ford omits biblical Evil Eye texts from his comparative analysis.

4. Ulmer gives only minimal attention to cross-cultural comparison and provides little theoretical analysis. She presumes, but fails to prove, a discontinuity between the understanding of the Evil Eye in the Hebrew Bible and the view of the rabbis, only the latter of which, she claims, accords with conventional views of the Evil Eye spanning the Circum-Mediterranean region (1994:1–7 and passim). She states only that "The evil eye was an *explicans* for occurrences both outside and within their religious experiences" (1994:ix; 1991:353). The title of her concluding chapter, "the Evolution of a Diseased Eye into an Evil Eye" (Ch. 11, pp. 183–90) is misleading. The chapter actually deals with suspected causes of eye illnesses and methods for healing a sick eye, including spitting into the eye (189–90). No evidence is provided to support her supposition that the notion of an Evil Eye evolved from the phenomenon of a sick eye. Ulmer, in fact, explicitly states: "The relationship of these cures and practices to the concept of the evil eye cannot be clearly established" (188). Her self-admitted *speculation* that "the rabbinic mind felt a need to make every effort to eliminate eye disease and restore the eye to full health in order to reduce the inherent danger of the evil eye" (188–89) remains unconvincing speculation.

4   Beware the Evil Eye

THE LITERARY EVIDENCE

The rabbinic sources record considerable concern about the Evil Eye(Hebrew: *'ayin ha-ra'*; lit., "(the) eye of the evil"; Aramaic: *'eina biša'*), its possessors and victims, its malignant effects down through history, and the means of averting its pernicious power. The Evil Eye occasionally also is spoken of as a "narrow eye" (*'ayin tsarah*) displayed by persons who are envious or stingy, ungenerous or give only begrudgingly. The phrases "narrow eye" and "Evil Eye" are explicitly equated in a passage of the Talmud which recounts that Jonathan, "a priest to a foreign god," nevertheless looked at an idol of that god with a *narrow eye, an Evil Eye*, and questioned the idol's existence (*y. Berakhot* 9, 13d). The phrases are also juxtaposed and equated in *b. Kiddushin* 82a and *Avot of R. Nathan* (I, 16, 31b).[5]

The belief appears to have been accepted by the rabbis without debate as based on a physiological reality. The rabbinic literature contains no discussion of its origins, its complex of features, or how it worked. The content of the texts indicates, nevertheless, that the Jewish understanding of the Evil Eye, its basic features and mode of operation, was, on the whole, that of its pagan and Christian neighbors. This included the concept of an active eye and an extramission theory of vision,[6] the association of the Evil eye with envy and other aspects of the Evil Eye complex, its presumed arousal by beauty and success, and the employment of apotropaics and amulets of the same materials, types and colors as found in Egyptian, Greek, Roman, and Christian apotropaics. On the whole, Hebrew and Aramaic terms and figures were substituted on the Jewish amulets for pagan ones.[7]

---

5. For "narrow eye" see also *b. Bava Batra* 75a; *b. Bava Metzi'a* 87a; *y. Sanhedrin* 10, 29b; *Genesis Rabbah* 61:3; *Numbers Rabbah* 7:5; *Esther Rabbah* 2:1; *Tanhuma*, ed. Buber, *Emor* 6, 43a, *Emor* 6 (printed edition), 4,36b; *Yalqut Shimoni* 2.73; and Ulmer 1994:15–20.

6. On the sense and crucial role of sight in rabbinic culture and an active eye see Neiss 2012, 2013. On the eye in ancient Jewish tradition see Rosenzweig 1892 (OT and Talmud); Seligmann 1922:501–7; Wilpert 1950; Deonna 1965 (eye symbolism); Michaelis 1967; Jenni and Vetter 1976:259–68; Opperwall 1982; Stendebach 1989:31–48; Avrahami 2011:263–73. For the rabbinic material see also Levy 1924 3:639–41; Jastrow 1950 2:1071–72. On the extramission theory of vision see Vol. 1:6–7, 23–25, 26, 54–58, 108; Vol. 2:18–19, 55–58, 63, 70,72–81, 115, 271; Vol. 3:17, 127–31.

7. "In post-talmudic literature," according to Noy (1971:997), "one of the following two explanations is generally found: (1) the evil eye contains the element of fire, and so spreads destruction (Judah Loew b. Bezalel ("Maharal") in *Netivot Olam*, 107d); (2) the angry glance of a man's eye calls into being an evil angel who takes vengeance on the cause of wrath (Manasseh Ben Israel in *Nishmat Hayyim*, 3:27; cf. *Sefer Hasidim*, ed. by J. Wistinetzki and J. Freiman (1924²), 242 no. 981.

The Evil Eye as Moral Failure

The Mishnah tractate, "Sayings of the Fathers" (*Pirke Avot*), includes several pronouncements on the Evil Eye.[8] One early text involves a discussion of Rabbi Johanan ben Zakkai (late first century CE) and his five disciples concerning "the good way to which a person should cleave" as distinguished from "the evil way that a person should shun":

> R. Eliezer said "a good eye" (*'ayin tovah*) and "an Evil Eye" (*'ayin ra'ah*); R. Joshua, "a good companion" and "an evil companion"; R. Jose, "a good neighbor" and "an evil neighbor"; R. Simeon, "one that sees what will be" and "one that borrows but does not repay"; and R. Eleazar, "a good heart" and "an evil heart." (*m. Avot* 2:9)

This contrast of good and Evil Eye recalls the similar contrast made by Jesus (Matt 6:22–23/Luke 11:34–35); see Volume 3, chapter 2.

In this same context, we read that Rabbi Yehoshua (c. 90 CE) used to say, "An Evil Eye (*'ayin har'ah*), an evil inclination, and a hatred of mankind drive a person from the world" (*m. Avot* 2.11).[9] Possessing and exercising an Evil Eye is ranked among the worst of human vices and has fatal consequences for the fascinator him/herself—a notion found also in biblical and Hellenistic Evil Eye lore; see Volumes 2 and 3. A parallel account in the Sayings of Rabbi Nathan equates an Evil Eye with a "narrow eye":

> R. Yehoshua says: the Evil Eye and the evil inclination and the hatred of mankind put a man out of the world. Evil Eye: This teaches that even as a man had regard for his own home, so should he look out for the home of his fellow. And even as no man wishes that his own wife and children be held in ill repute, so should no man wish that his fellow's wife and children be held in ill repute.
>
> Another interpretation: an Evil Eye: That a man's eyes should not be narrow upon another man's learning. There was once a certain man whose eye was narrow upon his companion's learning. His life was cut short and he died. (*Avot of R. Nathan* I, 16, 31b)[10]

In the case of this saying, it is the opposite virtuous behavior that the Evil Eye belief is said to uphold: concern for the well-being of the family of one's

---

8. See Billerbeck 1926 1:833–34; Ulmer 1994:33–61.
9. Billerbeck 1926 1:834 takes Evil Eye here to imply envy.
10. As cited in Ulmer 1994:10.

neighbor should match concern for one's own family. The second interpretation equates an Evil Eye with a "narrow eye" of someone who looks either enviously or begrudgingly at his companion's learning and so brings about his own death. "Narrow eye" with the sense of "envious Evil Eye" appears in a saying of Rabbi Akiva. This renowned teacher, it is said, had 12,000 disciples and all died at the same time "because they looked with a narrow eye at each other." Akiva explains that these disciples died "only because they were envious of each other in respect to the Torah" (*Genesis Rabbah* 61:3). "Narrow eye" (*'ayin tsarah*), implying a "begrudging Evil Eye," appears in a comment on Gen 18:6 and Abraham's request of Sarah for help in preparing a meal of hospitality to his heavenly visitors: "a woman looks with a more [grudging] narrow eye upon guests than a man" (*b. Bava Metzi'a* 87a).[11]

A contrast of four types of almsgivers in chapter five of *Sayings of the Fathers* (*m. Avot* 5:13) makes reference to the Evil Eye in connection with the first two types of almsgivers. The first almsgiver mentioned is "he who is minded to give, but not that others should give—his Eye is Evil (*'eno ra'ah*) concerning what belongs to others." The second is he who is minded that others should give, but not that he should give—his Eye is Evil (*'eno ra'ah*) concerning what belongs to himself." The saying links the Evil Eye with the occasion of almsgiving, as in the Old Testament book of Tobit (4:7, 16 in 4:1–21). As in Tobit and Deut 15:7–11, an Evil Eye denotes reluctant generosity, giving only begrudgingly, prompted by a disposition of miserliness (see also Deut 28:54–57; Prov 23:6; Sir 14:3, 5, 8, 10; 18:18; Matt 6:22–23/ Luke 11:34).[12]

In this same context of *Pirke Avot* 5, righteous disciples of Abraham are contrasted to wicked disciples of Balaam, with reference to good and Evil Eyes. Those who possess "a good eye (*'ayin tovah*), a humble spirit, and a lowly soul" are said to be the disciples of Abraham, in contrast to the followers of Balaam, who are marked by "an Evil Eye (*'ayin ra' ah*), a proud spirit, and a haughty soul" (*m. Avot* 5.19). Jacob Neusner's translation of the Mishnah aptly renders *'ayin tovah* as "a generous spirit" and *'ayin ra'ah* as its conceptual opposite, "a grudging spirit."[13] This text, in both its contrast

---

11. For further comments on a "narrow eye," see *y. Sanhedrin* 10, 29b (a certain Gehazi's narrow eye preventing the learning of Torah); *b. Bava Batra* 75a (R. Hanina said that one who has a narrow eye toward Torah scholars will have no entrance in the world to come (lit. "will have eyes filled with smoke in the world to come"). For texts see Ulmer 1994:15–20.

12. For "grudging" versus "generous" eye, see also *b. Bava Batra* 64b; *Avot of Rabbi Nathan* 1.40; *Sifre Leviticus* 25:23; *m. Terumot* 4:3; *y. Bava Batra* 4.14d, 10; *Exodus Rabbah* 31 (91c); *b. Sotah* 38b.

13. Neusner 1988:689; so also Billerbeck 1926 1:834 on "good eye" as "generous eye"("ein gütiges Auge").

of good and Evil Eyes and of generosity versus miserliness/reluctant giving, also recalls the saying of Jesus (Matt 6:22–23/Luke 11:34–35) where "good eye" has the sense of "generous eye" (cf. Prov 22:9) and "Evil Eye" denotes its opposite—a miserly person, who gives only begrudgingly.[14] Donors who give generously are praised for having a "good eye" (*b. Bava Batra* 71a; *m. Terumot* 4:3; *Numbers Rabbah* 21:15). Those who manifest an Evil Eye of stinginess and restrained giving are condemned (*Exodus Rabbah* 31:7). Whoever gives the most for the heave offering for priests (*terumah*), it was said, has a good eye; whoever provides the least has an Evil Eye.[15] The verdict illustrates the continued association in Israel's tradition of a good eye with generosity and an Evil Eye with the miserly begrudging of gifts.[16]

Rabbi Yitshaq, in declaring leprosy to be caused by an Evil Eye, explains that an Evil Eye is a "narrow eye" of someone never lending his vessels to anyone and so bringing on his household leprosy as divine punishment (*Numbers Rabbah* 7.5). A related teaching concerning leprosy as caused by an Evil Eye adds that the refusal to lend a friend an ax or a sieve is indicative of exercising an Evil Eye.[17] Moses, by contrast, is acclaimed as possessor of a "good eye," i.e. a generous eye, exemplifying Prov 22:9 ("He that has a good eye shall be blessed, for he gives of his bread to the poor") (*b. Nedarim* 38a). Possessors of the good eye were given the honor of reciting blessings: "We give the cup of blessing for the grace after meals to the one who has a good eye" (*b. Sota* 38b).[18] All these passages of *Pirke Avot* echo the typically biblical accentuation of the Evil Eye as a human moral disposition and action, rather than a transhuman demonic force attacking humans from without.

References to the Evil Eye Detected in Biblical Texts

The writings of the Talmud show that the rabbis perceived in numerous biblical verses references to the Evil Eye, upon which they then elaborated:

---

14. On the saying of Jesus, see Vol. 3, chap. 2.

15. *m. Terumot* 4:3; *Sifre Numbers* 110; Ulmer 1994:33–38.

16. See Deut 15:7–11; 28:54–57; Sir 14:8, 10; 35:8, 10; Tob 4:7, 16; Matt 6:22–23; 20:1–15. For further rabbinic texts illustrating the contrast of "good eye" and "Evil Eye" see Ulmer 1994:33–61. In the majority of these texts, "good eye(s)" signals a generous person (echoing Prov 22:9), and "Evil Eye," a withholding, miserly person.

17. *Deuteronomy Rabbah* 6:4; Ulmer 1994:29.

18. On the "good eye" see Goodenough 1953 2:238–39; 3:1066; Ulmer 1991:346–47; 1994:73–82 (on "God's eye of justice").

- "And the LORD will take away from you all sickness" (Deut 7:15) was interpreted as referring to illness caused by an Evil Eye.[19]
- The priestly Aaronic benediction ("The LORD bless you and keep you ..." (Num 6:24–26), according to rabbinic interpretation, offers protection against the Evil Eye.[20]
- A midrash ("interpretation") on Gen 32:17 indicates one manner of appeasing an Evil Eye. Jacob, fearing the Evil Eye of his angry brother Esau, offers to Esau a gift of animals from his flock in order to "satiate the eyes (Evil Eye) of that wicked man" (*Genesis Rabbah* 76:8; cf. Gen 32:13–21). To forestall the deadly effect of Esau's Evil Eyed envy of Jacob's abundant flock, Jacob gave his brother hundreds of goats and sheep, as well as numerous camels, cows, bulls and asses (Gen 32:13–14), "for he thought 'I may appease him with the present ... and perhaps he will accept me'" (Gen 32:20). The rabbis explain that it is Esau's Evil Eye that Jacob is intent on appeasing. This is a Jewish instance of the Evil Eye practice of the sop, known also to the Romans, as indicated in Vol. 2.[21]
- Jacob's dispatch of his sons to Egypt (Gen 42:1–5) was understood to include the warning that they should not all enter Egypt by the same gate so as to avoid exposing themselves as a group to a malevolent Evil Eye.[22] "And each one of the Israelites entered through one particular [and different] gate, so that the Evil Eye (*'eina' biša'*) had no power over them" (*Targum Yerushalmi I* Gen 42:5).
- A midrash on Gen 49:22 ("Joseph is a fruitful bough, a fruitful bough by a spring [*'ayin*])" explains the term *'ayin* as meaning "eye" rather than "well" (*Midrash ha-Gadol* Gen 49:22). Variants of this midrash regard it as a reference to Joseph who withstood the envious Evil Eye (*'ayin*) of his brothers and whose descendants enjoy immunity from the Evil Eye.[23]

---

19. *Baba Metzi'a* 107b; Brav 1992:46.

20. *Numbers Rabbah* 12; *Pesiqta Rabbati* 5:10; Brav 1992:46; Ulmer 1994:150–51; Yardeni 1991. For two amulets with the benediction see Yardeni 1991.

21. See Vol. 2:109, 157–58; also Ulmer 1994:108–9.

22. *Genesis Rabbah* 91:2, 6 on Gen 42:1; *Numbers Rabbah* 12:4; Brav 1992:46; Ulmer 1994:176.

23. b. *Bava Batra* 118a-b; b. *Bava Metzi'a* 84a; b. *Berakhot* 20a; *Midrash Ha-Gadol* Gen 48:15; Ulmer 1994:165–66.

- Joshua's command to those spying out the land (Josh 17:15) to hide themselves in the forest was thought to safeguard them and the people from an Evil Eye.[24]
- Rabbi Yehoshua b. Levi interpreted Prov 22:9 ("He who has a good [JPS, RSV: "bountiful"] eye shall be blessed, for he shares his bread with the poor," as the basis for giving the cup of blessing for the recitation of grace after meals "only to the one who has a good eye" (*b. Sota* 38b). In this context he also warns against accepting hospitality from people with an Evil Eye, citing Prov 23:6–7 ("Do not eat the bread of someone with an Evil Eye (*raʿ ʿayin*) nor desire that person's delicacies . . . That person says 'Eat and drink,' but does not mean it").

The rabbis also stated that Prov 28:22 ("The person with an Evil Eye hastens after riches") "refers to Ephron," a Hittite from whom Abraham wished to purchase the cave of Machpelah to bury Sarah, his wife (Gen 23:8–9). Ephron was reluctant to sell and "cast an (envious) Evil Eye on Abraham's goods" (*Genesis Rabbah* 58:7; *Exodus Rabbah* 31:17).

Targum Jerusalem/Yerushalmi I on Exodus and on Numbers adds two references to the Evil Eye to the Massoretic text. An account of Moses approaching the Tent of Meeting outside the camp (Exod 33:7–11) relates how, whenever Moses approached the tent, all the people would "look after Moses until he had gone into the tent." The Targum states that they "looked after him with an Evil Eye (*ʿeinaʾ bišaʾ*) (*t. Jerusalem/Yerushalmi I* Exod. 33:8). A second reference concerns the account of the Israelites preparing to enter Canaan and their instruction from Moses to drive out all the inhabitants of the land (Num 33:50–56). Any allowed to remain, according to the Massoretic text, "shall be as pricks in your eyes and thorns in your sides . . ." The Targum rendition reads, "they will become those who glare at you with an Evil Eye" (*Targum Jerusalem/Yerushalmi I* Num 33:55).[25] Rabbi Yitzaq, commenting on Gen 18:6 concerning fine flour desired by Abraham for preparing food for his guests, concludes: "This shows that a woman looks with a more grudging Evil Eye [lit. "narrow eye"] Eye upon guests than does a man" (*b. Bava Metziʿa* 87a).

Harm Caused by the Evil Eye

Beyond such commentary on biblical passages, there is additional rabbinical lore concerning the Evil Eye. The Evil Eye, for one thing, was thought to be

---

24. *b. Sota* 36b; *b. Bava Batra* 118a; Brav 1992:46.

25. *Targum Yerushalmi I / Pseudo-Jonathan* Num 33:55; Billerbeck 1926 1:834–35; Ulmer 1994:118.

a major cause of illness and death.[26] It was said to be one of several causes of leprosy (*Leviticus Rabbah* 17:3; *Numbers Rabbah* 7:5; *Deuteronomy Rabbah* 6:4). An envious Sarah cast an Evil Eye on Hagar, her co-wife, and caused her to miscarry (*Genesis Rabbah* 45:5; cf. Gen 16:4). When Hagar gave birth to Ishmael and he was in the desert, Sarah's Evil Eye also inflicted fever, stomach cramps, and thirst on Ishmael (*Genesis Rabbah* 53:13) "Wherever the sages cast their eyes, death or poverty results," it was said (*b. Nedarim* 7b). Rav, a prominent third century CE Babylonian Amora (Jewish scholar expounding on the oral law), commenting on the biblical passage, "The Lord will ward off from you all sickness" [Deut 7:15], declared, "This is the [Evil] Eye" (*b. Bava Metzi'a* 107b).[27] Going up to a cemetery, he said that of one hundred persons, "Ninety-nine [have died] of the Evil Eye, and one of natural causes" (*b. Bava Metzi'a* 107b).[28] The Palestinian Talmud attributes this saying to both Rav and R. Hiyya Rabbah: "Ninety-nine die from the [Evil] Eye and one by the hand of heaven" (*y. Shabbat* 14, 14c). It explains that Rav and R. Hiyya Rabbah lived in Babylon (thought to be the home of Evil Eye belief), "where the Evil Eye often appeared" (*y. Shabbat* 14, 14c). Babylonian Jews, particularly concerned about their vessels for food, sought to protect them and their contents with apotropaic inscriptions on the vessels according to Ludwig Blau (1898:154). The death of the many disciples of Rabbi Akiva was said to have been by their envious Evil-Eyeing of one another: "R. Akiva had twelve thousand disciples from Gabbat to Antipatris and all died at the same time. Why? Because they looked at each other with an Evil Eye [lit. 'narrow eye']" (*Genesis Rabbah* 61:3). To seven later disciples he explained: "My sons, the previous disciples died only because they were envious of each other in respect to the Torah; see that you do not act in this manner. Therefore they arose and filled the whole Land of Israel with Torah" (*Genesis Rabbah* 61:3).[29] Here a fatal Evil Eye is implied by death-dealing envy, as with the midrash concerning Sarah: the culprit was the disciples' envious Evil Eye. One can also damage another person's growing plants and crops by "overlooking" them with an Evil Eye, hence the prohibition of standing in a neighbor's field when the wheat is in its ear (*b. Bava Batra* 2b).

---

26. Ulmer 1994:21–31.

27. Manuscripts Firenze II.I.8–9 and Vatican 115 read "This is the evil eye." Manuscript Munich 95 omits.

28. Manuscript Firenze II.1.8–9 reads "Ninety-nine have died of the Evil Eye, and one of natural causes"; Manuscript Munich 95 omits.

29. On the Evil Eye as a major cause of death see also *y. Sanhedrin* 10, 28a.

Possessing and casting an Evil Eye also can shorten one's *own* life. Rabbi Joshua warned: "The Evil Eye, and the evil inclination, and hatred of mankind put a person out of this world" (*m. Avot* 2:11).[30]

The Evil Eye also is said to be the starting point of sin (*Seder Eliyahu Zuta* 9), one of the seven causes of sickness or disaster (*b. Arakhin* 16a), and the greatest of sins (*Derekh Eretez Zuta* 6; cf. Sir 31:13). The Evil Eye is said to have caused the breaking of the first tablets of the Law (*Numbers Rabbah* 12:4) and the death of Daniel's three companions in the fiery furnace (*b. Sanhedrin* 93a).[31]

Fascinators

Possessing an Evil Eye was deemed one of several negative characteristics of a blood-letter (physician) who was judged arrogant:

> Our rabbis taught: Ten things were said about a blood-letter: he walks haughtily, has a conceited spirit, leans back when sitting, has a grudging ("narrow") eye and an Evil Eye; he eats much and excretes little; and he is suspected of adultery, robbery and bloodshed. (*b. Kiddushin* 82a)[32]

It is difficult to control one's own Evil Eye:

> It is easy to make enemies, but difficult to make friends; it is easy to ascend heights, but difficult to descend; most difficult of all is the ability to combat the effect of one's own Evil Eye. (*Yalqut Shimoni* 1.845)[33]

And it is possible to Evil-Eye oneself (*b. Berakhot* 55b), as Greeks and Romans also thought.

Several biblical characters were considered by the rabbis to have been fascinators casting their envious Evil Eyes on rivals and victims. This included:

---

30. See also *Avot of Rabbi Nathan* I, 16, 31b.

31. On the Evil Eye as cause of Jerusalem's destruction in 586 BCE and of Israel's exiles in Egypt and Babylon, see Ulmer 1994:124–25.

32. "Narrow eye" and "Evil Eye" are linked and likely constitute a hendiadys—two words or expressions for the same phenomenon, similar to "Evil Eye" and "envy" in Greek and Latin texts).

33. Ulmer 1994:14.

- Cain against Abel,[34] and so marking "the evil eye [as] responsible for the first murder in the history of humanity";[35]
- the inhabitants of Sodom who cast an Evil Eye on wealthy people and robbed them day and night (*b. Sanhedrin* 109a);
- a childless Sarah casting an envious Evil Eye against co-wife Hagar, causing Hagar to lose her first child (*Genesis Rabbah* 45:5; cf. Gen 16:4);
- a malevolent Sarah casting a malicious Evil Eye on a twenty-seven year old Ishmael, son of Hagar, and causing his fever, stomach cramps, and thirst (*Genesis Rabbah* 53:13);[36]
- Ephron the Hittite, who envied Abraham and his wealth (*Genesis Rabbah* 58:7; *Exodus Rabbah* 31:17, citing Prov 28:22; cf. Gen 23:3–20);[37]
- Esau "hastening after riches" (*Exodus Rabbah* 31:17 as a midrash on Prov 28:22 and Gen 50:5; see also *Pirqe Rabbi Eliezer* 32);
- Esau's envious Evil Eye against Jacob (appeased by Jacob's gift to his brother of animals from his flock) (*Genesis Rabbah* 76:8; cf. Gen 32:17); and Jacob also feared Esau Evil-Eyeing Dinah (*Genesis Rabbah* 76:9; cf. Gen 32:23);
- Og, the giant king of Bashan, Evil-Eyeing the family of Jacob (*b. Berakhot* 54b; *Deuteronomy Rabbah* 1:25);
- Joseph's brothers casting an envious Evil Eye on Joseph, favored by his father (*Genesis Rabbah* 84:10; cf. Gen 37:8, 11; Acts 7:9);
- King Saul enviously Evil-Eyeing David with his "narrow eye" when assisting David in donning his armor (cf. 1 Sam 18:9);[38]
- Balaam for intending to injure the people of Israel (*Numbers Rabbah* 20:6–11) and the followers of Balaam (*m. Avot* 5:19);[39]
- the Persian King Ahasuerus "who had a narrow eye [=miserly Evil Eye] concerning money" (*Esther Rabbah* 2:1);[40]

---

34. *Exodus Rabbah* 31:17 as a midrash on Prov 28:22 and Gen 4:8.
35. Ulmer 1994:107.
36. See Brav 1992:46; Ulmer 1994:113.
37. Ulmer 1994:109–11.
38. *Tanhuma, Emor* 6, 43a (ed. Buber); *Emor* 4, 36b (printed edition); cf. 1 Sam 17:38; Ulmer 1994:121–22.
39. Ulmer 1994:119–21.
40. Ibid.:122.

- Queen Esther, who proposed to cast an Evil Eye upon King Ahasuerus "so that he will be envious of me and of Haman. And he will kill us and I will not see the suffering of Israel" (*Midrash Megillah* [*Otsar Midrashim* 60b]; *b. Megillah* 15b);[41]
- Haman, who cast an Evil Eye on Israel's festivals, was punished by God, and his downfall was commemorated by the new festival of Purim (*Esther Rabbah* 7:12).

"Those who cast their eyes at the better portion" (out of envy or greed) are listed among persons exposed to the Evil Eyed gaze (*b. Pesahim* 50b). But they are also likely to have been suspected of wielding an Evil Eye in accord with the sentiments of Prov 23:6; 28:22; Sir 14:10; and 31:12-13.

During this rabbinic period, *eminent Torah scholars* were added to the list of fascinators found in the Bible.[42] "Wherever the Sages cast their eyes in disapproval against someone," it was claimed, "death or poverty resulted."[43] It was said of Rabbis Eleazar ben Hyrcanus,[44] Simeon ben Yohai,[45] and Yohanan[46] that the burning rays of their Evil Eyes reduced the objects of their glances to heaps of bones.[47] R. Yohanan's "boiling" Evil Eye, killed a man who slandered Jerusalem.[48] This rabbi also is said to have slain his brother-in-law Resh Laqish with his Evil Eye (*b. Bava Metzi'a* 84a). When R. Yohanan subsequently met the young son of Resh Laqish conversing about Torah, the boy's mother, fearing his exposure to the rabbi's Evil Eye, "took him away and said: 'Go away from him, so that he [R. Yohanan] will not do to you what he did to your father'" (*b. Taanit* 9a). On another occasion, R. Yohanan confronted one who questioned his teaching concerning the meaning of Isa 54:12 ("I [God] will make your [Jerusalem's] pinnacles of agate, your gates of carbuncles and all your wall of precious stones"). The man, already once punished by God for his scepticism, was punished again by Yohanan for trusting only what his eyes perceived: "Yohanan lifted his eyes and glared at the man and he [the sceptic] was instantly turned into a

---

41. Ibid.:114.

42. See Lilienthal 1924:270; Ulmer 1994:83-104, on "the Sages' Powerful Eyes"; Sinai 2008.

43. *b. Nedarim* 7b; also *b. Mo'ed Qatan* 17b; *b. Ḥagigah* 5b.

44. *b. Bava Metzi'a* 59b; *b. Shabbat* 33b.

45. *b. Shabbat* 34a; *Pesiq. Rab Kah.* 90b; *b. Bava Metzi'a* 84a.

46. *Pesiq. Rab Kah.* 18, 136a-137a; *b. Bava Batra* 75a; *b. Sanhedrin* 100a.

47. Noy 1971:997.

48. *b. Bava Batra* 75a; *Pesiq. Rab Kah.* 18, 136a-137a. See Noy 1971:998; Ulmer 1994:87-88.

heap of bones."[49] Of Rabbi Sheshet it was said that he cast his eyes upon a heretic who immediately became a heap of ashes (*b. Berakhot* 58a). A man who persisted in requesting to marry Rav's daughter, but whom some sages suspected of being illegitimate, was slain by Rav's Evil Eye: "As the man refused to go away, [Rav] fixed his Evil Eye upon him and he died" (*b. Yevamot* 45a). The Evil Eye of R. Eliezer ben Hyrcanos caused extensive destruction: "a third of the wheat and a third of the barley crop . . . the calamity that occurred that day was great, since everything upon which R. Eliezer cast his eyes was burned" (*b. Bava Metzi'a* 59b). This was among the reasons given for his excommunication. Even his disciples feared his powerful Evil Eye (*b. Betsah* 15b).

Upon glimpsing two men throwing pieces of bread at one another and wasting a precious commodity, R. Yehudah "set his eyes upon them and there was famine" (*b. Taanit* 24b). Ulmer (1994:100) notes that it was held that "any critical remark by a rabbi could provoke his eye's destructive power." R. Shimeon b. Yohai, accused by a disloyal old man of having purified a cemetery (i.e. an unclean space), "cast his Evil Eye upon him and he [the old man] died." The account continues:

> He went out into the street and saw Yehudah, the son of proselytes.[50] He [R. Shimeon b. Yohai] said: 'That man is still in the world.' He [R. Shimeon b. Yohai] cast his eyes upon him [Yehudah] and he was turned into a heap of bones. (*b. Shabbat* 34a)

Rabbi Abaye, it was said, put to death with his Evil Eye the parents of his rival, Rabbi Papa, who had advanced an outrageous legal argument.

> Abaye said [to R. Papa]: "Where is your father?" He [R. Papa] said, "He is in town." "Where is your mother?" "In town," [R. Papa said]. [Abaye] set his Evil Eye [lit., "eyes"] upon them and they died. (*b. Yevamot* 106a)

The Evil Eye, in other words, was believed to cause illness and bring about scorched earth, famine, and death through burning rays emitted from the eye, even the eyes of prominent rabbis. This extramission theory of vision was consistent with that of the Mesopotamians, Egyptians, Greeks, and Romans and the biblical communities. Rabbis, it was believed, used their Evil Eye intentionally to punish insolence, disrespect by disciples, scepticism

---

49. *Pesiq. Rab Kah.* 18, 136a–137b; cf. *b. Bava Batra* 75a; *b. Sanhedrin* 100a; *Midrash Tehillim* 87:2.

50. This Yehudah, not to be confused with Rabbi Yehudah, was a traitorous informant who had betrayed the rabbi's secret discussion to the Romans (*b. Shabbat* 33b).

of rabbinic teaching, the use of specious, invalid arguments, heresy, fanaticism, and to mete out justice.[51]

Victims of the Evil Eye and Dangerous Situations

"Prominent men, beautiful women, and newborn babies—all of whom were likely to attract attention—are especially susceptible to the evil eye," David Noy points out.[52] This then led to efforts to deceive or thwart the Evil Eye by veiling the beauty, concealing the wealth, and covering the children or giving them ugly names. *Children*, as in Mesopotamia, Egypt, Greece and Rome, were deemed especially vulnerable to the Evil Eye (*b. Shabbat* 66b).[53] Children of elites were safeguarded with small bells, and those of the lower class with knots.[54] Grown children were also vulnerable. Jacob, according to one midrash, urged his handsome strapping sons, when visiting a strange town in Egypt (Gen 42:1), not to enter through the same gate as one group, lest their good looks attract an Evil Eye and they all be injured at once (*Genesis Rabbah* 91:2; cf. also 91.6).[55] *Targum Yerushalmi I* Gen 42:5 also takes Jacob's remark as referring to Evil Eye avoidance and describes the sons's entrance into Egypt accordingly: "And each one of the Israelites entered through one particular gate, so that the Evil Eye would have no power over them." According to another midrash, Joshua advised Ephraim and Manasseh to hide in a forest not just to gain some ground for residence (Josh 17:15) but also to avoid exposure to the Evil Eye (*b. Bava Batra* 118ab).[56] In reference to Gen 32:21-22 describing Jacob's noctural removal of his wives and entire family across the Jabbok river and away from Esau, Jacob, the sages said, hid his daughter Dinah from Esau's Evil Eye: "He put her in a chest, locked it, and said: 'This wicked man has an Evil Eye; let him not take her away from me!'" (*Genesis Rabbah* 76:9). The cover of night also was used to protect travelers from the Evil Eye (*Genesis Rabbah* 56:11).

Exposing a discovered object, such as a costly garment, to the view of visitors in one's home was inadvisable since this would make it visible

---

51. Ulmer 1994:87–97.

52. Noy 1971:998.

53. Blau 1898:164; 1907:280; Noy 1971:998; see Vol. 2:2–3, 29, 53, 143, 145–46, 152, 155, 251; and Vol. 3:4, 5, 63, 107, 225, 228, 231, 257–58, 263, 277.

54. Blau 1898:164.

55. Noy 1971:998. For an equivalent Arabic notion, see Ford 1998:223–24. Ulmer (1994:176) takes Jacob's remark to indicate that he feared that he himself would be envied for having ten handsome sons.

56. Noy 1971:998.

to the potential envy of the visitors's Evil Eyes (*b. Pesaḥim* 26b, *b. Bava Metzi'a* 30a).[57] Counting people also was discouraged because the action was thought to invite an Evil Eye attack on these persons.[58] Trading in cane (reeds) and jars was deemed dangerous, since their being visible and plentiful exposed them to Evil-Eyed envy (*b. Pesaḥim* 50b). The visibility of still others is dangerous for the same reason:

> traders in market-stands and those who breed small cattle, and those who cut down beautiful trees, and those who cast their eyes at the better portion, will never see a sign of blessing. What is the reason? Because people gaze at them (with an Evil Eye). (*b. Pesaḥim* 50b)

According to R. Yitshaq, "a blessing is found only in what is hidden from the (Evil) Eye" (*b. Bava Metzi'a* 42a). The school of R. Yishamel echoed this thought:

> In the school of R. Yishmael it was taught: blessing is only possible in things not under the direct control of the (Evil) Eye. (*b. Taanit* 8b)[59]

This conviction led to the practice among Jews, as in Greco-Roman cultures, of concealing one's children and valued possessions, and of denying one's good health, success in business and the like, so as not to attract an envious Evil Eye.[60] To this day there are persons who respond to the friendly question, "how are you?" not with any affirmative remark, but rather with the deflecting comment, "not too bad" or "it could be worse"—to avoid that pernicious or envious Evil Eye.

Beauty is likely to arouse praise and admiration. So both the condition of beauty and the act of *praise or admiration* of a child, a handsome person or object, or a person's good health, also was thought to arouse an Evil Eye, as held also in Greco-Roman culture:[61] "For this reason, Abraham sent his son Isaac home at night after the Akedah (*Genesis Rabbah* 56:11)" (Noy 1971:998). To counter the Evil eye and envy directed against objects praised, a custom developed among Jews analogous to the Roman practice of accompanying words of praise or admiration with the disclaimer, "no

---

57. Noy 1971:998–99.

58. Ulmer 1994:158, citing a comment of Rashi. For a similar Roman notion concerning counting see Vol. 2:15, 84, 151, 159.

59. See Blau 1898:156; Noy 1971:999; Ulmer 1994:173–81.

60. See Vol. 2:55, 112, 120, 156, 158–59.

61. See Vol. 2:15, 17, 32–33, 44, 64, 96, 99–100, 112, 113, 115, 129–30, 145–46, 149, 153–54, 155, 157–59, 168–69, 179, 181, 209, 274, 276.

Evil Eye (intended)." Paralleling the Roman expression *praefiscine dixerim* was the Jewish expression *bli 'ayin-harah* ("without an Evil Eye"), or in later Yiddish, *kein ein-horeh/genahora*, "no Evil Eye intended."[62]

Beside the victims of the Evil Eye already mentioned above in connection with fascinators and their targets, and in addition to prominent men and beautiful women, there were still *further victims* of the Evil Eye in the rabbinic tradition. Even rabbis themselves were vulnerable to the Evil Eyes of fellow rabbis. *Rava* (Rabbah bar Rav Nachman) was caused by the envious Evil Eye of the rabbis to suffer at the hands of the ruler King Shapur despite his payments to the government (*b. Ḥagigah* 5a–b). The *parents of Rav Papa* were struck dead by the Evil Eye (*b. Yebamot* 106a). Because of his excessive fasting and his testing himself with an oven's heat, R. Zera was scorched by other rabbis. "The rabbis cast an (Evil) Eye upon him and his legs were charred. After this he was called 'short and char-legged'" (*b. Bava Metsi'a* 85a).

Persons of high status were deemed vulnerable. When the people demanded that Rabbi Judah I go up from his seat of teaching to the lectern, his father, Patriarch Simon ben Gamliel said, "I have a dove among you and you want to destroy it"; i.e. leaving the audience and being promoted to joining the lecturers would expose him to the envious Evil Eye (*b. Bava Mezi'a* 84b).[63] Girls on the other hand, opined R. Chisda, do not attract the Evil Eye. So when the first child is a female, he stated, this is a favorable sign for the sons that might follow that they would escape the Evil Eye (*b. Bava Batra* 141a).[64]

Certain *situations* were opportunities for an Evil Eye to strike and therefore they called for precautionary measures. Being in a crowd posed a danger since in a crowd there would be many that might possess an Evil Eye, a notion found also among Greeks and Romans (*Genesis Rabbah* 91:2; cf. also 91:6).[65] "Two brothers," it was taught, "never enter a banquet hall together because of the (Evil) Eye."[66] According to *Midrash Tehillim* 7:2,

> A man who goes to a house where a feast is in progress does not take his sons with him, because he fears the Evil Eye in this assembly. Although Saul knew that the attribute of God's justice was about to strike him, when he went to war, he took his sons with him [and they died].

62. See Vol. 2:37–38, 44, 113, 154–55, 158, 169, 179, 209.
63. Blau 1898:154.
64. Ibid.
65. See Vol. 2:66, 69, 146, 155.
66. *Tanḥuma*, ed. Buber, *Miqets* 13, 99b.

In addition to its illustrating the act of concealing prompted by the Evil Eye, this passage makes a rare reference to "God's justice" about to strike Saul. The idea is close to that of the ancient Greek sense of *nemesis* as an expression of the Evil Eye of the gods executing justice.[67]

Related to this act of avoidance is the custom of not taking children to wedding feasts for fear of exposing them to an Evil Eyed person in the gathering (*Leviticus Rabbah* 26:7; *Midrash Tehillim* 7:2). Weddings, which were occasions of great joy, the assembling of many, and the presence of handsome youth, were particular moments of danger from the Evil Eye. According to a later ninth-century CE midrash on Num 6:24–26, 27 and 7:1, Rabbi Yehoshua of Sikhnin told a parable in which the Evil Eye prevailed over the preparations of a wedding. The father of the bride, a king, gave his daughter an amulet for protection against the Evil Eye. Rabbi Yehoshua compares this to the situation when God was about to give the Torah to Israel at Sinai. "However, the Evil Eye prevailed over the betrothal, and the tablets [of the Decalogue] were broken, as it is written, 'Moses . . . broke them beneath the mountain' [Exod 32:19]." Subsequently, however, R. Yehoshua continued, when Israel made the tabernacle, God gave them the blessing that the Evil Eye would have no power over them (*Pesikta Rabbati* 5:10).[68]

Valuable objects, such as seed-bearing plants and costly garments, also were considered vulnerable to the Evil Eye. Rab, a disciple of Rabbi Judah the Patriarch, forbad standing in a neighbor's field when the plants began to bear seed (lest the future crop be destroyed by an Evil Eye).[69] A costly garment that was found should not be spread over the bed and exposed to the view of any visitors, because "it will be scorched by the (Evil) Eye of the guests."[70]

On the other hand, certain *creatures and persons were considered invulnerable to the Evil Eye*. *Fish* of the sea were deemed safe from the Evil Eye (*b. Berakhot* 20a; *b. Bava Metzi'a* 84a). Accordingly, images of fish have been found on Jewish amulets against the Evil Eye.[71] According to one recorded opinion, *girls who are sisters of brothers* are likewise immune. "If a daughter [is born] first, it is considered a good sign for the sons that follow. Some say, because she rears her brothers. Others say, because the Evil Eye has no influence over them" (*b. Bava Batra* 141a). The rationale of the latter opinion is

---

67. See Vol. 2:19, 33, 100–101, 140, 167–68, 169.
68. See also *Midrash Aggadah* II, 89.
69. *b. Bava Metzi'a* 107a; *b. Bava Batra* 2b.
70. Noy 1971:998; cf. *b. Pesaḥim* 26b, *b. Bava Metzi'a* 30a.
71. Lilienthal 1924:255. On the fish as apotropaic see Dölger, (1922–27, 1943) esp. 2:181.

that the Evil Eye is not attracted to daughters (deemed inferior to sons) and so the birth of a daughter distracts the Evil Eye from any brothers that might follow. *Particularly pious persons*, according to Ulmer, also were thought invulnerable to the Evil Eye.[72]

Foremost among *immune persons*, and analogous to the immune fish of the sea, were the *descendants of Joseph*, who himself survived the Evil Eye hostility of his brothers.[73] Joseph's immunity, in turn, was thought to have been passed on to his descendants. This included Rabbi Yohanan (*b. Bava Metzi'a* 84a; see below).

Joseph and Solomon—Protectors against the Evil Eye

Both Joseph and Solomon were regarded as powerful protectors against the Evil Eye: Joseph because with God's aid he survived the Evil-Eyed envy of his brothers, and Solomon because of his divinely bestowed knowledge of the occult and his mastery of demons.

Joseph, Survivor of Evil-Eyed Envy

Joseph, favored son of Jacob (Gen 37:3), was remembered in rabbinic tradition and lore as a successful survivor of the envious Evil Eye, with the consequence that his descendents also were deemed immune from the Evil Eye.[74] The *Testaments of the Twelve Patriarchs*, as we have seen in Vol. 3, chap. 1, are an important Israelite witness to this traditional linkage of Joseph, envy and the Evil Eye. The rabbinic association was based on the Genesis account of Joseph's successful survival of the envy of his brothers in general (Gen 37–50; cf. Acts 7:9–15) and on a variant reading of Gen 49:22 in particular. As part of Jacob's final blessing of his sons prior to his death (Gen 49:1–27), Joseph's blessing stated: "Joseph is a fruitful bough, a fruitful bough by a spring/well . . ." (Gen 49:22 RSV). The Hebrew word translated "spring/well" (*'ayin*), however, can also mean "eye," as already noted above and as indicated in several rabbinic texts.

An example of this tradition is a Talmudic anecdote about Rabbi Yohanan, who claimed that being a descendent of Joseph protected him against the Evil Eye. A handsome and attractive man, his custom was to go

---

72. Ulmer 1991:352.

73. *b. Berakhot* 20a, 55b; *b. Bava Metzi'a* 84a; *b. Bava Batra* 118b; *b. Sotah* 36b.

74. See Blau 1898:154–55; Billerbeck 1926 1:834; Shrire 1982:114; Ulmer 1991:351–52; 1994:166–67. On the figure of Joseph in post-biblical Jewish history, see Niehoff 1992.

and sit at the gate of the women's ritual bath so that they could have children as beautiful as he.[75]

> "When the daughters of Israel ascend from the bath," he said, "let them look at me first, that they may bear sons as beautiful and as learned as I." The rabbis said to him: "Do you not fear an Evil Eye (when you expose yourself to be seen)?" He replied, "I am of the seed of Joseph, over whom the Evil Eye has no power." It is written: Joseph is a fruitful bough, even a fruitful bough by a spring/well (*'ayin*).... Rabbi Abahu said: "Do not read 'by a spring/well' but 'above [the power of] the (Evil) Eye." Rabbi Yose ben Rabbi Hanina said it from the following: "'Multiply abundantly like fish in the midst of the earth' (Gen 48:16). Just as fish in the sea are covered by water and the (Evil) Eye has no power over them, so also the seed of Joseph—the (Evil) Eye has no power over them. Or, if you prefer I can say: 'The Evil Eye has no power over the eye which refused to feed itself on what did not belong to it.'" (*b. Berakhot* 20a; *b. Bava Metzi'a* 84a)[76]

The question first addressed to R. Yohanan by the rabbis—"Do you not fear an Evil Eye when you expose yourself to be seen?"—alludes to the belief that putting beauty on display inevitably will attract an envious Evil Eye. This midrash also illustrates the belief that fish in the sea covered by water are not visible from the land and hence are considered immune to the Evil Eye. The notion that the Evil Eye is powerless over anyone refusing to benefit from what belongs to another, Ulmer suggests, "refers to the merit of Joseph, who refused to set an eye upon Potiphar's wife in his master's house in Egypt, when she tried to seduce him."[77]

According to another midrash, appeal was made to being of Joseph's lineage when entering a strange town in order to secure protection from an Evil Eye. The stranger joins his hands with each thumb in the palm of the other and recites the words: "I, so-and-so, son of so-and-so, am of the seed of Joseph over whom the Evil Eye has no power, as it says, 'Joseph is a fruitful bough, a fruitful bough by a spring/well' [Gen 49:22]" (*b. Berakhot* 55b). In regard to the saying itself, "I am of the seed of Joseph, over whom the Evil Eye has no power," Ludwig Blau has aptly observed that "the saying is Jewish, but the protective gesture is pagan."[78] Blau and Noy think the gesture

---

75. Blau 1898:154.

76. See also *b. Sota* 36b and *b. Bava Batra* 118b; Blau 1898:155; and Ulmer 1994:165–71 for texts illustrative of this Joseph tradition.

77. Ulmer 1994:167–68.

78. Blau 1898:155.

is similar to that of the *mano fica* gesture which also involves a thumb and an obscene gesture.[79] "The gesture (a 'fig')—universally used to avert the evil eye by putting it to shame (this originally meaning was probably unknown to sages who prescribed it)—took on a Jewish character by the pronouncement of the aggadic sentence that the descendants of Joseph are immune from the evil eye."[80]

Yet another midrash on Genesis declares that Joseph also protected others, notably Rachel, his mother, from the Evil Eye of Esau, by covering her with his body (*Genesis Rabbah* 78:10 on Gen 33:7).

Joseph as protector against the Evil Eye also was a recurrent motif on Jewish anti-Evil Eye amulets as we shall see below (pp. 25, 26, 29, 34, 35, 47, 155).

Solomon, Ruler of Demons and the Evil Eye

In Jewish and Christian tradition, Solomon was celebrated not only for his wisdom but also for his command of occult knowledge and his control over demons.[81] Flavius Josephus, in his *Antiquities of the Jews* (8.2.5), gives the following account of Solomon:

> Now so great was the prudence and wisdom which God granted Solomon that he surpassed the ancients; even the Egyptians, who are said to excel all men in understanding, were not only, when compared to him, a little inferior but proved to fall far short of the king in sagacity . . . He also composed a thousand and five books of odes and songs, and three thousand books of parables and similitudes . . . There was no form of nature with which he was not acquainted or which he passed over without examining . . . And God granted him knowledge of the art used against demons for the benefit and healing of men. He also composed incantations by which illnesses are relieved, and left behind forms of exorcisms with which those possessed by demons drive them out, never to return. And this kind of cure is of very great power among us to this day; for I have seen a certain Eleazar, a countryman of mine, in the presence of Vespasian, his sons, tribunes, and a number of other soldiers, free men possessed by demons, and this was the manner of the cure: he put to the nose of the possessed man a ring which had under its seal one of the roots prescribed by Solomon, and then, as the

---

79. Blau 1898:155 and n.3; Blau 1907:280; Noy 1971: 999.
80. Noy 1971:999.
81. See McCown 1922; Duling 1975, 1984, 1985, 1993; Verheyden, ed. 2012.

man smelled it, drew out the demon through his nostrils, and, when the man at once fell down, adjured the demon never to come back into him, speaking Solomon's name and reciting the incantations he had composed. Then, wishing to convince the bystanders and to prove to them that he had this power, Eleazar placed a cup or foot-basin full of water a little way off and commanded the demon, as it went out of the man, to overturn it and make known to the spectators that he had left the man. And when this was done, the understanding and wisdom of Solomon were clearly revealed, on account of which we have been induced to speak of these things, in order that all men may know the greatness of his nature and how God favored him, and that no one under the sun may be ignorant of the king's surpassing virtue of every kind.[82]

Proverbs attributed to Solomon and mentioning the Evil Eye (Prov 23:6; 28:22), as well as reference to the Evil Eye in the *Wisdom of Solomon* (4:12), have been discussed previously in Vol. 3, chap. 1. According to an Israelite pseudonymous writing, *The Testament of Solomon* (first–third centuries CE, possibly in Egypt), God granted Solomon "authority over all the spirits of the air, the earth, and the regions beneath the earth" (18:3).[83] The composition demonstrates the thwarting and curing power attributed to spoken words (18:5–10, 31, 36) written words and letters (18:22–30, 33, 37, 38, 40); ritual remedies (18:15, 20, 31, 33, 34, 35, 37) and inscriptions and amulets (18:16, 39, 40). Solomon received from God through the archangel Michael a powerful ring with a seal as a weapon against demons and the Evil Eye. This Seal of Solomon (*Sphragis Solomonis*) confined and bound demons, male and female (*T. Sol.* 7:3; 8:11 etc.), and played an important

---

82. Duling 1983:946–47, citing the LCL translation of Josephus by H. St. Thackery and R. Marcus, 593–97. On Solomon as master of demons, see also Schürer 1909 3:413, 418–20; Billerbeck 4/1 (1928):510–13 (on *b. Giṭṭin* 68a) and 533–535; Winkler 1931; DiTomasso 2012:317–20. For Solomon and the "Seal of Solomon" appearing on amulets and apotropaics see Schlumberger 1892b, 1895; Perdrizet 1903, 1922:6–7, 27–31; Peterson 1926:96–109; Meisen 1950:166, 171–72; Bonner 1950:208–15, 221, 302, (nos. 294–97); Goodenough 1953–1964 1:168; 2:226–38; 7:198–200; 9:1044–67; Delatte and Derchain 1964:261–64 (nos. 369–77); Bagatti 1971, 1972; Russell 1982; Russell, 1995:39–41 and fig. 6; Vikan 1984:79–81 and figs. 19–20; Gitler 1990:371; Limberis 1991:177–78; Meyer 1994:45–50; Michaelides 1994; Luck 1999:116–17. For Solomon appearing on amulets as a cavalier lancing an Evil Eye demoness, see Seligmann 1910:313–15 and figs. 230–233; Peterson 1926:96–109; Bonner 1950:302, (nos. 294–97 and Plate XIV); Bagatti 1971; Gitler 1990:371; Walter 1989–90. Bohak 2008:213; DiTomasso 2012:317–20. On Flavius Josephus's portrait of Solomon, see Feldman 1976.

83. On this text, see also Vol. 3, chap. 1.

role in exorcisms. Solomon, it is said, interrogated Beelzeboul, "prince of demons," as to his activities, to which Beelzeboul responded, "I inspire men to envy":

> I destroy kings; I ally myself with foreign tyrants. I impose my demons on men in order that they might believe in them and be destroyed . . . I also inspire men with envy, murder, wars, sodomy, and other evil things. And I will destroy the world. (*T. Sol.* 6:4–5)[84]

Beelzeboul, however, is aware that he is thwarted by almighty God, *Emmanouel*, whose great name is *Eloi* (*T. Sol.* 7:8). Solomon also confronted the demoness Obyzouth (*T. Sol.* 13:1–7), whose disheveled hair (13:1, 5, 7) recalls that of the Greek mythical figure, Gorgo/Medusa, caster of the Evil Eye.[85] Her activities, however, are also akin to the Mesopotamian demoness Lamashtu or the Hebrew demoness Lilith:

> "I do not rest at night," she states, "but travel all around all the world visiting women and, foreseeing the hour (when they give birth), I search (for them) and strangle their newborn infants . . . my work is limited to killing newborn infants, injuring eyes, condemning mouths, destroying minds, and making bodies feel pain." (*T. Sol.* 13:3–4)

Asked by Solomon by whom she was thwarted, she replied: "By the angel Raphael; and when women give birth, write my name on a piece of papyrus and I shall flee from them to the other world" (13:6). Solomon ordered the demoness to be bound by her hair and hung up in front of the Temple so that all could glorify the God of Israel who gave Solomon this authority (13:7). The demoness is not named explicitly as an agent of the Evil Eye, but this is made likely by her description here and its similarity to the graphic depictions of Solomon as cavalier slaying a prostrate demoness (in one instance named *Baskosynê*, "Evil Eye"); see below, pp. 24, 35, 105.

Among the *Greek Magical Papyri* is an amulet of Solomon with the words, "protect him, NN [bearer of the amulet], from all evil" (*diaphylaxon ton deina apo pasês kakias*); it perhaps was intended to induce a trance (PGM 4.850–929). This protective power of Solomon apparently was appropriated by contemporary Greeks, Romans, and Christians as well.

---

84. This is the reading of ms P; Duling 1983:968 n. e.

85. See Vol. 2:133–37, 145, 159, 174 and nn. 615, 206–7, 225, 227, 244–48 and illustrations 3–6, 28, 53, 54. For an obsidian Medusa on an amulet found on a Jewish corpse see Goodenough 1953 2:236 and n. 186.

Reference to Solomon is also made by the so-called Aramaic Incantation Bowls that were employed as apotropaics against the Evil Eye and other harmful forces. These bowls, "the size of soup tureens," Duling notes, have been found upside down in and around houses and at their corners. Almost all have ink Eastern Aramaic inscriptions written in spiral form on the bottom insides of the bowls. The function of the bowls was to trap and avert demons and thereby protect homes and inhabitants from demons, the Evil Eye, witchcraft, illness, and other evils.[86] "At least eighteen bowls refer to 'King Solomon, son of David,' and twelve or thirteen of them refer to his seal ring."[87] As a sample of these bowls and their incantations, Duling cites one that mentions the Evil Eye among the dangers to be averted:

> The demon NVVY', VVY QLY', BTY', Nuriel, Holy Rock. Sealed and countersealed and fortified are Axât, the daughter of Immâ; Rabbî, Malkî and Dipshi [and others named]—they and their houses and their children and their property are sealed with the seal-ring of El Shaddai, blessed be He, and with the seal ring of King Solomon, the son of David, who worked spells on male demons and female liliths. Sealed and countersealed and fortified against the male demon, and female lilith and spell and curse and incantation and knocking and Evil Eye and evil black arts, against the black-arts of mother and daughter . . . and against those of the presumptuous woman, who darkens the eyes and blows away the soul . . . In the name of the Lord. Lord, Hosts is His name, Amen, amen; selah. This charm is to thwart the demon Tîtînôs. Sealed are the bodies (?) of 'ŠQL [and others named].[88]

Solomon also figures prominently in amulets and apotropaics as a cavalier mounted on a horse and lancing a figure on the ground, usually a demoness, representing the Lilith and/or the Evil Eye (*Baskosynê*); see below, pp. 25, 31, 35–36, 41, 47, 49–50, 102, 105–6, 109, 115–17, 128, 133–44.

We turn now to the means employed to repel and thwart an Evil Eye as indicated not only by the literary but also the material evidence.

---

86. Duling 1983:947–48.
87. Ibid., 948.
88. Ibid., citing Gordon 1934:324–26 (Text B).

REPELLING AN EVIL EYE

Protective Words (Spoken or Written)

Spoken words included intoned charms, formulas, adjurations, conjurations, and blessings. These and other expressions eventually were written down on parchment, papyri, potsherds, bowls, and amulets.[89]

Appeal for help and protection against the Evil Eye was made to divine powers, as in Gentile practice, but in Israel specifically to the Hebrew God (Yahweh, Yah, Sebaoth, Shaddai) or to angels such as Michael, Gabriel, Raphael, and Uriel, or to prestigious persons of Israel's past who were successful in countering or controlling the Evil Eye, such as Joseph, David, and Solomon.[90]

The recitation of certain words that accompanied the manual gesture involving the two thumbs in opposite palms has already been mentioned. While pressing each of one's thumbs into the palms of their opposite hands, a person seeking protection from the Evil Eye declared: "I am of the seed of Joseph over whom the Evil Eye has no Power" (*b. Berakhot* 55b; cf. *b. Berakhot* 20a; *b. Bava Metzia* 84a).[91] The words appeal to the powerful figure of Joseph who, with God's help, survived the envious Evil Eye of his brothers. The manual gesture involving the thumbs is considered by Ludwig Blau to involve an "obscene gesture" similar to the *mano fica* of the Romans in which the thumb of the right hand is inserted between the second and third fingers of the same hand to simulate sexual intercourse.[92] This combination of words and gesture was recommended for anyone fearing an Evil Eye while entering a new town (*b. Berakhot* 55b). The rabbis linked this saying and gesture to the biblical words, "Joseph is a fruitful bough, even a fruitful bough by a well" (Gen 49:22), which words also were spoken for anti-Evil Eye protection (*b. Berakhot* 55b).[93] The words also appear on Jewish amulets discussed below.

Blessings (berakhot) also were spoken for protection.[94] Jacob, prior to his death, pronounced a blessing on Joseph and Joseph's two sons, Manasseh and Ephraim (Gen 48:1-22). Part of this blessing states: "the angel who has redeemed me from all evil bless the lads . . . and may they be teeming multi-

---

89. On apotropaics and amulets in general see Vol. 2:153-264.

90. See Dobschütz 1910:424-25; M. Gaster 1910:453; Ulmer 1994 passim.

91. See Blau 1898:155; 1907:280; Ulmer 1994:155, 166-68.

92. Blau 1898:155 and n. 3, though Blau opines that the rabbis no longer understood the gesture (1907:280).

93. Ulmer 1994:155.

94. Ibid., 148-50.

tudes in the midst of the earth" (Gen 48:16). This verse is regarded as potent against the Evil Eye (*'ayin ha-ra'*) because of its perceived two-fold power. First, it calls for angelic protection of the children of Israel. Secondly, the phrase, "may they be teeming multitudes" (*we-yidgu larov*) has a further sense of "may they multiply as fishes," and "fishes," in turn, alludes to creatures of the sea invisible to and safeguarded from the Evil Eye:

> Just as fish in the sea are covered by water and the [Evil] Eye has no power over them [because it cannot see them], so too [it is with] the descendents of Joseph—the [Evil] Eye has no power over them. (*b. Bava Metzi'a* 84a; cf. *b Sotah* 36b)

Joseph's descendants, alike fish below the water's surface, are, like Joseph himself, safe from the glance of an Evil Eye.

Pronouncing the words of the Aaronic benediction (Num 6:24–26) was thought to have apotropaic effect. This benediction, it was said, was God's gift of protection to Israel against the Evil Eye.

> When Israel made the tabernacle of the Holy One, blessed be He, He gave them the blessing first, in order that no Evil Eye might affect them. Accordingly, it is written, 'The Lord bless thee and keep thee' [Num 6:24, namely, from the Evil Eye]." (*Numbers Rabba* 12.4; *Pesiqta Rabbati* 5:10)[95]

Two silver amulets designed for wearing (c. seventh–sixth centuries BCE) were found in a burial cave in Ketef Hinnom in Jerusalem. They attest the apotropaic use of the words of this benediction in the first Temple period.[96] The benediction also is found on amulets of later time.[97]

Recitations of the Shema, Psalm 3, and Psalm 91 also were deemed effective.[98] Psalm 91 opens with reference to "abiding in the shadow of *Shaddai*," identifying God with this term. *Shaddai* ("Almighty") was an early name for the Deity prior to the name YHWH given to Moses,[99] and was rendered in the Greek Septuagint as *pantokrator*, "almighty." The word *Shaddai* was inscribed on numerous Jewish amulets and marks such amulets as

---

95. See Blau 1907a:547.

96. See Yardeni 1991; Ross 1991; Barkay et al. 2004; Barkay 2009:22–35, 122, 124, 126.

97. See Shire, *Amulets* 1982:164, Plate 41, lines 6–8. For the blessing in magic spells see Naveh and Shaked 1993:25–27.

98. Billerbeck 4/1 1928:528–529.

99. In the Priestly code of the Hebrew Bible, see Gen 17:1; 28:3; 35:11; 43:14; 48:3; Exod 6:3; and in older texts, Gen 49:25; Deut 32:8; Num 24:4, 16; Ps 18:14. It is also common in Job (5:17; 6:4, 14; 8:5 etc) and appears in Ps 68:15; Ezek 1:24; 10:5.

Jewish.[100] In later time, the divine name *Shaddai* and Psalm 67 were written in the form of a seven-branch candelabra. Words of the *Shema' Yisrael*, Israel's holiest confession (Deut 6:4), "Hear, O Israel, the LORD our God, the LORD is one," were written in Greek letters on a small rectangular gold leaf contained in a silver capsule amulet buried with an infant about eighteen months old. The site of the burial (c. third century CE) was a graveyard on a Roman estate in Halbturn, Austria, near the ancient Roman metropolis of Carnuntum in Pannonia Superior. The function of the amuletic capsule and its sacred content, as other *bullae* (Roman and Jewish) of its type, was to protect the Jewish infant from the forces of evil including the Evil Eye.[101] This practice of equipping the dead with amuletic protection mirrors that of Egyptian, Greek and Roman custom. It is another illustration of the Jewish use of selected biblical texts for apotropaic purpose. Biblical texts were also written on pieces of parchment worn as amulets on the body or inserted into capsules (*mezuzah*) affixed to the door-posts of homes; see below, under Amulets.

Conjurations, powerful oaths binding the forces of evil and compelling them to act according to the will of the conjurer,[102] against the Evil Eye were also employed. A conjuration used by Jews in Palestine, reads in part, "I adjure you, all forms of Evil Eyes, a black eye, a blue eye, a round eye . . . a male eye, a female eye . . . all forms of Evil Eyes in the world that look and speak evil." It then appeals to "the All Holy, Almighty and Highest Eye . . ." and in conclusion adjures "all forms of the Evil Eye to depart and be annihilated and flee far away from N. and his entire household, with no power over N . . . Amen."[103]

Anti-Evil Eye incantations in Aramaic (as in the Aramaic Magic Bowls) repeat features of Evil Eye belief manifested in Mesopotamian incantations millennia earlier, as shown by Ford.[104]

---

100. See Shrire 1982:73, 93, 137 and plates 1, 3, 4, 7, 11 (against the Evil Eye), 17, 24, 34, 38, 40, 43 (reverse side of Jewish-Christian amulet), 49, 51b, 53; Trachtenberg 1939:158.

101. On the discovery, details and significance of the amulet see Lange and Eshel 2013; and Eshel, Eshel, and Lange 2010.

102. M. Gaster 1910:451–52.

103. The full text is given by Seligmann 1910 2:358–59, with no date indicated.

104. Ford 1998; for incantations against the Evil Eye in various dialects of Aramaic see Hazard 1893:284–86; Gollancz 1912: Codex A §23, §39; cf. §54; Codex B §9; Codex C §19, cf. §1; Driver 1937, 1938; 1943:152, 170; Neveh and Shaked 1987:133; cf. pp. 40–45, 172–75; 1993:99–101, 120–22; Ford 1998:202 n.1; Tarelko 2000.

28   Beware the Evil Eye

Potent words once spoken or chanted eventually were *written* on parchment, papyri, potsherds, bowls, and amulets, thereby imbuing the objects with anti-Evil Eye power.[105]

Protective Actions, Objects, and Gestures

Post-biblical Israel continued defending against the Evil Eye with the protective practices prescribed in the Bible.

Leather *phylacteries* (*tefillin*), a pair of small, black, leather boxes containing pieces of parchment inscribed with verses from the Torah, were donned by men for daily morning prayer and bound to forehead and left arm.[106] The Greek designation of these *tefillin* as "phylactery" (*phylaktêrion*, from *phylassô*, "protect") indicates their safeguarding use. *Tefillin* and amulets (*qame'ot*) were often mentioned in tandem by the sages.[107]

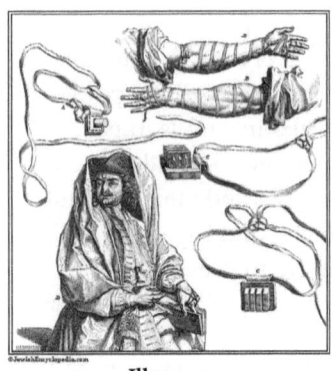

Illus. 1.1
Jewish Phylacteries/*Tefillin*
(*Jewish Encyclopedia* 1906 10:24), reproducing an engraved drawing from Bernard Picart, 1725.

Also worn was a *prayer shawl with blue fringes/tassels* (*tzizzit*) attached on the four corners.[108] These four blue tassels were considered potent and protective against evil demons and the Evil Eye.[109]

Mezuzahs (*mezuzot*; sing. *mezuzah*), small capsules containing pieces of parchment inscribed in Hebrew with words of Torah (Deut 6:4-9; 11:18-21), were attached to door posts (Hebrew *mezuzah* = "door post") of dwellings to protect them and their inhabitants from the Evil Eye.[110] This means for protecting homes resembles the Roman practice of affixing what they considered a potent amulet, namely the *fascinum,* a representation of the phallus and testicles, to the door post of

---

105. M. Gaster 1910.

106. Exod 13:9, 16; Deut 6:8; 11:18; Matt 23:5; *m. Shevu'ot* 3:8, 11; *m. Menaḥot* 3:7, 4:1. See Billerbeck 4/1 (1928):250-76. On the tefillin in Israel and the ancient world, see Cohn 2008.

107. *m. Shabbat* 6:2; *m. Mikwa'ot* 10:2; *m. Kelim* 23:1.

108. Num 15:37-41; Deut 22:12. See Matt 9:20; Mark 6:56 for their assumed healing power.

109. *Targum Canticle* 8:6; cf. *m. Mo'ed Katan* 3:4 *m. Menahoth* 4:1; see Billerbeck 4/1 (1928):277-92.

110. *m. Berakoth* 3:3; *n. Gittin* 4:6; *y. Peah* 1, 15d; Trachtenberg 1939:146-52; Kosior 2014. See also Vol. 3:127 and Illus. 3.5

Roman homes, as at Pompeii and elsewhere.[111] Christians of the post-biblical period followed a similar practice of affixing potent inscriptions to the door posts of their homes.[112]

The *forehead-band* (*totefot*) worn by Torah-observant Israelites, according to R. Joseph, is a kind of *knot* that protects against the Evil Eye (*b. Shabbat* 57b; cf. Exod 13:16; Deut 6:8; 11:18). Ludwig Blau regards the adornment mentioned in *m. Shabbat* 6:1 (bands of wool, head-straps, forehead bands, necklaces, nose-rings, finger ring without a seal) as similar "originally magical means of protection."[113] Evil Eye malice is projected from the eye, and therefore is averted, it was believed, by a red-colored apotropaic placed between the eyes.[114]

A *manual gesture*, discussed above, was the pressing of the thumbs of each hand into the palms of their opposite hands and declaring, "I am of the seed of Joseph over whom the Evil Eye has no power" (*b. Berakhot* 55b).[115]

Illus. 1.2
Jewish prayer shawl (*tallit*) with four blue tassels/fringes (*tzitzit*), worn by observant Jewish males during weekday morning services, averting harm and evil, including the Evil Eye

Bells were used for apotropaic purposes, akin in function to those attached to the high priest's robe (Exod 28:33–34; 39:25–26). They were suspended on the foreheads and necks of horses (Zech 14:20).[116] Children were protected by hanging small bells on their clothing or necklaces with knots around their neck (*b. Shabbat* 66b).[117] They also were safeguarded by *threads of red or blue* attached to their wrists.[118]

The *color red* was used to ward off the Evil Eye, as in Roman custom.[119] Tree trunks were painted red: "If a tree lets its fruit fall, it should be painted

111. See Vol. 2:193–207.

112. See below, chap. 2.

113. Blau 1898:165.

114. Ibid., 166; Schrire 1982:57–58; Teman 2008.

115. On the gesture's similarity to the obscene gesture of the *mano fica* see Blau 1898:155 and n. 3; Blau 1907:280; and Noy 1971:999.

116. *b. Pesaḥim* 53a. This Talmudic passage provides an explanation of Zech 14:20 (the "bells of the horses" inscribed with "Holy to the Lord").

117. So Blau 1898:164, noting the similiarity to Greco-Roman practice.

118. On this practice see Trachtenberg 1939:133; Moss and Cappannari 1976:7; Teman 2008. See also Vol. 3:100–102.

119. See Vol. 2:220–21, 254–55, 256–58; Vol. 3:100–102. Pliny, *NH* 18.86; Blau

red and loaded with stones" (*b. Shabbat* 67a).[120] Blau finds the rationale for this action in the ambiguity of the verb *sqr*, which can mean not only "to paint/color" but also "to fascinate with an Evil Eye." Guided by the principle of "like influences like," he proposes, one took a further step and from the outset protected trees from the Evil Eye by painting them with red paint.[121] The red/crimson thread suspended between the eyes of a horse, as mentioned in *b. Shabbat* 4:5, also served as protection against the Evil Eye. The color red, like the color blue, continues to be used among Jews in modern time to avert the Evil Eye.[122] In Islamic countries, where most of the populations are brown-eyed, people with blue eyes are thought to possess the Evil Eye. Ulmer opines that "this may go back to the medieval confrontation with the crusaders" (strange blue-eyed warriors from the north).[123] Blue, however, had been a protective color against the Evil Eye for centuries, as far back as ancient Mesopotamia and Egypt.[124]

Horses also were protected by hanging between their eyes a *foxtail* (*t. Shabbat* 4.5 [115.14]); *b. Shabbat* 53a)[125] or *small bells* (*b. Pesaḥim* 53a).

Spitting repeatedly to protect oneself and others from the Evil Eye may have been practiced by Jews of this period, given Paul's reference to the practice among the Galatians,[126] its practice among Greeks and Romans,[127] and the Jewish use of spitting and spittle for curing maladies.[128]

Someone afraid of his own Evil Eye and of fascinating himself was told to "look at the side of his left nostril" (*b. Berakhot* 55b).[129]

Concealment was a form of shielding from harm. Concealment of infants and prized possessions from the intentional or inadvertent gaze of

---

1898:166.

120. See also *t. Maʿaser Sheni* 5.13 (96); *y. Maʿaser Sheni* 5.55d; Blau 1989:165, 166. The verb *sqr* can mean "dyeing red" or "fascinate with the Evil Eye"; see Blau 1898:165 and Blau 1907:280. The rabbinic interpretation of *b. Shabbat* 67a stresses that red attracts peoples' attention and subsequently their prayer on behalf of the tree.

121. Blau 1898:166. On red, as well as blue, as a potent apotropaic color, see Prov 31:21, and Vols. 2 and 3.

122. See Einszler 1889:206–7; Canaan 1914:28–32; Moss and Cappannari 1976:7; Ulmer 1994:164 and note 55; Furtst 1998; Teman 2008 (red thread).

123. Ulmer 1994:164 and n. 55.

124. See Vol. 1, chap. 2; Vol. 2:254–56.

125. Blau 1898:155.

126. See Vol. 3, chap. 2.

127. Theocritus, *Idyls* 6.39; Pliny, *NH* 28.35, 39 etc.; cf. Vol. 2:28, 62, 125, 140, 155, 166, 175–76.

128. See *b. Sanhedrin* 101a, *b. Shevuot* 15b; Mark 7:33, 8:23; and John 9:6. See also Ulmer 1994:189–90.

129. Blau 1898:155; 1907:280.

an Evil Eye was a regular practice in the ancient Circum-Mediterranean world.[130] Children were not taken to public places because of the Evil Eye: "A man who goes to a house where a feast is going on does not take his sons with him, because he fears the Evil Eye" (*Midrash Tehillim* 7:2; *Leviticus Rabbah* 26:7). Jacob hid his daughter Dinah from the Evil Eye of Esau (*Genesis Rabbah* 76:9). Women were concealed and protected from potential Evil-Eye gazing by the veils they wore (*b. Shabbat* 65a; *y. Shabbat* 5,7b).[131]

Related steps for escaping an Evil Eye were *avoidance of crowds* and large gatherings, as at banquets, and *minimizing one's visibility* in public spaces, as we have noted above.[132]

Changing a person's name or *substitution of another name* was a method for concealing a person's identity from the envious Evil Eye of others (Ulmer 1994:156-158). Thus a male was called a *kushi* or a female a *kushit*, i.e. a Cushite ("Ethiopian" or "black person"), as in the case of Moses's wife (Num 12:1), in order to confuse potential fascinators and thereby protect from the Evil Eye (*b. Rosh Hashanah* 16b; *Midrash Tanhuma*, Tsav 13, 10a).

An *action* that was *prohibited* was *standing in a neighbor's orchard or field* so as not to inadvertently cast an Evil Eye and ruin the fruit (*b. Bava Batra* 2b).

Amulets and Other Apotropaic Objects and Images

Amulets and Other Apotropaic Means

In the rabbinic period, the *use of amulets and other apotropaic objects* for protection against all kinds of hostile forces was pervasive in Israel, and generally permitted by the rabbis. There was extensive syncretistic borrowing among pagan, Israelite, and Christian populations in respect to words, actions, and amulets for warding off evil forces, including the Evil Eye.[133] Jewish and Christian literature and practice also attest the borrowing and adaptation of pagan apotropaic devices and practices. Within both Israel and Christianity there was tension concerning the strict prohibition of the

---

130. See Vol. 2:155-57.
131. Ulmer 1994:175.
132. See above, 15-16, 30.
133. See Aune 1986:216-19. There is evidence of pagan borrowing of Israelite names for God (*Iao, Sabbaoth, Adonai, Eloi*) biblical names of angels (*Michael, Raphael, Gabriel*) and humans (e.g., Solomon), and of powerful words, as attested in the Greek Magical Papyri.

use of amulets and apotropaic means, on the one hand, and, on the other, unrelenting resort to apotropaic strategies and amulets.[134]

Amulets and apotropaics appear to have been deemed effective on the same principle emphasized by Greeks and Romans in relation to both amulets and medicine; namely, *similia similibus*, "like influences like." One example of rabbis appealing to this principle is the statement of R. Abbaye that eating fish can cure an aching eye because eating fish had created the ache in the first place: "Abbaye said, "It refers to one whose eyes ache; fish is harmful to the eyes. If it is so, he should eat fish" (*b. Nedarim* 54b).[135]

Various amulets worn on the body and other objects were employed by Jews of this period against the Evil Eye. Protective designs were included in art, architecture, mosaics, and household vessels. The personal amulets were frequently composite in nature, with material, shape, symbols, inscriptions, and legends all combining their respective powers.[136]

Before the turn of the Common Era, the soldiers of Judas Maccabeus wore on their bodies amulets (*hierômata*, lit. "consecrated objects") for protection in battle (2 Macc 12:40).[137] The wearing of amulets and use of apotropaics in *Israel* goes back much earlier, as noted in Vol. 3, chap. 1. The Hebrew term for "amulet," *qameʻa*, is mentioned in the Mishnah,[138] where it designates a folded piece of parchment with writing on it or a capsule containing also drugs.[139] The term appears in the midrash of *Numbers Rabbah* 12:4, which states that when a king is about to give his daughter in marriage, he gives her an amulet and says to her, "keep the amulet upon you so that the Evil Eye may have no power over you any more." Strips of leather parchment with Bible verses were placed in capsules or *bullae*,

---

134. On Jewish anti-Evil Eye amulets and apotropaic objects from this period see Blau 1898:152–76, 1907a, 1907b; Montgomery 1910–1911; Billerbeck 4/1 (1928):529–32 (amulets, *bullae*, stones, knots, herbs), 250–76 (*tefillin*); 277–92 (*tzizzit*); Friedenwald 1939; Trachtenberg 1939:132–52; Bonner 1950:97–100, 302–7 (nos. 294–303, 306, 309, 311), and for illustrations, Plates 14–15, nos. 294–303, 306, 309, 311; Goodenough 1953, 2:164, 227–41, 244 n.262; vol. 3: figs. 1049, 1063, 1065; vol. 11.3 (1964), fig. 352 (photo of the Dura-Europus synagogue ceiling and the two Evil Eye tiles); Koetting 1954:474–76; Noy 1971; Budge 1930:212–38 (Hebrew); 258–71 (Samaritan); 283–90, 446–47 ("Babylonian terra-cotta Devil traps" = Aramaic Incantation Bowls); Engemann 1981:290–91, figs 7, 8; Russell 1982:540, figs. 1, 2; 541; Schrire 1982:50, 56–58, 102, 114, 139–72 (appendix and plates 2, 5, 12, 14, 16, 50); Naveh and Shaked 1987:40–41, 44–45, 98–99, 102–3, 120, 133, 172–73; Naveh and Shaked 1993; Ulmer 1994:158–65; for later periods beyond Late Antiquity, see Trachtenberg 1939; Schrire 1982/1966.

135. Ulmer 1994:185.

136. On "the typical Hebrew amulet," see Schrire 1982:17–19.

137. The *hierômata* were consecrated to the idols (of the Jamnites).

138. *m. Shabbat* 6:2, cf. 8:3; *b. Shabbat* 78b; *m. Kelim* 23:1; *m. Mikwaʼot* 10:2.

139. M. Gaster 1910:454; see also *ḥippah* for amulet.

which were then worn as pendants around the neck,[140] similar to the Roman practice. Among the amulets were also stones, gems, knots, and herbs.[141] As with Mesopotamians, Egyptians, Greeks, and Romans, the jewelry (neck pendants, rings, bracelets etc.) worn by Jews usually had a double purpose of both adornment and protection from evil forces including the Evil Eye. Again, like their neighbors, Jewish infants and children, in particular, were equipped with *bullae* (capsules) as neck pendants for protection (*b. Qiddushin* 73b). Many such amulets were designed and worn as protection not only against the Evil Eye but against other dangerous forces as well. Additional anti-Evil Eye amulets might also be mentioned.

Small bells, similar to those attached to the bottom of the High Priest's robe, were hung on horses;[142] their sound was thought to drive away the Evil Eye. Bells were used by the Romans (*tintinnabula*) for the same purpose.[143] According to Rabbi Eleazar, "all the bells which are hung on a horse between its eyes shall be holy unto the Lord," commenting on the passage of Zech 14:20, "And on that day there shall be inscribed on the bells of the horses, 'Holy to the Lord'" (*b. Pesaḥim* 50a).

"A leather bag containing pearls" was another amulet used to ward off the Evil Eye from animals (*b. Sanhedrin* 68a).

An obsidian Medusa/Gorgo image, a popular apotropaic in Greco-Roman culture, was found on an amulet protecting a Jewish corpse.[144]

A representation of an eye on the prow of a ship was thought to safeguard the ship and its cargo from the Evil Eye (*b. Nedarim* 50a).[145] This custom is typical of the Mediterranean world—even to this day—and goes back to Egyptian custom.[146]

An amulet from Palestine against the Evil Eye consists of a nine-line Hebrew inscription on a strip of bronze foil. The inscription reads in part:

---

140. Billerbeck 4/1: 529–31; Ulmer 1994:159.

141. Billerbeck 4/1: 531–32; Schrire 1982:12–19 and *passim*; Ulmer 1994:159.

142. Seligmann 1910 2:275.

143. Seligmann 1910 2:274–76; Budge 1930:215. See Vol. 2:193, 197 and Illus. 21; 198; 203 and Illus. 27; 204, 214–15, 254.

144. Goodenough 1953 2:236, cf. n. 186. For further post-biblical Jewish depictions of the Gorgo/gorgoneion/Medusa image, see Goodenough 1953 1:168, 195, 217, 218, 239; 2:231, 249 and note; 3: figs. 383, 493, 991, 993; 5:60, fig. 67; 7:63, 102, 219, 224–29, figs. 285–91; 8:77; 11: (illustrations), fig. 107; 12:153, 156. On Medusa/Gorgo, see also Vol. 2.

145. Levy 1924 3:639, sub *'ayin*, describes this literally as "a 'calf's eye,' the name of a precious stone."

146. See Vol. 1, chap. 2; see also Vol. 2:230, 231 and Illus. 41, 42, 43.

> [Protect the ... and the body of Georgios, son of Pagatios, from all evil and from the eye of [his father] and from the eye of his mother and from the eye of women and from the eye of men and from the eye of virgins. [YHWH] Sebaoth is with us, the God of Jacob is our refuge. Selah, Amen, Amen, Amen ...[147]

The language, divine names, and provenance identify it as a Jewish amulet. The presence of a cross whose arms terminate in a circle could suggest its use by Christians as well by Jews. The amulet demonstrates that even family members were feared of casting an Evil Eye on their own children, a concern among Greek and Romans that Plutarch also had voiced in his treatise on the Evil Eye (*Quaest. Conv.* 5.7.4, *Mor.* 682A, 682D).[148] The serial listing of eyes ("of father, mother, women, men, virgins") recalls the similar serial wording found in Mesopotamian incantations centuries earlier.[149]

As indicated above, two silver amulets (c. sixth century BCE) found in a burial cave in Ketef Hinnom in Jerusalem attest the apotropaic power attributed to the Aaronic benediction.[150]

A Jewish amulet for averting the Evil Eye made for Abraham, son of Falgona, was found in Marseille, France. Written in Hebrew on parchment it adjures numerous evil forces and "every form of Evil Eye, black eye, yellow eye, ... pierced eye... staring eye... and words of an evil tongue."[151] Beside indicating various epithets for "Evil Eye," it also illustrates the linking of Evil Eye and Evil tongue, as found also in Greek and Roman sources. Then it prays for a helping eye, a holy eye, a pure eye, an eye full of compassion, ... an eye that watches over Israel.[152]

These contrasting positive ocular and moral features, especially the eye watching over Israel, may be alluding to the watchful and protective eye of God.

Reference to *Joseph as a powerful protective figure*, appears repeatedly on Jewish anti-Evil Eye amulets. Citations of Gen 49:22 ("Joseph is a fruitful bough, a fruitful bough by a spring") occur on several Jewish silver amulets. Among the fifty Jewish inscribed silver amulets and their inscriptions listed by Theodore Shrire in his appendix, several were designed to ward off the

---

147. Montgomery 1910:280–81, with photograph. See Ulmer 1994:159.
148. See Vol. 2.
149. See Vol. 1, chap. 2.
150. See Yardeni 1991; Ross 1991; Barkay et al. 2004
151. The full text of both obverse and reverse sides of the parchment is given by Seligmann 1910 2:359–61. Date and other identification are not indicated.
152. Ibid.

Evil Eye.[153] Plate 5, lines 3–4 of a silver pointed pendant (Kurdistan) reads: "I am from the seed of Joseph by descent whom the Evil Eye does not affect." This is followed (lines 5–7) by a citation of Gen 49:22: "Joseph is a fruitful bough, a fruitful bough by a spring/eye (*ayin*) of water whose branches run over the wall."[154] This is one of several amulets citing Gen 49:22 and, by implication, appealing to Joseph's power in withstanding the envious Evil Eye of his brothers.[155]

There are numerous amulets from Palestine and Syria depicting the Evil Eye being attacked, with several also mentioning *Solomon* or depicting him as a cavalier slaying an Evil Eye demoness. It is not clear, however, which of these is exclusively Jewish or Christian, if any. Solomon also is reckoned in Islam as a potent defender against hostile forces, including the Evil Eye, and appears similarly on Islamic amulets.[156]

On several amulets Solomon is depicted as a cavalier on horseback lancing a figure on the ground, usually a demoness, representing the Lilith and/or the Evil Eye (*Baskosynê*).[157] A fourth-century CE bronze amulet (unknown provenance) with a suspension loop (see Illus. 1.3 below) depicts on the obverse a figure of Solomon with nimbus on horseback spearing a prostrate demoness symbolizing the Evil Eye, with lion below. The encircling inscription reads, "There is only one God who conquers the evil forces" (EIS THEOS HO NIKON TA KAKA).[158] On the reverse side, an Evil Eye is attacked from above by a trident, from lions on each side, and from other unclear animals/serpents. The inscription reads, "Iao Sabbaoth" (*Iaô Sabaô*)

153. Shrire 1982:139–72, Plates 2, 5, 10, 1112, 134, 16, 18, 22, 26, 50.

154. Ibid., 143.

155. See also ibid., Plates 12, 14, 26, 50.

156. See Al-Saleh 2000 on "Amulets and Talismans from the Islamic World."

157. For Solomon as cavalier on Jewish amulets lancing a demon/demoness see also Schlumberger 1892b:12, no. 13; 74–75; 1895, vol. 1:120, 134, 293; cf. also 1:118 n.1; 120 n.2; 122 n.3; 124 n.5; 125 n.7; 126 n.8; 127 n.9; 128 n.11; 129 nn.12, 13; 130 n.14; Perdrizet 1903:47–50; 1922:5–7, 27, 29–31; Gollancz 1910; Seligmann 1910:313–15 and figs. 230–233; Leclercq 1924:1847–50; Peterson 1926:96–109; Leclercq 1936:1939–40 (copper plaque with cavalier on one side and on other, an Evil Eye under attack and pierced by three daggers [fig. 8990]; the rider is Solomon, and the eye attacked is the Evil Eye of the envious, whether of hostile humans or demons [so Russell 1995:41]); Bonner 1950:302, Plate 14 and nos. 294–97; Goodenough 1953 1:68; 2:226–28; 7:198–200; 8:1044–67; Delatte and Derchain 1964 (no 371); Levi 1941:221 (figs. 101a and b); Bagatti 1971; Budge 1930:276 (Syriac "Book of Protection" with a figure of King Solomon as cavalier lancing a demoness [British Museum ms., Orient, No. 6673]); Vikan 1984:79–81 and figs. 19–20; Bohak 2008:213; Walter 1989–90. Nine samples of amulets with Solomon are in the Cabinet des Médailles of the Bibliothèque Nationale, Paris. See also Vol. 3, chap. 1.

158. Gitler 1990:371.

36   Beware the Evil Eye

Another apotropaic was designed for Christian use, but was a product of both Jewish and Christian tradition. A copper amuletic medallion from Smyrna in Asia Minor depicts on the obverse side Solomon with nimbus as cavalier piercing a prostrate female demon with a lance adorned by a cross. The encircling inscription reads *pheuge, memisimeni, Solomôn se dioke, Sisinnios Sisinnarios* ("flee, you loathsome demoness, Solomon is pursuing you, Sisinnios, Sisinnarios"). It identifies the protecting cavalier as Solomon, along with Sisinnios and his brother. See below, chapter 2, Illus. 2.6. The reverse depicts an Evil Eye attacked from above by three daggers, by lions on each side, and from below by a scorpion, serpent and ibis. The word *phthonos* ("envy") appears over the daggers and the whole is encircled by the inscription, *Sphragis Solomônis apodioxon pan kakon apo tou phorountos* ("Seal of Solomon, drive away all evil from the bearer").[159] This "Seal of Solomon" (*Sphragis Solomonis*) was included on numerous Jewish and Jewish-Christian amulets designed to repel the Evil Eye.[160] The cross and references to Sisinnios and Sisinnarios identify the amulet as intended for Christian as well as Jewish use. The name Solomon relates it to Jewish amulets of the same type. Christian cavalier amulets with an Evil Eye attacked and mentioning Solomon are discussed below in chapter 2. In Christian tradition, Solomon as cavalier attacking an Evil Eye is paralleled by the cavalier saints Sisinnios and George.

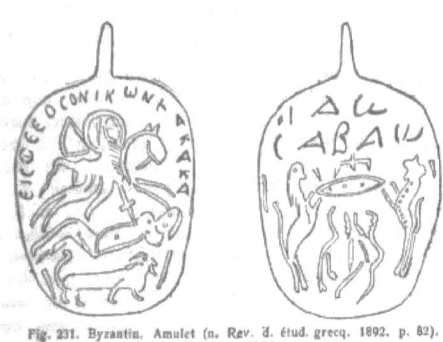

Fig. 231. Byzantin. Amulet (n. Rev. d. étud. grecq. 1892, p. 82). (Zu Seite 314.)

Illus. 1.3
Byzantine bronze amulet: on obverse, King Solomon as cavalier lancing a prostrate demoness, lion below, with inscription: "there is only one God, who conquers evil." On reverse, an Evil Eye attacked by an array of beasts (from Seligmann 1910 2:314 and p. 445, fig. 231).

A Syriac amulet exhibiting both Christian and Jewish detail illustrates the cultural cross-fertilization typical of amulet production and use. Among the pernicious forces it aims to bind and destroy is "the "Evil and envious

---

159. Schlumberger 1892a: 74; Perdrizet 1903: 47–48 and figs. 3–4; 1922:27, figs. 7–8; Seligmann 1910 2:443, fig. 230 with description on pp. 313–14; Levi 1941:221, fig. 101 a and b; Dunbabin and Dickie 1983:33 and Plate 8c.

160. On the *Sphragis Solomonis* see also Leclercq 1924:1847–50 [inscriptions and figures of amulets with Solomon]; Goodenough 1953 1:68; 2:226–38; 7:198–200; 9:1044–67.

Eye," here further identified as "the eye that smiteth and pitieth not, the green-coloured eye":

> By the power of those ten holy words of the Lord God, by the Name, I am that I am, God almighty, Adonai, Lord of Hosts, I bind, excommunicate, and destroy, I ward off, cause to vanish, all evil, accursed, and maddening (lit. "misleading") pains and sicknesses, adversaries, demons, rebellious devils, also the spirits of lunacy, the spirit of the stomach, the spirits of the heart, the spirits of the head, the spirits of the eyes, the ills of the stomach, the spirit of the teeth, also the evil and envious eye, the eye that smiteth and pitieth not, the green-coloured eye, the eye of every kind, the eye of all the spirits of pain in the head, pain on one side of the head, sweet and soft (doleful) pulsations, seventy-two such sweet and mournful noises, also the fever, cold and hot, visions fearful and false dreams. as are by night and by day; also Lilith, Malvita, and Zarduch, the dissembling (or "compelling") demon, and all evil pains, sicknesses, and devils, bound by spell, from off the body and the soul, the house, the sons and daughters of him who beareth these writs, Amen, Amen![161]

Four Jewish amulets from Palestine and Syria also were designed to avert the Evil Eye or provide healing from its harmful effect. Texts and translations are given in Naveh and Shaked (1987).

One amulet of the four (particular provenance unknown) assures God's healing of a certain Quzma, son of Salminu, from all the pain . . . from the eye of cataract (?), from the eye of spell . . . from the eye of the house, and from the eye of the open space (?), and from the eye of . . ."[162] The "eye" ('yn') is identified as the source of evil and the Evil Eye is implied, according to Naved and Shaked,[163] though the full phrase "Evil Eye" does not occur. They note a similarity to a much later Jewish amulet from Warsaw (1867) where an eye and a hand are prominently represented.

A second amulet (provenance: Horvat Kanaf, found at the ancient synagogue near Kibbutz Nirim, Negev desert), is designed to "heal Ya'itha, the daughter of Marian, from the fever and the shiver and the Evil Eye. Abrasax [sic] Ya Ya Yahu . . ."[164]

---

161. Cited by Goodenough 1953 2:164, derived from Gollancz 1912.

162. Naveh and Shaked 1987:40–41, Amulet 1, lines 11, 16–17, fig. 1 (p. 43) and Plate 1, from the collection of R. Hecht, Haifa.

163. Ibid., 45.

164. Naveh and Shaked 1987:44–45, Amulet 2, lines 1–3, fig 2 (p. 48) and Plate 2, Golan Archaeological Museum, Qacrin, no. 3164.

A third amulet, a small bronze tablet (c. fifth–sixth century CE) found in the apse of a synagogue at Nirim, Negev desert) reads in part: "[A]n amulet proper for Esther, daughter of T'tys, to save her from evil tormentors, from the Evil Eye ('yn byšh), from spirits, from demons, from shadow-spirits, from [all] evil tormentors, from the Evil Eye ('yn r'h) . . . from imp[ure] spirits . . ."[165]

A fourth amulet (specific provenance unknown) reads in part: "[This amulet is for Shim]'on, son of Shappira, against every . . . and Satan and Evil Eye and fever [and shiver . . . and every] spirit that shakes. In the name of the God of Israel . . ."[166]

The *hand and images of the hand* were long considered powerful apotropaics against the Evil Eye, as noted previously in Volume 2.[167] A representation of a hand (palm displayed outward and fingers upward) was employed by Jews to avert the Evil Eye. They called it the "Hand of Miriam" (sister of Aaron and Moses) and *Hamesh*, which is Hebrew for "five," referring to the five digits. Images of this Hand of Miriam continue to be worn in our own time as an object of adornment and perhaps also of protection.

Illus. 1.4
Jewish silver amulet: Hand of Miriam (*Hamesh*) with inscribed *Shaddai* ("[God] Almighty") in the palm (from Seligmann 1910 2:193, fig. 162).

A Muslim equivalent to the Jewish *Hamesh* is the *Hamsa* (likewise meaning "five"). It designates the "Hand of Fatima," after the prophet's honored daughter, Fatimah Zahra. This Hand of Fatima is ubiquitous in Islamic and Middle Eastern cultures. Depictions are found on jewelry and pendants and are affixed to walls of homes, building facades, mosques, and other objects to be protected.[168] According to Siegfried Seligmann, at the entrance to the Alhambra in Granada, Spain, an apotropaic hand once was displayed above

---

165. Naveh and Shaked 1987: 98–101, Amulet 13, lines 1–11, fig. 15 (p. 100) and Plate 11, Israel Department of Antiquities, No. 57.744.

166. Naveh and Shaked 1987:102–3, Amulet 14, lines 1–3, fig. 16 (p. 101) and Plate 12, collection of J. Samuel, Munich.

167. For ancient hand amulets and apotropaic images of hands see, for example, Jahn 1855, Plate 4, nos. 2a,b, 3 (*mano pantea*), 9 and 10 (*mano fica*); Plate 5, nos. 1 (hand), 2 (*mano fica*) and 3 (hands). On the apotropaic hand see also Seligmann 1910 2:164–88 and figs. 83, 145–64; Elworthy 1958/1895:235–76; and Budge 1930:467–69.

168. See Seligmann 1910 2:168, 170–72, 176–78; Herber 1927; Probst-Biraben 1933, 1936; Budge 1930:467–71; Kötzsche 1986:467–69.

the horseshoe arch of the Torre de Justicia.[169] E. A. Wallis Budge regards it as "probably a development" of the earlier Egyptian open hand amulet signifying "liberality and generosity."[170] In some amulet replicas of this apotropaic hand, an eye in the midst of the palm intensifies its anti-Evil Eye power.[171]

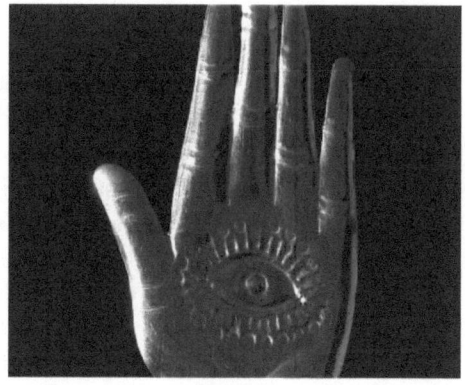

Illus. 1.6
Metal amulet of protective hand with eye in palm, El Santuario de Chimayo, New Mexico (John H. Elliott collection)

Illus. 1.5
Images of the Islamic protective Hand of Fatimah (*Hamsa*) on façade of a modern building, Spain (photo by John H. Elliott)

Bowls of clay on which were written incantations in Aramaic and which were employed to drive away the Evil Eye and other evil forces were mentioned previously in connection with apotropaic Mesopotamian bowls (see Vol. 1:114, 153). The Aramaic Incantation Bowls found in Iran and Iraq had been used by Babylonian Jews in the Talmudic period (226–636 CE) to ward off evil forces, including the Evil Eye.[172] The bowls average sixteen cm in diameter by five cm in depth and are

169. Seligmann 1910 2:169 and fig. 155. For Islamic amulets, see de Vaux 1910: 457–46.

170. Budge 1930:173. For illustrations of Jewish hand amulets (often inscribed with *Shaddai*, "Almighty," one of the traditional names for God), see Seligmann 1910 2:176–77 and figs. 162–64.

171. See the depiction of an Israeli anti-Evil Eye amulet on the cover of Dundes 1992—an upright hand with an eye in its palm (from the private collection of Barry and Reneé Ross); see also Potts 1982:13, figs. 13–19; and Kunesh 1998 on "The Eye in the Hand."

172. On the Aramaic incantation bowls (found primarily at Nippur) and their texts, see Montgomery 1913; Gordon 1937; Isbell 1975; Budge 1930:283–90, 446–47

inscribed inside in various Aramaic dialects (Babylonian Talmudic, Syriac, Mandaic). About the size of soup bowls, they were used to trap or drive off evil spirits, including the Evil Eye demon. The bottom insides of the bowls were covered with spiraling inscriptions adjuring the demons. They were turned upside down (to contain the demons) and often buried in the ground of private homes. Though inscribed with Jewish proper names and epithets for God, the bowls were used not only by Jews but also by others. Their purpose included assurance of a safe childbirth, protection of barren women, and the binding of the demon Lilith hostile to children and of other demons and harmful spirits. Lilith was feared in Israel as a demon attacking and killing mothers and newborns, similar to the demon Gylou dreaded by the Greeks and the demon Lamashtu feared by the earlier generations of Mesopotamians. Pregnancy and birth were precarious matters. Births were premature (Eccl 6:4–5); miscarriages frequently occurred (Exod 21:22–25); delivery was accompanied by pain (Isa 13:8; Jer 13:21; 22:23; 30:6; 49:24) and often by the mother's death (Gen 35:16–20; 1 Sam 4:19–21; 2 Kgs 19:3). The bowls were intended to provide some modicum of protection from the evil spirits and the Evil Eyes threatening mothers and newborns. A Babylonian terracotta incantation bowl with a spiral inscription was designed as an amulet (*Kamiah*) and was intended to protect its owner and kin "from banning, and baleful visions . . . and cursings . . . from evil spirits . . . from the Evil Eye, and from sorceries practiced by men or women."[173]

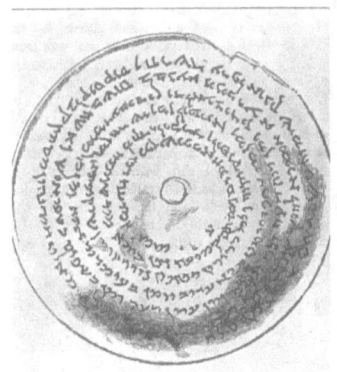

Illus. 1.7
Babylonian Incantation Bowl with Aramaic script protecting owner and kin from all evil spirits and the Evil Eye (from Budge 1978/1930:289)

Testament of Solomon 16:7 (first–third century CE), speaks of a bowl into which the demon Kunopegos was cast and is a likely reference to an earlier version of these later Aramaic incantation bowls.[174]

("Babylonian terra-cotta Devil traps" =Aramaic incantation bowls); Duling 1983:947–48; Aune 1986:217–18; Naveh and Shaked 1987:172–73 (bowl 8), 1993; Schiffman and Schwartz 1992; Ford 1998:212 n.30; Segal and Hunter 2000. For a photograph of one such incantation bowl see *ISBE* 1986 3:218.

173. Budge 1930:288 and fig. IV, p. 279, labelling the bowl a "Babylonian Terracotta Devil-trap."

174. On the *Testament of Solomon*, see also Vol. 3:86–89, 109, 110.

One such Aramaic bowl inscription included the Evil Eye among the powers to be overcome:

> Sealed, countersealed and fortified against the male demon and female lilith and spell and curse and incantation and knocking and Evil Eye and evil black-arts, against the black-arts of mother and daughter, and against those of daughter-in-law and mother-in-law, and against those of the presumptuous woman, who darkens the eyes and blows away the soul, and against the evil black-arts that are wrought by men and against everything bad.[175]

The "seal-ring of El Shaddai" and the "seal-ring of King Solomon, the son of David, who worked spells on male demons and female liliths" are also enlisted in this inscription for protection.

Another bowl, from Mesopotamia and now in the Israel Museum, has words written on it intended to safeguard the home and residents of a certain Khwaday, son of Pali, from the Evil Eye and other hostile forces:

> I. Bound are the demons, sealed are the devs, bound are the idol-spirits, sealed are the evil liliths, male and female, bound
>
> II. bound is the evil eye (*'yn' bištah*) away from the house of Khwaday, son of Pali, from this day to eternity. Bound is the evil eye (*'yn'*).
>
> III. Bound is the evil eye (*'yn' bištah*) from the house of Khwaday, son of Pali, from his house and from his . . . (and) from
>
> IV. . . . and from Adur-dukh and from her sons from this day to eternity.
>
> Amen, Amen, Selah.[176]

A bowl (No. 33 [=A.O.17.284]) included in a corpus of Syriac incantation bowls from Late Antiquity edited by Marco Moriggi (2014) has an inscription reading, "bowl for the protection of the house" (par. 1). The inscription seeks protection of a father, mother, sons and daughters (par. 7). May four angels, the inscription requests, protect and "preserve them and hinder and keep away the Evil Eye and [preserve them] from the envious

---

175. Gordon 1934:324–26 (Text B, lines 5–8); also in Duling 1993:948.

176. Naveh and Shaked 1987:172–73 (bowl no. 8) and Plate 24 (Israel Museum, N. 69.20.265); translation by authors; date and specific provenance not given. This text also appears in Vol. 1:106

glance and from the plotting of the evil heart and the slanderous tongue" (par. 8).[177]

J. A. Montgomery commented in 1913 on mention of the Evil Eye in the Aramaic incantation texts on bowls found at Nippur (c. 600 CE, in modern Iraq). He noted that "[t]he longest pertinent passage in the Nippur texts is Text 30:3–4. It is a charm for two men and a woman against specified diseases and demons, the eye of man or woman, the eye of contumely, the eye that looks right into the heart."[178]

A late anti-Evil Eye incantation appearing on a Hebrew-Aramaic amulet adjures the Evil Eye along with other threatening forces. It mentions the various types and colors of Evil Eyes, the variety of their possessors (fascinators), and their injuring by means of a fiery glance:

> I adjure you, every sort of evil eye (*'yn' byš'*) and every sort of plague and pestilence and demons and spirits and liliths, black eye (*'yn' 'wkm'*), brownish/tawny (lit. "yellow") eye (*'yn' ṣhwb'*), blue eye (*'yn' tklt'*), green eye (*'yn' yrwq'*), long eye, short eye, narrow eye, straight eye, crooked eye, round eye, sunken eye, bulging eye, eye that sees (*'yn' rw't*), eye that gazes (*'yn' mbṭt*), eye that bursts, eye that sucks up, eye of a male, eye of a female, eye of a man and his wife, eye of a woman and her daughter, eye of a woman and her sister, eye of a woman and her female relative, eye of a young man, eye of an old man, eye of a virgin, eye of a non-virgin, eye of a widow, eye of a married woman, every sort of evil eye (*'yn' biš'*) that exists in the world that desires to burn (people) by gazing upon them with a strengthening of the element fire from the east, west, south and north.[179]

In addition to pointing out examples of amulets inscribed in Aramaic, Ford aptly insists that such amulets, found relatively infrequently, must be studied in connection with "Mandaic and Syriac incantations, such as the *Šapta d-Pišra d-Ainia*, preserved in late manuscripts," and that these incantations provide "eloquent witness to the continuity of the Aramaic magical tradition" and "invaluable aid to the interpretation of (the much earlier Ugaritic incantation) KTU^2 1.96."[180]

---

177. Moriggi 2014:155. A Christian bowl (No. 24) in this collection, now in the Bible Lands Museum, Jerusalem (0070), states in its opening line, "May it be smitten—the Evil Eye that smote him [the owner]" (translation by Moriggi 2014:134). It concludes, "May the power of Christ arise and help."

178. Montgomery 1913:89, text on p. 221.

179. Naveh and Shaked 1987:133, Fig. 21 (Jewish amulet printed in Warsaw in 1867, transliterated text and translation in Ford 1998:241.

180. Ford 1998:212 n.30. On this Ugaritic anti-Evil Eye incantation, see Vol. 1,

Postbiblical Israel 43

The Dura-Europus Synagogue

The Dura-Europus synagogue of third-century CE Syria and its two anti-Evil Eye ceiling tiles is a striking example of how the Evil Eye belief influenced Jewish architecture and art, as it did also Christian and Islamic traditions. On the tiled ceiling (234 tiles) of the synagogue, are two fresco depictions of eyes—most likely Evil Eyes, though this interpretation is not unanimous.

Dura-Europus, located on the west bank of the Euphrates River in Syria, was a Roman military outpost from 165 CE, with a mixed Hellenistic, Parthian, and Roman history. Founded by the Seleucids of Macedonia in 303 BCE, the city was captured by the Romans in 165 CE and later fell to a Sassanian siege in 256–257 CE. It was deserted thereafter until the archaeological expedition of 1928 under the leadership of Yale University and the French Academy of Inscriptions and Letters. Remains of a Jewish synagogue (244–256 CE) and a Christian church (233–256 CE), both adapted from private dwellings, were found there. The synagogue was built in two stages, the latter stage was an expansion begun in 245 CE. On the tiled ceiling of this building are two tiles displaying eyes. The tiles were placed there during the synagogue's second renovation (245 CE).[181]

One tile, according to a reproduced sketch made by R. Du Mesnil du Buisson when it was first discovered,[182] depicts an (Evil) eye attacked by three daggers from above, by two serpents (or birds) from each side, and by a crab or scorpion or insect from below. The letters I A O appear to stand above the daggers and there are descending lines below the eye. The uncertain detail around both eyes, however, allows for conflicting interpretations.[183]

---

chap. 2.

181. On the synagogue see Goodenough vols. 9–11 (1964, 354 illustrations, 21 color plates). Vol 11.3, fig. 352 shows a reconstruction of the entire ceiling including both tiles, as well as figures of both tiles (11: figs. 46, 47). Goodenough refers to the eyes as "magical eyes" (9:54–55; 12:159). On this synagogue and the tiles see also Cumont 1926; Bauer-Rostovtzeff et al. 1929–69; Du Mesnil du Buisson 1939; Contenau 1947:261 (fig. 24); Kötting 1954:476; Kraeling 1956:41, note 28, 48–49 and figs. 11–12; Engemann 1975:38, figs. 8 and 9; Hopkins 1979 (p. 141 on the two eye tiles); Seawright 1988; Hachlili 1998, Plate III–2.:.

182. Du Mesnil du Buisson 1939:136 (Plate LIX, fig. 96.1).

183. For variant illustrations see Du Mesnil du Buisson 1939:136 (fig. 96) and 137 (fig. 97); Contenau 1947:261 (fig. 24); Kraeling 1956:48–49 (figs. 11–12); Goodenough 1964, vol. 11: fig. 46; Hopkins 1979:141; Engemann 1975:38–39 and figs. 8, 9.

44   Beware the Evil Eye

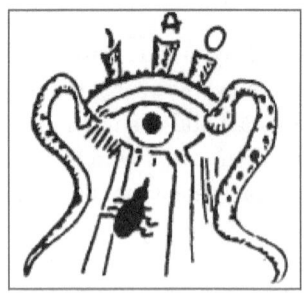 

Illus. 1.8
Dura-Europus synagogue (245 CE): two ceiling tiles protecting against the Evil Eye. Line drawing by Dietlinde Elliott, after Hopkins 1979:141.

Interpreting the letters above the eye of the first tile as *IAO* (a Hellenized version of YHWH, Israel's Hebrew name for God), led Goodenough to conclude that this is not an Evil Eye image but a symbol of the beneficent eye of God and immortality.[184] This interpretation, however, is justly opposed by other scholars. Noting the similarities between this depiction and numerous representations of the Evil Eye attacked by a menagerie of creatures, they regard this as another depiction of the Evil Eye akin to Hellenistic specimens discussed above in this chapter and previously in Vol. 2. Franz Cumont lead the earliest archaeological investigation of Dura-Europus (1922–1923). In his published account he provides a sketch in black and red of an Evil Eye pierced from above by a dagger and harpoon.[185] Above that is a bird of prey flying at the eye; on each side and from below are attacking serpents.[186] Josef Engemann offers a cogent critique of Goodenough, noting also the similarity of the image to iconographic depictions of Envy,[187] and, we might add, other depictions of Evil Eyes under attack. Georges Contenau also regards this figure as an Evil Eye attacked (according to Contenau, by two birds, a serpent and a scorpion).[188]

A second tile with an eye and very unusual detail is located in a different part of the ceiling and faces the opposite direction of the first eye tile.[189]

184. Goodenough 1953 2:238–41; 1964 9:54–55.
185. Cumont 1926:137ff. and fig. 31.
186. On this tile as representing an Evil Eye see also Contenau 1947:259–63; Bonner 1950:97–99; Kötting 1954:476 (three nails above the eye and a poisonous insect below); Kraeling 1956:48–49 and figs. 11–12 and 41 n.28; on amulets with the Evil Eye under attack see above, 35–38.
187. Engemann 1975:38–39 and figs. 8 and 9.
188. Contenau 1947:261.
189. See Goodenough 1964 vol 11. fig. 352 for an illustration of a reconstruction of

Kraeling notes "the central feature of this eye is the black iris set in a white eyeball."[190] Upper (outlined in red) and lower (black) eyelids accentuate the eyebrows; knobby yellow lampstands, each surmounted by a lamp, flank the eye; the bolster below the eye is green and adorned with three pink stripes cut by red lines; perpendicular red lines overlap the eye and the bolster. These lines, he reports, were taken by Du Mesnil du Boisson to depict "a flame kindled in the cushion and ready to destroy the eye."[191]

Goodenough, on the other hand, views this eye also as a good eye, with the bolster representing cushions used at banquets and the framing symbols of light representing a menorah, which in turn symbolizes the eyes of God.[192] Above the eye, according to Goodenough, is the "sun ship," which, in Egyptian iconography, represents the ship of immortality. Below the eye, is "the bolster of sacramental and eschatological banquets." On the whole, the image, according to Goodenough, symbolizes divine blessing, immortality and hope.[193]

Again, most scholars disagree with Goodenough's interpretation and consider this image as well to be that of an apotropaic Evil Eye. Bernard Kötting, for example, sees this unusual design as a depiction of an Evil Eye consumed by flames emerging from the cushion/bolster below the eye.[194] Because of the poor condition of the tile, Engemann remains agnostic, while allowing that it could represent a good eye.[195] As possible eyes under attack, both images have apotropaic force and illustrate the influence of Hellenistic Evil Eye tradition on the Jews of this period and their art.

House Plaque, Tombstone

A *clay plaque* from fifth-century Syria-Palestine was likely used to safeguard a house and its Jewish inhabitants from the Evil Eye.[196] The plaque currently is in the Israel Museum, Jerusalem. Its complex of Jewish symbols identify it as Jewish in origin with a protective function similar to that of a mezuzah.

---

the entire ceiling; for illustrations of this second eye see du Mesnil du Buisson 1939:136 (fig. 96, no. 2); Kraeling 1956:48 (fig. 11); Goodenough 1964:11, fig. 47; Engemann 1975:38–39 and fig. 9.

190. Kraeling 1956:48.
191. Ibid.
192. Goodenough 1953 2:55, 221.
193. Ibid., 2:238–41; 9:55
194. Kötting 1954:476.
195. Engemann 1975:39.
196. See Weitzmann 1979, no. 357 of the Catalogue of the exhibition of the Metropolitan Museum of Art, New York, Nov. 19, 1977—Feb. 12, 1978.

Illus. 1.9
Clay door plaque defending a home against the Evil Eye, Syria Palestine, fifth century CE

The symbols on the plaque depict the wall of a synagogue. In the center is a niche that is flanked by two lateral doorways. In the front of each stands a menorah. Two round blue stones, appear in the central niche, one above and one below. Above each menorah also appears a similar blue round stone. The base of the plaque is decorated with a frieze of three birds. The blue stones, shaped like eyes, are likely to have been intended as defense against hostile and envious Evil Eyes.

A Jewish tombstone found in Gaul has on it the word *shalom* ("peace" in Hebrew) and was decorated with a menorah, shofar and lulab. Its Latin inscription reads: "In the holy name of God . . . May envious (evil) eyes burst (*oculi invidiosi crepent*) . . . From the gifts of God, Jona made this."[197]

Evil Eye belief and practice in early Islam is discussed below at the conclusion of chap. 2.

CONCLUSION OF CHAPTER 1

A plethora of evidence indicates that Evil Eye belief and practice flourished in the house of Israel long into the period of Late Antiquity. The complex of basic notions associated with this belief and supporting its plausibility continue to be evident: an understanding of the eye as active not passive and emanating hot rays that scorch and destroy all persons and objects struck by its glance; its conveying the dispositions of envy and miserliness, as contrasted to a good eye conveying generosity and liberality toward others; its unintentional as well as intentional operation; its particular danger to newborn babies and their mothers; its being a crucial cause of illness, injury, and death; its possession by persons across classes and even by those of respected occupations such as teachers of the Mosaic Law, who with their eye punish erroneous teaching; and the possibility of its aversion or deflection through a range of apotropaic words, formulas, conjurations, gestures, symbols and images and amulets. These apotropaics, on the whole, involve the same *types*

---

197. Noy 1993:267–70 (inscription no. 191). On this and other examples (third–seventh centuries CE), see also Gregg 2000.

of words, symbols, actions, and amulets as encountered in the Greek and Roman materials. The chief difference involves the employment of Hebrew or Aramaic words and the names of Israel's deity, angels, and honored powerful persons (e.g., Joseph, Solomon); citations of Israel's sacred scriptures; and amulets and apotropaic gestures reflecting Israelite belief and tradition (e.g., phylacteries/*tefillin* accompanying prayer, blue prayer shawl fringes [*tzizzit*], mezuzahs for protection of homes; bells on priestly robes; hand gestures and accompanying invocation of association with Joseph; amulets bearing the "Seal of Solomon" and images of Solomon as cavalier lancing a prostrate demoness symbolizing the Evil Eye). The places, private and public, providing protection in the Jewish world included—beside homes, public buildings, and gravesites—synagogues, locations of Jewish weddings, gatherings for daily prayer, and places of assembly.

As in the biblical communities, the belief served to explain causes of illness, misfortune, and death. It contributed to the condemnation of envy, miserliness, and greed and encouraged the values of generosity and charity.

Evil Eye belief and practice have continued in Palestine of modern times. The belief and practice was common among Jews, Muslims, and Christians through the end of the nineteenth century, as described anecdotally by Lydia Einszler (1889), reporting on Muslim and Christian communities. Those with blue eyes and separated front teeth as well as beardless males were suspected to be Evil-Eyed fascinators.[198]

Among contemporary Jewish communities in general across the globe, various customs have their roots in Evil Eye lore: the avoidance of crowds, of compliments, of strangers, or accompanying praise and admiration with the Hebrew expression *bli 'ayin hara'* or the Yiddish equivalent *kein einhore* ("no Evil Eye intended"), the breaking of glass at weddings, the wearing of objects colored red or blue, the attachment of red or blue strings on the wrists of newborns, the use of holy verses and the powerful name of God on amulets which are then worn; the Hand of Miriam (*Hamesh*) worn as ornament and protective; and the employment of manual gestures—all are practices evident in Jewish communities of our own time. They attest a lively continuation of ancient Evil Eye belief into the modern era and illustrate how a general set of beliefs and practices has been adapted to a particular cultural and religious tradition.[199]

198. Einszler 1889:201; Seligmann 1910 1:82. See also Montgomery 1910:280–81; Hanauer 1935.

199. On Jewish Evil Eye belief and practice in the modern period see Thomson 1880; Trachtenberg 1970; Moss and Cappannari 1976; Spooner 1976:76–84; Schrire 1982; Brav 1992; Dundes 1992:257–312; for further literature see, previously, Vol. 1, chap. 1.

2

EARLY CHRISTIANITY (AND ISLAM) THROUGH LATE ANTIQUITY

INTRODUCTION

BEYOND THE BIBLICAL PERIOD (treated in Vol. 3) and down through Late Antiquity (second through sixth centuries CE), dread of the Evil Eye continued unabated in Israel and the Christian communities, as it did in the Mediterranean world generally. This is evident from the abundant literary, epistolary, iconographical, and archaeological evidence. In this period, the Evil Eye continues to be feared, Silke Trzcionka has observed, as "the most prominent and pervasive threat in the Graeco-Roman world."[1] As in the case of the rabbinic sages, the Christian commentators on the Evil Eye shared with the Greco-Roman world of Late Antiquity most of the concepts belonging to the Evil Eye belief complex, as it had developed from earliest Sumerian incantations down through Hellenistic lore. On the whole, Christians adopted and adapted existent Evil Eye traditions, with minimal additions or modifications. The most significant and influential development in the Christian communities is the association of the Evil Eye with the devil, alias Satan, the prince of demons. The continued

---

1. Trzcionka 2007:101.

worry over demons in general in this period is illustrated by a comment of Justin Martyr in his dialogue with Trypho the Jew:

> For we do continually implore God by Jesus Christ to preserve us from the demons that are hostile to the worship of God, and whom we served in time past, in order that after our conversion by him to God, we may be blameless. For we call him Helper and Redeemer, the power of whose name even the demons do fear; and at this day, when they are exorcised in the name of Jesus Christ, crucified under Pontius Pilate, governor of Judaea, they are overcome. (Justin, *Dialogue* 30, mid-second century CE)

In these centuries, the Greek terminology for "Evil Eye" and paronyms remained words of the *bask-* family, along with the phrase *ophthalmos ponêros*. *Phthonos* and paronyms continued to serve as partners of, or stand-ins, for *baskania* and its family of terms. The equivalent Latin remained *fascinare, fascinatio, fascinus,* and *fascinum,* with *invidia, invidere,* and paronyms as the partners of, or stand-ins for, *fascinare* and paronyms. *Oculus malus, oculus nequam, oculus invidiosus,* etc. continued as the Latin alternatives of *ophthalmos ponêros,* as the terminology of Jerome's Vulgate illustrates.

These terms are found both in the literature and in the large body of iconographic material: Evil Eye amulets and apotropaics found in excavated houses, vestibule mosaics, public buildings and walls, synagogues, churches, and grave sites. The type and amount of evidence identified as Jewish or Christian resembles that of the Greco-Roman material. Between Jewish and Christian Evil Eye tradition there is evidence of extensive cross-fertilization in terms of shared apotropaic words (e.g., names of the Deity, angels), formulas, prayers, figures (such as Solomon and the cavalier image), combinations of motifs and types of amulets. E. R. Goodenough, summarizing his research on Jewish amulets in the Greco-Roman period,[2] noted the extensive overlap of Greco-Roman, Jewish, and Christian cultural traditions in amuletic design and content. Some amulets, but by no means all, can be identified as "indisputably Jewish" or "indisputably Christian" because of the presence of only Jewish or Christian details (Jewish: Jewish emblems such as the menorah, or Jewish words, names, and heroes; Christian: Jesus Christ, cross, Christus monogram, etc.) Most amulets, however, illustrate the merging and interpenetration of pagan, Jewish, and Christian elements.[3]

---

2. Goodenough 1965 12:58–63. On Jewish amulets see also Goodenough 1953 2:208–95; 1953 3: nos. 379–381, 999–1209.

3. For Christian apotropaics in general, but including Evil Eye apotropaics, and on

We shall proceed by first examining the literary and written evidence of Christian Evil Eye belief and practice from second to sixth centuries, in roughly chronological order. The conventional terminology for the Evil Eye will be indicated and the association of the Evil Eye with the Evil-Eyed demon, envy, and the Devil will be noted. Personal correspondence will illustrate the day-to-day reality of Christian anxiety over injury from the Evil Eye. Turning to the material and iconographic evidence, we shall examine the various apotropaic means (words, physical gestures, amulets) that were employed by Christians for warding off the Evil Eye, specific liturgical and ecclesiological practices, and remedies for treating injury from an Evil Eye.

The emergence of Islam at the end of this period and its complex of beliefs and practices concerning the Evil Eye—so similar to that of Jews and Christians—are important contemporary developments. The topic of Islamic Evil Eye tradition is noted only briefly here as one germane to developments in Israel and Christianity. It an issue exceeding the limits of the present study, however, and deserves a full and separate treatment.

---

the Church Fathers concerning the Evil Eye see King 1873; Hazard 1893; Elworthy 1895/1958:213–14, 229–32, 247–49, 265–69, 279, 285–88, 294–300, 390–94; Perdrizet 1900, 1903, 1922:25–27; Reizenstein 1904 (Jewish and Christian phylacteries against the Evil Eye); Prentice 1906; Montgomery 1910–1911; Seligmann 1910 2:319–20, 324–41, 348–50, 357–58, 362–64; Seligmann 1912–13, 1922, 1927; Dobschütz 1910:413–30 (of Christian origin, 425–28: name of Jesus, biblical texts [passages from Psalms, Gospels; Lord's Prayer, liturgical formulae [e.g., Trisagion; "Christ conquers"; "Christ reigns"; "Kyrie, eleison"], prayers; the holy cross and making the sign of the cross; the sacraments and sacramentalia [holy water, incense, salt, oil, wax from candles, bread; relics; pictures/icons); Gollancz 1912; Eitrem 1921; Leclercq 1924, 1936:1936–41; Peterson 1926:96–109; Perdrizet 1922; Dölger 1932a, 1932b; Stegemann 1934: (nos. xxv, xliii, xlv); Staude 1934, 1954; Merlin 1940; Bonner 1950; Eckstein and Waszink 1950:407–10; Meisen 1950:157–77 (on Basil, Jerome,Gregory of Nazianzus, Cyprian; and amulets); Meisen 1952; Goodenough 1953 passim; Cavassini 1954; Kötting 1950:334–42, 403–13; Kötting 1954:480, 1978; Menzel 1955; Robert 1965; Brox 1974; Grabar 1974 (expanding Bonner's list); Engemann 1975:37–48 (Jewish and Christian), 1980; Merkelbach and Youtie 1975 (athletes fallen victim to the envy demon); Budge 1930:127–32 (Coptic amulets), 177–99 (Ethiopian amulets), 272–82 (Christian amulets from Syria); Gollancz 1912:275 (on Evil Eye spells), 274–80 (on cavalier figures including Solomon), 336–53 (apotropaic cross and crucifix); Maloney 1976; Bonneau 1982; Russell 1982; Bartelink 1983; Dunbabin and Dickie 1983; Seeliger 1989 (Christ monogram); Bernand 1991; Limberis 1991; Meyer-Smith-Kelsey 1994:49–50; Dickie 1995, 2001:202–321, 1994, 1995, 1997; Maquire 1990, 1994, 1995, 1997; Maquire, ed. 1995; Maguire et al., eds. 1989:212–17 and nos. 133–36 (cavalier, Evil Eye attacked); Walter 1989–1990; Manganaro 1995; Mantanseva 1994; Russell 1995, 2001; Rakoczy 1996:216–26; Ford 1998; Fauth 1999; Tarelko 2000; Olszewski 2001; Kotansky 2002; Aquaro 2004:71–100 (focus on envy rather than Evil Eye), 96–100 (on "Solomon, St. George and the Evil Eye"); Kahl 2006; Trzcionka 2007, 2011; Soderlund and Soderlund 2013; Tilford 2015, 2016.

THE LITERARY AND WRITTEN (EPISTOLARY) EVIDENCE

The Apostolic Fathers

The earliest Christian references to the Evil Eye outside the New Testament appear in two of the second-century compositions of the so-called Apostolic Fathers: Ignatius's *Letter to the Christians of Rome* and the *Martyrdom of Polycarp*.

Ignatius of Antioch, Letter to the Romans

Ignatius, bishop of Antioch, Syria, in his letter to a group of Christians at Rome (c. 106 CE), speaks twice of the Evil Eye, once using the verb *baskainô* (*Rom.* 3:1) and once the noun, *baskania* (*Rom.* 7:2). Writing en route to Rome and under Roman military guard (*Rom.* 5.1–3), Ignatius seeks the support and prayers of the Christians at Rome for a successful outcome of his forthcoming appearance and Christian witness in Rome and his eventual martyrdom (*Rom.* 1–2). He praises his readers with the words, "You have never Evil-Eyed (*ebaskanate*) anyone; you taught others" (*Rom.* 3:1). The familiar Loeb Classical Library translation by Kirsopp Lake (1952:229) renders the relevant words, "you never have *envied* anyone." The new LCL edition, translated by Bart Ehrman, is similar: "At no time have you been envious of anyone." Both translate *ebaskanate* according to its inferred sense, rather than literally.[4] The verb, however, is identical to that employed by Paul in his letter to the Galatians (3:1), with the meaning "to Evil-Eye," not "to envy." Evil-Eyeing and envying, as we have seen, are so closely related in Evil Eye lore that the verb could have the secondary sense of envying here: you have never enviously wished harm on others, but rather instructed and gave freely to others. The context of the letter, however, indicates that Ignatius is concerned not with whether his friends in Rome are envious or not, but whether they will oppose his intention to die as a witness to Jesus Christ (*Rom.* 1:1–2; 2:2; 3:2–3). Although the statement is in either case a compliment, it is more likely designed to win their support for his wish to die as a martyr. To this end Ignatius hopes that his prospective hosts will continue to be free of an Evil Eye when he arrives and not be miserly or ungenerous toward him in withholding or begrudging their cooperation and support of his plan to die and rise with Jesus Christ (*Rom.* 3:2—4:3). Its sense is: "you have never begrudged anyone (the opportunity of martyrdom)." The

---

4. So also Schoedel 1985:171; Holmes 2007:229.

explicit use of *zêloô* in *Rom.* 5:3 has, in this context, a similar sense—less of envy[5] than of "begrudge": "May nothing of the things seen or unseen begrudge me (*me zêlôsai*) my attaining to Jesus Christ." Begrudging, spiteful withholding, as we have seen in previous volumes, is an occasional feature of the Evil Eye as well (e.g., Sir 14:10; Tob 4:7, 16; Plutarch, *Quaest. conviv.* 5.7, *Mor.* 681D).

Later in the letter, Ignatius repeats his request for the cooperation of his friends in Rome that they not resist his martyrdom and thereby aid the "prince of this world" (i.e. the devil) wishing "to tear me in pieces" (*Rom.*7:1). His second mention of the Evil Eye has a similar motive: "Let no Evil Eye malice dwell among you (*Baskania en hymin mê katoikeitô*). Even if, when I come, I should ask you myself [to rescue me], do not be persuaded by me, but rather obey the things I am now writing to you" (*Rom.* 7:2).[6] Ignatius draws several clear contrasts in *Rom.* 7:1–3 between the prince of this world (the devil) and God (v. 1a), the Roman believers and the devil (v. 1b), Jesus Christ and the world (v. 1c), the Roman believers and the Evil Eye (v. 2a), death and life (v. 2c), and transient things versus the bread of God and Jesus Christ (v. 3). In respect to the Evil Eye, Ignatius is urging his Roman readers not to allow Evil Eye malice in their midst, for this would put them on the side of the devil and this world rather than on the side of Ignatius, God, and Jesus Christ. Here *baskania* likely implies, like *zêlôsai* in 5:3, a begrudging attitude on the part of the Roman believers, which Ignatius seeks to avert and forestall. They should neither begrudge him nor stand in his way of attaining life with God. His words imply a connection in his mind between an Evil Eye and the devil as prince of this world hindering Ignatius from attaining his goal. But this is not stated explicitly. A few decades later, however, this connection of Evil Eye and the devil is explicitly made in the account of the martyrdom of Polycarp.

The Martyrdom of Polycarp—*The Evil Eye and the Devil*

The *Martyrdom of Polycarp* (c. 160–170 CE) is an account of the recent death of Polycarp, bishop of Smyrna in Asia Minor. The details of his death, which occurred c. 155–157 CE under the Roman proconsulship of Statius Quadratus (21:1), are contained in a letter from the church of the city of Smyrna to the church of Philomelium (*Prescript*). Toward the end of the description of his execution and the events leading to it (chs. 3–18), the letter emphasizes

---

5. Against Lake 1952:233.

6. *Baskania* is translated "envy" by Schoedel (1985:178) and Holmes (2007:233).

the role that the Devil played in the treatment of Polycarp's charred corpse. *Martyrdom of Polycarp* 17:1 reads:

> The envious (*antizêlos*), Evil-Eyeing (*baskanos*) and evil (*ponêros*) One [i.e. the Devil, cf. 2:4], who resists the family of the righteous [i.e. the Christian community], however, when he saw the greatness of his [Polycarp's] martyrdom, and his life-long blameless career, and that he [Polycarp] was crowned with the crown of immortality and had carried off the unutterable prize, he [the Devil] saw to it that not even his [Polycarp's] poor body should be carried away by us, though many desired to do this and to have a share in his holy flesh.[7]

The Devil is not explicitly mentioned but is clearly implied by the epithets and the context as the transcendent agent directing the action here. An earlier passage of the letter describing the modes of torture and death used against the Christians concludes, "For the Devil used many wiles against them" (2:4). This same thought of the Devil manipulating human agents appears in 17:2: "Therefore he [the Devil] put forward Niketas, the father of Herod, and the brother of Alce, to petition the governor not to give his [Polycarp's] body" [to the Christians]. "The envious, Evil-Eyeing, and evil one," the letter states, is the Devil working his malice through human hands.

This is the first direct Christian association of the Evil Eye with the Devil, Satan, the prince of demons. It is the beginning of a tradition that continues in Christian circles down to the present. In this tradition, the Evil Eye, as well as envy ("through the Devil's envy death entered the world," Wis 2:24), are attributed to the Devil, Satan, who then infects humans and enlists them as his agents of the Evil Eye and envy. This association of the Evil Eye with the Devil has been labeled a "paradigm shift" that constitutes a distinctive *Christian* perspective on the subject.[8] While a significant development, it is must be pointed out, however, that this association of the Evil Eye and the Devil in particular begins not with Jesus or the writings of the New Testament, but only in the post-biblical period. Throughout the Bible, the Evil Eye is described as a *human* characteristic and not as a demonic external power, as it is presented in various Greek and Roman sources. This "shift" is later than the biblical writings and the nascent Jesus movement. In actuality, it represents a *turning* or *return* in the post-biblical period to the conceptuality of the pagan world and the attribution of the Evil Eye to an Evil Eye demon (*baskanos daimôn*).[9]

---

7. Holmes (2007:325) renders, "But the jealous and envious Evil One..."
8. Rakoczy 1996:216–26, 277–78.
9. On the *baskanos daimôn* in pagan sources, see Geffcken 1930; Meisen 1950,

This coupling of the Evil Eye and the Devil, once established in the Christian communities, had a lasting influence on future generations. It set the stage for an association of the Evil Eye with heretics as well as with witches (*Hexen* and *Hexenaugen*—witches and witches' eyes)—both classified as enemies of God and the church. Consequently in the Middle Ages, casting an Evil Eye became equated with bewitching (*verhexen*) as an action of the Devil and his minions operating through witches (*Hexen*) as human agents, accompanied by the gradual disappearance of the Greek and Latin terms *baskainein* and *fascinare*.[10] Witchhunts included searches for possessors and wielders of an Evil Eye, now deemed a telltale and malignant feature of witches. Whereas the Greeks thought of the Evil-Eyeing envy of the gods and imagined Evil-Eyeing demons, the Christian church, demonizing the phenomenon of the Evil Eye, saw humans as under the sway of an envious Evil Eyeing Devil and as pawns of Satanic Evil Eyeing malice. In this regard there was no separation of a pagan popular religiosity, on the one hand, and on the other, an enlightened Christian theology tolerant toward the relics of pagan culture.[11]

Before we leave the Apostolic Fathers, it should be noted that one writing, the *First Letter of Clement* from Rome to Corinth (c. 96 CE), while making no reference to the Evil Eye, underscores the noxious effect of the Evil Eye's partner in malice, envy, throughout the history of Israel and the nascent Jesus movement. *First Clement* 3:1—6:4 addresses the disruptive force of envy (*zêlos, phthonos*) at the church of Corinth and in Israel's past (Cain and Abel, Jacob and Esau, Joseph, Moses, Aaron and Miriam, Dathan and Abiram, David and Saul, Peter and Paul, Christian women persecuted as Danaids and Dircae, Christian wives estranged from husbands, and great cities and mighty nations all overthrown by envy and strife [*zêlos kai eris*, 6:4]).[12]

1952; Capelle 1953; Bartelink 1983 (and Christian sources); Rakockzy 1996:117-29; and Vol. 2 of the present work.

10. So Rakoczy 1996:276-77.

11. Rakoczy 1996:217 n.799. This is made clear by Engemann (1975:22-23), who uses the example of the Evil Eye to show the parallels between pagan and Christian means employed for warding off evil.

12. For the conventional linkage of Evil Eye and envy in later Christian literature see, e.g., Basil, *Homily 11, Concerning Envy/Peri phthonou/De invidia* (PG 31.372-85); Jerome, *Letter 69* (to Oceanus); John Chrysostom, *Hom. Jo. 48.1* (PG 59.269); *Hom. Act. 5* on 2:14 (PG 60.50); *Hom. Act. 25* on 11:19 (PG 60.195); *Hom. 1 Cor. 12* on 4:6 (PG 61.106); *Hom. 1 Cor 33* on 13:4 (PG 61.262); *Hom. Gal.* on 3:1 (PG 61.648); *Hom. Col. 8.5* on 3:5-7 (PG 62:357-59); *Hom. Col. 11* on 4:11 (PG 62.380). On the devil as envious see Irenaeus of Lyons (c. 140-c. 202), *Adversus Haereses* 5.24.4; Theophilus of Antioch (c. 181/182 CE) as the first to quote Wis 2:24 to explain death as caused by the

Further References to the Evil-Eyeing Demon and the Devil

Address to the Greeks

A further text of this early post-biblical period, the *Address to the Greeks* (*Cohortatio ad gentiles*), attributed to Justin Martyr, refers in its conclusion (ch. 38) to the Sibyl's prediction of the coming of

> our savior Jesus Christ who . . . restored to us the knowledge of the religion of our forefathers, which those who lived after them abandoned through the *teaching of the Evil-Eyeing demon* (*didaskalia baskanou daimonos*) and turned to the worship of those who were not gods. (*Address to the Greeks* 38; PG 6.307–308B)[13]

Here the Greek designation for the Evil-Eyeing demon (*baskanos daimôn*) is used in reference to the Devil of Israelite and Christian parlance, as in the *Martyrdom of Polycarp* 17:1.

A Christian inscription in the Catacomb of Priscilla on the Via Saleria, Rome, one of the largest and oldest of the catacombs, illustrates this association of the Evil Eye and the Devil. It names the Devil *baskanos pikros* ("spiteful fascinator/Evil-Eyer").[14] The catacomb was used for Christian burials from the mid-second to fourth centuries CE.

Tertullian of Carthage

Tertullian of Carthage, North Africa (c. 160–225, *fl.* 190–220) speaks of the Evil Eye in relation to the custom of women wearing veils.[15] Like his pagan neighbors, Tertullian also considers the veil to afford effective protection against the Evil Eye.[16] In a treatise on the sexual modesty and purity of women, this Church Father urges the Christian virgins of Carthage to veil themselves as protection against scandalous gossip, suspicion, whispering,

---

Devil's envy (*Ad Autolycus* 2.9); see similarly Athanasius of Alexandria (275–373 CE), *On the Incarnation* 5.2–3; on the devil as envious, see also the commentary below on Basil and John Chrysostom.

13. See also Justin, *Monarchia* 1 regarding the Evil Eye (PG 6.313A: *baskania*) or envy (PG 6.313B, *invidia*), which turned humanity away from the worship of the Lord of all to the making of idols.

14. Meisen 1950:158 ("Envier par excellence"), citing Kaibel, *Epig. Gr.* ed. 1878, no. 734.

15. On Tertullian and the Evil Eye, see Dickie 1995:26–28.

16. Compare, e.g., Euripides, *Iphigenia in Taurus* 1217–1218; and Virgil, *Aeneid* 3.405–407.

rivalry, and envy. Mention of envy (*livor*) then leads him to speak of the Evil Eye (*fascinum*), its closely related cousin, and to relate it to the Devil:

> For there is something feared also among the pagans (*ethnicos*) which they call the Evil Eye (*fascinum*), the unhappy consequence of excessive praise and fame. We [Christians] sometimes attribute it [i.e. *fascinum*, the Evil Eye] to the Devil (*diabolo*), for he hates the good. Sometimes we ascribe it to God, for He judges arrogance by exalting the humble and demoting the high and mighty. For this reason, because of the Evil Eye (*in nomine fascini*), a really chaste virgin will fear the adversary [= the Devil], on the one hand, and God, on the other, the envious essence (*lividum ingenium*) of the one [Devil] and the judging eye (*censorium lumen*) of the Other [God], and she should rejoice for being known [because of her veiling] only to herself and God. (Tertullian, *De virginibus velandis* 15.1–3)[17]

Christians, like their non-Christian neighbors, he declares, acknowledge the existence of the Evil Eye, which is closely linked with envy and aroused by excessive praise and fame.[18] What he then states about further Christian thought on the Evil Eye is both surprising, if not singular. His observation that Christians sometimes ascribe the Evil Eye to the Devil (15.2) is in line with the *Martyrydom of Polycarp* (17.1). That Christians also sometimes ascribe the Evil Eye to God, on the other hand, is a statement without parallel in the Christian tradition.[19] However, it does echo the notion of ancient Greek thought that the envious Evil Eye of the gods, alias Nemesis, strikes down human excess and unrestrained ambition.[20] His point is that, with respect to this Evil Eye, virgins have reason to fear both the Devil's Evil-Eyeing envy of their beauty and God's judging Eye on their vanity. Keeping themselves and their beauty veiled, however, maintains their purity and keeps them safe from any and all Evil Eyes. Tertullian is aware of the conventional association of Evil Eye and envy as well as of the widespread notion that it is praise and success that arouse an envious Evil Eye.

On another occasion, Tertullian records two further features of Evil Eye belief; namely exercise of the Evil Eye by old women, and children as its

17. Tertullian, *De virginibus velandis* 15.1–3, PL 2. 959; Bulhart, ed., CSEL 76, 1957:100.

18. For Greco-Roman texts on this motif, see previously Vol. 2. Dickie (1995:26–28) oddly and unconvincingly concludes from this passage that Tertullian "rejected what he called *fascinus* in its pagan understanding" (1995:26; cf. also 28). Rakoczy (1996:223–26) presents a more balanced and cogent interpretation.

19. So also Rakoczy 1996:223–26.

20. On nemesis, see Vol. 2, as illustrated by Herodotus and others.

targets (Tertullian, *De carne Christi* 2.2, PL 2.800). These reflect conventional wisdom on the Evil Eye from Sumerian incantations onward. Refuting Marcion's heretical denial of the Lukan record of Jesus' nativity and infancy, Tertullian mockingly recreates what he claims Marcion thinks about the infant Jesus's presentation in Temple and the reaction of the eighty-four year old prophet Anna (Luke 2:36–38): "Let the old woman [Anna, Luke 2:36–38] be silent, lest she cast an Evil Eye (*fascinet*) upon the child [Jesus])" (Tertullian, *De carne Christi* 2.2, PL 2.800). Here Tertullian employs the standard Latin verb *fascino*, meaning, as in the Vulgate of Gal 3:1, "injure with an Evil Eye."

Eusebius of Caesarea

Eusebius of Caesarea (c. 260–340 CE) attributes the misfortunes of the Church, especially the persecution of Christians, to the *baskanos daimôn*, the Evil-Eye demon and rival of God (*Life of Constantine* 1.45; 2.73; 3.1.1; 3.2.1; 3.59.1; 4.41.2).[21] Beginning with his historiographical writings, *phthonos baskanos daimôn/nemesis* were ascribed influential roles in historical events and identified as enemies of the Church and adversaries of God. As the Christian Church gradually morphed into the Christian state, the Evil Eye demon, now identified with the Devil, was depicted as archenemy of both church and state.[22]

This Christian identification of the Evil Eye with the Devil runs parallel to the shift noted by Peter Brown taking place from 300–600 CE in ascribing various kinds of misfortune, witchcraft, and sorcery not simply to humans but to the Devil. Writing on "sorcery, demons and the rise of Christianity,"[23] Brown notes that in this period of intense conflict over positions of power, resort was made to sorcery and sorcery accusations by holders of articulate power against "holders of ambiguous positions of personal power."[24] This resort to sorcery accusations against rivals was accompanied by an attribu-

---

21. Bartelink 1983:396–97. For further linking of the Devil and Evil Eye see, e.g., Gregory of Nazianzus, *Carmina* 1.1.7.66 (PG 37.441A); 1.1.27.8 (PG 37.499a); 1.347 (PG 37.1476a); *Poemata de se ipso* 55 (PG 37. 1599). The same verses of this quasi-conjuration, only slightly modified, are found on a gold neck pendent serving as an anti-Evil Eye amulet (IG 14.2413.18); see DACL 1.2 cols. 1743–45. See further Basil, *Hom.* 11.4 (PG 31.379–380).

22. So Hinterberger 2010:201, citing Eusebius, *Eccl. Hist.* 8.1.6; 5.21.2; 10.4.14.1; 10.8.2.2; and *Life of Constantine* 1.49.2; 2.73; 3.1.1; 3.59.1; 4.41.1. Hinterberger (2010) discusses shifting meanings of *phthonos, baskanos daimôn, and nemesis* in writings of the medieval period; Hinterberger (2013) offers a fuller treatment.

23. Brown 1970; see also Brown 1972:119–46.

24. Brown 1970:21–22.

tion of misfortune to the Devil more than to human agency. "On Christian amulets," he observes, "we may be sure that *Invide*, 'O Envious one,' refers, not to the Christian's neighbour, but to the Devil."[25] "Where the teachings of the Fathers of the Church clash with popular belief, it is invariably in the direction of denying the *human* links involved in sorcery (they will deny, for instance, that it is the souls of the dead that are the agents of misfortune), in order to emphasize the purely *demonic* nature of the misfortunes that might afflict their congregations."[26] In these unstable times, the witch is now seen in Christian circles as one who has made a binding compact with the Devil. The sorcerer is no longer the pagan outside the Christian community and the sorcerer's power is gained not by skill but by compact with the Devil and renunciation of Christ.[27] The increased coupling of the Evil Eye with the Devil follows this same pattern.

By the time of Eusebius of Alexandria (fifth–sixth century CE), the adaptation of the old Greek attribution of the Evil Eye to a demonic force, a *baskanos daimôn*, had become standard practice among the Fathers, who trace the Evil Eye to the Devil, Satan, prince of demons.[28] Writing later than Basil, Jerome, and John Chrysostom, who make this connection, Eusebius of Alexandria still laments that there are some persons blaming fellow humans for casting an Evil Eye when they should be accusing the Devil. In a homily criticizing improper Christian observance of the Sabbath,[29] he attacks inappropriate conduct such as concern for what day and hour it is, or preoccupation with the cries of birds, and includes blaming the destruction of some valuable object on the Evil Eye of passers-by. Instead, he insists, they should accuse the Devil, for it is actually the Devil who works evil through human beings, and in the cross Christians have a means of protection against Satan. Both notions are common patristic themes. Accusing humans of casting an Evil Eye, of course, was conventional practice in the Greco-Roman world, as was dread of an Evil Eye demon (*baskanos daimôn*). The biblical communities likewise inveighed against humans injuring others with their Evil Eyes. The argument of Eusebius illustrates, on the one hand, continuation far into the late Roman and Byzantine period of the conviction that *humans* cast an Evil Eye. On the other hand, it shows how intent some Church Fathers were

---

25. Ibid., 32, citing Diehl, ILCV 1 (1961), no. 2388 (pp. 462–63).
26. Ibid.
27. ibid., 36.
28. Bartelink 1983; Dickie 1995.
29. Eusebius of Alexandria, Sermon 7, *De Neomeniis et Sabbatis et de non observandis avium vocibus* (PG 86.1, cols. 354–357). On this passage see Dickie 1995:28–29.

to attribute the Evil Eye solely to the Devil, while dismissing its attribution to humans as ignorant and pagan superstition.

Terminology: *Bask-* Word Family, *Ophthalmos Ponêros*

Beside terms of the *baskanos* word family, a further Greek expression for Evil Eye, *ophthalmos ponêros*, also was employed at this time.[30] The biblical scholar Origen of Alexandria (184–254 CE), in *Against Celsus* (c. 250 CE), his defense of Christianity against the pagan philosopher Celsus, mentions the Evil Eye in citing a passage from Mark 7:20–22 in connection with how one properly sees God:

> For that which sees God is not the eye of the body. It is the mind that is made in the image of the creator, and that God in his providence has rendered capable of that knowledge. To see God belongs to the pure of heart, out of which no longer proceed "evil thoughts, murders, adulteries, fornications, thefts, false witness, blasphemies, the Evil Eye (*ophthalmos ponêros*)," or any other evil thing. Origen, *Against Celsus* 7.33.17)[31]

Gregory Thamaturgus of Pontus (c. 213–c.270 CE) and disciple of Origen in Palestine, commenting on Matt 6:22–23 and *ophthalmos ponêros*, takes the saying as a contrast not of eyes but of opposing forms of love. The integral eye stands for an unfeigned love that enlightens the body; an Evil Eye represents a "pretended love, which is also called hypocrisy." Hypocrisy turns the light of genuine love into consuming darkness, he asserts.[32]

The expression *ophthalmos ponêros* for the Evil Eye occurs less frequently than terms of the *bask-* word family, and appears mostly in quotations of biblical texts that employ the phrase (Sir 31:13; Matt 6:23; cf. Luke 11:34; Matt 20:15; Mark 7:22).[33] In this literature, the standard expressions for "Evil Eye" are terms of the *bask-* word family.

30. The phrase appears earlier in Sir 14:10; 31:13; and Mark 7:22—biblical texts.

31. See also Tatian, *Diatessaron* 20.38; John Chrysostom, *Hom. Gal.* 3:1 (PG 61.648); *Hom. Col.* 8.5 (PG 62.357–60); *Hom. 1 Cor.12.13* on 4:6 (PG 61.105–6).

32. Gregory Thaumaturgus, *Fragmentum in evangelium Matthaei* (PG 10. 1189); cf. *Ante-Nicene Fathers*, vol. 6:179 (S. D. F. Salmond, trans.).

33. A TLG search indicates that *ophthalmos ponêros* appears in the post-biblical period only rarely and only in Christian writings. See, e.g., Origin, *Against Celsus* 7.33.17; Tatian, *Diatessaron* 9.42 (on Matt 6:22–23); 20.38 (on Mark 7:22); Gregory of Nyssa, *Oratio funebris in Meletium episcopum*, vol. 9.447.4; Basil, *Enarratio in prophetam Isaiam*, Ch. 16.315.16; John of Damascus, *Sacra parallela*, PG 96.217.25, 30; Antiochus Monachus, *Pandecta scripturae sacrae*, Homily 3, line 9, and *Catena in Matthaeum*, page 161, line 27 (referring to Matt 20:15 and Sir 14:10). A single instance

The Evil Eye in the Apocryphal Acts

The Acts of Thomas

The *Acts of Thomas* (third century CE, Syria), one of the Christian New Testament Apocryphal writings, makes mention of the Evil Eye. This Christian Gnostic romance of Syrian provenance tells of the apostle Judas Thomas and his mission to India. On one occasion he encounters a beautiful woman tormented by the Devil ("the adversary") for five years (*Acts Thom.* 5.42–43). Appearing in the forms of both a young man and an old man, this figure, the Devil, she explains to Thomas, raped her over this five year span. Knowing that demons and spirits and avengers (*daimones kai pneumata*) are subject to the apostle, she begs Thomas to drive out the demon (*daimona*) and set her free. Thomas then addresses the demon:

> O evil (*ponêria*) not to be restrained! O shamelessness of the enemy! O Evil-Eyeing One (*baskanos*) never at rest . . . O you from the devil (*tou diabolou*) that fights for the aliens . . . (*Acts Thom.* 5.44)[34]

The demonic enemy (*daimôn*), acknowledging the apostle's superior power, leaves the woman and vanishes (*Acts Thom.* 5.45–46). The story is another illustration of how in the post-biblical period Christians associated the Evil Eye with the Devil as a *demon*, an external force afflicting humans from without. Like their Greek and Roman neighbors, they conceived of the Evil Eye as a *baskanos daimôn*.

A second reference to the Evil Eye in *Acts of Thomas* appears in chapter 9. The narrative concerns an encounter of the apostle and an elite noblewoman by the name of Mygdonia recently married to a certain Charisius (*Acts Thom.* 9.82–118). Thomas wins this woman to the Christian faith (9.88) but is repeatedly accused by her husband, Charisius, kinsman of and minister to the king, Misdaeus, of being a stranger practicing magic or sorcery and of alienating the affection of his wife, who refuses to sleep with him [Charisius] (9.89–98).[35] Charisius laments to his wife:

---

of the plural, *ophthalmoi ponêroi*, appears in Artemidorus of Ephesus (second century CE), *Onirocriticon* 1.26, line 68.

34. Greek Text: *Acta Apostolorum Apocrypha* 2.2 (M. Bonnet, ed., 1959:161). Translation with minor modification according to "Acts of Thomas" (translated by G. Bornkamm, with English translation by R. McL. Wilson) in Hennecke-Schneemelcher, eds., *New Testament Apocrypha* (1965 2:467).

35. The accusation of magic and sorcery recurs; see also *Acts Thom.* 9.99, 101, 102, 106, 107, 114, 116, 117; 10.123, 131; 11.135 ("malefactor"), 138; 13.152, 162, 163.

> Woe to me, most beloved, and to you also! For I have been too quickly deprived of you . . . Neither son nor daughter have I of you, that I might rest upon them. You have not lived with me a full year, when an Evil Eye (*baskanos de ophthalmos*)[36] snatched you from me. Would that the violence of death had taken you! (*Acts Thom.* 9.100).[37]

Charisius's lament amounts to an Evil Eye accusation directed against Thomas, similar to the Evil Eye accusation mounted against the apostle Paul by his opponents in Galatia. Charisius adds to this loss the ignominy of suffering all this "from the hands of a stranger" (*hypo xenou*; *Acts Thom.* 9.100). The nobleman seeks to discredit Thomas by stressing Thomas's suspiciousness as "stranger" (9.100) and accusing him of "separating my sister Mygdonia from me" (9.99) by means of magic and deceit (9. 96) and an Evil Eye (9.100). This text provides us another example of an Evil Eye accusation employed to denounce and discredit an opponent, along with the labels "magician" and "sorcerer." The repeated stress on Thomas as a "stranger" further illustrates the continued association of an Evil Eye with not-to-be-trusted strangers, outsiders, and aliens, as was the case with Paul in Galatia.[38] In this accusation, Charisius is charging Thomas with being a human agent of the Evil-Eye demon, as Church Fathers later speak of humans being the agents of the Evil-Eyeing Devil.

Finally the *Acts of Thomas* provide a clear example of reckoning according to the principle of "like influences like" (*similia similibus*). In an interchange in which King Misdaeus is requesting Thomas's aid in restoring Mygdonia to her husband Charisius, the king states: "Some drugs make other drugs ineffective" (*Pharmaka hetera dialuei hetera pharmaka*) (*Acts Thom.* 10.127).

This is the basic principle of sympathy and antipathy—powerful force neutralizes powerful force—underlying the assumed effectiveness of all amulets and apotropaics, including those against the Evil Eye.

---

36. This is the reading of Ms U (Codex Vallicellanus, eleventh century CE). Ms P (Paris Codex, eleventh–twelfth century CE) reads similarly: *baskanos . . . ophthalmos* which is then identified immediately as a *ponêros daimôn* ("evil demon"). Ms H (Escorial, twelfth century CE) reads *phthoneros daimon* ("envious demon").

37. Greek Text: *Acta Apostolorum Apocrypha* 2.2 (M. Bonnet, ed.) 1959:212. With minor modification this is the translation of Bornkamm and Wilson, in Hennecke-Schneemelcher, eds., *New Testament Apocrypha* (1965 2:494).

38. For Thomas as stranger see, e.g., *Acts Thom.* 9.95, 99, 100, 101, 106, 117; 10.120, 123; 11.136; *Acts Thom.* (Martyrdom of Thomas) 163 ("runaway" to India). In attracting another noble wife to the Christian faith, Tertia, spouse of King Midaeus (*Acts. Thom.* 11, 134–138), Thomas was accused by the king also of being a sorcerer and malefactor (*Acts. Thom.* 11.134), who "bewitched (*epharmakeusen*) Tertia" (*Acts. Thom.* 11.138).

The Acts of John

The *Acts of John,* another of the New Testament Apocrypha, is a Christian Gnostic writing (c. second–fourth century CE) focused on the powerful actions and teaching of the apostle John of Zebedee after Jesus's resurrection. It represents the ascetic Encratite tradition of Syria and Asia Minor. In the first of two accounts of John's two visits to the city of Ephesus (chs. 1–57), the apostle encounters a certain Lycomedes, a wealthy official (*stratêgos*) of the city, who tells him that "the God whom you preach has sent you to help my wife who has been paralyzed for the past seven days and is lying there unable to be cured" (ch. 19). John immediately went with Lycomedes to the latter's house. Upon seeing his dying wife, Cleopatra, Lycomedes lamented to John,

> See, my Lord, this faded beauty; look at her youth; look at the flower-like grace of my poor wife, at which all Ephesus was amazed! Wretched man, I am the victim of envy (*ephthonêthên*). I am humbled. My enemies' (Evil) Eye (*ophthalmos echthrôn*) has fallen upon me. (*Acts of John* 20)[39]

Lycomedes sees himself as the victim of an enemy's envious Evil Eye that has robbed him of his beautiful wife and then expires (chs. 20–21). The details of the illness are consistent with the notion of an envious Evil Eye as cause: the youth and beauty of Cleopatra, her fading and wasting away, her great value to her husband who is the actual target of his enemies' envy, and their ocular projection of that envy. Through John's mediation, however, God raises from the dead first Cleopatra and then her husband (chs. 22–23). Lethal envious Evil Eye attack from human enemies is countered by the resurrecting power of God and the Lord Jesus Christ, so that new recruits may be gained for the faith (ch. 22).

Cyprian of Carthage on Envy

Cyprian, bishop of Carthage (died 258 CE). had composed a Latin treatise on envy and rancor, *De zelo et livore* (PL 4. 637–652). This treatise preceded Basil's homily on envy and the Evil Eye. Cyprian does not mention the Evil Eye explicitly in this treatise, but his linking of envy with ocular action and with machinations of the Devil suggests that he envisions an Evil Eye as the physical mechanism by which envy is directed at its victims. A comparable

---

39. Greek Text: *Acta Apostolorum Apocrypha* 2.2 (M. Bonnet, ed.) 1959:161. Original German translation by K. Schäferdieck, with English translation by G. C. Stead, in Hennecke-Schneemelcher, eds., *New Testament Apocrypha* 1965 2:216.

treatise by Plutarch, *On Envy and Hate* (*De invidia et odio/peri phthonou kai misous*) a century earlier, had discussed envy and contrasted it to hate. The English translation of the title of Cyprian's treatise as "On Jealousy and Envy," is misleading.[40] The treatise focuses not on jealousy, but on envy, as is clear in its account of the features of the emotion.[41] Cyprian employs various Latin terms for envy which he uses as synonyms: *zelus, zelare; invidia, invidere, invidus; aemulatio*.[42] *Livor*, with which envy is coupled, denotes "rancor," "malice."[43] The treatise as a whole is a discourse on the malice of envy that originates with the Devil and that Christians are to ponder and avoid. Cyprian traces envy to the instigation of Devil, the "adversary" and "enemy" who himself envied from the beginning (*De zelo* 1, 2, 3, 4, 11, 16, 17). After linking envy with the Devil (*De zelo* 1-2), Cyprian discusses the origin and magnitude of the vice (*De zelo* 3-5). Envy (*zelus, invidia*) began with the Devil envying the first human made in God's image. Because of this envy, the Devil was cast from heaven and by instigating envy among humans he deprived them of the grace of immortality. Henceforth "envy (*invidia*) rages on earth" and whoever is envious (*zelat*) imitates the devil, the master of perdition, in accord with Scripture: "Through the devil's envy (*invidia diaboli*) death entered the world" (*De zelo* 4, quoting Wis 2:24). Among humans, Cain envied (*zelat*) Abel, Esau envied Jacob, Joseph's brothers envied Joseph, Saul envied David, and there was the envy of the Judaeans of Jesus's day whose eyes were blinded from seeing Jesus's divine works (*De zelo* 5). Turning to a description of the vice, Cyprian declares that envy is "the root of all evils, the source of disasters, the nursery of sins, the substance of transgressions." From it, hatred arises; because of it, brotherly love is violated, truth is adulterated, heresies and schisms emerge, the clergy are disparaged and superiors are resented (*De zelo* 6). Envy turns the good things of another person to one's own evil. Envy involves being tormented by the prosperity of famous persons, it is to make the fame of others one's own punishment. It lacerates us with internal tortures. No food or drink

40. As, for example, is the inadequate translation of Coxe in the *Ante-Nicene Fathers*: "Treatise 10. On Jealousy and Envy," *Ante-Nicene Fathers*. Volume 5: *Hippolytus, Cyprian, Caius, Novatian* by A. Cleveland Coxe et al. 1886.

41. On the definition and distinction of "jealousy" and "envy"in this study, see Vol. 2.

42. See *zelus et livor* (chs. 3, 13, 17) = *invidia et livor* (ch. 3); *zelus* (chs. 3 [2x], 4 [3x], 5 [4x], 6 [5x], 7, 9 [3x], 10 [2x], 11, 12, 13 [2x], 17, 18); *zelare* (1, 3, 4, 8, 10, 11, 13, 1); *livor* (3, 4 [2x], 5 [3x], 6, 7, 17); *invidia et livor* (3, 5); *invidia* (3 [3x], 5 [2x], 11); *invidere* (5, 6, 7, 10, 17); *invidus* (7 [2x], 9); *aemulatio* (translated envy) 5 (synonymous with *invidia, livor,* 6, 10).

43. For the treatise's combination of *zelus et livor* as a hendiadys see chs. 3, 13, 17; for *invidia et livor,* see chs. 3, 5.

can be pleasing to the envious. Other evils have an end, but not envy (*zelus*); the more one who is envied (*invidetur*) succeeds, the greater the flame of envy (*zelus, De zelo* 7). The symptoms of envy include the threatening look, the savage appearance, facial pallor, trembling lips, gnashing teeth, violent words, frenetic insults, hands moved by hatred and given to violence (*De zelo* 8). The envious are their own worst enemy. Envy is their master (*zelo dominante*), brings harm to enviers themselves, and there is no remedy (*De zelo* 9). When Jesus's disciples inquired as to which of them was the greatest, Jesus cut off all envy (*aemulationem*) with his reply, "he who will be the least among you all will be great" (*De zelo* 10, quoting Luke 9:46-48). To engage in envy (*zelus, invidia*) is to return to the devil and become like Cain. Christians, however, are to imitate not Cain but Christ (*De zelo* 11). Followers of Christ are to avoid envy (*zelus*) and rather love one another (*De zelo* 12). Paul stated that love does not envy (*non zelat*) [1 Cor 13:4]. Whoever is magnanimous and kind toward others is free of envy and malice (*zeli ac livoris; De zelo* 13).

Christians are to recall their baptism and not become entangled in deadly snares of the devil but rather love both neighbors and enemies (*De zelo* 14-15). Resisting the darts of the Devil calls for sound thinking, ceaseless prayer, and spiritual action. Not envying (*zelare*) others but loving the community has as its reward love and peace (*De zelo* 16). Whoever was possessed by envy and rancor (*zelo et livore*) must abandon all that malice (*malitiam*) by which he/she was previously held, undergo a reformation of conduct, and be cleansed of the rancor of the serpent (*livor serpentinus*). "Esteem those whom you envied (*invidebas*) with unjust disparagements" and rather imitate the good and engage in the fellowship of love and the bond of brotherhood (*De zelo* 17) "Ponder paradise, where Cain, who destroyed his brother through envy (*zelo*), does not return." Consider that we are under God's eyes and are running a course that God himself is observing and judging, so that we can finally succeed in seeing Him (*De zelo* 18). In this conclusion, the condemnation of looking with eyes of envy gives way to meditating on *God's eyes*, his *looking* with mercy, and finally succeeding in *seeing* God. Though Cyprian does not mention the Evil Eye specifically in this treatise, the stress on ocular action throughout and its repetition here in the conclusion hints strongly at an Evil Eye as a concomitant tool of the Devil and the physical mechanism conveying the envy which Cyprian condemns. On most points, Cyprian reflects conventional thinking on envy, but as a Christian, he typically associates it with the Devil and condemns it as inconsistent with being a follower of Jesus Christ.[44]

44. On envy see also Gregory of Nazianzus, Cappadocia (329-390 CE), archbishop

This understanding of envy from Late Antiquity, including its inseparable connection with the Evil Eye, is echoed centuries later in Francis Bacon's celebrated essay, "Of Envy" (1625). These key features of envy, minus the reference to the Devil as the prime motivator of human envy, also reappear in the definition of envy given by Immanuel Kant (1724–1804), which Helmut Schoeck in his comprehensive study of the subject (1987), regards as "one of the most complete definitions" ever offered:

> Envy (*livor*) is a tendency to perceive with displeasure the good of others, although it in no way detracts from one's own, and which, when it leads to action (in order to diminish that good) is called qualified envy, but otherwise only ill-will (*invidentia*); it is however only an indirect, malevolent frame of mind, namely a disinclination to see our own good overshadowed by the good of others, because we take its measure not from its intrinsic worth, but by comparison with the good of others and then go on to symbolize that evaluation.[45]

The Writings of the Fourth Century Church Fathers— Evil Eye, Envy, and the Devil

The fourth century Church Fathers are the main source of the literary evidence concerning the Evil Eye in the Christian Roman-Byzantine period. Of particular importance are the theologians Basil of Caesarea in Cappadocia, John Chrysostom of Antioch in Syria, and Jerome, translator of the Latin Bible, the Vulgate.[46]

---

of Constantinople, *Oration* 6 (PG 35. 721–752); *St. Gregory of Nazianzus. Select Orations* (translated by Martha Vinson) 2003:3–20 (*Oration* 6). John Chrysostom, Homily 40 on Matthew 12:9–10, PG 57.439–46; NPNF series 1, vol. 10:254–57; Homily 1 Cor. 12:13 on 4:6 (PG 61.105–6; APNF, series 1, vol. 12, 184–85); Cyril, patriarch of Alexandria (died 444 CE), in his *Commentary on Joel* (3:1–3), illustrates the conventional identification of envy and Evil Eye in his rendition of *baskania* with *invidia* (PG 71.38.235d).

45. Quotation in Schoeck 1987:201.

46. The two other Cappadocian Fathers, namely Gregory of Nyssa, brother of Basil, and Gregory of Nazianzus, friend of both Basil and Gregory of Nyssa, make occasional but less sustained references to the Evil Eye. On the Church Fathers and the Evil Eye and envy see Kötting 1954; Nikolaou 1969; Brox 1974; Engemann 1975; Russell 1982, 1995; Dunbabin and Dickie 1983; Bartelink 1983; Limberis 1991; Dickie 1995 (1995:18–21 on Basil; 1995:21–24 on John Chrysostom; 1995:24–26 on Jerome; 1995:26–28 on Eusebius of Alexandria; 1995:28–30 on Tertullian; 1995:30–34 on the Fathers in general); Maguire 1995; Rakoczy 1996:216–226; Aquaro 2004; Trzcionka 2007, 2011.

The period from the fourth to sixth centuries was marked by great unrest, massive political struggles for power, and a growing sense of insecurity concerning a center not holding in unstable and tumultuous times. Noticing the rise in accusations of sorcery during this period, Peter Brown has proposed that these accusations synchronized with changes in the structure of the governing class in mid-fourth century and then eventually declined in the sixth century with the return of political and social stability.[47] This period saw a clash between two systems of power: articulate power (agreed upon by all) and inarticulate power (involving intangibles and advantages of certain groups). In this time of struggle, resort was made to accusations of sorcery by holders of articulate power against "holders of ambiguous positions of personal power."[48] Sorcery accusations among rivals figured in the purges of emperors Constantius II, Valentinian I, and Valens. Libanius (c. 314–393 CE), famous orator of Antioch and possible teacher of John Chrysostom, employed such accusations and, because of his ill-defined power, was a target himself.[49] All classes of society, including charioteers and denizens of the demi-monde, came under attack. Christians, linked with this demi-monde, also were charged with sorcery.[50] The attacks subsided as political stability returned.[51] The Christians themselves, shifting to "explanations of misfortune through *suprahuman* agencies," blamed demons as the cause of all misfortune and sorcerers as manipulators of the demons.[52] The Christian church, according to Brown, "offered an explanation of misfortune that both embraced all the phenomena previously ascribed to sorcery, and armed the individual with weapons of satisfying precision and efficacy against its suprahuman agents."[53]

The correlation between sorcery accusation and times of social instability explains as well the continuation of fear of the Evil Eye and resort to a host of apotropaics and amulets to protect against it. This period saw a marked increase in concern about the Evil Eye among all classes of society, including Jewish and Christian segments of the population. Anxiety over the Evil Eye also reckoned as a factor in the growing hostility between Christians and Jews in this period. Canon 49 of the Council of Elvira (306 CE), for example, expressly forbade Jews from standing among the ripening

47. Brown 1970:20.
48. Ibid., 20–21.
49. Ibid. 23–24.
50. Ibid., 26.
51. Ibid., 27.
52. Ibid., 28.
53. Ibid.

grain fields of Christians, lest they cause the crops to wither by their malevolent glances. This is an ominous forerunner of the later medieval equation of the Evil Eye and "Judenblick" ("Jew's glance").[54]

The re-focusing of the Christians on *external* suprahuman agents of evil and on the Devil as ultimate manipulator of human pawns applies as well to their practice concerning the Evil Eye. Evil and envy were traced to Satan, and religious heresy was linked with the magical arts.[55] The increase in these centuries in literary references to the Evil Eye[56] as well as in the material evidence (apotropaics and amulets) is striking, as is the similarity in amuletic design and use among Christians, pagans, Jews, and Romans.

Basil of Caesarea

Basil of Caesarea in Cappadocia, Asia Minor (c. 330–379 CE) composed a notable homily on envy (c. 364 CE) that makes explicit reference to the Evil Eye and that illustrates the assumed association of envy, the Evil Eye, and the Devil (*Homily 11, Concerning Envy/Peri phthonou/De invidia* [PG 31.372–85]). This is one of the fullest extent ancient descriptions of the perniciousness of envy in its everyday reality and its connection with the Evil Eye.[57] "From the point of style," Gonzalo Fernandez de la Mora notes in his reference to this text, this homily of Basil is "the peak of Greek writing on envy, and the same may be said from its conceptual point of view . . . It is more dense and precise than the studies of Plutarch, Justin and Cyprian. It is the highlight of the ancient world on the theme of envy."[58] Basil, however, is clearly indebted to Plutarch, both his "On Envy and Hatred" and his treatise on the Evil Eye, as Dickie has shown.[59] Basil goes beyond Plutarch, however, in attributing the Evil Eye to the figure conceived by Christians as the cosmic adversary, the Devil, operating through human pawns.

Urging his community to renounce envy in all its forms, Basil opens his homily by contrasting the good character of God to the wickedness of the Devil as the source of all iniquity. He then immediately connects the

54. See Moss and Cappannari 1976:8.

55. See Engemann 1975; Bartelink 1983; Rakoczy 1996:216–26; Dickie 1995, 2001:251–321; Trzcionka 2004.

56. A search of the *Thesaurus Linguae Graece* computer database in this time frame indicates 986 occurrences of the *bask*-family of terms in thirty-four sources, with high totals among particular ecclesiastical writers and theologians.

57. See Limberis 1991; Elliott 1992:58–59; Dickie 1995:18–21; Rakoczy 1996: 220–23.

58. De la Mora 1987:24.

59. See Dickie 1995:19 and nn. 30 and 31 for parallels.

prince of evil with envy and the Evil Eye, spelling out the pernicious features of Evil-Eyeing envy:

> As freedom from envy (*aphthonia*) is consistent with the good [and with God who is good], so the envious Evil Eye (*baskania*) relates to the Devil. Therefore, brothers and sisters, let us shun the vice of envy (*phthonou*)... and not be sharers in the works of our Adversary... No feeling (*pathos*) more pernicious than envy (*phthonos*) is implanted in human souls. This passion is first and foremost a personal detriment to the one guilty of it and does not harm others in the least. As rust wears away iron, so envy corrodes the soul it inhabits. More than this, it consumes the soul that gives it birth, like vipers which are said to be born by eating their way through the womb that conceived them. Now, envy (*phthonos*) is pain caused by our neighbor's prosperity. Hence, an Evil-Eyeing person (*ton baskanon*) is never without cause for grief and despondency. If his neighbor's land is fertile, if his (neighbor's) house abounds with all the goods of this life, if he, its master, enjoys continual gladness of heart—all these things aggravate the sickness and add to the pain of the Evil-Eyeing person (*tôi baskanôi*). He is exactly like one, who, stripped of his clothing, is being pierced with wounds from all quarters. Is anyone brave and vigorous? This is a blow to the Evil-Eyeing person (*ton baskanon*). Is someone else handsomer than he? Another blow to the Evil-Eyeing person (*tôi baskanôi*). Does so-and-so possess superior mental endowment? Is he looked up to and emulated (*zêloutai*) because of his wisdom and eloquence? Is someone else rich and eager to lavish his wealth in alms to the poor and charitable contributions, and does he receive great praise from the beneficiaries of his charity? All these blessings are like so many blows and wounds piercing the envious man to his heart's core. The worst feature of this malady, however, is that its victims cannot reveal it to anyone, but he hangs his head and is mute. He is troubled and he laments and is utterly undone by this vice. When he is questioned about his state, he is ashamed to make known his sad condition and say, "I am an Evil Eyeing person (*baskanos eimi*), and bitter, and the good fortune of my friend distresses me. I am grieving over my brother's joy and I cannot endure the sight of others' blessings. The happiness of my neighbors I make my own misfortune." This he would say if he were willing to tell the truth. But, not choosing to reveal these sentiments, he confines in the depths of his soul this illness (*tên noson*) which is gnawing at his vitals and consuming them...What could be more fatal than this illness? It ruins our

life, perverts our nature, arouses hatred of the good bestowed on us by God, and places us in a hostile relation toward God. (PG 31. 372.32–376.7)[60]

Basil's juxtaposing of the terms *baskania*, *phthonos* and *zêlos* throughout the homily demonstrates how, for him, envy and the Evil Eye are virtually synonymous.[61] He traces the origin of envy, the most fatal of vices, to the Devil, "that author of evils" (PG 31. 372.26–32; 376.8; 380.46–48). Filled with bitterness against God because of God's "lavish generosity" toward mankind (PG 31. 376.10), the Devil, Basil stresses, wreaked vengeance upon mankind. Cain envious of Abel, Joseph's brothers envious of Joseph, and Saul envious of David were among his victims and pawns (PG 31.376.13—377.30). Jesus, too, was an object of envy because of his generosity to the needy and his gift of life to mankind (PG 31.377.31-44). All this was wrought by the Devil, who continues to afflict mankind and rejoice at all those destroyed by envy and the Evil Eye (PG 31.372.45–50).

In the course of his homily, Basil mentions numerous features that we have found to be conventionally associated with envy and the Evil Eye. Among these familiar characteristics is the feeling of hostility toward someone enjoying prosperity even though he has in no way caused your own possessions to decrease (PG 31.376.23-27). King Saul's Evil-Eyeing envy of David (1 Sam 18:9) is given by Basil as an example,[62] but the behavior fits as well the envious Evil-Eyed laborers of Jesus's parable (Matt 20:1–15).[63] Basil recalls the wise counsel in Proverbs (23:6) that dining with an Evil-Eyeing person (*baskanos*) should be avoided as well as any further social contacts (PG 31. 377.51–53). Envy, he notes, is virulent among friends and close neighbors, citing a passage of Ecclesiastes (4:4) to that effect (PG 31. 380.1–15) while also echoing Aristotle. This feature of envy is conventional from Aristotle onward and also recalls Jesus' parable of the laborers in the vineyard (Matt 20:1–15). Membership in groups, moreover, should be avoided where Evil-Eyeing persons (*baskanoi*) are present.

---

60. Here and in the following quotations of Basil, I am citing with modification, the translation by M. Monica Wagner, "Homily 11. Concerning Envy," *The Fathers of the Church*, vol. 9 (1950):463–474.

61. Terms of the *bask-* family appear 26x in the homily; terms of the *phthon-* word family occur 35x; and of the *zêl-* family, 7x. Professor Vasiliki Limberis (1991) in her detailed examination of the homily offers an instructive examination of the Evil Eye and envy in the cultural context of Mediterranean society in Basil's time.

62. On this text see Vol. 3, chap. 1.

63. For the discussion of this text see Vol. 3:168–98.

> Among acquaintances, it is neighbors and fellow workmen, or those who are otherwise brought into close contact, who are envied and among these again, those of the same age and kinsmen and brothers. In short, as the red blight is a common pest to corn, so envy is the plague of friendship. (PG 31.380.10–14)

Envious persons, he is eager to warn, damage themselves with their envy:

> As arrows shot with great force come back upon the archer when they strike a hard and unyielding surface, so also do the movements of envy strike the envious person himself. (PG 31.380.17–19)

This notion, too, is conventional and parallels the idea that persons with an Evil Eye can inflict harm on themselves.[64]

In the same breath, however, Basil denies that this Evil-Eyeing envy actually harms others:

> they [the movements of envy] do not at all harm the object of his spite. Who, by his feelings of annoyance, ever caused a neighbor's goods to be diminished? (PG 31.380.20)

This curious distinction between harm to self but no harm to others illustrates an ambiguous stance on envy and the Evil Eye marking the entire homily and Basil's thinking on the Evil Eye in general, as Dickie (1995:21, 30–31) has stressed.

Then, directly addressing the customary association of envy and the Evil Eye, Basil observes that

> persons who suffer from this malady of an envious Evil Eye (*hoi nosountes tên baskanian*) are supposed to be even more dangerous than poisonous animals, since these [latter] inject their venom by piercing their victim; then, gradually, putrefaction spreads over the infected area. But some think that envious persons (*tous phthonerous*) cause damage (*tên blabên*) merely by a glance [lit, "through their eyes, *di' ophthalmôn*], so that healthy persons in the full flower and vigor of their prime are made to pine away by their [the enviers's] Evil-Eyeing gazing (*par' autôn katabaskainomena*), suddenly losing all their plumpness, which dwindles and wastes away under the gaze of the envious (*tôn*

---

64. See above, Cyprian, *De Zelo*; also John Chrysostom, *Hom. Gen. 46*, PG 54.427–28; *Hom. Matt. 40* on Matt 12:9–10, PG 57.439–46; *Hom. 31 on 1 Cor. 12:13*, PG 61.262–64; *Hom. 2 Cor 27*, PG 61.586–88; *Hom. Rom. 7*, PG 60.447–52. See also Vol. 2:53–55, 60, 62, 118, 149.

phthonerôn ophthalmôn), as if washed away by a destructive flood." (PG 31.380.24–35)[65]

At this point Basil registers a demur concerning popular opinion regarding the Evil Eye and envy; namely, that harm can be wrought through emanations from a malicious eye:

> For my part, I reject this [preceding] account (*ton logon*) as popular supposition and old wives' gossip. (PG 31. 380.35–36)

Without pausing, however, he goes on to stress that Evil-Eyeing persons do in fact exist and are, in reality, pawns of the Devil and his demonic minions—a fact that his audience must take with utmost seriousness.

> But this I do say: the demons (*daimones*), who hate all that is good, make even the eyes of envious Evil-Eyed persons (*ophthalmois tôn baskanôn*) serviceable to their own purposes. You should not shrink, therefore, from making of yourself a pawn for the dread demon/Devil (*daimonos*) and submitting to wickedness, by which you become an enemy to persons who have not harmed you in any way and an enemy also of God who is good and without envy (*aphthonou*). (PG 31. 380.36–45)[66]

The envious (*hoi phthonountes*), he elaborates, have tell-tale features by which they can be detected:

> Their eyes are dry and lusterless; their cheeks, sunken; their brow grown together (*ophrys sympeptôkuia*),[67] their mind, distorted and confused by their passion and incapable of making valid judgments in handling their own affairs. (PG 31. 380.50–53)

Like vultures and flies attracted to ill-smelling places and wounded flesh, these envious Evil Eyed fascinators (*hoi baskanoi*) avert their gaze from the brightness of life and the loftiness of good actions and fix their attention upon rottenness (PG 31. 380). Like incompetent painters, they focus

---

65. On the drying up and withering conventionally associated with the Evil Eye see also Gregory of Nyssa, *De beatitudinibus* 7 (PG 44.1288b); Rakoczy 1996:220 and n. 815 (Evil-Eyed enviers also have dry eyes, sunken cheeks, boney visages); for further characteristics of the Evil-Eyed envier see Nikolaou 1969: 35–36; Dunbabin-Dickie 1983:10–12.

66. On God as "without envy" see van Unnik 1971, 1973 and, previously, Vol. 3, Chap. 1.

67. Eyebrows grown together, knit eyebrows, were considered a conventional telltale indicator of a fascinator. As noted in Vol. 3, the first physical description of Paul explicitly mentioned his knit eyebrows (*synophryn, Acts of Paul and Thecla* 3); see Vol. 3:245, 247–48, 257, 260.

on ugliness and deformity. They pervert praise into something despicable, courage into recklessness, generosity into profligacy, thrift into stinginess (PG 31. 380–381). His hearers therefore are exhorted to "flee from so abominable a vice":

> It is a lesson taught by a serpent, an invention of demons, the seed of discord, a pledge of punishment, a barrier to holiness, a path to hell, and a cause for losing the kingdom of God. (PG 31. 380.46–49)

Approaching his conclusion, Basil shifts from denunciation of Evil-Eyed envy to advice on avoiding this malice and striving after virtue (PG 31. 384.43—385.36). His audience is urged to cease desiring transitory things such as health, prosperity, status and renown, and instead to focus on what is real and eternal: benevolence of character and generosity toward others (PG 31.384.30), just as God and Jesus are generous (PG 31.376.10-11; 377. 34–44). The honorable person is one who "will be generous (*aphthonos*, lit. 'without envy') in giving of his abundance to the needy, and he will offer physical assistance to the infirm and regard that part of his wealth which is superfluous as belonging to any destitute person as much as it does to himself" (PG 31.384.1–5). The stress on generosity as the opposite of the Evil Eye and envy, though Basil does not explicitly note it, echoes a refrain of numerous biblical Evil Eye texts (Deut 15:7–11; 28:53–57; Sir 14:3; Tob 4: 5–19; Matt 6:22–23/Luke 11:34). Hypocrisy, "the fruit of envy" (PG 31. 385.20), is what the churchman's hearers must eschew, along with envy itself and the desire for things not under one's personal control. What all believers must pursue is that which is within their power to attain, namely personal virtue, the more lasting good (PG 31.385.2–19). This concluding emphasis on benevolence and generosity to those in need, while generally minimal in pagan comment on envy and the Evil Eye, is entirely consonant with the repeated antithesis of the Evil Eye and generosity found in the biblical texts, as we have seen in Vol. 3. In contrast to the social divisiveness of Evil-Eyeing envy and miserliness, generosity, moreover, contributed to the unity and harmony of the community.

Even with his rejection of certain notions of Evil Eye belief as "popular supposition and old wives' gossip," (PG 31.380.35–36), Basil's view of the Evil Eye and envy accords in many respects with the conventional view prevalent among his pagan neighbors[68] and also with Christian tradition.

---

68. Dickie (1995:19), in fact, sees Basil relying directly on Plutarch's *De invidia et odio, On Envy and Hate* (*Mor.* 536E–538E), where Plutarch clarifies envy by comparing and contrasting it to hate. Dickie compares Basil, *De Invidia* PG 31.373 and Plutarch., *Mor.* 537E (the envious never admit to envy); Basil, *De Invidia* PG 31.373 and Plutarch.

He assumes that the eye is an active organ and that an Evil Eye projects envy and other emotions. The demons, he says, "make even the eyes of the Evil-Eyed (*tois ophthalmois tôn baskanôn*) serviceable to their own purpose" (PG 31. 380). In affirming the possibility of self-fascination, he compares the action of the eye conveying envy to "arrows shot with great force [that] come back upon the archer when they strike a hard and unwielding surface" (PG 31. 380). "Envy is hurled (*epiballein*) from the eyes," as Vasiliki Limberis observes, in her insightful study.[69] The comparison of an Evil Eye and envy to a bow shooting arrows appears as early as Aeschylus (*Agamemnon* 241, 468; *Persians* 81–82) and again centuries later in Plutarch's treatise (*Quaest. Conv.* 5.7, *Mor.* 681E). The distinguishing features of the envier—withered, haggard appearance and contracted or knit eyebrows (PG 31. 380.57)—are those likewise associated conventionally with the Evil-Eye.[70] The envious Evil-Eyeing person can injure himself; he "is consumed and pines away with grief" (PG 31.380.23). The effect of envy as a "wasting and rotting" and a wearing away of vigorous health[71] is synonymous with the conventional view of the harm caused by an Evil Eye.[72] Basil's definition of envy as "pain caused by our neighbor's prosperity" and the wish that this good fortune be lost (PG 31.373) echoes the seminal definition of Aristotle and others. Basil ranks envy as the worst of the human vices (PG 31.372). We recall that in the Bible, Sirach said the same of its cousin, the Evil Eye (*ophthalmos ponêros*) (Sir 31:13). The worst aspect of this envy is "that its victim cannot reveal it to anyone because of the profound shame it brings." So "he confines this illness in the depths of his soul, [an illness] which is gnawing at his vitals and consuming them" (PG 31.373). These features of the envious that Basil delineates (PG 31. 380.49–381.26) are those conventionally associated with the envious and Evil-Eyed. The antithesis of the envious Evil Eye is generosity, as numerous passages of the Bible have also stressed.

This all shows that Basil's stance on the subject is strikingly ambiguous, a point stressed by Dickie as well. "Despite his dismissal of Plutarch's

---

Mor. 538B-C (misfortune of the envied puts a stop to envy); Basil, *De Invidia* PG 31.376–377 and Plutarch *Mor.* 538C-D (doing good to the envious exacerbates their envy rather than stopping it). The theory of *baskania* that Basil rejects, Dickie argues (1995:19), is that spelled out by Plutarch in his treatise on the Evil Eye (*Quaest. Conviv.* 5.7; *Mor.* 680C–683B) and Basil's "description of the effect of *baskania* on bodies in their prime comes from Plutarch's explanation of why good-looking young men in their prime may fascinate themselves if they see their image reflected in water." Plutarch, in turn, closely followed Aristotle's description of envy.

69. Limberis 1991:165, noting PG 31.373.43–74; 380.53.
70. See above, 62, 71.
71. Limbris 1991:164.
72. See above, 62, 71.

theory as to how the Evil Eye operates, Basil has more in common with Plutarch than perhaps he would want to admit: he too believes that the eyes of the envious may cause hurt," but "appeals to the notion of envious demons using envious human beings as the instruments of their will."[73] Though discounting the possibility of an Evil Eye causing physical harm to *others* (PG 31.380.20–21), he allows for the possibility of *self-injury* via an Evil Eye (PG 31.380.19, 23). He likewise took seriously the power of potions/spells (*pharmaka*) and binding tablets (*katadesmoi*). In speaking of voluntary and involuntary homicide, he lists the preparation of potions causing death as an example of a spell: "This is the sort of thing that women frequently do. They seek to attract love to themselves by means of potions and tablets and they give to them [their victims] charms that make their thinking cloudy" (Basil, *Epistles* 188.8, c. 360 CE).[74] Basil appears to accept an envious Evil Eye as a personal *psychological* reality that harms the self, while disallowing any physiological possibility of an ocular gaze that can harm others (PG 31.372–373). Certain aspects of the belief are dismissed as specious (PG 31. 380.35–36), while other features of the Evil Eye are deemed to have dangerous consequences. One thing, however, for Basil is paramount: behind the malice of the Evil Eye and envy lurks the Devil "the author of all evils" and "destroyer of our lives" (PG 31. 372.24–27; 376.8–9; 377.45–50; 380.36–45). Satan can and must be resisted through virtuous living, avoidance of hypocrisy, and the practice of generosity.

Envy, he notes, is aroused by a comparison of our lot with that of those close to us and sees their sudden gain as a diminishment of our status. It is resentment at not having that to which we believe ourselves entitled. Our envy begrudges both the good fortune of beneficiaries and generosity of benefactors although in actuality these in no way diminish our own condition. It gnaws away at our own health, perverts our nature, and endangers the social cohesion and well-being of the community. This Christian description of envy involves features of the Evil Eye complex, including envy, that we have already met in Greek and Latin sources. Though never referring to Aristotle by name, Basil's words seem a virtual echo of the philosopher's comments six hundred years earlier. "Envy," Aristotle had indicated in his essay on rhetoric, "is a disturbing pain excited by the prosperity of others."

> We feel it towards our equals [in birth, relationship, age, disposition, distinction or wealth] not with the idea of getting

---

73. Dickie 1995:20–21.

74. On other contemporary Christians and their belief in the magical arts see Brox 194; Gager 1992:260–64; Dickie 1995, 2001:202–321; Russell 1995; H. Maquire 1995b; Trzcionka 2007.

something for ourselves, but because other people have it . . . We feel envy also if we fall but a little short of having everything . . . Ambitious men are more envious than those who are not . . . and small-minded men are envious, for everything seems great to them . . . The deeds or possessions which arouse the love of reputation and honor and the desire for fame, and the various gifts of fortune, are almost all subject to envy. This is especially so if we desire the thing ourselves, or think we are entitled to it, or if having it puts us a little above others, or not having it a little below them. . . We envy those who are near us in time, place, age or reputation . . . hence the saying, 'Potter against potter.' We also envy those whose possession of, or success in, a thing is a reproach to us: these are our neighbors and equals . . . We also envy those who have what we think we ought to have, or who have got what we once had. Hence old men envy younger men; and those, who have spent much, envy those who have spent little on the same thing. And persons who have not obtained a thing, or have not obtained it yet, envy those who have obtained it quickly. (Aristotle, *Rhetoric* 2.10 1387b–1388a; cf. also 2.9)

Basil's homily on envy represents, according to Vasili Limberis, a "direct effort to wrest control over the evil eye for the church." She is surely on the right track in affirming that the homily also "demonstrates how Basil continued to work within the indigenous code of Mediterranean social behavior that was dominated by honor, shame, revenge, and envy. Basil's solution to "the grave problem of envy" . . . is really a recasting of the pursuit of virtue, which "is rewarded by the most valued possession: honor" (Limberis 1997:163–64).

Basil affirms that, from his Christian perspective, envy and the Evil Eye are more than mere *human* vices. Ultimately they originate with the Devil/Satan, the "author of evils" (PG 31. 372.24–27, 376.8–9; 377.45–50), and they alienate the believer from God. The devil uses the eyes of the envious for his own malignant ends (PG 31.380 24–42). In linking envy and the Evil Eye with the prince of demons, Basil goes beyond what is stated in the biblical writings where both envy and Evil Eye are solely *human* vices. Basil's position, however, is less the "paradigm shift" that Rakoczy (1996:216–226) has claimed for the church fathers than a return to the Greek notion of a *baskanos daimon*, an Evil-Eye demon, now equated with the Devil/Satan, demon and "author of evil."[75] This coupling of envy, the Evil Eye and the Devil is consistent with the thinking of most Christian authors in the post-biblical period, including Cyprian, and sets the pattern for the medieval

---

75. Basil, *Homily 11 on Envy* (PG 31.376).

church and beyond. This return to Greek and Roman thinking concerning the Evil Eye and the demonic is hardly surprising given that these authors were themselves steeped in Greek and Roman *paideia*, as noted by Peter Brown and Stephen Black among others.[76]

In the last analysis, Basil, along with other church fathers, remains ambivalent on the subject of Evil Eye and envy, as Dickie has concluded. Although Dickie problematically regards the Evil Eye as a form of magic, his point about the vacillation of the fathers on these matters is still valid.

> The fathers of the church have no reservations about condemning all forms of magic-working, in which category they certainly included the casting of the evil eye . . . They condemn magicians as frauds and charlatans, but sometimes speak of them as though they posed a real threat. They have no doubt that magic is the devil's work, but they are not at all certain whether the demonic forces magicians enlist to aid them do in fact afford any real help or only create the illusion of change. (Dickie 1995:10)

This vacillation of the fathers, he continues, includes their ambivalent stance on the Evil Eye.

> The attitude of the fathers of the church to the evil eye is a profoundly ambiguous one: they are not prepared to accept that the eyes of envious men can on their own inflict harm, but they are willing to concede either that the virtuous and fortunate do have something to fear from envious forces or that a supernatural force may use the eyes of the envious to cause harm . . . In essence they continue to believe in the evil eye, but qualify the expression of their belief to make it philosophically and theologically respectable.[77]

Basil, Dickie affirms, "is not prepared to deny that the eyes of the envious may be dangerous, if demons use them, let alone that there may be envious demonical and diabolical forces out there intent on destroying what is fair and good."[78]

The fathers thus shared the belief with educated pagans, along with the terms and presuppositions that the pagan philosophers have established for thinking about it. Basil, Dickie perceptively observes, by "bringing the demonic or the divine into the explanation, puts the explanation on a plane

---

76. Brown 1992; Black 2005.
77. Dickie 1995:10–11; see Brox 1975 for a similar position.
78. Dickie 1995:21.

that excuses the further exercise of the critical [human] faculty."[79] As a consequence of no little import, humans are now held less accountable for exercising an Evil Eye than they are in the Bible, for "the Devil made them do it." In this process of demonization, Basil shifts from a natural to a supernatural explanation of the Evil Eye that will influence Christian thinking and practice for centuries to come.

Gregory of Nyssa

Gregory of Nyssa (c. 335–c. 395 CE), the younger brother of Basil and another church father from Cappadocia, referred to the Evil Eye less often than his elder brother, but on the whole appears to have shared the views of Cyprian and Basil. Envy, he laments, is

> the passion which causes evil, the father of death, the first entrance for sin, the root of wickedness, the birth of sorrow, the mother of misfortune, the basis of disobedience, the beginning of shame. Envy banished us from Paradise, having become the serpent to oppose Eve. Envy walled us off from the tree of life, divested us of holy garments, and in shame led us away clothed with fig leaves. Envy armed Cain contrary to nature and instituted the death which is vindicated seven times. Envy made Joseph a slave. Envy is the death-dealing sting, the hidden weapon, the sickness of nature, the bitter poison, the self-willed emaciation, the bitter dart, the nail of the soul, the fire in the heart, the flame burning on the inside... (Gregory of Nyssa, *The Life of Moses* 2. 256–259, esp., 256; SC 1, 282–284)[80]

In his *Encomium on the Forty Martyrs*, Gregory of Nyssa states that it was the outstanding virtue of the martyrs that aroused the Evil Eye and envy of the Devil. The demonic Adversary, the Devil, also saw himself wronged by Job's renown, so "the one born by nature to oppose the good looked with an Evil Eye (*eide ponêrôi tôi ophthalmôi*) on these mighty opponents and was unable to endure such maturity of character in one so young" (Gregory of Nyssa, *Encomium in xl martyres*, PG 46.760c).[81]

In his funeral oration for Meletius, bishop of Antioch (d. 381 CE), Gregory similarly attributes the death of the revered bishop and the grief of the mourners to the personified power of Envy

---

79. Ibid.
80. Translation by Malherbe and Ferguson, in *Gregory of Nyssa, The Life of Moses*, 1978:120. On "envy as the chief sin" for Gregory and Athanasius see Louth 1984.
81. See Dickie 1995:34.

> that has an eye for all things fair [and] casts a bitter glance upon our blessedness. . . . What Evil Eye (*ophthalmos ponêros*), what wicked Evil-Eyeing malice (*baskania kakê*) has intruded on that church ? What is there to compensate her loss? (*Oratio funebris in Meletium*, PG 46. 856)

Envy casts a bitter glance and is synonymous with an Evil Eye and Evil-Eyed malice.

This comment also makes clear his adherence to the conventional extramission theory of vision, with its notion of an active eye. Similarly, in his treatise on the premature deaths of infants, Gregory observes briefly that the eye has a natural light within itself that actively apprehends external kindred light: "The eye enjoys the light by having the light within itself seize its kindred light; the finger or any other limb cannot effect the act of vision because none of this natural light is present in any of them."[82]

Gregory of Nazianzus

Gregory of Nazianzus (329–389 CE) is another Cappodocian father and colleague of Basil and Gregory of Nyssa. He not only links the Evil Eye with the Devil, but designates the Devil/Satan as *baskanos* ("The Evil Eyed One") in a kind of conjuration that works like the cry of an educated Christian in fear of Satan (Gregory Nazianzus, *Poemata de se ipso* 55 [PG 37. 1599]). The same formulation, slightly modified, is found on a gold amulet neck pendent at the cathedral of Monza.[83] In his *Poemata* he also substitutes *phthonos* for *baskania* as he repeats the belief recorded by Plato (*Phaedo* 95b) that loud speech attracts a punishing Evil Eye.[84]

Jerome

Jerome (c. 347–420 CE), vaunted translator of the Hebrew and Greek testaments of the Bible into a Latin version dubbed the *Vulgata* ("speech of the common people," c. 404 CE), reveals his thinking on the Evil Eye both in his Latin biblical translations and in his commentary on Galatians, composed c. 387/388 CE.[85]

---

82. Gregory of Nyssa, *On Infants' Early Deaths* (*De infantibus praemature abreptis labellum*), in *Sermones, pars 1*, in *Gregorii Nysseni Opera*, vol. 9.1 1992:447.

83. See IG 14.2413.18 and DACL 1.2 cols. 1743–1745.

84. Gregory Nazianzus, *Poemata de se ipso* 55 (PG 37.2.1052).

85. On Jerome's stance on the Evil Eye see Dickie 1995:24–26; Rakoczy 1996:

His Latin translations of biblical passages mentioning the Evil Eye employ a variety of standard expressions for "Evil Eye": terms of the *fasc*-word family (*fascinatio*, Wis 4:12; *fascinare*, Gal 3:1) as well as other expressions: *oculus malus* (Ecclus/Sir 14:10; 31:14; Mark 7:22); *oculus nequam* (Ecclus/Sir 14:8; 31:14, 15; Matt 6:23; for *nequam* also: Sir 14:5, 6; Luke 11:34); *oculus lividi* (Ecclus/Sir 14:8; cf. also *vir lividus*, Ecclus/Sir 37:12); *oculus cupidi* (Ecclus/Sir 14:9); *invidere* (Deut 28:54, 57; Prov 28:22; Ecclus/Sir 14:6, 8); *homo invidus* (Prov 23:6); *homo lividus* (Ecclus/Sir 14:3); terms of the *aemul-* root (Ecclus/Sir 37:12; cf. 1 Sam 2:32); and *zelare* (Ecclus/Sir 37:7). The formulation of 1 Kgdm/1 Sam 18:9, *non rectis oculis adspicere*, is rare but also a likely relevant Latin expression in the negative for David's looking at King Saul with an Evil Eye: "from that day Saul did not look at David with [lit.] straight eyes" (*non rectis ergo oculis Saul adspiciebat David a die illa*). An "oblique eye" (*oculus obliquus*) that looks askance is one of the Latin synonyms for Evil Eye and may have influenced Jerome's phrasing here in 1 Reg/1 Sam 18:9.

Jerome's commentary on Paul's letter to the Galatians offers further information on what he knew and thought about the Evil Eye. He renders Paul's standard Greek verb for "injure with an Evil Eye," *ebaskanen*, with its standard Latin equivalent, *fascinavit*.[86] This is a word of everyday speech, Jerome notes, though it does not mean, he claims, that Paul hereby recognizes the existence of an Evil Eye (*fascinum*) that is commonly supposed to do harm (Jerome, *Comm. Gal.* on 3:1 [PL 26.346–48]).[87] The term *baskanos*, akin to the verb *ebaskanen*, Jerome points out, occurs in Ecclus/Sir 18:18: "The gift of an Evil-Eyed person (*baskanou*) dims the eyes." Jerome renders *baskanou* here with *invidi* ("envious man").[88] "The word for 'envious person' (*invidus*) in our [Latin] language," he notes, "is recorded more meaningfully in Greek as *fascinator* ("Evil-Eyed person" [*baskanos*]). *Baskania*, he continues, appears in Wis 4:12, which Jerome renders with *fascinatio*, the standard Latin term for Evil Eye. "By these examples," he goes on,

---

217–18.

86. Ambrose renders similarly: *O insensati Galatae! Quis vos fascinavit?* "All who are fascinated [by an Evil Eye]," he explains, "pass from good to evil, just as they [the Galatians] passed from liberty and security to servitude and anxiety (*omnis enim qui fascinatur, de bono transit in malum, sicut et hi de libertate et securiatate ad servitium et sollicitudinem transierunt*), Ambrose, *In Epistolam Beati Pauli ad Galatas* (PL 17 372A).

87. See also Jerome, *Explicatio in epistulam ad Galatas* (PL 30.847).

88. His Vulgate translation of Ecclus/Sir 18:18, on the other hand, renders *baskanou* with the term *indisciplinati* ("undisciplined person") not conventionally associated with the Evil Eye).

we are shown either that the envious man (*invidus*) is tormented by the happiness of another, or he, in whom there are some good things, suffers harm by another who fascinates (*fascinante*), that is, by one who envies (*invidiante*)" (*Comm. Gal.* on 3:1, PL 26.346 and more briefly, *Exp. in ep. ad Gal.*, PL 30. 847).[89]

Jerome here renders Greek terms of the *baskainô* word family with Latin terms of the *fascino* word family, while also considering the terms *baskainô* and paronyms and *fascino* and paronyms as synonyms meaning "envy," "envious" (*invidere, invidus*)[90] He rejects the notion that an Evil Eye causes physical harm and regards Paul's verb *ebaskanen* to mean not "injured with an Evil-Eye" but "envied" (you). The terms in Sir 18:18 and Wis 4:12 he likewise takes to mean only "envy," with no implication of physical harming through ocular glance.[91] Nevertheless, he is familiar with the common notion that the Evil Eye (*fascinus*) harms infants and young children. As illustration of this feature, he cites the oft-quoted passage of Virgil (left unnamed), "someone has fascinated/Evil-Eyed (*fascinat*) my tender lambs" [Virgil, *Eclogues* 3.103] (Jerome, *Comm. Gal.*, PL 26.347). Jerome gives no explanation of, or support for, his dismissing the conventional meaning of *baskainô* as "injure with an Evil Eye" and his claim that it means only "to envy." He leaves this a bare assertion. At the same time, he seems to register some uncertainty on the Evil Eye (and not just envy) as an actual cause of harm.

Jerome posits a connection between the pagan notion that an Evil Eye harms young children (as expressed in the quotation of Vigil) and the injury done to the Galatians of which Paul speaks. In the latter case, it is harm to those who are young in the faith:

---

89. Thomas Scheck's recent translation of Jerome on Galatians (Scheck 2010: 47–275) obscures and misleads in respect to Jerome's remarks on Gal 3:1a. Jerome employs terms of the *fascin-* family (*fascinavit, fascinum, fascinatio, fascinator, fascinante, fascinate*) eleven times in this comment on Gal 3:1a, with Scheck using renderings such as "bewitched," "bewitching," "witchcraft," and "cast a spell." His rendition of Jerome on Gal 3:1a, "O senseless Galatians, who has bewitched you?" (2010:110) mistranslates Jerome's *fascinavit* (standard Latin for "injure with an Evil Eye") with "bewitched." Scheck continues this mistranslation also with respect to Jerome's citation of Sir 18:18 ("envious"), Wis 4:12 ("bewitching"), and Virgil, *Eclogues* 3.103 ("bewitches") (Scheck 2010:112–13). This translation shows that Scheck himself appears unclear concerning ancient Evil Eye belief, Jerome's familiarity with the Evil Eye. and the meaning of *fascinavit* in Gal 3:1.

90. Commenting on Matt 20:15 Jerome equates *ophthalmos ponêros* with envying another (*Letter* 69.1, to Oceanus); for this juxtaposition and apparent equation see also *Letter* 77.12 (also to Oceanus)

91. Noted also by Dickie 1995:112.

We think that the reason he [Paul] has now taken this example from popular thinking is that, just as the tender age is said to be harmed by the Evil Eye (*fascino*), so also the Galatians, recently born in the faith of Christ and nourished with milk, not solid food, have been injured. It is as though someone has Evil-Eyed (*fascinante*) them and they have vomited up the food of the Holy Spirit. For they are sick to their stomachs in respect to the faith (Jerome, *Comm. Gal* [PL 26. 348]).[92]

The notions that the Evil Eye hurts children in particular and that it also causes diners to vomit up their food are both features of Evil Eye lore with long pedigrees.[93] In regard to the harm that an Evil Eye does to children, Jerome declares, "whether or not this is true, God alone must decide." He concedes, furthermore, that "it is possible that demons (*daemones*) assist with this sin. And whomever they spot initially busy in God's work or already well advanced, this one they divert from doing what is right" (*Comm. Gal.*, PL 26. 347). His position seems the same as that of Basil and later John Chrysostom; namely, that demons, or the chief of demons, the devil, manipulate the Evil Eye and envy of humans, a view shared by most of the Fathers. This association of the Evil Eye with a demon or demons and the demonization of envy likewise have a long pagan pedigree.[94]

There is a marked ambivalence in Jerome's position. On the one hand, he takes *fascinô* to mean "a person's being able to harm someone else" with an ocular glance, especially infants (citing Virgil), and to cause the vomiting of food. Yet he considers the verb of Gal 3:1, *ebaskanen/fascinavit*, to mean "to envy" rather than "to harm with an Evil Eye," and denies that Paul uses the verb in its conventional literal sense. In addition, similar to Basil, he allows that in the act of fascination and envy demons also may be at work. It is thus uncertain whether Jerome completely rejected the actuality of an injurious Evil Eye, even though taking Paul in Gal 3:1 to be referring to envy rather than ocular glance.[95] Also uncertain is the extent of the role that Jerome assumed demons played in the fascination or envy of which Paul was

---

92. Translation by T. P. Scheck 2010:112–13, with modifications by John H. Elliott. For Jerome on the Galatians as children see also PL 26.384, 385 etc.

93. See Vols. 1–3 passim on children as victims. On vomiting at dinner caused by an Evil Eye, see Pseudo-Aristotle, *Problemata Physica* 20.34 926 b21–31; Prov 23:6. See also Rakoczy 1996:142 and nn.469, 470.

94. See Euripides, *Troades* 768; Sophocles, *Philoctetes* 776; Plutarch, *Vita of Dio*; Rakoczy 1996:104–20, 218–19; and in the present work, Vol. 1, chap. 2 on Mesopotamian Evil Eye incantations and Vol. 2 for Greek and Roman texts.

95. Dickie (1995:26, 30) sees Jerome, Basil and John Chrysostom rejecting as "incredible" the notion of an injurious ocular glance.

speaking. In any case, Rakoczy is surely correct in viewing this association of the Evil Eye with the devil and demonic activity actually a "pagan popular belief in Christian clothing."[96]

Jerome, in sum, mentions aspects of Evil Eye belief with which he is familiar, and in his linking the Evil Eye and envy with demons, takes a position similar to that of Basil. Though dismissive of the conventional notion of the Evil Eye causing harm, Jerome, like Basil, assumes that behind the Evil Eye and envy lies the malice of demons who manipulate human beings to their malevolent ends.[97] In the last analysis, his position, like that of Basil, is ambiguous. Dickie's concluding observation on Jerome's view of the Evil Eye captures this ambiguity:

> What emerges from all of this is Jerome's concern that Paul not be thought to subscribe to belief in *fascinatio* in what Jerome imagines is its popular acceptance, and at the same time his willingness to entertain the possibility that demons may use envious men to further their own purposes, presumably acting through their envious gaze. *Fascinus* in its popular acceptance for Jerome apparently means a person's being able to harm someone else, though the means by which this is done are not specified.[98]

Two other fourth-century Christian commentators on Galatians, Marius Victorinus Afer and an author named Ambrosiaster by Erasmus centuries later take *ebaskanen* (Gal 3:1) to refer to harm by an Evil Eye and envy.[99] Dickie observes that though they explain what *ebaskanen* means, they "have nothing to say either about whether Paul subscribes to the belief that men can fascinate or whether there is anything to the belief" (Dickie 1995:26). Victorinus, he notes, however, "writes in such a way as to suggest that he accepts the belief."[100]

---

96. Rakoczy 1996:218.
97. So also Dickie 1995:25.
98. Ibid.
99. Marius Victorinus, *In epistulam Pauli ad Galatas liber 1* (PL 8.1166–67); Ambrosiaster (Pseudo-Ambrosius) *Comm.* [on Gal 3:1] (PL 17.372).
100. Dickie 1995:26. Victorinus, *In epistulam Pauli ad Galatas liber 1* (PL 8. 1166–67): "Only those are victims of the Evil Eye who are rich in something good; and they are victimized by the malicious and the envious (*non patiuntur fascinum, nisi qui in bono aliquo pollent, et patiuntur a malignis et invidis*)."

John Chrysostom

The renowned theologian, biblical expositor, and preacher, John Chrysostom of Antioch and Constantinople (354–407 CE) makes frequent reference to the Evil Eye and regards it as a "known, actual reality" (Rakoczy 1996:219).[101] His terminology for "Evil Eye" includes *baskania, baskanos, baskainein, baskanos ophthalmos, ophthalmos ponêros, ophthalmoi tôn baskanôn*. He often links these terms with envy (*phthonos, zêlos*), the malice of the Devil, the Evil-Eyed envy of the Jews, and, on occasion, Joseph and David as victims of Evil-Eyed envy. His repeated invective against Christian apotropaic practices to avert the Evil Eye makes it clear that in his day, among Christians as well as their pagan neighbors, fear of the Evil Eye and measures taken to avoid it were as pervasive as ever.

John the "Golden-mouthed" was educated in Antioch, Syria, home of the renowned pagan orator Libanius, and was ordained there to the Christian priesthood in 386 CE. He later became bishop and patriarch of Constantinople (398 CE).[102] His extensive writings do not include a homily on envy (and the Evil Eye) similar to that of Basil. However, several of his homilies make reference to the topic.[103] Though profoundly critical of the persistence of Evil Eye belief and practice in Christian circles in his time, Chrysostom too reveals a vascillation on the subject similar to that of Basil and Jerome.[104]

Chrysostom's series of homilies on Genesis and on certain books of the New Testament (Matthew, John, Romans, Galatians, 1–2 Corinthians, Colossians, Ephesians, 1–2 Timothy, Titus) was aimed at the instruction and moral reformation of the Christian residents of Antioch (c. 386–398 CE). He refers repeatedly to their ignorant and persistent use of protective charms and amulets. They even encircle their heads and feet with copper

---

101. Rakoczy points to Chrysostom, *Hom. Gen.* 14.1 (PG 53.111); *Serm. Gen.* 1.4 (PG 54.586); *Hom. Matt.* [on Matt. 12:4] (PG 57.207); *Paralyt.* (PG 51.49); *Delic.* 2 (PG 51.348); cf .also Nikolaou 1969:36–37.

102. Chrysostom was elected as bishop of Constantinople in October/November of 397 and consecrated in February 398 CE.

103. See *Hom. Gen.* (PG 54.525-32); *Hom. Matt.* 40 [on Matt 12:9–10] (PG 57.439–46); *Hom. Rom.* (PG 60.447–51); *Hom. 1 Cor.* (PG 61.262–64); *Hom. 2 Cor.* (PG 61.568–70, 586–90); *Hom. 1 Tim.* (PG 62.518–520) and notes below. See also De Wet 2007 on Chrysostom's homilies on 1 Corinthians 12 and especially pp. 181–201 noting the association of envy and Evil Eye.

104. On Chrysostom, envy and the Evil Eye, and apotropaics in general see Nikolaou 1969; Dickie 1995:21–26, 29–34; 2001:281–83; Rakoczy 1996:218–20; Trzcionka 2007:106–17, 121–27 and passim; Trzcionka 2011. On sorcerers and sorceresses from Constantine to the end of the seventh century, see Magie 2001:273–321. On the the Evil Eye in Syrian and Palestinian Christianity see Dickie 1995; Trzcionka 2007, 2011.

84   Beware the Evil Eye

coins/medallions of Alexander of Macedon, placing their hope of protection from evil in the image of a former Greek ruler, when they should be trusting only in the power of God, Jesus Christ, and the Cross.[105] These Antioch Christians, he complained, were still immersed in the pagan practices of their neighbors in their preoccupation with amulets, incantations, apotropaic rituals, and women singing charms instead of trusting exclusively in the protection and power of the Christian God.[106] Their fear of malignant demons should have ended with their entrance to the Christian community. They should rather be declaring, "I leave your ranks, Satan, and your pomp, and your service, and I join the ranks of Christ, and never go forth without this word."[107]

Chrysostom's repeated criticism of belief and behavior inappropriate for Christians[108] is a rich source of information about ongoing Evil Eye belief and practice in his day. Among the graphic descriptions of vulgar belief and practice that he inveighs against are numerous references to Evil Eye belief and practice.[109] Chrysostom speaks often of the Evil Eye (*ophthalmos baskanos*) as a known and actual fact.[110] In his 64th homily on the Gospel of John (11:41–42), he states that Jesus was suspected by his hearers of breaking the law and being an enemy of God. "They looked at him with an

105. John Chrysostom, *Catech. illum.* 2.5 (PG 49.240). Several such amulets with Alexander in the character of Hercules on one side and, on the other, a she-ass with her foal, a scorpion, and the name of Jesus Christ are in the Cabinet of Medals, Paris. Another in the Vatican Library displays an image of Alexander on one side and on the other, a Christ monogram

106. John Chrysostom, *Catech. illum.* 1.2 (PG 49.223–40). The Council of Laodicea, meeting c. 365 CE and approving a set of sixty canons, also confronted the continued production, sale, and use of amulets. Canon 36 specifically prohibited the clergy from making amulets and distributing them to the faithful. Augustine likewise denounced the amulets and the frauds who dispensed them (*On Christian Doctrine* 2.20; Letter 245.2 [to Possidius, bishop of Calama, Numidia]). A sermon of Caesarius, archbishop of Arles (c. 470–542 CE) makes it evident, however, that the production and distribution of amulets remained an ongoing enterprise (PL 39.2272).

107. John Chrysostom, *Catech. illum.* 2 (PG 49.240.53–55).

108. See, e.g., *Hom. 8 on Col.* (PG 62.358). Also *Hom. 4 on 1 Cor* (PG 61.38.14–20); *Hom. 10 on 1 Tim.* (PG 62.552); and *Catech. illum.* 1.2 (PG 49.223–240). On the cross as apotropaic see John Chrysostom, *Catech. illum.* (PG 49.246); *De adoratione pretiosae crucis* (PG 58.838); *Hom. Col.* (PG 62.357–359).

109. On John Chrysostom and the Evil Eye see Dickie 1995:21–24, 30–34; Dickie 2001:281–83; Rakoczy 1996:218–20; Trzcionka 2007:101–20; 2011. Nikolaou 1969:16 treats *phthonos* and *baskania* in John Chrysostom's works as synonyms referring to the same affect. On Chrysostom and the erotic gaze see Leyerle 1993.

110. See, e.g, John Chrysostom, *Hom. Gen. 14.1* (PG 53. 111); *Hom. Gen. 1.4* (PG 54.586); *Hom. Matt. 12.4* (PG 57.207); *Paralyt.* (PG 51.49); *Delic.* (PG 51.348), *Hom. 1 Cor. 12.13 on 4:6* (PG 61.105–6); Rakoczy 1996:219.

Evil Eye (*to baskainein*) and were ill-disposed toward him, because he declared himself equal to God."[111] Consistent with convention, both pagan and Christian, he frequently juxtaposes and often equates envy (*phthonos, zêlos*) and Evil Eye (*baskainein, baskania, ophthalmos ponêros*).[112] In his Second Homily on Philippians (1:8–11), he seeks to dissuade his audience from envying and Evil-Eyeing the rich (twice juxtaposing *envy* and *Evil Eye*).[113] The generous giving of alms, on the other hand, liberates one from the vice of envy.[114] In his tenth homily on Ephesians, he discusses the relation of head and feet within the church as Body of Christ. He urges those symbolized by the head not to be high-minded against the feet, and those symbolized by the feet not to Evil-Eye the head and eyes.[115]

Commenting on the unity that should prevail in the Christian community as the Body of Christ according to Paul's first letter to the Corinthians, Chrysostom insists that "nothing so divides and separates as envy and the Evil Eye (*phthonos kai baskania*)" that grievous sickness which in some respects is even worse than covetousness, the root of all evils (*Homily 31 on 1 Corinthians* 12:25, PG 61.262-264). His description here of envy (and the Evil Eye) in Homily 31 repeats many of the characteristics conventionally associated with envy and the malignant Eye: envy transpiring between neighbors; its being a displeasure and a pining away at the sight of the prosperity and success of others; its being worse than covetousness since the covetous person "rejoices at some acquisition of his own" whereas the envious person "delights in some else failing to receive"; its perceiving the misfortune and loss experienced by others as a benefit to self; its being a "grievous sickness," far removed from praiseworthy emulation, and worst among the vices; its having a "continual worm gnawing through the heart" and "collecting a fountain of poison more bitter than any gall," so that the fever of envy devours the very bones of the envious and destroys

---

111. *Hom. Jo.* 64.1, PG 59.382.

112. Nikolaou goes so far as to regard *phthonos* and *baskania*, "envy" and "Evil Eye," in Chysostom's writings as synonyms "describing one and the same affect" (Nikolaou 1969:16).

113. John Chrysostom, *Hom. Phil. 2* (on 1:8–11), PG 62.198, 214. For the frequent juxtaposition in other writings of Chrysostom see also PG 47.371, 430, 434; 48.785; 49.101, 140, 169, 198, 267; 50.607, 754–755; 54.450, 463, 525, 530; 50.821; 55. 59, 279, 365, 502, 503, 516, 565; 57.375 (2x), 442; 58.612, 613, 640, 661, 721, 764, 767, 769, 777; 59.210 (2x), 250, 269, 299, 309, 329, 528, 763; 60.50, 65, 66, 132, 195, 284, 342, 401, 447, 610, 619, 671, 697, 699, 734 (2 x); 61.106, 262, 263, 569, 590; 62.173, 198, 214, 411, 412, 468, 633; 63.155, 201, 576, 677, 698, 718, 771.

114. See Plassmann 1960: 8–10.

115. John Chrysostom, *Hom. Eph. 10* on 4:5 (PG 62.76).

all self-control in the soul. It is an "evil fever" and "more grievous than any gangrene."[116]

In this homily Chrysostom distinguishes envy (always negative) from emulation, which can be laudable:

> If indeed you wish to emulate him [a prosperous brother in the faith], I do not forbid it. Do emulate, but with a view to be like him who is approved—not in order to depress him [as envy would desire] but that you may reach the same lofty point, that you may display the same excellence. This is wholesome rivalry, imitation without contention: not to grieve at the good things of others [= envy] but to be vexed at our own evils. Envy results in the exact opposite of this.[117]

The noxious nature of envy is then described:

> For neglecting its own evils, it pines away at the good fortune of other men. And thus the poor is not so distressed by his own poverty as by the abundance of his neighbor. What can be more grievous than this? Yes, in this respect the envious person, as I said before, is worse than the covetous one. The latter rejoices at some acquisition of his own, while the former delights in someone else failing to receive.[118]

The envious deserve our prayers as well as our tears and lament, for the envious devour themselves:

> For they are the injured persons, having a continual worm gnawing through their heart, and collecting a fountain of poison more bitter than any gall. Come now, let us beseech the merciful God, both to change their state of feeling and that we may never fall into that disease: since heaven is indeed inaccessible to him that has this wasting sore, and before heaven too, even this present life is not worth living in. For not so thoroughly are timber and wool wont to be eaten through by moth and worm abiding

---

116. Excerpts from Homily 31 on 1 Cor. 12:21–26, translated by Talbot W. Chambers, *Saint Chrysostom: Homilies on the Epistles of Paul to the Corinthians* in NPNF, Series 1, Vol. 12:184–85. Chris Len De Wet (2007) offers an English translation of Homily 31 (2007:202–12), which incorporates and modifies that of Chambers, along with an overview of envy and the Evil Eye in the ancient Mediterranean world, the Bible, and John Chrysostom (2007:181–201).

117. Translation by Chambers.

118. Ibid.

therein, as does the fever of envy devour the very bones of the envious and destroy all self-command in their soul.[119]

Chrysostom denounces as ridiculous many practices of his time undertaken to protect vulnerable children from harm and the Evil Eye when Christians have a more powerful protective on hand. This includes the practice of bringing old women into the home to cure illness with incantations, even though the families are devout Christians and invoke the name of God. They are a trap, he states, laid by the Devil. How preposterous that they should claim regarding a sick child that an Evil Eye had stolen it and taken it away (*Homily 8 on Colossians*, PG. 62.357–59).[120] In another homily he lambasts

> the amulets and the bells, which are hung upon the [infant's] hand, and the scarlet thread, and the other things full of such extreme foolishness, when they [the nurses] ought to invest the child with nothing else than the protection of the Cross. (*Hom. 1 Cor 12.13* on 4:6, PG 61.105–6)

Bells and red threads had been employed for centuries in pagan and Jewish communities as protectives against the Evil Eye. They remained popular apotropaics among the Syrian Christians as well.[121] Their use still continues among the Syrian Lebanese in modern time.[122]

Chrysostom also condemns the apotropaic practices of Christian midwives, nurses and female slaves at the baths. These women, attempting to protect their infants from the Evil Eye (*ophthalmos, baskania*) and envy (*phthonos*), use mud from the bottom of the bath and with their finger smear it on the foreheads of children. "It turns away the Eye," they say, "both the Evil Eye and envy."[123] Resorting to such procedures, he says, compromises the children's having been sealed with the cross by the priest at their baptisms.

---

119. Ibid. For the envious as victims of their own envy see also *Homily 27 on 2 Cor* (PG 61.586–588); *Homily 46 on Genesis* (PG 54.427–428); *Homily 7 on Romans* (PG 60.447–452) and the same point in Basil, *Homily 11, on Envy* (PG 31.371–86).

120. See also John Chrysostom, *Catech. illum.* 2.5 (PG 49. 240).

121. On bells and scarlet thread as protectives against the Evil Eye see, previously, Vols. 2 and 3. Russell (1995, fig. 11) displays a photo of such an apotropaic bell (discovered at Anemurium in Asia Minor).

122. See Naff 1965.

123. *ophthalmon apostrephei, phêsi, kai baskanian kai phthonon*. John Chrysostom, *Hom. 1 Cor. 12.13* on 4:6 (PG 61.106). On the baths as a dangerous place of exposure to the Evil Eye see Dunbabin 1989.

Chrysostom's repeated objections to such practices indicate that both fear of the Evil Eye and apotropaic defense were still widespread in his day. They were of such seriousness that the Christian preacher could not turn a blind eye, as it were, or refrain from pastoral admonition. His tactic, it is interesting to note, was not to argue the implausibility of the belief. Instead he maintained that the apotropaic use of mud and other means for warding off the Evil Eye denied the effectiveness of the protection that Christian baptism conferred on the infants. Signing with the cross is a more effective anti-Evil Eye protective than daubing with mud. This response is an important indication of Chrysostom's view of the Evil Eye. He does not challenge the reality of the Evil Eye and the harm it causes, but only the means of its deflection. His regular move is to denounce the Evil Eye as an instrument of the Devil: to claim, when a child falls ill, that "an (Evil) Eye has caught the child" and is, in actuality, "satanical" (*Hom. Col. 8.5* on 3:5–7, PG 62.357–58). This is the pattern we have seen with Basil, Jerome, and other church fathers as well. In pointing out the powerlessness of the mud and clay, Chrysostom challenges the claim that these substances "avert all the host of the devil." The devil operates by introducing evils into human life, arousing envy, and laughing at the pathetic human attempts at resistance (*Hom. 1 Cor. 12.13* on 4:6, PG 61.106).

These homilies reveal the continuation of several aspects of Evil Eye belief and practice in Chrysostom's time: the notion that the Evil Eye causes harm and especially to children; that colored threads tied to the newborns' wrists were thought effective;[124] that a finger was used to smear the mud (most likely the middle finger [*digitus medius* = *digitus infamis*], the finger also raised against the Evil Eye)[125]—all features conventionally associated with the Evil Eye.[126] The new element found in the Christian tradition since the *Martyrdom of Polycarp* is the coupling of the Evil Eye and envy with Satan, the Devil, and the use of distinctively Christian symbols (baptism, prayer, the sign of the cross) for averting it.

This coupling of the Evil Eye and the Devil is evident in Chrysostom's exposition of Galatians 3. Commenting on Galatians 3:1, Chrysostom sees *ebaskanen* implying "the malignity of a demon whose breath had blasted their prosperous estate," as well as a human act of envying (*Hom. Gal.*, PG 61.648). Paul's human opponents were acting as agents of the Evil One. Here,

124. John Chrysostom, *Hom. 1 Cor. 12.13* on 4:6 (PG 61.105).

125. Compare the similar details of the ritual performed centuries earlier by a nurse in Petronius's *Satyricon* (131.4); see Vol. 2:148–49.

126. Leaving children dirty, rather than smearing them with mud, as protection against an Evil Eye, is practiced in modern time among Arabs in Iran, India, Tunisia, Greece and elsewhere; see Maloney 1976:64, 81, 122; Jahn 1855: 82.

as elsewhere, Chrysostom also equates the Evil Eye (*baskainein, baskania, ophthalmos ponêros*) with envy (*phthonos*). The Galatians, he surmises, were victims of envy because of something admirable about them. This, he observes, actually speaks well of them for having something worth envying. So Paul's rebuke, "who has injured you with an Evil Eye?" implies a hint of praise.[127] *Ebaskanen* in Gal 3:1, however, Chrysostom takes to mean "envy" and points to the Gospel (Matthew 6:22–23) where *ophthalmos ponêros*, he maintains, means the same. It is envy and not a harm-producing eye that Paul and Jesus have in mind, he claims.

> And when you hear of envy (*phthonon*) in this place [Gal 3:1], and in the Gospel [Matt 6:23] of an Evil Eye (*ophthalmon ponêron*), which means the same, do not suppose that the glance of the eyes (*hê tôn ophthalmôn bolê*) has any natural power to injure those who look upon it.[128] For the eye (*ophthalmos*), that is, the organ (*to melos*) itself, cannot be evil (*ponêros*). But Christ in that place [Matt 6:23] is speaking of envy (*ton phthonon*). The function of the eye is simply to behold (*to. . .horân*), but to behold in an evil manner belongs to an internal depravity of mind. Since through this sense [viz. the eye] knowledge of visible objects enters the soul, and because envy (*ho phthonos*) is, for the most part, generated by wealth, and wealth, sovereignty and their protection are perceived by the eye, therefore he [Jesus Christ] calls the Eye Evil (*ponêron ophthalmon*)—not as simply beholding (*ton horônta*), but as beholding with Evil-Eyed malice (*ton meta baskanias horônta*) from some evilness of soul (*tês kata psychên ponêrias*). (*Hom. Gal.* [on 3:1], PG 61.648)

Chrysostom, in other words, asserts that both *ebaskanen* in Gal 3:1 and *ophthalmos ponêros* in Matt 6:23 refer only to the internal emotion of envy and not to the capacity of a human Evil Eye to physically injure or harm. The eye in itself, he states, is neither evil nor good, but simply an organ of the body that beholds and takes in information.[129] It is rather in the soul

127. The Antiochan rhetorician Libanius also echoed the conventional wisdom that praise of persons, especially young persons, attracted envy and an Evil Eye; see Libanius, *Epistle* 127.1.

128. Rakoczy (1995:219 n.810) points out that this phrase *hê tôn ophthalmôn bolê* had been used centuries earlier by Homer in the *Odyssey* (4.150) in reference to the bolts projected from the eyes of Telemachus.

129. This concept of the eye's operation is more in line with an intromission theory of vision, than with the more prevalent extramission theory of vision held by Plutarch and most ancient authors; see Plutarch, *Quaest. Conviv.* 5.7, *Mor.* 681A; Apollonius of Rhodes *Arg.* 4.1559–1670 and Alexander of Aphrodisias, *Probl.* 2.53. Chrysostom, however, does not expand on this point and the extramission theory of vision remains

that evil arises. Envy, prompted by what is seen, is conveyed outward by beholding with malice aforethought. Yet he also believes that envy involves the eye and an act of beholding in a malicious manner, which has harmful effect—mutilating what exists, subtracting from what is complete, and ruining the whole (see below).

His reasoning amounts to what Dickie calls "an extremely tortured explanation" that leaves unclear what Chrysostom actually thinks about the eye as a vehicle of harmful envy (Dickie 1995:22). On the one hand, he views the eye as a passive organ. On the other hand, he considers the act of beholding to have a possible harmful effect on the viewer and the object viewed. "By this," Dickie speculates, "Chrysostom may mean that while the eyes of the envious are not bad in the sense that they can do harm; they are bad in the sense that envy distorts the vision and causes it to put an evil construction on what is seen" (Dickie 1995:22–23).

Chrysostom then returns to the issue of the meaning and implication of *ebaskanen* and Paul's point in Gal 3:1.

> Therefore in saying "who has harmed you with an envious Evil Eye" (*tis hymas ebaskanen* [Gal 3:1]), he [Paul] indicates that the persons in question [Paul's opponents] acted not from concern, not to supply defects, but to cut off what existed. For envy (*phthonou*), rather than supplying what is lacking, subtracts from what is complete, and ruins the whole. And he says this, meaning not that envy (*tou phthonou*) had any power of itself, but that the teachers [Paul's opponents] envied with Evil-Eyed malice (*dia baskanian*). (*Hom. Gal.* [on 3:1] (PG 61. 648)[130]

Dickie takes *ebaskanen* in Gal 3:1 as Paul's "asking who has put an *envious spell* on them" (Dickie 1995:22). He claims that Chrysostom reads Paul to be saying that "the Galatians have suffered the assault of a demon fiercely hostile to their success" and that they "have drawn envy on their heads" (Dickie 1995:22). Chrysostom sees this, Dickie avers, as "a reference to a demonic assault and not to fascination by a human eye" (Dickie 1995:22, 23). "Both Chrysostom and Basil present a unified voice in seeing *baskania* as a form of envious demonic assault" (Dickie 1995:24). Dickie appears intent on liberating Paul, Basil and Chrysostom from holding a belief in a human Evil Eye; but the evidence, as Dickie himself has acknowledged, is far from

---

dominant throughout Late Antiquity and beyond. Dickie's claim (1995:23–24) that Chrysostom as well as Basil had definitively adopted an intromission theory of vision in contrast to that of Plutarch, whose treatise they echo, states more than the evidence allows.

130. Translation of Gross Alexander (NPNF Series 1, 13:23–24), modified by J. H. Elliott; cf. Dickie 1995:22.

clear. The positions of Basil and Chrysostom rather seem to embrace, or oscillate between, notions of human and demonic agency.

Chrysostom, in this extensive reflection on Galatians 3 and Paul's reference to the Evil Eye, denies that an eye can physically injure others. He takes *ebaskanen* to mean "envy" and describes envy as a vicious internal emotion entailing malice that, when given rein, as in the case of Paul's opponents, diminishes and destroys. In this exposition, the physical force of a human Evil Eye is denied and the concept is psychologized.[131] This envy of the teachers opposing Paul and damaging the Galatians, however, is then traced in its origin to the "malignity of a demon" operating on and through Paul's opponents.

Chrysostom's intense interest in another type of ocular gaze, the erotic gaze, on the other hand, illustrates a concern about an active and aggressive power of the eye. "Nowhere did the perils of sight impress themselves on him [John Chrysostom] more forcefully," Blake Leyerle observes, "than in his consideration of the viewing of women."[132] Commenting on Jesus's warning against adultery and his admonition, "If your right eye offends you, pluck it out and throw it away" (Matt 5:29), Chrysostom "focuses on the visual aspect of eroticism."[133] This saying, he states, is "about those who are close to us."[134] He is referring to monks living with virgin housemates in "spiritual marriages." Inveighing against this practice, Chrysostom charges that these monks "must be guilty of ten thousand adulteries, daily beholding them [virgin housemates] with desire . . . although you have not touched her with your hand, yet you have caressed her with your eyes" (*Hom. Matt. 17.2*, PG 57. 257).[135] He even goes so far as to claim that "Jesus did not permit a man even to look into the eyes of a woman, but threatened those who did so with the penalty laid on adulterers."[136] At the same time, Chrysostom accuses certain unchaste women of "exercising a bruising and imperious dominion over men, through their eyes."[137] Lustful glances, according to Chrysostom, have dire eschatological consequences. In the last judgment, a wrongful glance and a wanton gaze will earn perpetual torment in hell.[138]

---

131. So also Rakoczy 1996:219
132. Leyerle 1993:163.
133. Ibid., 166.
134. John Chrysostom, *Hom. Matt. 17.3* (PG 57.258); cf. *Hom. Jo. 57.2–3* (PG 59. 314).
135. Leyerle 1993:166 n.35.
136. Ibid., 167.
137. Ibid., 168.
138. John Chrysostom, *Oppugn.* 3.1 (PG 49.350).

Over this scene sits God, the great "Unsleeping Eye."[139] Chrysostom "aims to bring the erotic eye under the control of shame."[140] He portrays men as passive feminized objects of the female gaze and women as ravished objects of the libidinous glance. Both, he insists, must be alert to the grave dangers of the erotic gaze. This is particularly so for couples in spiritual marriages, whom he sought to convince to renounce the practice. His own sight, on the other hand, he aligns with the ever-vigilant eye of God, thereby investing his point of view with divine authority[141] These are hardly the thoughts of someone who discounts the active power of the eye.

On the whole, Chrysostom, like Basil, appears ambivalent on the subject of the Evil Eye, as noted by Dickie and Rakoczy. On the one hand, Chrysostom distances himself from the idea that an eye is active rather than passive and can cause harm to others. Evil results from envy that is generated by demons and the Devil. On the other hand, as Dickie emphasizes, "[e]ven John Chrysostom when his guard is down speaks as if the eyes of envious men can cause harm."[142] As illustration, Dickie points to the passage we have considered above, where Chrysostom condemns the practice of nurses smearing children with mud to protect them against the Evil Eye (*Hom. 1 Cor. 12.13* on 4:6, PG 61.106). His attack is directed not at the nurses' belief that an Evil Eye can harm, "but at the measures they take to protect the child"—smearing the forehead with mud rather than marking it with the sign of the cross. This protection afforded by the cross would only be a point of consideration if the infants indeed were deemed vulnerable to Evil Eye attack.[143] Chrysostom had no hesitancy in attributing to the cross apotropaic power and encouraged its use for warding off evil,[144] just as he attributed apotropaic power to texts of the Gospels.[145] Basil and Chrysostom are further illustrations of the fact that in the post-biblical period Christians demonized the Evil Eye and envy, and divinized the effective protection

---

139. Leyerle 1993:171. For God as unsleeping Eye see *Oppugn.* 3.21 (PG 49.386); *Adv. Jud.* 8.8 (PG 48.941); *Hom. Gen.* 7.3 (PG 53.64); *Hom. Gen.* 8.66 (PG 53.75); *Hom. Jo.* 3.6 (PG 59.46); ibid. 4.4 (PG 59.52); *Hom. 1 Cor 12.* (PG 61.101); *Stat.* 20.4 (PG 49.203); *Laz.* 1.8 (PG 48.973).

140. Leyerle 1993:171.

141. Ibid., 174.

142. Dickie 1996:31.

143. Rakoczy (1996:219–220) reaches a similar conclusion.

144. See John Chrysostom, *Adv. Jud.* 8.8 (PG 48.939–942); *Hom. Matt.* 54.4 (PG 58.536–38); *Hom. 1 Cor 12.13* (PG 61.105–6); *Hom. Col.* 8.5 (PG 62.357–60).

145. John Chrysostom, *Stat., hom.* 19. 4 (PG 49.195–98); *Hom. Jo.* 32.3 (PG 59. 186–88); *Hom. 1 Cor.* 43. 4 (PG 61. 372–374). Contrast Jerome's rejection of the use of Gospel texts and wood fragments of the cross as amulets to ward off evil (*In Matthaeum* 4.23.5, CCL 77:212).

from both. Envy and the Evil Eye were ascribed to the malice of demons and the devil, who worked on and through human beings. The issue of an active or passive eye and of a damaging Evil Eye was left unresolved. On the other hand, these fathers represent the firm conviction that protection from, and victory over envy, the Evil Eye, and these demonic forces are provided by the Triune God and the powers of holy baptism, the cross, the words of sacred scripture, and actions of the Christian liturgy.

Other Patristic References to the Evil Eye

There are numerous other references to the Evil Eye by the Church Fathers, some of a more esoteric nature. The prayers of Cyprian, bishop of Carthage (died 258 CE), make repeated reference to the Evil Eye.[146] Ambrose, bishop of Milan (c. 339–397 CE), in his *Exposition of the Christian Faith*, remarked that Christians who question the eternity of the Son of God are in danger of joining Jews in looking at Jesus Christ with Evil-Eyed envy, alluding to Matt 27:18/Mark 15:10.[147] Gregory Nazianzus the Elder and his wife Nonna curiously named their daughter "Gorgonia."[148] Her name recalls the myth of Gorgo/Medusa, and the protection against the Evil Eye afforded by the gorgoneion, the image of Medusa's severed head. Perhaps the name was intended to provide her lasting protection from the Evil Eye. She died in 375 CE of natural causes. Said to have cured herself of two severe illnesses, she was venerated as patron of those afflicted with bodily sicknesses, as one might expect of someone with this moniker. Her feast day is observed on December 9 in the western church and on February 23 in the eastern church.[149]

Augustine, bishop of Hippo, North Africa (354–430 CE), recounted in his *Confessions* how he himself had sinned at an early age and how children are not innocent of evil behavior. As illustration of this latter point, he recalls his once viewing two babies nursing at the same breast. Whenever the one saw his foster-brother nursing, "he would grow pale with envy (*zelantem*)" (*Confessions* 1.7.12). This is a classic example of envy between rivals, and the mention of one infant "seeing" the other nursing implies the likely role

---

146. Schermann 1903:311, 313–14, 316–20, 323 and passim.

147. Ambrose, *Exposition of the Christian Faith* 1.10.67.

148. Gregory Nazianzus (the Younger), *Oration 8: Funeral Oration for His Sister Gorgonia* (PG 35.789–817).

149. For further references among the fathers to the Devil, fascination and the Evil Eye (endangerment of mother's milk, Evil Eye injury of animals, death of a son fascinated in public) see Meisen 1950:159.

of an Evil Eye in this incidence of sibling envy. In his *City of God*, Augustine describes and denounces pagan festivals where obscene rites involving Priapus and Pater Liber were undertaken to ward off the Evil Eye (*fascinatio*) and assure fertility. *Fascini* (male phalluses) were mounted on carts, exhibited at crossroads and forums, and honored publically by matrons. "In this way, it seems, the god Liber was to be propitiated, in order to secure the growth of seeds and to repel the Evil Eye (*fascinatio*) from the fields" (*City of God* 7.21, 24; cf. 4.11).[150] In his letter to Maximus of Madaura, the grammarian (c. 390 CE), Augustine refers to a marketplace where a statue of a man is placed over against two images of the god Mars. The man is making a prophylactic gesture with his hand. With three extended fingers (*porrectis tribus digitis*) the man's hand would restrain the injury that the god would willingly inflict on the citizens (*Epistle* 17.1). The gesture of three fingers is unusual and differs from the *mano cornuta* that involved only two extended fingers. It is therefore uncertain, in fact unlikely, that this gesture is intended as protection against an Evil-Eyed Mars.

Like his contemporaries, Augustine was greatly concerned about demons and the pastoral problems they presented. In general, Augustine condemned as superstition all such forms of idolatry or contracts with devils, under which he subsumes "all amulets and cures which the medical art condemns, whether these consist in incantations, or in marks which they call 'characters,' or in hanging or tying on . . . certain articles" (*On Christian Doctrine* 2.20). Absence of any mention of the Evil Eye here is noteworthy. His stance on the subject was ambiguous, similar to the ambiguous position of his theological colleagues on the Evil Eye.[151]

The Antiochene father, Theodoret, bishop of Cyrrhus, Syria (c. 393–c. 458 CE), makes an unusual reference to the casting of the Evil Eye by Eve in the Garden of Eden. In a treatise against the Monophysites, Theodoret portrays a certain Eranistes ("Beggar") representing the Monophysites in a dialogue with Orthodoxus (= Theodoret himself). Eranistes, mentions the sin of Eve and Adam in partaking of the tree of knowledge and death as their divine punishment. Orthodoxus then asks, "Why, then, when soul and body have both sinned together, does the body alone undergo the punishment of death?" Eranistes replies:

> It was the body [of Eve] that cast its Evil Eye upon the tree, and stretched forth its hands, and plucked the forbidden fruit. It was the mouth that bit it with the teeth, and ground it small, and

---

150. On this custom see Vol. 2:167, 193–94, 205.

151. See Brox 1974:173 and the informative study of the everyday piety of Augustine's time by Zellinger 1933.

then the gullet committed it to the belly, and the belly digested it, and delivered it to the liver; and the liver turned what it had received into blood and passed it on to the hollow vein and the vein to the adjacent parts and they through the rest, and so the theft of the forbidden food pervaded the whole body. Very properly then the body alone underwent the punishment of sin.[152]

Among the ancient Christian luminaries thought to have *possessed* an Evil Eye were Porphyry, bishop of Gaza,[153] and the empress Theodora, wife of Justinian I.[154] Centuries earlier, the author of *1 Clement* (c. 95 CE) had presented an extensive list of biblical figures who were considered subjects or objects of Evil-Eye envy. *First Clement* 4:1-13, focusing on the subject of envy, lists biblical exemplars of *zêlos kai phthonos*:

—Cain envious of Abel (*1 Clem.* 4:1-7; Gen 4:3-8) resulting in fratricide

—Jacob fleeing from the envy of Esau (*1 Clem* 4:8; Gen 27:41-38:22)

—Joseph, the victim of his brothers' envy (*1 Clem.* 4:9; Gen 37:11) (*ezêlôsan de auton hoi adelphoi autou*).[155]

—Moses fleeing from Pharoah and what Clement takes to be the envy of his kinsmen (*1 Clem.* 4:10; Exod 2:11-15).[156]

—Aaron and Miriam, understood by Clement as directing *zêlos* toward Moses and being forced to lodge outside the camp (*1 Clem.* 4:11; Num 12:1-14).[157]

—Dathan and Abiram are regarded by Clement as rebelling against Moses out of envy and accordingly were punished with death (*1 Clem.* 4:12; Num 16:12-14)

---

152. Theoret, *Dialogue* 3; ET in *Theodoret, Jerome, Gennadius, and Rufinus: Historical Writings*, NPNF, series 2, 3:217.

153. See Mark the Deacon (fifth-century Egyptian monk and biographer), *The Life of Porphyry* 19.

154. Procopius of Caesarea Palestine (c. 500-565 CE and last major historian of the ancient world), *Secret History* 9.26.

155. See also Rachel envying (*ezêlôse*) her sister Leah for the four sons she bore Jacob while she herself was childless (Gen 29:31—30:1).

156. See also Moses envied by Joshua for selecting prophets (Num 11:29).

157. Num 12:1-14 actually states that Mirian and Aaron spoke against Moses because of the Ethiopian women he took and that only Miriam was punished with a skin disease and forced outside the camp seven days. The narrative also contains an interesting comment on spitting: "And the Lord said to Moses, 'If her father had only *spit in* (*eneptusen*) her face, would she not be ashamed seven days?" (Num 12:14). This would have constituted a lesser punishment for her and Aaron's insolence in speaking against Moses because of the Ethiopian women he took (Num 12:1).

96 Beware the Evil Eye

—David was envied by not only strangers but even by Saul, king of Israel, for David's greater popular acclaim (*1 Clem.* 4:13; 1 Sam 18:6–9). The Hebrew of 1 Sam 18:9 states, "And Saul *eyed* David from that day on."[158] This text makes clear that the author of *1 Clement* appears to have followed convention in considering envy as conveyed through looking and an Evil Eye.

The Divine Liturgy of St. Mark (Alexandrian rite) illustrates in one of its prayer formulas how fear of envy/*phthonos* was addressed in the liturgy.[159] The prayer of the First Antiphon, linking envy with the works of Satan and evil men, reads: "But all envy, all terror, all temptation, every working of Satan, every plot of wicked men, drive far from us, O God, and from Thy Holy Catholic and Apostolic Church."

In his discussion of the Fathers and the Evil Eye, Dickie maintains that these Christian theologians, while sharing much of the conventional pagan view on the Evil Eye, took the further step of demonizing it and tracing it *exclusively* (emphasis added) to the wiles of the devil. Jerome, Chrysostom, and Basil, he claims, as well as Tertullian and Eusebius of Alexandria, rejected the pagan view delineated by Plutarch that a *human eye* by itself could inflict harm. Instead these fathers held that *baskania/fascinatio* denoted "supernatural force envious of good fortune, prosperity, beauty, and virtue," which they attributed to the devil.[160] On the one hand, Basil and Jerome, Dickie states, "suggest that the devil or his demons use men's envious eyes to accomplish their own envious purposes." Other fathers, including Tertullian,[161] John Chrysostom (as cited above) and Eusebius of Alexandria,[162] Dickie claims, "exclude the action of human intermediaries and put down the reverses that the fortunate suffer to the direct action of the devil."[163] Dickie, however, detects inconsistency on this point—even in the thinking of individual fathers.[164] This inconsistency means, however, that the skepticism toward the phenomenon of a *human* Evil Eye that Dickie finds among the church fathers may not be as certain and extensive as he

---

158. Contrast LXX: "And it appeared evil in the eyes of Saul concerning this matter" (*Kai ponêron ephanê to rhêma en ophthalmois Saoul peri tou logou toutou*). On this text see Vol. 3:19, 20, 53, 65–66, 69, 70, 105–7, 183, 253.

159. See Brightman 1896 1:114.

160. Dickie 1995:30.

161. Terullian, *De virginibus velandis* 15 (PL 2:959).

162. Eusebius of Alexandria, Sermon 7, *De Neomeniis et Sabbatis et de non observandi avium vocibus* (PG 86.1.354–357).

163. Dickie 1995:30–31.

164. Ibid., 18–34.

claims. The assertion of Eusebius of Alexandria is in response to the fact that there were in his time people who ascribed *baskania* to fellow *human beings* rather than the devil. Eusebius criticizes this notion; blaming humans for *baskania*, he insists, is a form of Judaizing. He ends his sermon with a statement that the cross is the Christian phylactery against the *baskania* of the devil.[165] It thus appears that, although some fathers are intent on thoroughly demonizing the phenomenon of an Evil Eye, they are not quite successful in eliminating the notion that human beings were channels of Evil Eye malice. Behind human envy and Evil-Eyeing can lie the devil's malice. This, however, does not exclude humans from malignant Evil-Eyeing, but maintains that in their Evil-Eyeing they are tools of the devil.

Dickie concludes his important study of the church fathers and the Evil Eye by suggesting that it is ultimately not a vague Evil Eye attack that Christians of late antiquity feared, but rather the specific danger of envy.[166] This, however, goes beyond what the evidence indicates. What Dickie has shown is the persistent ambivalence of the church fathers on the phenomenon of the Evil Eye and how it operates. They employ traditional pagan terminology for the phenomenon and repeat conventional notions associated with the belief. The concept of children, for example, as particular victims of the Evil Eye, and the association of the Evil Eye and envy are thoroughly consistent with pagan belief. Pagan amulets against the Evil Eye are not eliminated but replaced with Christian ones. Moreover, Dickie's reading of the relevant texts at crucial points is unsupported by probative evidence. His claim, for instance, that John Chrysostom and other Fathers espoused an intromission theory of vision over against the prevailing extramission theory held before, during, and after the patristic period lacks substantial evidentiary support and strains credibility. This extramission theory of vision was dominant in the patristic period and was not abandoned for over one thousand years. "Envy" and "Evil Eye," *phthonos* and *baskania*, moreover, continued to be employed as equivalent terms, making it additionally inadvisable to attempt drawing fine lines between the two.

Silke Trzcionka questions Dickie's relating the attitude of the church fathers concerning the Evil Eye to earlier pagan presuppositions and discourses. She contends that the ambiguities in the church fathers's attitudes to the Evil Eye can be related to "social conceptions of *baskania* and envy, and are thus not so much related to a 'pagan' past and present, but a broad Greco-Roman worldview evident throughout Mediterranean society,

---

165. Ibid., 29.
166. Ibid., 33.

irrespective of the religious adherence of the members of that society."[167] In actuality, this thesis is not that different from Dickie's. The valid point of both is that the Christian church fathers share at numerous points the social and conceptual worldview of their neighbors, including many conventional features of Evil Eye belief and practice.

What the church fathers thought concerning the Evil Eye in the final analysis remains rather cloudy and their positions rather ambivalent. Vacillation rather than consistency is what we have found. Whether the Evil Eye is still considered a physical means of harm or is taken as an alias for envy seems to vary not only from theologian to theologian but even from writing to writing of the same church father. No consensus is evident other than the equation of Evil Eye and envy and the common attribution of both to the malice of the Devil and his demonic minions working hand in hand with humans or using them as pawns. This association of the Evil Eye and envy with the Devil, the enemy of God, is a noteworthy tactic of the Christian church fathers, and has no parallel, for instance, in rabbinic teaching on the Evil Eye. This association, furthermore, of the Evil Eye with the prince of demons—not found in the biblical texts—is a return to the pagan concept of a *baskanos daimôn*, an Evil-Eye demon. Similarly, the association of envy with the Devil, as Rakoczy aptly notes, "is in reality still a remnant of the ancient notion of the envy of the gods (*phthonos theôn*) in Christian dress, even if now transferred to an entirely negative power" (Rakoczy 1996:226). However much "envy" (*phthonos*) is the term on which attention is focused, dread of the Evil Eye still looms in the shadows. For "where there is envy, as we have seen, the Evil Eye is not far removed" (Rakoczy 1996:226). Whatever doubt these fathers may have harbored concerning the physiological reality of a human Evil Eye, and whatever the inconsistencies in their comments, the material evidence in this period makes it patently clear that envy and the Evil Eye of humans and demons remained as dreaded as ever. The epistolary and iconographic evidence tells a consistent story of a fear of the Evil Eye and envy that knows no alteration or diminution.

Christian Personal Letters—"Unharmed by the Evil Eye"

Before turning to the iconographic material, we do well to consider another written source of information about the harmful Evil Eye and steps to avert it. This is the evidence in *Christian personal letters* of the period. Joining the Greco-Roman personal correspondence cited previously in Vol. 2 are several examples from Christian correspondence. These are the letters that

---

167. Trzcionka 2011.

include the prophylactic wish that the addressees, their children and families, remain "unharmed by the Evil Eye."[168] Two examples from Egypt date from the third century CE; two further letters are from the fourth century.

A personal letter (third century CE) from a certain Ammonius to Theodosius (a Christian name) addresses the intended recipients as "brother" or "sister" (in the faith). Ammonius includes the conventional protective wish (lines 25–26), "may your children remain unharmed by the Evil Eye (*ta abaskanta sou paidia*)" (P.Ryl. 4.604).[169]

In a late third-century CE personal letter, Aurelius Artemidorus writes to the wife of Aurelius Apollonius about her husband's impending trial. He includes the customary wish that her children "remain unharmed by the Evil Eye (*ta? abask?[an]t?a? s[sou] paidia*)." He concludes by praying for them all "in the Lord God (*en kyriôi theôi*)" (P.Oxy. 20.2276).[170]

A fourth-century Christian papyrus letter possibly from Oxyrhynchus, Egypt,[171] includes the same apotropaic wish. A certain Antoninus writes to his patron Gonatas, complaining about the patron's camel-driver who assaulted Antoninus. The letter opens with the conventional expression for the good health of the recipient and the wish that his children remain unharmed by Evil Eye: "To my lord brother Gonatas the landowner, [from] Antoninus, very many greetings . . . I pray for your health . . . I greet your children—may they be unharmed by Evil Eye (*ta abaskanta sou tekna*)."[172]

Another fourth-century letter, probably Christian, from the archive of Flavius Abinnaeus, commander of a fortress at Dionysias in the Fayum, Egypt (between 342–351 CE) concludes with a greeting of the recipient and his children, "who, I pray, may be unharmed by the Evil Eye" (P.Abinnaeus 35.28–29).[173]

These letters illustrate the Christian adoption of the epistolary convention of the apotropaic Evil Eye wish. Like their neighbors, Christians also considered children especially vulnerable to Evil Eye attack. Some babies

168. On Christian papyri letters, see Ghedini 1923; Cavassini 1954; Naldini 1968 (collecting Christian private letters from Egypt, second–fourth centuries CE); Horsley, *New Docs* 1981 passim); Snyder 1985:149–58. For examples of Greek correspondence with the apotropaic Evil Eye wish see previously, Vol. 2:1–4.

169. Cavassini 1954; Snyder 1985:155–56.

170. Cavassini 1954; Naldini 1968, no. 18; Snyder 1985:155.

171. Editio princeps: G. Vitelli, *PSI* 8 (1927):180–81 (= SB 10841); see also Naldini 1968, no. 64, pp. 267–70.

172. Horsley 1981 1:134–36, no. 85 (Greek text and ET on pp. 134–35). Horsley (1981 1:70) notes that "a similar phrase (*meta tôn abaskantôn paidiôn*) occurs at *PSI* 7 (1925) 825.21–22 (provenance unknown, IV¹, = Naldini, no. 44)." See also P.Mich. 8 (1951) 519.3–7 (Karanis, fourth century) = Naldini, no. 67.

173. See also P.Abinnaeus 30.23–24; 37.4.

actually were given the proper name *Abaskantos/Abascantus* ("unharmed by the Evil Eye") as a protective.[174] The letters show that Christians took the Evil Eye threat as seriously as did their non-Christian contemporaries and in their personal communication employed the same tactics for safeguarding the vulnerable.

CHRISTIAN AMULETS AND OTHER APOTROPAICS: THE MATERIAL AND ICONOGRAPHIC EVIDENCE

The importance of the material evidence of Christian Evil Eye belief in this period has been aptly described and stressed by James Burton Russell:

> Just how widespread their use [anti-Evil Eye amulets] was may be deduced from the archaeological context of the objects under consideration, which provides a more objective record of how ordinary people coped with the evil eye in their daily lives than the prejudiced testimony of most literary texts.[175]

The diverse means that Christians employed for warding off the Evil Eye and other forces of evil in this post-biblical period included invocations, powerful letters of the alphabet, formulaic phrases, acronyms and symbols associated with the Christian deity, plaques, graffiti and epigrapha on walls, mosaics at domestic thresholds, and amulets beyond number.[176] These apotropaics were in great part identical to those employed throughout the Roman world, but were lightly modified with specifically Christian words or symbols. James Nathan Ford demonstrates through his comparison of ancient Mesopotamian texts with post-biblical Jewish and Christian texts (Syriac, Mandaic, Coptic, and Ethiopian) the remarkable stability and continuity of motifs, themes, topics, and terminology associated with the

---

174. See Robert 1944, 1951:146, no. 55.

175. Russell 1995:38.

176. On specifically Christian amulets and apotropaics see Elworthy 1895/1958:285–89, 390–94; Reizenstein 1904; Seligmann 1910 1:385, fig. 71; 2:137 and passim; 1912–13; 1922; 1927; Dobschütz 1910; Leclercq 1924; Meisen 1950; Budge 1930:126–32 (Coptic); 177–99 (Ethiopian); 239–49 (Mandaean); 272–82 (Syriac); Engemann 1975; Dickie 1995; Ford 2000:224–28, 232–35, 238–39, 257–69. On Jewish and Christian amulets from Syria and Palestine see Robert 1965, 1981:29–30; Trzcionka 2007, 2011. On Christian amulets from Asia Minor, Russell 1995. On a Coptic incantation against the Evil Eye, see Meyer et al. 1994:49–50. On the Evil Eye in Abyssinian Christian art, see Staude 1934; for Ethiopia see also Worrell 1909, 1910, 1915; Dobberahn 1976:28, 63; Reminick 1976; Vecchiato 1994.

Evil Eye and the extensive cultural cross-fertilization that these apotropaics illustrate.[177]

Celsus, second-century pagan critic of the Christ movement, at one point mentioned disparagingly the following actions and objects that he claimed were practiced and taught by Christians:

> processes of purification, or expiatory hymns, or spells for averting evil, or [the making of] images or resemblances of demons, or [various sorts of antidotes against poison to be found in] clothes or in numbers, or stones, or plants, or roots, or generally in all kinds of things . . . [and] barbarous books containing the names and wondrous acts of demons. (Origen, *Contra Celsum* 6.39, 40)[178]

Origin of Alexandria (c. 240–250 CE) countered Celsus's charge by declaring it to be ignorant and baseless and motivated by intense hatred of the Christians. Followers of Jesus Christ, he declared, were not engaged in such things (*Contra Celsum* 6. 39, 40). In actual fact, the Christians, like their Greek, Roman and Jewish neighbors, employed a wide range of strategies and means for protecting themselves against evil forces, including the malicious Evil Eye. Celsus's claim about Christian activities was not far from the mark, though the practices he mentioned were hardly evidence of ignorance on the part of the Christians, since in his Hellenistic world they were the common practice of educated and commoners, Greek intellectuals and Christian believers, alike.

Christian apotropaics against the Evil Eye in particular closely resembled in form and detail those employed by their pagan and Jewish neighbors. They comprised, on the whole,

> (1) *words* (e.g., incantations/charms; formulas; and calling on the names of God, Jesus, angels, Solomon, and various saints;);
> (2) *actions* (e.g., gestures, touching, binding, making knots, anointing, bathing and cleansing; use of vapors, making noise [bells]); and
> (3) *objects* (e.g., plants, herbs, stones, metals, gems, jewelry, coins, medallions, bells, and crosses).[179]

---

177. Ford 1998:256–68 and passim. His attempt, on the other hand, at denying the appearance of Evil Eye belief in the Hebrew Bible (Ford 2000) is rather odd, unexpected, and thoroughly unsuccessful.

178. See also *Contra Celsum* 1.6 regarding the suspected Christian use of the names of demons and incantations for expelling evil spirits.

179. Dobschütz 1910:422–24.

Efforts were made, by way of modification and addition, to give conventional pagan apotropaics a distinctive Christian character and, ideally, a power granted by the Christian God, the angels, and saints. In his 1910 article on ancient Christian charms and amulets, Ernst von Dobschütz discussed apotropaics of specifically Christian origin and their identifying characteristics: the name of Jesus, biblical texts (passages from the Psalms, Gospels, and the Lord's Prayer), liturgical formulae (e.g., Trisagion ["Holy, Holy Holy"]; "Christ conquers"; "Christ reigns"; "Kyrie, eleison" ["Lord, have mercy"]); prayers; the holy cross and making the sign of the cross; the sacraments and sacramentalia (holy water, incense, salt, oil, wax from candles, bread); relics; and pictures/icons.[180]

A later compilation by the German folklorist Karl Meisen (1950) lists as Christian characteristics of apotropaics: (1) invocations of God and God's name, often with the sign of the cross; (2) the Christus Rex monogram (Chi Rho); (3) the Greek letters Alpha and Omega; (4) the Greek letters Chi, M, G; (5) the formula *ICHTHYS* ; (6) the cross and the sign of the cross; (7) the names of angels (Michael, Gabriel, Raphael, Uriel, Archaf); (8) the names of saints and patron saints (Solomon, Daniel in the lions' den; the three children in the fiery oven; the magi from the East at Jesus's birth, the four evangelists; Saint Sisinnius, Saint Theodore, Saint John, Saint Veit); (9) Christian writings (excerpts of the written Gospels, the Lord's Prayer, the Trisagion, amens and alleluias); (10) the combination of protective symbols, as found throughout the ancient world (Evil Eyes under attack; appeal to Solomon; cavalier images lancing the figure of an Evil Eye [fourteen examples]; the figure of an owl accompanied by a protective inscription against the Evil Eye [eight examples]; and (11) apotropaic inscriptions on houses (six examples).[181] Meisen concludes that the material evidence shows a wide distribution of Evil Eye belief and practice down through Late Antiquity and beyond in the cultures of the Circum-Mediterranean, including the Christian populations. This includes a broad distribution among Christians of all social levels in the Near East, North Africa, and Europe. Christian practice, as always, was influenced by its matrix, the melting pot of ancient cultures marking Greco-Roman civilization. Christian belief and practice absorbed the ancient traditions and gave them, where necessary, new Christian content.[182]

Josef Engemann, covering pagan and Christian apotropaic practice in this same period, concurs. He adds that the apotropaics were in public as

---

180. Ibid., 425–28
181. Meisen 1950:157–77.
182. Ibid., 176–77.

well as private use,[183] and were employed by clergy as well laity.[184] Christians, he stresses, shared the fear of the Evil Eye that was found in non-Christian populations of the time,[185] with Christian theologians also believing in the effectiveness of the "magic arts."[186] Engemann discusses Jewish and Christian use of the Evil Eye images on amulets,[187] paintings in cultic areas,[188] relics and eulogies,[189] crosses, Christograms, and the use of the acronym ICHTHYS for protection of building portals.[190]

Christians, like their neighbors, considered the *fish* to have apotropaic power.[191] The individual letters of the Greek word for "fish," ICHTHYS, also formed an acronym representing the Greek words Iêsous CHristos, THeou Yios Sôtêr ("Jesus Christ, God's Son, Savior"). The term ICHTHYS thus was considered and employed by Christians as a powerful apotropaic. Where found as an inscription, the acronym generally identifies distinctly Christian apotropaics and amulets.[192] An amulet in the Berlin Bode Museum (previously the Kaiser Friedrich Museum) shows two fish under a cross.[193] A phallus amulet shaped like a fish at one end and having at its other end a *mano fica* is a composite amulet, which shows even more clearly the Christian association of fish, phallus, and *mano fica* as related conventional designs for warding off the Evil Eye.[194] The Christus Rex ("Christ the King") monogram on phylacteries also was ascribed apotropaic power and marked the phylacteries as Christian.[195]

Commenting on the Evil Eye in the early Byzantine Period and the apotropaic items found at Anemurium, Asia Minor, Russell observes that

183. Engemann 1975:22, (qualifying Brox 1974, who focused primarily on private use).

184. Ibid., 23, 48.

185. Ibid., 24.

186. Ibid., 23, 48 (so also Brox 1974).

187. Ibid., 37–38.

188. Ibid., 38–40.

189. Ibid., 40–42.

190. Ibid., 42–48.

191. On the fish and its symbolism and potency in antiquity see Dölger ICHTHYS, 5 vols., 1922–1943; Engemann 1969.

192. On the Christian use of this ICHTHYS acronym for apotropaic purposes and in combination with other apotropaic symbols, see Dölger 1928 1:243–57; Engemann 1969:1043–47 and 1085–95. Compare also the Christian Egyptian prophylactic inscription cited below.

193. Dölger 1922 2:119.

194. See ibid., 2:444, and 1922 3, Plate 77.4.

195. Eckstein and Waszink 1950:409.

"[i]n antiquity, householders inscribed apotropaic formulae to accompany the cross on their doors.[196] They also uttered special prayers to avert danger, sometimes even with ecclesiastical authority.[197] They addressed their friends or named their children *Abaskantos*: "Unharmed by the Evil Eye."[198] Above all, people wore amulets, rings, and other protective devices inscribed with potent symbols and formulae to avert the bewitching glance of the envious."[199]

Silke Trzcionka has dealt extensively with the evidence of Evil Eye belief and practice in fourth-century Syria and Palestine. Her impressive 2007 study, *Magic and the Supernatural in Fourth-Century Syria*, references the Evil Eye on several occasions[200] and does an excellent job contextualizing the ancient evidence. She notes that the Evil Eye was seen as "the most prominent and pervasive threat in the Graeco-Roman world."[201] She identifies and illustrates many of its salient features such as its connection with envy, the vulnerability of children, the variety of apotropaics, its description in the pagan sources, and its condemnation by the Christian church fathers.

In a subsequent study, Trzcionka writes on "A Syrian-Christian Perspective on the Supernatural,"[202] again noting how Christians, like pagans, feared and took precautions against the dreaded Evil Eye. Anti-Evil Eye apotropaics included the image of the Evil Eye under attack, the symbol of the cavalier or "rider saint," the Alexander medallions,[203] and various symbols and inscriptions found on amulets, clothing,[204] lamps, household articles,[205]

---

196. The most common formulas, according to Russell (1995:38 n.6), were the Trisagion, *kyri boêthi* ("Help, o Lord!"), "One God alone" (*Eis theos monos*), XMG (probably for Christ [X], Michael [M] and Gabriel [G]). and ICHTHYS; see also Prentice 1901. For formulas averting *phthonos* by name, see IGLSSyr, no. 1909; Robert 1965; Gregoire 1922, no.230.

197. As examples of prayers Russell mentions a prayer of Gregory Theologos (Delatte 1927, 243.11) and the prayer (with ecclesiastical authority) in the *Mikron Euchologion* (M. Saliveros, ed.) quoted in French translation by L. Arnaud 1912:386–87.

198. Robert 1944:41–42; 1951:146 n.55.

199. Russell 1995:37–38, 40 (and n.17 for further literature).

200. Trzcionka 2007:101–4, 107–11, 113–19 and endnotes on 191–97.

201. Ibid., 101; see especially 101–20 on "the Apotropaic."

202. Trzcionka 2011.

203. On these medallions see above in this volume, p. 84 and below, p. 131.

204. See Maguire 1990; 1995:61, 63–64.

205. Russell 1995:45; also Dunbabin and Dickie 1983:21–22; Engemann 1975:26, 29; Bonner 1950:99; and E. D. Maguire et al. 1989:3–4, 194.

decorative features,[206] and buildings.[207] In Syria and Palestine, the anti-Evil Eye devices included gems inscribed with the seal of Solomon or amulets with Solomon as cavalier,[208] coins and medallions,[209] formulaic phrases,[210] and representations of certain animals (such as those attacking an Evil Eye).

As illustration of the continuing Christian belief in the Evil Eye in the fifth century, Dickie mentions a mid-fifth-century inscription from I'gâz in Syria whose Christian author calls on the Holy Trinity and God to drive away Envy (*Phthonos*). Showing no awareness of any violation of Christian teaching and confident in Christ's role in relieving pain, the author adds that "he will not fear the plans of the demon who wreaks ill nor the hate-filled and unlawful eye of man."[211] An Egyptian Christian papyrus (fourth–fifth centuries CE) designed to protect a house and its inhabitants from an Evil Eye reads in part: "protect this house and its inhabitants from every evil, from the Evil Eye of every spirit of the air and the human [Evil] Eye."[212] *Baskosynê* is the term for Evil Eye here, which is attributed to both (demonic) spirits of the air and malevolent humans. Both these apotropaics illustrate the continued juxtaposition of demonic and human agents of harm and the continued association of the Evil Eye with *human* agents, despite efforts of many church fathers to brand the Evil Eye as a tool only of the devil. *Baskosynê* appears also on an amulet (fifth–sixth centuries CE, provenance unknown) of a Christian asking Jesus for protection "from every disease, every

---

206. Levi 1947 1:28–34, 262–263, 321–323. See also Dunbabin 1999, esp. pp. 169, 341; Heintz 2000:163 and H. Maguire 1990:216.

207. Prentice 1906; Downey 1962:133–34; Robert 1965; see also John Chrysostom, *Hom. Matt.* 54.4 (PG 58.537).

208. On Solomon as cavalier on horseback lancing a prostrate female figure or demoness occasionally identified as "Evil Eye" (*Baskosynê*) see Perdrizet 1903, 1922:32–35; Bonner 1950:208–13; Goodenough 1953 2:227–32; Menzel 1955; Bagatti 1971, 1972; Delatte and Derchain 1964:261–64, nos. 369–377 (texts and description in also in Bernand 1991:102–3); Russell 1982, 1995:39–41 and fig. 6; 541; Vikan 1984. For specimens from Syria see also SEG 7.232; 36.1313–1318, 35.1558. For Solomon on Jewish amulets, see chap. 1 in the present volume.

209. Several have depictions of Alexander the Great. On this and on the use of coins as apotropaic devices see Maguire 1997 (on Alexander, p. 1040); see pp. 42, 69 and below, 84, 101, 104–5, 109, 128, 131–49.

210. See, e.g., the Syrian and Palestinian amulets in Bonner 1950:208–28.

211. IGLS 4.1599.6–7; Dickie 1995:31.

212. PGM 2, P 3: *diaphylaxon ton oikon touton meta tô enoikountôn apo pantos kakou, apo baskosynês pasês aerinôn pneumatôn kai anthrôpinou ophthal[mou]*; see Dickie 1995:31 and note 67 for the Greek text; Cf. also PGM P 9.10 (*ton daimona probaskanias*). On this apotroaic see also below, p. 125.

fever, every shivering, fit, and every headache (?), as well as from every Evil Eye (*pasês baskosynês*) and every evil spirit."[213]

Many of the apotropaics employed in this period are *composite* in nature, combining factors of shape (e.g., phallic), color (e.g., red, blue), image (e.g., eye attacked, cavalier) and inscription (*KAI SY, ICHTHYS*, "Scram Evil Eye!" and the like). Determination of specifically Christian design and employment is rendered difficult where specifically Christian features are not present, and where provenance and dating are uncertain. The pagan appropriation of Christian divine names, formulas and the like on their apotropaics makes this determination even more difficult.

Writing on Christian charms and amulets, Ernst von Dobschütz classifies them—whether of pagan, Jewish, or Christian origin—as "defensive," "productive," or "malevolent" in aim: (a) "defensive" (for purposes of prophylaxis, countering evil forces, curing illness, and detection of harming agent), (b) "productive" (for the positive purposes of promoting fertility of families and fields, securing favorable weather, assuring safe birth and health for mother and child, gaining the love of another); and (c) "malevolent" (with negative intentions to harm victims via curse tablets [*defixiones*], anathemas, laming race horses, causing illness, or taking life.[214] Christian apotropaics adopted and adapted pagan means and methods, "Christianizing" them by, for instance, the replacement of names of pagan deities with the names of God, Jesus, and the apostles. Similarly, powerful pagan words were replaced with biblical terms, Christian symbolism was found in certain herbs, and Christian symbols were inscribed on gems and stones.[215] Christians thus took over the same *media* as pagan apotropaics (stones, metals, herbs and plants, animals and birds, human body parts [e.g., eye, hand, hair, nails, spittle, excrement, urine], apotropaic colors [red, blue], sounds [by bells, rattles], waxen images and effigies, scarecrows).[216] They likewise engaged in the same *actions* (making manual gestures, spitting, touching, crawling, binding, tying knots, anointing, bathing, using vapors, making noise, uttering or writing powerful words [charms and spells, conjurations, enumeration of dangers, letters of alphabet or groups of letters, formulas]).[217] Apotropaics of *Jewish* origin employed the names of God, angels, and Solomon, the image of Solomon as cavalier/rider on horseback,

---

213. P.Turner 49.4, in Horsley 1983 3:115 (114–19) §93. Horsley, the editor, renders *baskosynês* as "bewitching."
214. Von Dobschütz 1910:416–21.
215. Ibid., 421–22.
216. Ibid., 422–23.
217 Ibid., 423–24.

and the seal of Solomon.[218] Apotropaics of *Christian* origin employed the name of Jesus, the Chi Rho monogram, biblical formulas, texts from the Gospels and Psalms; liturgical and ecclesiastical items (Trisagion, expressions such as "Christ reigns," Christ conquers," Trinitarian formulas, Lord's Prayer, Kyrie eleison; prayers; the holy cross; the sacraments of baptism and eucharist; sacramentalia [holy water, incense, consecrated salt, wax from altar candles, oil, bread, as antidotes to illness]); relics; and icons/pictures of saints.[219] Archaeological excavations since Dobschütz's overview have richly supplemented the evidence he presented. In what follows, we concentrate on apotropaics employed by Christians in the post-biblical period and down through Late Antiquity for thwarting the Evil Eye. This includes (1) the *speaking* of protective words, phrases, formulas or *inscribing* them on various objects and surfaces; (2) the *placing* of anti-Evil Eye formulas, designs or symbols on houses, sarcophagi, churches and monuments or their inclusion in mosaics; (3) the *wearing of personal amulets* with similar designs or symbols and the *use of apotropaic gestures and objects* such as phalluses and phallic-shaped objects, bells, fishes, crosses, sacramentalia, and relics.

The Speaking and Inscribing of Potent Words, Phrases, and Formulas

Uttering certain powerful words, formulaic phrases, the names of God, Jesus, and the angels, liturgical expressions, and incantations were all considered by Christians as effective means for warding off or repelling the Evil Eye.[220] Examples of such expressions also are found in written form on amulets and are presented below.

—*Calling upon God for help and protection against the Evil Eye and inimical powers*. For example, a Christian amulet of the fourth century (now in Oslo) meant to provide protection against all possible inimical powers, including the Evil Eye, uses the formula "through the name of the highest god" (*dia to onoma tou hypistou theou*) and adds the name of Jesus to older protective powers.[221] Beside the speaking or writing of the name "Jesus,"[222] other spoken and written formulas include: "There is one God who conquers evil" (*Eis theos ho nikôn ta kaka*), or simply "There is one God" (*Eis*

---

218. Ibid., 424–25.
219. Ibid., 425–28.
220. See Meisen 1950:160–176, with documentation; Brox 1974.
221. Eitrem and Fridrichsen 1921:23–25
222. Origen, *Con. Cels.* 1.6 (GCS 2.59; SC 132.92); Brox 1975:165.

108   Beware the Evil Eye

theos); house blessings ("Christ lives here" or "Jesus, the Nazarean, born of Mary, the Son of God, lives here");[223] a door lintel inscription reading "Emmanuel is with us, God is our help."[224] The name *Iaô* (an abbreviation of *Yahweh*) also is inscribed on amulets, gems, and potent metal nails.

—The *naming of children "Abaskantos"* ("Unharmed by the Evil Eye") and the regular speaking of that name also were deemed effective prophylaxis.[225]

Potent apotropaic words, phrases, formulas and abbreviations, and longer incantations have been found *written down* in literary works, personal letters, and *inscribed* on pieces of parchment and personal amulets worn on the body or engraved on walls of residences, tombs, catacombs, and churches. In Christian circles, as in Israel, this also involved words or phrases from Sacred Scripture, especially the Pentateuch and the Psalter, the names of God, Jesus Christ, angels; or verses from prayers, worship, and liturgy.[226] Meisen lists the following:[227]

—The *Chi Rho monogram* is a symbol formed by the superimposition of the first two Greek letters of the name CHR*istos* (X + R, *chi* + *rho*). As a Christian symbol it was used widely since emperor Constantine (fourth century CE) to identify all things Christian.[228] It recalls the crucifixion of Jesus and his confession to being a king of a kingdom not of this world (John 18:36). It also served Christians as a popular apotropaic, especially in Syria but also across the Mediterranean world including Gaul and Spain. The monogram was put over doors and windows, at entrances to churches and grave sites, on sarcophagi, on the shields of Constantine's soldiers (where previously the crescent moon had stood to ward off the Evil Eye) and also on the helmets of the emperor and his sons. It is on the sarcophagus of archbishop Theodore of Ravenna, on the columns of the Antonius and Faustina temple in Rome, and, with a Byzantine cross and Alpha and Omega, on Rome's Porta Latina.[229] It often appears in conjunction with other Evil Eye apotropaic symbols and inscriptions.[230]

---

223. Meisen 1950:161; Gitler 1990:371.

224. Meisen 1950:161.

225. Robert 1944:41–42; Robert 1951:146, no. 55; see above, pp. 100, 104; and on *Abaskantos* as a personal name, see also Vol. 1:117, 139–40; Vol. 2:36–38.

226. Dobschütz 1910:425–28; Kötting 1954; Trachtenberg 1939:104–13; Schrire 1982:10, 12–138.

227. Meisen 1950:160–76; see also Brox 1975:165–72.

228. See Snyder 1985:17, 27, 29, 143, 147–49.

229. Meisen 1950:161–62.

230. Ibid., 160.

—The *first and last letters* of the Greek alphabet, *alpha and omega*, appear in Rev 1:8; 21:6, and 22:18 as the letters by which God and Christ identify themselves in the book of Revelation. These letters were inscribed on parchments and papyri, on buildings (in Syria above the house portals), amulets, jewelry boxes, medallions and on bells, in the company of other anti-Evil Eye words and symbols (Meisen 1950:162).

—*Other letters* of the Greek alphabet also were used to form potent abbreviations: CH M G (= "CHrist-Michael-Gabriel," or "Mary bore Christ" [*Christon Maria Genna*]). These were used for exorcistic purposes and also as protection against the Evil Eye.[231] The Greek word *ICHTHYS*, "fish," consists of letters forming the acronym, "Jesus Christ, Son of God, Savior," as already noted. This acronym was deployed against the Evil Eye, especially in Syria, and placed above the entrances to homes, graves, and on amulets and gems. The letters often were used together with the names of angels, Gryllus, C M G, the anchor cross, the Tau cross, a dove, a lamb, a shepherd, and fish.[232]

—*Biblical passages* were employed for protection against the Evil Eye and other evil forces.[233] Biblical passages (e.g., 1 Kg 17:45, Ps 19:8 [20:8], Prov 18:10; Mark 16:17 and many others) were written on small fragments of parchment and placed in capsules/containers (*bullae*) worn around neck as protectives, similar to Roman *bullae* and Jewish phylacteries.

—Figures of *Christian crosses* were inscribed on amulets, buildings, churches, sarcophagi, and tombs. Christians in Egypt removed from buildings the images of the deity Serapis (pagan protector against the Evil Eye) and replaced them with the cross of Christ.[234] The use of crosses themselves and making the sign of the cross to counter the Evil Eye are discussed below.

—The *names of angels* (e.g., Michael, Gabriel, Raphael, also Uriel Archaf) were thought to have apotropaic power.[235] They too were inscribed on amulets, lamina, put at thresholds and above the entrance to churches and grave sites, along with other words and symbols.

—*Holy persons* likewise were ascribed power as protective patrons against the Evil Eye. Under this heading Meisen's illustrative list includes Solomon, Daniel in the lion's den, the Three Young Men in the fiery furnace, the Magi at Jesus's birth, the four Evangelists, St. Sisinnios, St. Theodore, St.

231. Meisen 1950:163.

232. So ibid., 163–64; see also Dölger 1928 1:248–372, and his addendum in the 2nd ed. (1928:⁺1–21⁺).

233. Meisen 1950:170; Brox 1975:170–72.

234. So Meisen 1950:164–65.

235. Ibid.:165–66.

John, and St. Veit. Their names appear on amulets and apotropaics, often in combination with other prophylactics against the Evil Eye.[236] Some of these amulets and apotropaics are identified and discussed below. To Meisen's list Joseph the patriarch should also be added.

—*Written incantations* provide appreciable information on important details of Christian Evil Eye belief, and also show noteworthy parallels to much earlier Mesopotamian incantations.

A Syriac Mandaic incantation of the late Roman period in the *Šapta d-Pišra d-Ainia* ("Scroll for the Exorcism of [Evil] Eyes") elaborates on the many types of Evil Eye possessors. It reads:

> And he said: "As for the eye of your neglected (?) father, and the eye of evil neighbours against (?) their sons, and the eye that goes, and the eye that comes, and the eye of those who are far away, and the eye of those who are near, and the eye of little boys, and the eye of little girls, and the eye of a whoremonger (?), and the eye of a male prostitute (?), and the eye of the entire world, and the eye that struck N. son of N.—may a raven take it and ascend to a lone palm tree, may it sit on a branch and rip it into piece(s), may it shake what it rips off from it; during the shaking (?) some of it will drop (down) among the flock, so that the bulls shall trample it, and ewes shall trample it." (*Šapta d-Pišra d-Ainia*, Drower 1937:592, lines 30–36)[237]

This listing of various Evil Eye possessors, as Ford observed in his study of Mesopotamian texts, is one of the several stable features of anti-Evil Eye incantations that harks all the way back to Mesopotamian incantations.[238] The Evil Eye remains as well an active eye that "strikes" its victims and inflicts harm even on family members and neighbors.

A Christian Syriac incantation of the late Roman period illustrates a similar listing of fascinators, including neighbors and strangers, insiders and outsiders ("barbarian," "heathen," "infidel"). This incantation, published by Hermann Gollancz in *The Book of Protection* (1912) reads:

> I bind you and ban you and overthrow (you), O evil and envious eye (*'yn' byš t' wḥsmt'*), eye (*'yn'*) of seven evil and envious neighbors, eye (*'yn'*) of every sort, eye (*'yn'*) that strikes and does not pity, eye (*'yn'*) of a father, eye (*'yn'*) of a (text: her) mother, eye (*'yn'*) of a barbarian, eye (*'yn'*) of heathens, eye (*'yn'*) of a

---

236. Ibid., 166–70, 172–73, with documentation.

237. Ford 1998:238–39 provides a transliteration and translation of the original.

238. Ford 1998:238; for these Mesopotamian texts such as VAT 10018:3–4, see Vol. 1, chap. 2.

barbarian, brownish/tawny eye (*'yn' šhlnyt'*), jealous [JHE: more accurately, *envious*] eye (*'yn' ṭ nnyt'*), blue eye (*'yn' zrq'*), {eye} eye of those who are far away, eye of all evil people, eye of those who are far away, eye of those who are near, eye of every sort, {eye} eye of men and women, eye of old men (and) old women, eye of evil and envious people (*'yn' dbnynš' byš' wḥsm'*), eye of an infidel . . .²³⁹

The Evil Eye in this Christian Syriac incantation is explicitly identified as "envious" (*'yn' ṭ nnyt'*).²⁴⁰ This association of the Evil Eye with envy, as we have seen, is one of the most prominent and enduring features of Evil Eye tradition down through the centuries and across cultures.

The elaboration of Evil-Eyed persons (fascinators) was a conventional and stable feature of such anti-Evil Eye incantations. This feature appears centuries earlier in Mesopotamian incantations; see Vol. 1:83–104. In his study of Mesopotamian and Ugaritic incantations, Ford (1998:238–240) lists similar Christian texts from centuries later; for a Hebrew-Aramaic amuletic text see Ford 1998:214. An ancient anti-Evil Eye amulet from Palestine, a Hebrew nine-line text on bronze foil, similarly enumerates the potential fascinators from whom protection is sought: "his father, his mother, eye of women, eye of men, eye of virgins."²⁴¹ The cross accompanying other signs might suggest a Christian charm, however the text also could be solely Jewish.

In the Christian Syriac incantation above, which lists fascinators and types of eyes, the reference to the "blue eye" (*'yn' zrq'*) is also noteworthy.²⁴² As indicated above and in Vols. 1 and 2, blue is one of two colors, the other being red, that is most often associated with the Evil-Eyed fascinators across cultures and down through the centuries.²⁴³

239. Gollancz 1912: lxxxii–lxxxiii, Codex C, §19, Transliterated text and translation according to Ford 1998:239–40. Further texts from Gollancz are included below.

240. As also in the Syriac Mandaic *Šapta d-Pišra d-Ainia* ("Scroll for the Exorcism of (Evil) Eyes"): "The eye that envies (*aina d-hasma*) children, male and female, envies it (sc. the child), strikes it and torments it" (Drower 1938:2, lines 2–23; Ford 1998:224). See also the phrase "envious Evil Eye" (*aina bišta hasumtia*), Drower 1938:4, line 16; Ford 1998:224 n.75. For further texts on envy expressed by an Evil Eye and the harm it causes, see Ford 1998:224–28.

241. Montgomery 1910–1911:280–81.

242. Translated "the caerulean eye" by Drower (Ford 1998:239 n.135).

243. Ford (1998:239 n.135) finds the expression "more or less synonymous with *'yn' zrwqt'*" (translated 'the blue-coloured eye' by Gollancz), which occurs in the parallel incantation in Codex B §9, pp. 69–70, where "green eye" (*'yn' yrwqt'*) and blue eye (*'yn' zrwqt'*) are paired. Ford traces this combination to the fact that "blue and green physiological eyes are similarly classed together in the Arabic physiolognomical

The Syriac Mandaic incantation of the late Roman period in the *Šapta d-Pišra d-Ainia* ("Scroll for the Exorcism of [Evil] Eyes"), like Mesopotamian incantations centuries earlier,[244] envisions the Evil Eye as a demon with its own body: "and descend and seize the evil and glaring Eye [*aina bišta ukauitha*] by the hair of its head, by the tassels of its girdle, and by the fringes of the lower skirt of its legs and cast it . . . !"[245]

A Coptic Christian apotropaic for driving away "the cursed Evil Eye" and written on many parchment amulets, narrates an account of Jesus and his disciples encountering an old woman by the shore of the Sea of Tiberias. Here the Evil Eye takes the form of this old woman of terrifying visage, with teeth and claws like those of a lion, flashing eyes, and flames of fire shooting from her mouth. To Jesus's question, "Who is this?" his disciples responded,[246]

> The terrible Evil Eye. When she glances at a ship, she capsizes it. When she glances at a horse, she knocks off its rider. When she glances at a cow, she cuts off its milk. When she glances at a woman and her child, she destroys them . . . (Ford 1998:213)[247]

A Syriac Christian incantation against the Evil Eye, "the Anathema of the Angel Gabriel, which is of avail for the Evil Eye," appears in the Syriac manuscript, *The Book of Protection*. It too depicts the Envious Evil Eye as a female figure destroying a variety of victims that are listed. Its formulation, "the Evil Eye went forth," shows the survival of an ancient Mesopotamian incantation formula ("the Evil Eye went forth . . . to destroy"),[248] even though written as late as 1804. The translation reads:

---

treatise"; see Mourad 1939:64, lines 7–8. For an Aramaic Magic Bowl (*AMB* 113, Late Antiquity) adjuring the Evil Eye along with other threatening forces and mentioning various types of fascinators, Evil Eyes and their colors, among which are blue and green eyes see Vol. 1:112–13.

244. See previously, Vol. 1:83–104; see also Ford 1998:212–13.

245. Ford 1998:213.

246. The Ethiopian version given by Budge (1930:185–86; cf. 361–62) has the disciples as the questioners and Jesus as the respondent.

247. Ford (1998:213) gives the German translation of H. A. Winkler (1931:34), rendered here in English by J. H. Elliott; see also Budge 1930:185–86, 361–62, for a slightly different version and identifying it as an Ethiopian spell. For Ethiopic/Abyssinian parallels see Worrell 1909, 1910:87–88; 1914/1915:102–3, 111–12, and Dobberahn 1976:20, 63; for Arabic parallels, see Winkler 1931:27–33. For a Coptic anti-Evil Eye incantation see M. Meyer et al. 1994:49–50. On the Evil Eye in Abyssinian Christian art, see Staude 1934.

248. See previously, Vol. 1:83–104.

> In the name or the Father, the Son, and the Holy Ghost. The Evil Eye ['*yn' byšt'*] went forth from the flinty rock, and the angel Gabriel came upon her. He said unto her: "Where are you going, Daughter of Destruction?' She said to him, "I am going to destroy men and women, and boys and girls, the lives of cattle and birds of the sky." [The angel] Gabriel said to her: "Have you never entered Paradise and seen the Great God, He whom thousands upon thousands and myriads upon myriads of angels surround and sanctify him? In His name you are bound by me, and I bind thee, O Evil and Envious Eye ['*yn' byšt' wḥsmt'*], Eye of seven evil neighbors, and you may approach neither the body nor the soul, nor the spirit, nor the connections of the sinews, nor the three hundred and sixty-six members which are in the frame of the one who carries these formulae." By the prayer of my Lady, the blessed Mary, and Mar John the Baptist. Amen![249]

An eighteenth-century Ethiopian (Geʻez) incantation similarly urges the Evil Eye (*Ainat* as an illness) to "go forth" driven away by God,

> you great accursed one who eats flesh and drinks blood—Eye of the Muslim, Eye of the Christian, Eye of the Jew, Eye of the Heathen, Eye of Saiṭānāt, Eye of demons! Go forth in red and in black ... and do not return ... Do not come near the soul and body of your handmaid, Walatta Māryām![250]

Ford sees the reference to the eating of flesh and drinking blood as a predilection ascribed to demons in Mesopotamian incantations and Egyptian sources centuries earlier as well as in later Aramaic incantations.[251] The cavalier amulets discussed below are a graphic illustration of the conceptualization of the Evil Eye as a female demon, which is attacked by a rider on horseback.

A scroll in Syriac six feet long and two inches wide (900 words on 244 lines) includes a Christian incantation meant to protect a girl against the Evil Eye and other evil forces. The text reads in part:

> Further, through the power of the Lord Jesus Christ we begin the safeguard of a man [human being]. The Holy Gospel of the Lord Jesus Christ, the proclamation of John [Here follows the quoted text of John 1:1–5] ... By the power of these holy words

---

249. Gollancz, *The Book of Protection* 1912:xl–xli; Codex A §23; translation according to Ford 119:213–14. See also Goodenough 1953 2:164; Budge 1930:275.

250. Ford 1998:233 cites the German translation of Worrell 1914–1915:95–96, rendered in English here by J. H. Elliott.

251. Ford 1996:230–33.

> of the glorious Godhead, and in the name [of] . . . El-Shaddai, Adonai, Lord Sabaoth [and] by the power and by the command of the Lord Jesus Christ, I bind and I expel and I objurate the evil and bewitching eye, and the eye green and heavy, and the eye of men and the eye of women, and the eye of every kind of man and beast. And I bind wounds . . . and all sicknesses and all diseases and all plagues and all rebellions and all *incubae* of nights, of demons, and of rebellious devils, and satans. And I bind all evil fevers and evil strokes . . . from the body and soul of Gauza, the daughter of Shima, who bears these incantations (or charms). (Hazard 1893:284–86, lines 1–50)[252]

Here the green color of the Evil Eye is noted, its possessors are named (human and animal), and its being bound is indicated, along with its cohorts (*incubae*, demons, devils, satans).

In this same scroll there follows a binding spell by Mar Abd-Ishu to protect the girl Gauza (lines 51–113).[253] Thereafter it presents "the prayer and petitions and requests and supplications of Mar Giwargis, the illustrious martyr" (lines 148–180) (Hazard 1893:290–92). The prayer includes the following words:

> And everyone who writes the Holy Name and suspends it upon himself, and my name—Thy servant Giwargis—may he not have the evil and envious (fascinating) eye, nor fear, nor tremor . . . and may they not be brought near to Gauza, the daughter of Shima . . .

The Syriac Christian *The Little Book of Protection* (Codex A dated 1802) was edited and translated by Hermann Gollancz in 1912 as *The Book of Protection*. The work is "a collection of charms," E. A. W. Budge notes, "which was probably written for, or compiled by, a native of the country which lies to the north of Mosul" (in current day Iraq).[254] Edited from four manuscripts of the eighteenth–nineteenth centuries, which, in turn, represent earlier tradition, it contains a variety of spells aimed at binding and warding off the Evil Eye, among other noxious forces.[255]

---

252. Hazard (1893:284–86) gives the Syriac text and English translation. The text was obtained in Persia but date and provenance are not stated.

253. Ibid., 287–88. On the legend of Mar Abhd-Isho and the Evil Eye (and its many names), see Budge 1930:278–79.

254. Budge 1930:272. On the content of this work and nine facsimiles of its illustrations, see Budge 1930:272–82.

255. A fourth manuscript of this work is in the British Museum (Orient., no. 6673).

Early Christianity (and Islam) through Late Antiquity   115

Accompanying certain spells are vignette images of riders on horseback (cavaliers) spearing prostrate demons including the Evil Eye demoness.[256] Accompanying "The Anathema of the Angel Gabriel, which is of avail for the Evil Eye," is a vignette of the angel Gabriel mounted as a cavalier on a white horse and spearing a prostrate demoness of the Evil Eye.[257] Accompanying "The Anathema of Rabban Hurmizd, which is of avail for mad dogs," is a figure of Rabban Hurmizd as a cavalier spearing an animal, to which is affixed the description, "This is a lion or a mad dog."[258] The spell "Binding the mouth of wolves from off the sheep and larger animals" is accompanied by a vignette of "Daniel the prophet" also as cavalier spearing "the cunning wolf lying in ambush for the sheep."[259] Further vignettes of cavaliers in *The Book of Protection* include Mar George of Lydda spearing

Illus. 2.1
The angel Gabriel as cavalier spearing a prostrate demoness representing the Evil Eye (from Gollancz, *The Book of Protection* 1912:xl, Codex A, §23, p. 34).

Illus. 2.2
Rabban Hurmizd as cavalier spearing a prostrate lion or mad dog (from Gollancz, *The Book of Protection* 1912:xlii, Codex A, §27, p. 38; reproduction in Budge 1978/1930:280).

256. Two of the Budge facsimiles depict cavaliers lancing prostrate demonesses representing the Evil Eye: the angel Gabriel (Budge 1930:274) and King Solomon (Budge 1930:276).
257. Codex A, §23, p. 34; Gollancz 1912:xl-xli; facsimile in Budge 1930:274. For another vignette of "Mar Gabriel and the Evil Eye" see Codex C, p. 58a.
258. Codex A, §27, p. 38; Gollancz 1912:xlii.
259. Codex A, §35, Gollancz 1912: xlvi; facsimile in Budge 1930:278.

116   Beware the Evil Eye

the prostrate Great Dragon;[260] Mar Thomas spearing a prostrate "spirit of lunacy,"[261] Thaumasius, a Christian martyr, spearing a prostrate figure of the "spirit of the daughter of the moon,"[262] and King Solomon spearing the prostrate demon Asmodeus.[263]

Illus. 2.3
Daniel the prophet as cavalier spearing "the cunning wolf lying in ambush for the sheep" (from Gollancz, *The Book of Protection* 1912:xlvi, Codex A, §35, p. 47; reproduction in Budge 1978/1930:278)

Illus. 2.4
Mar Thomas as cavalier spearing the spirit of lunacy (from Gollancz *The Book of Protection* 1912:xxxii-xxxiii, Codex A, §12, p. 20)

The spells themselves against the Evil Eye are varied in intention and content. One charm requests that a family cow be safeguarded from "the evil and envious eye" and well-disposed toward her mistress and son:

> In the name of the Father, the Son, and the Holy Ghost. We beg of Thee, O Lord, God of Hosts, that by thy exalted and strong arm, this beast may be fond of and subject herself to her mistress and her son. Guard her against the evil and envious eye, by

260. Facsimile in Budge 1930:275.
261. Codex A, §12, p.20, Gollancz 1912:xxxii–xxxiii.
262. Codex A, §27, p. 38, Gollancz 1912:xl–xli; facsimile in Budge 1930:279.
263. Perdrizet 1922:12, fig. 5 (reproducing Gollancz, *The Book of Protection* 1912, Codex A, p. 55). Budge 1930:276 has a facsimile of a different vignette from *The Book of Protection* showing "King Solomon spearing a devil."

the power of thy beloved Son, our Lord Jesus Christ, and by the power of the angels who minister before Thee both night and day, who exclaim and repeat, 'Holy, Holy, Holy is the Lord God of Hosts, the heaven and the earth are full of his glory!' Make this cow at peace with her mistress A. the daughter of B., so that she may milk her by thy living and holy command, by the sanctification of those on high, and the action of those below, through the prayer of my Lady, the blessed Mary, and Mar John the Baptist. Amen! (Codex A, §24, Gollancz 1912:xl–xli)

Another charm seeks to protect cattle and sheep and their owner from hateful visitations, pestilence, and the Evil Eye. In regard to the Evil Eye it reads:

May no malady or sickness of Kûs, or sickness of Mosul, or evil and envious eye, or the wily eye of wicked men (approach him): but may evil demons and (their) cursed practices be removed from the sheep of the servant of Christ, A., the son of B. Amen!; (Codex A, §26; Gollancz 1912:xli–xlii)

Another spell likewise is intended to protect cattle from the injurious and destructive Evil Eye. It reads:

Illus. 2.5
King Solomon as cavalier spearing the prostrate demon Asmodeus (from Perdrizet 1922:12, fig. 5; cf. Gollancz, *The Book of Protection* 1912, Codex A, p. 55)

In the name of the Father, the Son, and the Holy Ghost. [I said] to the seven accursed brothers, sons of the evil and accursed man: "Whither are you creeping along on your knees, and moving upon your feet, and crawling upon your hands?" The wicked sons of the wicked and accursed man replied: "We are creeping along on our knees, walking upon our hands, and moving upon our feet, so that we may eat flesh, and drink [blood] in our palms." And when I saw them, I cursed them in the name of the Father, the Son, and the Holy Ghost, which is Eternal and a third of God (saying), "You are accursed and bound in the name of Gabriel, Michael, and Azrael, the three holy angels; in the name of that angel who judged the woman that combed (the hair of) her head on the eve of holy Sunday; and in the name of the Lord of the angels; so that you may not proceed on your way, nor finish your journey. May God break your teeth, and cut the veins of your head, and the nerves of your teeth, (keeping them off) from the cattle of the one who carries these writs. As the smoke vanishes from before the wind, may they vanish, in the name of the Father, the Son, and the Holy Ghost; in the name of the Father, the Fatherhood, in the name of the Son, the Lordship, and in the name of the Holy Ghost, the Emanation: in the name of the glorious Trinity, now, and for all time, for ever and ever. Amen!" (Codex A, §39, Gollancz 1912: xlviii–xlix)[264]

A charm that concerns a "benediction for vineyards and corn-fields" seeks safety from "the Evil and Envious Eye":

> Pronounce the benediction over the seed:—
> In the name of the Father, the Son, and the Holy Ghost. Glory to Thee, O God! Glory to Thee, O Planter of all trees, bearing fine fruit for the enjoyment of his servants. Bless, O my Lord, the seed and all the crops of the one who beareth these writs, also his vineyard, whatever he hath, and whatever he will have, that they may be covered with joyous fruits. Remove from them the evil and envious eye; and may drought and hard growth, hail and locust, and the worm, and all plagues, be annulled from off his seed, his vineyard, his crops, his field, and from all that he hath, and will have, namely, the one who beareth these writs. Amen. (Codex A, §29, Gollancz 1912:xliii)

A prescription for determining the source and duration of sicknesses includes a method for reckoning the precise time when an illness caused by the Evil Eye first began and how long it will last. Figuring on calculations based of the numerical value of an ill child's name and that of his mother indicates that

> on the first day of the week (Sunday) the illness began; at sunset the Evil Eye took a hold on him from the head, and from the shoulder, and from the neck. Nine days it lasts. [In] the monastery of Mar John [you will find] the prescription (lit. 'writing') for the Evil Eye. (Codex A, §54, Gollancz 1912: lvii–lx)

A charm to safeguard its bearer against all "evil men, cursed and deceitful demons, hinderers and devils, fear and trembling and dread, and all sicknesses and diseases" includes a binding and expulsion of the Evil Eye:

---

264. Compare Codex B, §10.

we bind, and anathematize, and expel, and prevent, and distance evil demons and accursed devils, rebellious Satans, wicked and envious people, the wiles of Emirs, fear, trembling, fright and surprise, anxiety and heaviness, the evil and envious eye, sweet and harsh sounds, evil spirits, all calamities and all opposition, [we expel these] from the body and members of the man who bears these writs. Amen! (Codex B, §5, Gollancz 1912: lxxx–lxiv)

An anathema issued in the name of Mar George, "the glorious martyr," includes the request that the bearer of the charm be safeguarded from "the envious and evil eye and various other afflictions:

no harm shall happen unto him carrying these writs, nor fear, nor trembling, nor surprise, nor evil visions, nor the evil and envious eye. Remove from him pains and sicknesses, fear and trembling, and those visions which come by night and by day ... (Codex B, §8, Gollancz 1912:lxx)

A spell intended to bind "the evil and envious eye" lists a variety of Evil Eyes, Evil-Eye possessors, victims, and its destructive effects:

The Evil Eye went forth from the eye of the heart, and the angel Gabriel met her, and said unto her, 'Whither goest [lxxi] thou, O daughter of destruction?' She replied unto him: 'I am going to destroy men and women, male and female children, and the souls of beasts and fowls.' The angel Gabriel addressed her: 'Have you not been to Paradise and seen the great God—Him whom thousands upon thousands, and myriads upon myriads of angels surround? By his Name may there be bound by me, and I bind you, O Evil and Envious Eye, the eye of strangers, the eye of those dwelling in our midst, the eye of people far off, the eye of those who are near, the green-coloured eye, and the blue-coloured eye, the dark-grey eye, and the tearful eye, and the eye of the seven evil ones, from off the body and members, from off the servants, from off the sheep and oxen, from off the vineyards and fields of him who carries these writs, through the prayers of my blessed Lady Mary, and of Mar John the Baptist. So be it. Amen!" (Codex B, §9, Gollancz 1912:lxx–lxxi)[265]

Another spell, "On the Evil Eye," identifies itself as a charm transmitting the words of the angel Gabriel, who enumerates various kinds of Evil Eyes and their possessors and announcing his binding and destroying them:

---

265. Compare Codex A § 23.

> ... boys and girls, the soul of cattle, the fowl of heaven; and Gabriel, the angel, said unto her [the Evil and Envious Eye]: "Hast thou not been up to Paradise, nor seen the Living God, Him to whom thousands upon thousands, and myriads of myriads of holy angels minister, and who sanctify his Name? You are bound by me, and I bind you, and excommunicate you, and destroy you, O Evil and Envious Eye, eye of the seven evil and envious neighbours, eye of all kinds, the eye that woundeth and pitieth not, the eye of the father, the eye of the mother, the eye of the foreigner, the eye of the gentile, (the eye of the foreigner), the dark-grey eye, the jealous eye, the caerulean eye, (the eye of those far off), the eye of all wicked men, the eye of those far off and those near, the eye of all kinds, the eye of man and woman, the eye of old men and old women, the eye of evil and envious men, the eye of the infidel, from the house, from the possessions, from the sons and daughters, from whatever else there may be to him who bears this charm, Amen! (Codex B, §19, Gollancz 1912:lxxxii–lxxxiii)[266]

Codex C of the *Book of Protection* likewise contains several spells against the Evil Eye. One spell merges a binding of the Evil Eye and other evil forces with opening words from the prologue of the Fourth Gospel. A charm intended for binding, warding off and destroying all forms of evil, illness, demons and the Evil and Envious Eye, it reads:

> By the power of our Lord we write the *Book of Protection*, Amen! In the name of the Father, the Son, and the Holy Ghost, the holy gospel of our Lord Jesus Christ, the preaching of John: In the beginning was the Word, and that Word was in the beginning with God, and God was [the Word]. In the beginning it was with God. And all was by his hand, and without him there was not one thing that existed. In him was life; and the life was the light of men. That light lighteth the darkness, which overcame it not. By the power of those Ten Holy Words of the Lord God, by the name, I am that I am, God Almighty, Adonai, Lord of Hosts, I bind, excommunicate and destroy, I ward off, cause to vanish, all evil, accursed, and maddening (lit. "misleading") pains and sicknesses, adversaries, demons, rebellious devils, also the spirits of lunacy, the spirit of the stomach, the spirits of the heart, the spirits of the head, the spirits of the eyes, the ills of the stomach, the spirit of the teeth, also the evil and envious eye, the eye that smiteth and pitieth not, the green-coloured eye, the eye of every

266. Compare Codex A § 23; Codex B §9.

kind, the eye of all spirits of pain in the head, pain on one side of the head, sweet and soft (doleful) pulsations, seventy-two such sweet and mournful noises, also the fever, cold and hot, visions fearful and false dreams, as are by night and by day; also Lilith, Malvita, and Zarduch, the dissembling (or "compelling") demon, and all evil pains, sicknesses, and devils, bound by spell, from off the body and soul, the house, the sons and daughters of him who beareth these writs, Amen, Amen! (Codex C, §1, Gollancz 1912:lxxiii–lxxiv)

A prophylactic prayer of Mar George the Martyr at the point of his martyrdom is meant to protect its bearer from an assortment of pains, wounds, accursed demons, rebellious Satan, and envious evil ones, and the eye of all wicked men and rebellious ones:

In the name of the Father, the Son, and the Holy Ghost. The prayer, petition, and supplication of Mar George, the triumphant martyr, which he prayed and asked of God, the Saviour, at the time of martyrdom, placing his knee in (the attitude of) prayer, and said: "O Lord God, All-powerful, as for everyone who will make mention of thy Holy Name, O Lord, Jesus Christ, and the name of Georgis, may there not come to him either terror, trembling, anxiety, or anger, nor one of the evil pains, sicknesses, accursed demons that lead astray; rebellious Satan and envious evil ones; fearful visions and the faces of evil devils, demons, and the evil spirit; the eye of all wicked men and rebellious ones; nor fear, trembling, visions demoniacal, fright, bonds of magic; nor Lilith and Zaduch, the demon Malvita, mother of strangled children, boys and girls, the souls of the birds of heaven, all pains, evil sicknesses, rebellious ones, and visions fearful; nor the sweet sounds of the head, seventy-two evil sounds, and accursed adversaries that lead one astray, rebellious and envious, evil ones; may all wounds, and all dire sicknesses be kept away from the house of him who carries these scraps, Amen! (Codex C, §2, Gollancz 1912:lxxiv)[267]

A portable protective charm has an incantation spoken by the angel Gabriel serving to bind and destroy the Evil and Envious Eye and all its various possessors:

... and Gabriel, the angel, said unto her: "Hast thou not been up to Paradise, nor seen the Living God, Him to whom thousands upon thousands, and myriads of myriads of holy angels

---

267. Compare Codex A, § 5, Codex B, § 8.

minister, and who sanctify his Name? You are bound by me, and I bind you, and excommunicate you, and destroy you, O Evil and Envious Eye, eye of the seven evil and envious neighbours, eye of all kinds, the eye that woundeth and pitieth not, the eye of the father, the eye of the mother, the eye of the foreigner, the eye of the gentile, (the eye of the foreigner), the dark-grey eye, the jealous eye, the caerulean eye, (the eye of those far off), the eye of all wicked men, the eye of those far off and those near, the eye of all kinds, the eye of man and woman, the eye of old men and old women, the eye of evil and envious men, the eye of the infidel, from the house, from the possessions, from the sons and daughters, from whatever else there may be to him who bears this charm, Amen! (Codex C, §19, Gollancz 1912: lxxxii–lxxxiii)[268]

The Placing of Protective Formulas, Designs, or Symbols for Safeguarding Homes and Sites

Prayers, incantations, formulas and symbols were variously placed to protect Christian homes and households, sarcophagi and burial sites, churches and monuments. Some of them mention and portray the protective power of the cross.

A Christian prayer on papyrus (Cairo, Egypt, fourth–fifth centuries CE) requesting protection of a home and its inhabitants from the Evil Eye reads:

> protect (*diaphylaxon*) this house and its inhabitants from every evil, from the Evil Eye (*baskosynês*) of every spirit of the air (*aerinôn pneumatôn*) and the human (Evil) Eye (*anthrôpinou ophthalmou*), from terrible suffering, the sting of the scorpion and bite of the serpent...[269]

Included are the formula "through the name of the most high God," (*dia to onoma tou hypistou theou*), the name of Jesus, and other protective signs and powers (CMG, T +, Chi Rho, Alpha and Omega, Ichthys, Amen, Iao, Sabaoth, Solomon).

---

268. Compare Codex A, §23; Codex B, §9. This text is cited in Ford 1998:239 (with minor variations) and was previously quoted in Vol. 1, chap. 2, of the present work.

269. Eitrem and Friedrichson 1921:25; Dölger 1928 1:16+–17; Robert 1981:29–30 (text on p. 30 n.18); Dickie 1995:31 and n.67 for the Greek text.

On a doorpost of a house in Simkhar, North Syria, are the words intended to repel any malicious glance from passers-by and to return it to its sender:

> God is one. ICHTHYS (fish symbol). In the Year 398. Back to you double as much as you say.
>
> EIS TH[eos]. ICHTHYC. Etous 398 Kai soi, osa (legeis) ta dipla.[270]

The expression "back to you double as much as you say" has the same apotropaic function as the similar phrases *kai sy* and *kai soi* (Greek, "also to you") and their Latin equivalent, *et tibi*.[271]

An inscription of eleven verses on a house in I'djaz, Syria, announces, in part, its owner's confidence in the protection from demons and an Evil Eye afforded by the living Christ:

> The eternally living Christ raises his suffering-relieving hand; therefore I will not tremble before the cunnings of evil-working demons nor before the terrible and wicked human [Evil] Eye (*omma*).[272]

An inscription on the doorpost of a house in Sabba, Syria, dated 546 CE, announces the protection afforded by the Lord and the cross against the Evil Eye. It reads:

> In the year 858 in the month Peritos: the Lord will protect the entrance and exit of this house; for where the cross is displayed, the Evil Eye will have no power (*[t]o[u] staurou gar prokimenou ou[k] [i]schys[ei ophthalmos baska]nos*).[273]

An inscription on a door lintel (Antioch, Syria), accompanies a cross and declares that the composite design was intended to repel the Evil Eye. It reads: "Of this house the Lord shall guard the entrance and the exit; for the cross being set before, no Evil Eye shall prevail against it."[274]

The inscriptions for averting the Evil Eye from residences are frequently matched in formulation and detail by inscriptions designed for warding off envy.

The cross, for example, was employed similarly as a prophylactic against envy. On the capital of a house in Tepedshi, Syria, was found a globe

---

270. Grégoire 1922:78, no. 230 ter; Meisen 1950:175.

271. On these apotropaic phrases in Greek and Roman cultures, see, previously, Vol. 2:170–74.

272. Leclercq 1933:195–99; cf. also *DACL* 10.1 (1931):1112. Meisen 1950:175.

273. Dölger 1928 1:247, no. 230; Meisen 1950:175.

274. See Downey 1962:133; also Prentice 1906:141.

124   Beware the Evil Eye

with a cross on top and an inscription reading: "Where the cross (S[ta]urou) is present, envy (phthonos) has no power."[275]

A sixth-century stone found in Khamissa southwest of Souk-Ahras, Algeria, bears a Christ monogram, an Alpha and Omega, a Latin cross, and an inscription reading:

> O Envy, why do you injure those who you think are prospering? / You are your own tormentor. The wounds you suffer you bring on yourself.
>
> In[v]ide, quid laceres illos quos crescere sentis? / Tu tibi tortor, tu tecum tua [v]ulnera portas.[276]

A door lintel inscription on a fortification in Oviedo, Spain, likewise displays a cross and reads:

> Place a sign of salvation, Lord, / in these dwellings, so that you do not allow the slaying angel any entrance.
>
> Signum salutis pone domine / in domibus istis, ut non permittas introire angelum percutientem.[277]

Further apotropaics designed to protect homes from envy are virtually identical to those aimed at averting the Evil Eye.[278] A door lintel in Asia Minor bears the inscription, "you see the cross . . . envy, scram; evil is vanquished."[279] A door lintel from Nessan in Palestine has acclamations to Christ followed by a malediction against envy.[280] Another door lintel from Syria has three crosses flanked by an Alpha and an Omega, with an inscription declaring: "In the presence of the cross, envy has no power" (*Staurou prokeimenou, ouden ischyei ho phthonos*).[281]

A door lintel inscription from Bardoune in Syria is similar to that of the house in Sabba, Syria, cited above (p. 123). It is marked with three crosses, and flanked by the letters, Alpha and Omega. It reads: "The cross being present here, envy has no power" (IGLS 4 [1955].1909). These similar

---

275. Grégoire 1922:78; Meisen 1950:175.
276. CSEL 1929; Gsell et al. 1922, no. 1971; cf. also no. 113; Meisen 1950:175–76.
277. Hübner 1871:81, no. 253; cf. p. 80, no. 249 and p. 81, no.252; Meisen 1950:176.
278. See Bernand 1991:103–4.
279. Robert and Robert 1966:346, no.89.
280. Robert and Robert 1965:179, no. 441.
281. See IGLS 4 (1955) n.1909 (=Robert and Robert 1956:176–77, no. 325). See also Bonner 1950:97 for an amulet against personifed *Phthonos* reading, "Envy, bad luck to you."

apotropaics protecting homes illustrate the equivalence of Evil Eye and Envy in the minds of the owners.

Other apotropaics on Christian houses appeal to the power of the Holy Trinity or Jesus: "May the Trinity, (our) God, drive envy far away"; "Jesus the Nazarene, who was born of Mary, the son of God, lives here. Let nothing evil enter here!" (PAES III.B 1018, IGLS 2 [1939].424).

An inscription from Christian Egypt and incorporating Christian, Jewish and Egyptian themes was designed to protect a house and its occupants from the Evil Eye and other harmful forces. It reads:

> CH M G [XMG]] Hor Hor Phor, Yao Sabaoth Adonai, Eloe, Salaman, Tarchei, I bind you, artemisian scorpion, 315 times. Preserve this house with its occupants from all evil, from all bewitchment of spirits of the air and the human Evil Eye and terrible pain and sting of scorpion and snake, through the name of the highest god, Naias Meli, 7 times, XUROURO AAAAAA BAINCHOOOCH MARIIIIII ENAG KORE. Be on guard, O Lord, son of David according to the flesh, the one born of the holy Virgin Mary, O holy one, highest god, from the holy spirit. Glory to you, O heavenly king, Amen. ALPHA OMEGA ALPHA OMEGA ICHTHYS.[282]

An inscription from Greco-Roman Egypt, either Jewish or Christian, found at Cheihk Zoude, on the Mediterranean coast of the Sinai peninsula, between Rafah and Al-Arish, was meant to protect a piece of art against envy (*ton phthonon*) and the "eyes of Evil-Eyed malice" (*ommata baskaniês*) (Bernand 1969: 96–97, no. 122b).

Protection against the Evil Eye was also sought by Christians at gravesites. A Christian funerary inscription in iambic verse found in a cemetery in Rome, indicates that the deceased suffered an evil fate from the Evil Eye (*baskanôi*) (CIG 4.9688).

A late imperial age inscription from a necropolis at Tyre records the protective warning on a stone that closes off a grave loculus: "God [is our] helper; flee O Evil-Eyed one; you have spoken well (*theos boêthos. baskane, pheuge. kalôs ipes*)" (*I. Tyre* 1.160).[283]

A twenty-six line inscription (date unknown) was found engraved in uncial lettering on the column of a Christian church in the Phrygian village of Seidilar (ancient Dokimion, site of famous marble quarries). It denounces envy as abhorrent to God and warns enviers of how their Evil-Eyed envy ends up choking them:

282. See Meyer 1994:49–50; Aquaro 2004:80.
283. See Horsley 1982 2:208.

Envy is a very evil thing, but it has some good that is greater. It dries up those who envy and it punishes evil. O Envy (Leclercq: "Evil Eye")[284] what are you envying?[285] [you are looking at] nothing more than drying up yourself.[286] Everything belongs to God who is without envy (*aphthonos*);[287] and he gives his help to all who hope in him. But you, o envier (Leclercq: "Evil Eye"), tell me, wanting to help, you are not able; you are thus choked by your own evil. God completely abhors those who are evil and envious (Leclercq: "have an Evil Eye"). (JHE trans.)

> *Ho phthonos esti kakistos, echi d'agathon ti megiston. Têki tous phthonerous, elegchô tên kakiên. O phthonere, ti phthonis; ouden pleon ê têkis (s)eauton. Theou gar esti ta panta hos aphthonôs parechi pasan tois elpizousin eis auton. Sy de, leg', ô phthonere, ke thelôn parechin ou dynase, 'ke phthonôn eischueis ouden. Anxê oun eis tên kakian sou. Tous de kakous ke phthonerous ho Theos pantote misi.*[288]

Another Christian mosaic inscription on envy from the Byzantine period and now in the National Museum of Beirut, makes a similar point with similar words. It was part of a threshold mosaic of a wealthy house in the center of Byzantine Beirut. Its purpose was to protect the residence and its inhabitants from envy and the Evil Eye:

> Envy (*ho phthonos*) is a great evil.
> However, it has some beauty,
> for it consumes the eyes
> and the heart of the envious (*phthonerôn*).[289]

A similar saying about envy also concludes a funerary inscription from Lyon, France. It is a further illustration of the popularity and wide dissemination of this sentiment:

---

284. Leclercq's translation (1924:1844) renders *phthonos* as "Evil Eye" (*mauvais oeil*), assuming the equivalence of envy and Evil Eye).

285. Leclercq: "what are you looking at with your Evil Eye?"

286. Leclercq adds as explanation in parentheses: "you turn your Evil Eye on yourself").

287. Leclercq: "does not have an Evil Eye."

288. Published and commented on by Perdrizet 1900:294-99; see also Ramsey 1897:745 n.689; Leclercq (1924:1843-44) gives the text and variant readings. His translation, *mauvais oeil*, takes *phthonos, phthoneros, phthonein* here as references to the Evil Eye. On the Dokimion envy inscription, see also Perdrizet 1936, 1937-38.

289. The mosaic sometimes is erroneously referred to as the "jealousy mosaic." The Greek, however, speaks not of jealousy, but twice of "envy" (*phthonos*).

How evil envy is!
Still it has something good about it:
it dries up the eyes and heart of the envious.[290]

On a temple in Syria, the conclusion of a dedication includes the phrase *kai soi*, familiar from Evil Eye texts and an equivalent to *kai sy* ("you too").[291] Here it is part of a wish that God save the reader from envy: "and to you (*kai soi*), O reader, may God come to your aid, and contend and not begrudge [assistance]. May the envier, however, burst asunder."[292]

These Christian envy inscriptions and the epigram illustrate the conventional notion that the envious are consumed by their own envy, like the Evil-eyed are injured by their own Evil Eye, thus paralleling the iconographical depictions of personified Envy engaged in self-strangulation.[293]

An inscription on the wall of a house in Syria requests that the mother of the house, Marcellina, and her infants and others of the household prosper with God's help, and "may Envy burst asunder" (*ho phthonôê* [sic] *rhagêtô*) and thus be incapable of harming the home's inhabitants.[294]

A Christian lintel-inscription in iambic trimeter from the area of Halicarnassus, Asia Minor (modern Bodrum, Turkey) reads: "As long as the cross is present, *Phthonos/Envy* is not in the least powerful (*staurou [parontos] ouden ischyei phthonos*)."[295] Compare the similar formulation of the door lintel inscription from Sabba, Syria, cited above, pp. 123, 124.

An inscription found on a public building in ancient Beirut declared to the passers-by: "keep going and don't envy!" (*parage kai mê phthoni*).[296]

These inscriptions against envy are virtually identical to those used to protect houses and homes from the Evil Eye. They illustrate the equivalency of Evil Eye and envy in numerous apotropaics and in popular thought.[297]

---

290. *ho phthonos hôs kakon estin. Echi gar ti kalon en autô. têki gar phthonerôn ommata kai kardiên*. Text according to Leclercq 1924:1845.

291. On the *kai sy* formula in Greek and Roman cultures, see Vol. 2:170–74.

292. *kai soi, (ô) anagenôskon, boêthêsê soi ho Theos, kai erize kai mê phthoni. Ho de phth(oneros) rhagêtê (rhagêtai)*. Cf. Aristides (129–189 CE) *Orationes* 50: "may the Evil-Eyers (*tois baskanois*) burst asunder (*rhêgnusthai*)."

293. See Dunbabin and Dickie 1983; Dunbabin 1991.

294. Waddington 1870, no. 2415; Perdrizet 1900:294; Leclercq 1924:1845 (with full Greek text). See also Dunbabin and Dickie 1983: 32 and nn.32, 33.

295. Faraone 2009:231. For two parallel Syrian Christian door lintel amulets warding off *phthonos*/envy, see Robert 1965:265.

296. Waddington 1870, nos. 2360, 2406; Perdrizet 1900:293; Leclercq 1927:1844, regarding it as Christian.

297. Meisen 1950:175–76.

Of three similar door lintel inscriptions from Syria, one, eleven verses in length, mentions "the mercy-dispensing hand of the living Christ" removing fear of "the wiles of the evil-working Demon/Devil (*daimonos*) or the fearsome and wicked human (Evil) Eye (*omma*). Another reads, as cited above (p. 124), "In the presence of the cross, envy has no power";[298] A third Syrian door lintel inscription reads: "God is one (*Eis th[eos]*)—Ichthys—In the year 398—Back to you twice as much (*Kai soi hosa ta dipla*)."[299]

The final words involve another variant (*kai soi*) on the *kai sy* expression, whose aim was to return to Evil-Eyed passers-by any envy and Evil-Eyed malice they directed at the residence and its inhabitants.[300]

Many of these are composite apotropaics, like their pagan counterparts, with several features or motifs combined for increased apotropaic effect. "The commonest [Christian] formulae employed," according to Russell,[301] "are the Trisagion, *kyri boêthi* ["Help, O Lord!"] or some variant, *Eis theos monos* ["One God alone"], CHI-M-G (probably for CHristos, Michael, Gabriel) and ICHTHYS."

At the Roman villa of Buthrotum, modern Butrint, an Aegean port settlement in southwest Albania, were discovered various objects to protect a private residence and its Christian inhabitants. A mosaic pavement in front of the main doorway of the residence, which was expanded in the fourth–fifth centuries CE to palatial proportion (Triconch Palace), displayed the design of a large Evil Eye surrounded by a variety of motifs, including crosses. Apotropaic images, including the Chi Rho monogram and crosses, also were incorporated into the four main windows of the dining hall. A further image of an Evil Eye under attack was found on a bone intaglio plaque displaying a large hunting dog leaping over, and defending against, this Evil Eye. A two-sided copper medallion designed for wearing also joins this Evil Eye material. It depicts a haloed cavalier, probably Solomon, lancing a prostrate figure, probably the Evil Eye demoness, *Baskosysnê*. This is made likely both by analogous amulets and by the reverse side, which shows an Evil Eye attacked by a trident, spears and entourage of creatures including a lion, serpents and scorpion.

298. Grégoire 1922:78, no. 230; Meisen 1950:175.

299. Dölger 1928 1:12, no. 88; Meisen 1950:175.

300. For two further examples of door lintel inscriptions in Latin from Algeria and Spain protecting residences from envy and the Evil Eye see Meisen 1950:175–76. On *kai sy/kai soi* see Vol. 2:170–74.

301. Russell 1995:38 n.6.

Early Christianity (and Islam) through Late Antiquity 129

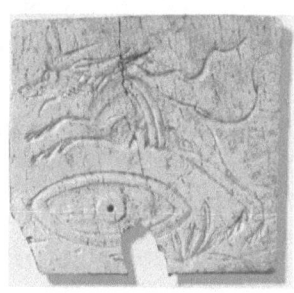

The accompanying inscription reads, "Iao [Yahweh] Lord of Hosts, Michael, help!" The Albanian material illustrates that dread of the Evil Eye that was as typical of elites as of commoners, and of Christians as well as pagans, down through late Roman antiquity.[302]

The Wearing of Personal Amulets and Use of Apotropaic Gestures and Objects

An engraved gold *lamella* from Asia Minor or Syria, dated early second century CE, was worn by a Christian as an amulet for dispelling a headache. Its inscription invokes the aid of Jesus in overcoming "the Grim-faced One": "turn away, O Jesus, the Grim-Faced One (*tên Gorgôpa*) and on behalf of your maidservant, her headache to (the) glory of your name, IAO ADONAI SABAOTH . . ."[303] It is likely that here "Grim-faced One" refers to the Gorgo, who, given the association of Gorgo/Medusa and the petrifying Evil Eye, stands in for the Evil Eye as the cause of the headache.[304] The amulet illustrates the Christian adoption of pagan Evil Eye lore and its varied motifs.

A fourth-century amulet from a tomb in Beirut, Lebanon, likewise was designed to protect a certain Alexandra against an Evil Eye and other sources of harm. Consisting of a strip of silver (*lamella*) encased in a bronze tubular capsule, the amulet has an inscription that begins with an adjuration

---

302. On ancient Butrint, see Hodges et al., eds. 2004.

303. For the Greek text and translation and analysis see Kotansky 2002:37–46, text and translation on 37–39.

304. Ibid., 42.

for protecting the girl from demons, sorceries and binding-spells. It then calls on angels, the God of Abraham, Isaac and Jacob to protect Alexandra from a wide range of harmful forces, including an Evil Eye:

> . . . protect Alexandra whom Zoe bore from demons and sorceries and dizziness and from all passions and from all frenzy. I adjure you by. . . that all male <demons?> and frightening demons and all bindings-spells flee from Alexandra whom Zoe bore, to beneath the founts and the abyss of Mareôth, lest you harm or defile her, or use magic drugs on her, either by a kiss, or from an embrace, or a greeting; either with food or drink; either in bed or intercourse; either by the (evil) eye or a piece of clothing; as she prays, either on the street or abroad; or while river-bathing or a bath. Holy and mighty and powerful names, protect Alexandra from every demon, male and female, and from every disturbance of demons of the night and of the day.[305]

The amulet illustrates the Christian familiarity with both pagan and Jewish Evil Eye traditions.

A Christian amulet for wearing around the neck (CIG 4.9065b) bears an inscription stating that it protects against the devil, evil and an Evil Eye (*baskan[os] oph[thalmou]* . . .). An epigram on a Christian amulet (fifth century CE) addressing evil powers similarly reads: "Flee, Beliar, dragon . . . Evil-Eyed One (*Pheuge, Beliar, Drakôn . . . baskanos daimôn*) . . ."[306] In this context, it appears that *baskanos daimôn*, like *Beliar* and *drakôn* identifies the Devil/Satan. This is illustrative of the merging of the Evil Eye with the Devil as found in the Christian literary texts discussed above.

An amulet consisting of an inscribed leaf of tarnished silver encased in a bulla was worn to protect mother and/or daughter Syntyche from "the spirit of fever, all epilepsy, all hydrophobia, every Evil Eye [*ton baskanon ophthalmon*], every violent sending of spirits, all poisoning."[307]

An amulet concerning the Virgin Mary is inscribed in Latin and displays a broad array of Christian symbols (crosses, Alpha and Omega, names of God, of the Magi, and figures of the Virgin Mary and St. Anthony of

---

305. Text according to Trzcionka 2007:103, following the text and translation of Kotansky1994:270–300, amulet no. 52, lines 71–121). For discussion, see Trzcionka 2007:103–5. For two additional anti-Evil Eye amulets, see Trzcionka 2007:107–10, 113–19.

306. Kaibel, *Epig. Gr.* ed. 1878:512, no. 1140.

307. Bonner 1950:100; Kotansky 1991:119. Originally published by W. Froehner in 1867, the amulet was once in the Louvre Museum (inv. Bj 87), Paris, but is now long lost. The wearer, Bonner adds, was supposed to speak the charm.

Padua) and appeals to Christ for aid and forgiveness. It was designed for protection against fire, pestilence, the Evil Eye and other inimical forces.[308]

Apotropaic Alexander Medallions

A popular type of amulet worn by Christians in the fourth and fifth centuries at Antioch and adopted from Greek practice, was a medallion bearing an image of Alexander the Great of Macedon. The use of these amulets was mentioned and condemned by John Chrysostom.[309] Amulets of this type, many in the Cabinet of Medals, Bibliothèque Nationale de France, Paris, show Alexander in the character of Hercules on one side, and, on the other, a she-ass with her foal, a scorpion, and the name of Jesus Christ. A Christian amulet in the Vatican Library with the picture of Alexander bears on the reverse the Christ monogram.[310]

Apotropaic Depictions of an Evil Eye under Attack

Apotropaic depictions of an Evil Eye under attack (alias "the much-suffering eye") were even more popular, as noted previously in Volume 2. They took various forms, as they were employed to protect individuals or residences.[311]

An anti-Evil Eye amulet found in Beirut in 1965 has a mutilated image on its obverse and, on the reverse, an inscription reading, "protect (*phylaxon*) Constantinus, son of Christina. *Eis Theos*." Below this inscription is a representation of an Evil Eye attacked by a circle of enemies: two lions, ibis, serpent, scorpion, and below this two daggers.[312]

Designs of the Evil Eye under attack also appear on gems and medallions worn by individuals. Campbell Bonner lists a gem now in the Metropolitan Museum of New York showing an Evil Eye attacked, with an owl perched on the Eye.[313] Gems and lamellae with similar designs were shown

---

308. Described by Budge 1930:353, citing Villiers and Pachinger 1927.

309. John Chrysostom, *Catech. illum.* 2.5 (PG 49.240); cf. Trzcionka 2007:106 and 192 nn.24, 25.

310. *Catholic Encyclopedia* online, sub "Christian amulets"; http://www.catholic.org/encyclopedia.

311. See. e.g., Schlumberger 1892a:74–75; Perdrizet 1922 and figs. 1–11; Bonner 1950:97–99, ch. 15, 302–7 and nos. 294–304, 306, 311; Meisen 1950:166, 170–73. See Vol. 2:170–74; 202–4, 216, 233–43.

312. Robert 1981:32.

313. Bonner 1950:98–99.

earlier by Jahn[314] and Elworthy.[315] Elworthy describes one of these engraved gems as "blood-red" and of Graeco-Egyptian provenance.[316] It shows an Eye with an owl perched above and surrounded by a serpent, stag, scorpion, dog, lion and thunderbolt. Bonner also mentions "a specimen in the Borgia collection,"[317] a circular gold lamella showing an Eye surrounded by eight small figures (lizard, flying swan, serpent, dog, lion, winged phallus, scorpion, thunderbolt), with a crescent moon above the Eye. Also in Bonner's list of Evil Eyes attacked is a terra cotta medallion (found at Königshoffen in Alsace) fastened to an urn. Though fragmented, it shows various animal heads directed toward a central point, presumably an Evil Eye.[318] Many cavalier amulets, as we shall note, likewise show an Evil Eye being attacked.[319]

These depictions of an Evil Eye under attack were used to protect not only individuals but also dwellings and graves. As examples, Bonner (1950:98–99) mentions the Woburn marble relief discussed by Jahn; a threshold mosaic found on Rome's Caelian hill in the vestibule of the sanctuary of Cybele, with an owl perched on an Evil Eye attacked by a coterie of animals and birds; another attacked Eye;[320] and a funerary stele found on the site of ancient Auzia in Algeria.[321] It depicts the donor, his wife and two children (boy and girl) all standing. At the feet of the adults and between the two children an Evil Eye is attacked by a scorpion, snail and lizard. The design protects a sepulchral monument.

These Christian apotropaics displaying images of an Evil Eye under attack are joined by others employing further designs to protect homes and their inhabitants.[322]

---

314. Jahn 1855, Plate 3.1–5.
315. Elworthy1958/1895:130–33 and figs. 14–19.
316. Ibid., 131–32 and fig.19.
317. Bonner 1950:98–99; Zoega 1810:457, no. 19. The collection of the *Museo Borgiano* was transferred in 2001 to the Museo Civilico-Archaeologico of Velletri, Italy.
318. Bonner 1950: 99.
319. See Bonner 1950:99–100 on Palestinian, Syrian, Christian specimens, also Plate 14, nos. 294–99 and Plate 15, nos. 300–303, 306, 309, 311.
320. See Bienkowski 1893; illustrated by Perdrizet 1922:29, fig. 9, and described by Bonner 1950: 98.
321. Bonner 1950: 99.
322. See Meisen 1950:175–176.

Early Christianity (and Islam) through Late Antiquity   133

The Apotropaic Figure of Solomon, the Seal of Solomon, and Solomon as Cavalier

Many Christian amulets include representations of, and appeal to the patronage of, the biblical figure of King Solomon. As already noted, Solomon was renown in Israel for his great wisdom (1 Kgs 4:29-34), occult knowledge, and power over demons.[323] He was revered as a protective figure by Christians as well. Solomon's authority over demons and evil spirits is especially stressed in the *Testament of Solomon* (first-third cenury CE), a composition involving both Jewish and Christian traditions.[324] Christian amulet makers adopted and adapted Jewish lore concerning Solomon as master of wisdom and ruler of spirits. They made extensive use of his name, his seal, and his portrait.[325]

A glass paste oval amulet from Anemurium, Asia Minor, inscribed on both sides, shows on the obverse a Trisagion, a standard formula used by Jews and Christians to avert evil, and *Sab[ao]th*. The inscription on the reverse reads: "The Seal of Solomon restrains the Evil Eye" (*Sphrag[is So]lomonis [e]chi tên baskanian*).[326] Similarly, each of a group of oblong amulets of red haemetite (i.e. a protective color) is inscribed with "Solomon" on one side and, on the reverse, "Seal of God" (*Sphragis Theou*).[327] The inscription "Seal of Solomon" also appears on amulets depicting an Evil Eye under attack, as discussed below.

Closely related to this glass amulet from Anemurium are two oval amuletic disks of thin copper sheeting found together at Anemurium. One depicts an Evil Eye pierced by two oblique spears from the left and a triangular bladed dagger from above. Below the Eye is a half-circle of creatures attacking it, including two serpents, a scorpion, an ibis, a lion and a leopard.

---

323. See Josephus, *Ant.* 8.2.5; *T. Sol.*; and above, chap. 1 of the present volume.

324. See Duling 1983:941-51. For Christian material and redaction, see, e.g., *T. Sol.* 11:6; 12:3; 15:10-15; 17:4-5; and for Christian tradition on Solomon, see Duling 1983:949-51.

325. For Solomon on amulets and apotropaics see Perdrizet 1903; Perdrizet 1922:6-7, 27-31; Winkler 1931; Meisen 1950:166, 171-72; Bonner 1950:208-13, 302, nos. 294-97; Goodenough 1953 2:227-32; Delatte and Derchain 1964, nos. 369 ff.; Bagatti 1971, 1972; Vikan 1984; Russell 1995:39-41 and fig. 6.

326. See Russell 1995:39 and figs. 2-4; cf. also Russell 1982:539-40 and figs. 1-2. On the Seal of Solomon see Perdrizet 1903; Perdrizet 1922:32-35; Bonner 1950:208-13; Meisen 1950:166; Goodenough 1953 2:227-32; Delatte and Derchain 1964, no. 371; Bagatti 1971, 1972; Dunbabin 1991:33; Russell 1995:39 n.15. There are nine Solomon specimens in the Cabinet des Médailles, Bibliothèque Nationale, Paris.

327. Meisen 1950:166.

The legend above the scene reads, "Help, O Lord" (*kyri boêthi*).³²⁸ The second disk shows a "nimbate cavalier in military garb," probably Solomon (see below), lancing a supine demoness representing the Evil Eye.³²⁹ The motifs of both amulets, according to Russell, are found on numerous apotropaic objects from around the eastern Mediterranean world, "not only on oval or round plaques such as these, but also on rings, incised gemstones, and bracelets."³³⁰ Russell compares the second disk with a copper amulet from Smyrna in Asia Minor (see below) depicting Solomon as a cavalier surrounded by the inscription, "Flee, you loathsome demoness; Solomon pursues you" (*Pheuge, memisimeni: Solomôn se dioki*). On the reverse is an inscription reading, "Seal of Solomon, drive away all evil from the bearer" (*Sphragis Solomonos apodioxon pan kakon apo tou phorounto[s]*).³³¹ This leads us to a more detailed consideration of the connection of Solomon and depictions of anti-Evil Eye cavalier (rider on horseback) apotropaics.

Solomon and Anti-Evil Eye Cavalier Apotropaics

On numerous pagan amulets, representations of an Evil Evil under attack are often combined with the motif of a cavalier (rider on horseback) spearing from his horse a prostrate female figure (demoness). Cavalier amulets have been traced back to Egypt and to at least the Ptolemaic period.³³² Jewish and Christian amulets of this type from Syria and Palestine (generally in the Byzantine era) identify the cavalier as Solomon or as a Christian counterpart, Saint Sisinnios.³³³ These cavalier amulets are a graphic illustration of cultural cross-fertilization and adaptation. In Christian tradition, Solomon

---

328. Russell 1995:40 and fig. 5.
329. Ibid., and fig. 6.
330. Ibid., and for literature, nn.17 and 18.
331. Ibid., n.18. Russell compares this with another amulet displaying an Evil Eye under attack over which was the legend PHTHONOS (Envy); cf. also Russell 1987:39, 45–47, fig. 8, Plate VII, 11; Schlumberger 1892a:74–75; Perdrizet 1903:47–48.
332. Perdrizet 1903, 1922. See Vol. 2:236–37, 243–44 and n.928.
333. Schlumberger 1895 1:120, 134, 293; Perdrizet 1903, 1922; Leclercq 1924:1847; Meisen 1950:166, 171–72; Bonner 1950:99–100, 208–12, 302 nos. 294–304; Pl. 14, nos 294–99; Pl. 15, nos. 300–303, 306, 309, 311; Goodenough 1953 2:238–41; Menzel 1955; Budge 1930:272–82; Piccirillo 1979; Russell 1982, 1995; Vikan 1984; E. D. Maguire, et al., eds. 1989:212–17, nos. 133–36 and 25–28 on the holy rider; Limberis 1991:177–78; and Vol. 1:145–47, 155. On Solomon in Israelite tradition as master over the forces of evil see Blau 1898:12; Perdrizet 1903:42; 1922:7; Winkler 1931; see also *T. Sol.* 13:1–7 (Solomon controlling the demoness Obyzouth, slayer of birthing mothers and newborn infants).

as cavalier attacking an Evil Eye is joined by the cavalier saints, St. Sisinnios and St. George.[334]

Writing on an "intaglio of Solomon in the Benaki Museum and the origins of the iconography of warrior saints," C. Walter notes that

> [t]he type of Solomon himself, as represented on the Benaki intaglio, may be as early as the third century. By the fourth century it was being christianized. In the next stage, perhaps as early as the fifth century, the rider became anonymous and a beast or serpent was being substituted for the prostrate woman. By the sixth century the rider was receiving a new identity, that of a Christian saint, and, more specifically, that of a warrior: Theodore, George and, later, Demetrius. However, the essential "message" of the iconographical type did not change: the rider receives from God the power to triumph over evil.[335]

The connection of Israel's King Solomon and the Evil Eye under attack is illustrated by the Israelite pseudepigraphical writing, the *Testament of Solomon* (see above, pp. 22–24, 40, 133). At one point in the *Testament*, Solomon interrogates the thirty-six heavenly bodies, "the world rulers of the darkness of this age," and learns of their specific identities, their pernicious powers, and what thwarts them (18:1–42).[336] The thirty-fifth of these spirits reports his name to Solomon: "My name is Rhyx [*Rex*?] Phtheneoth [*Phthonos*?] (Lord Envy) I cast an Evil-Eye on (*baskainô*) every human. My power is annulled by the inscribed image of the much-suffering eye (*ho polypathês ophthalmos*)" (*T. Sol.* 18:39).[337]

Bonner (1950:97) uses this expression, "the much-suffering eye," as designation for amuletic representations of the Evil Eye under attack. I prefer the designation "Evil Eye attacked/under attack." This highlights the aggressive power of the apotropaic directed against the Evil Eye rather than the suffering of the Evil-Eyed and envious.

The many specimens of anti-Evil Eye apotropaics discussed by Bonner[338] include several Christian amulets (Palestinian and Syrian provenance) of the cavalier type depicting a rider on a horse, sometimes identified as Solomon, lancing an Evil Eye or a prostrate female figure/demoness.[339] An

---

334. On Sisinnios, see further, Leclercq 1950; Greenfield 1989; Spier 1993; Fauth 1999. On St. George and the Evil Eye, see Aquaro 2000:96–110.

335. Walter 1989–1990:42.

336. See Duling 1993 *OTP* 1:977–81.

337. Following the numeration and translation of Duling 1993 *OTP* 1:981.

338. Bonner 1950:97–100 (Evil Eye), 208–12 (Solomon as cavalier).

339. For samples of cavalier amulets (rider on horseback spearing prostrate objects)

elaborate bronze medallion for wearing as an apotropaic pendent is clearly a Christian amulet. It shows on the obverse a cavalier with nimbus spearing a lioness with a human, female face. An angel with nimbus blesses the rider with his raised wing. The inscription reads: "One God who conquers evil." In the margin is a cross accompanying the words, "He who dwells in the help of the Most High will abide in the shelter of the God of heaven. He will say to the Lord . . ." The reverse shows an enthroned Christ surrounded by the four animals of the Apocalypse (ox, man, eagle, lion) and, below, a lion, snake, two cobras (?), and a crab. In the field are the inscription, "Holy, Holy, Holy, Lord Sabaôth" and certain powerful characters. In the margin is a cross and the words, "The seal of the living God, guard from every evil him who carries this amulet."[340] Several of these cavalier amulets depict on the reverse an Evil Eye under attack.[341]

These combinations of an attacked Evil Eye on the reverse and a cavalier image on the obverse are eloquent testimony to the merging of Evil Eye motifs in both Jewish and Christian traditions, as well as their adaptations from apotropaics of the Circum-Mediterranean world in general.

A Christian Byzantine silver/copper medallion from Smyrna, Asia Minor, is typical of this combination. It depicts on the obverse (left) side a cavalier with nimbus piercing with a lance adorned by a cross a prostrate female demon. The encircling inscription reads "Flee, you loathsome demoness; Solomon, [along with] Sisinnios [and] Sisinnarios, is chasing you" (*pheuge, memisimeni, Solomôn se dioke, Sisinnios Sisinnarios*). The protecting cavalier is identified as Solomon accompanied by St. Sisinnios and his brother.[342] The cross and references to Sisinnios, Sisinnarios as well as to Solomon identify the amulet as intended for Christian use. The reverse (right) shows an Evil Eye attacked from above by three daggers, by lions on

---

see Kelsey Museum, University of Michigan, nos. 26092 (cavalier spearing prostrate demoness; on obverse, "Seal of God"; Bonner 1950, no. 294); and from Syria, no. 26140 (obv. "Seal of God"; cavalier spearing a prostrate demon; Bonner, *Studies* 1950:208–10); 26114 (cavalier with nimbus, obv. "One God who conquers ev[il]"; Bonner 1950, no. 309); 26115 (on obverse, cavalier with nimbus spearing prostrate demoness, "One God who conquers evil"; on reverse, Evil Eye attacked by a lion, ibis, serpent, scorpion, leopard?, trident, and spear, "Iao Sabaoth Michael, help"; Bonner 1950, no. 299); 26140 (cavalier spearing prostrate demon [obv.] "Seal of God" [rev.]; Bonner 1950:208–10); 261165 (cavalier with nimbus spearing prostrate demoness; Bonner 1950, no. 323).

340. Bonner 1950, no. 324; Kelsey Museum, University of Michigan, no. 26119.

341. Bonner 1950:302–7, and for illustrations, Plates 14–15, nos. 294–306, 309, 311; Meisen 1950:171–72; and Kelsey Museum collection, University of Michigan, no. 26115 = Bonner 1950, no. 299).

342. Schlumberger 1892a:74; 1903:47 and figs. 3–4; Seligmann 1910:2:443, fig. 230; Perdrizet 1922:27, figs. 7–8; Dunbabin and Dickie 1983:33 and Plate 8c; Russell 1995:40 n.18. See also above, p. 36.

each side, and from below by a scorpion, serpent and ibis. The word *phthonos* ("envy") appears over the daggers and the whole is encircled by the inscription, "Seal of Solomon, drive away all evil from the bearer" (*Sphragis Solomônis apodioxon pan kakon apo tou phorounto[s]*).

Illus. 2.6
Byzantine silver Seal of Solomon medallion amulet depicting, left, Solomon as cavalier spearing a prostrate demoness and, right, an Evil Eye (alias *phthonos*/envy) under attack (from Seligmann 1910 2:443, fig. 230; description in Vol. 2:313–14)

A depiction of an Evil Eye appears on an oval copper plate with a loop (from Jaffa and now in the Museum of Notre-Dame de France in Jerusalem). On the obverse an Evil Eye is attacked by three daggers, and from below by an ibis, scorpion, serpent, and two erect lions. Above is the inscription, "*Iaoth, Sabaoth, Michael*." The reverse shows Solomon in military attire lancing a demoness on the ground, under which is a striding lion on the right and the inscription "There is one God, who conquers Evil" (*Eis Theos, ho nikôn ta kaka*).[343]

A similar depiction of an Evil Eye under attack appears on a Byzantine bronze amulet from Beirut, Syria. On the obverse, an Evil Eye is assaulted from above by three daggers and a trident, from below by an ostrich, scorpion, and serpent, and from the sides by two erect lions. Above, the inscription reads, "Yah[weh] Sabao[th]" (*Iaô Sabaô*)." The reverse shows Solomon as cavalier lancing a prostrate demoness and below that a striding lion. The inscription reads, "There is one God who conquers evil" (*Eis Theos ho nikôn ta kaka*).[344]

---

343. Perdrizet 1903:49; Meisen 1950:171. For an amulet (now in Brussels) with a virtually identical design see Perdrizet 1903:49 n. 1; Meisen 1950:171; and Gitler 1990:371.

344. Schlumberger 1892a:82, no. 10 with illustration XVI; Schlumberger 1903:49 and figs. 5 and 6; Meisen 1950:171.

A bronze amulet from Syria, with a loop for wearing as a pendent, depicts on its obverse a cavalier with nimbus lancing a prostrate demoness, with a lion below, and the inscription, "One God who conquers evil." The reverse displays an Evil Eye attacked by a lion, an ibis, a snake, a scorpion, a leopard (?), a trident, and a spear and an inscription reading, "*Iaô Sabaôth Michael, help!*"[345]

An amulet from Syria, with a loop for wearing as a pendent, has on the obverse an Evil Eye beside which is an ibis with spread wings and bearing a serpent. In the background is an unidentifiable object. Above stands the inscription, *Iaô Sabaô Pinô*. On the reverse side is a galloping cavalier with nimbus, spearinging a demoness lying on the ground, with the same inscription, *Iaô Sabaô Pinô*.[346]

A bronze amulet from Beirut, Syria, with the same cavalier and inscription on its reverse side, shows on its obverse an Evil Eye under attack with an inscription reading, PIPOCN OILOSEIB ISEUTHEIA KOLEANDR OSTROUTHO KAMHLOS APOLLO, to be read, *hippos, noilos (moilos), eibis, eutheia kôlê andros, strouthokamêlos, Apollô* ("horse, Nile-Ibis, male member, ostrich, Apollo").[347] Below is a lion turned toward the right with mane and open mouth.

A bronze Byzantine amulet from Cyzicus in Phrygia, Asia Minor (late third century) is replete with particular detail. On its reverse side (right) an angel (Araaf) on the right faces a cavalier (Solomon), who from his horse is spearing a demoness lying on the ground. Above the horse, a star, and below, a serpent, move toward the demoness. The inscription reads: "Flee, Loathsome One, Solomon, along with the angel Araaf, is chasing you" (*pheuge memisimeni. Solomonos dioki se angelos Araaph*). The reverse side (left) shows busts of Sun and Moon with burning torches and between them a Trisagion beneath which are the letters R P S S S.[348] Beneath them is a serpent and a lion with open mouth springing over a prostrate demoness and charging to the right to attack a large Evil Eye. The inscription reads: "Michael, Gabriel, Uriel, Raphael: protect the bearer [of this amulet]" (*Michael, Gabriel, Uriel, Raphael, diaphylaxon ton phorounta*).[349]

345. Bonner 1950, no. 299; Kelsey Museum, University of Michigan, no. 26115.

346. Schlumberger 1892a:81, no. 8; Meisen 1950:171.

347. *BCH* 3 (1879): 267; and Schlumberger 1892a:89, no. 7; Meisen 1950:171–72. Meisen reads *noilos (moilos) eibis* as *neiloseibis* ("Nile-Ibis"), as proposed by Perdrizet 1922:31–32 and accepted by Meisen 1950:172.

348. Seligmann 1910 2:315, without explanation, takes the letters RPSSS to represent the number 666, the number of the beast in Rev 13:18. The Greek letters Π Ι Π Ι individually surround the entire scene.

349. Perdrizet 1903:46–47 and figs. 1, 2; Seligmann 1910 2:440, fig. 233, description

Early Christianity (and Islam) through Late Antiquity 139

Illus. 2.7
Christian Byzantine bronze medallion amulet from Cyzikus, in Mysia, Asia Minor, depicting (obverse, left) an Evil Eye attacked by a charging lion and (reverse, right); Solomon as cavalier spearing a prostrate demoness (from Seligmann 1910 2:449, fig. 23); description in Vol. 2:314-15

A medallion amulet from Lydia, Asia Minor, shows Jesus Christ with a cross-nimbus, and on right and left a Sun and Moon and two bowing angels. Below the demoness representing an Evil Eye is a creeping serpent and springing lion. The surrounding inscription reads, "Seal of the living God, protect the bearer. Holy, holy, holy" (*Sphragis tou zôntos Theou. Phylaxon ton phorounta. Hagios, Hagios, Hagios*). On the reverse is Solomon as cavalier lancing the Evil Eye demoness toward which a serpent creeps. Depicted also are a star, the angel Araaph with nimbus, a cross with Christ monogram and the letters Alpha and Omega. The surrounding inscription reads, "+ Flee, Loathsome One, Araaf the angel and Solomon chase you from the bearer." (+ *Pheugê, misimenê, Araaph ho angelos se dioki ke Salomon apo tou phorout[os]*).[350]

A medallion amulet from Carthage shows on one side an angel boring a demon with a cross-lance, with the inscription (following a cross), "Flee, Loathsome One, Araaf the angel is chasing you" (+ *Pheugê, misimenê, dioki se ho angelos Araaph*). On the reverse, Christ stands between two angels, and below Solomon as cavalier slays a demon with his lance. The surrounding inscription reads, "Seal of Solomon, Help John" (*Sphragis Solomounos, Boêthi Ioannou*).[351]

---

on 2:314-15;Dunbabin 1991:33 and Plate 5, fig. d.
    350. *BCH* 1893: 638; Perdrizet 1903:48-49, no. 4; Meisen 1950:172.
    351. Perdrizet 1903:48, no. 3; Meisen 1950:172.

Illus. 2.8
Christian Byzantine copper medallion amulet depicting, on the damaged left, the Three Wise Men and the Virgin Mary with the infant Jesus, and, right, Solomon riding a lion attacking an Evil Eye and prostrate demoness below (from Seligmann 1910 2:315 and p. 453, fig. 234).

A Byzantine copper medallion from Constantinople, severely damaged, has a hole indicating its use as a pendent for wearing. On its reverse side (left) it depicts a seated Virgin Mary with the infant Jesus, the three Magi standing before her and in the background the inscription "Christ conquers you" (*Christos nika se*). Below her are the words, "Emma[nuel], Go[d]" (*Emma[nouê]l The[os]*). The surrounding inscription reads, "+ Flee, Loathsome One, the angel Araaf, along with Uriel, is chasing you; flee, Loathsome One" (+ *pheuge memisimeni. dioki se ho angelos Archaph kai Ouriêl, pheuge misoumenê*) The reverse (right) shows a cavalier (Solomon) with lance on top of a lion charging right toward a prostrate demoness; on right, a small demon with upraised arms, a serpent devouring an Evil Eye, and above this a row of potent letters. Above the whole scene are depictions of Sun (behind which is the word *ENEISOS* [?]) and Moon deities, other signs, a star, and a crescent moon. The surrounding inscription reads: "The Son of the highest God is chasing you" (*Tokos Theou hypa[t]ou diokei se*) and "the Lo[rd] Go[d] with a sharper dagger" (*Ky[rios] The[os] machera oxuteron ileos*).[352]

A bronze amulet from Beirut, Lebanon, partially damaged, shows a lion advancing on an Evil Eye. Of the legend, only the names Gabriel and Uriel are discernable.[353]

On a damaged copper medallion with loophole (the Brussels Cabinet of Medallions),[354] the only discernable features are the rear part of a lion,

---

352. Schumberger 1892a:77, no. 3 with illustration; Meisen 1950:173.
353. Schlumberger 1892a:81–82, no. 9 with illustration; Meisen 1950:173.
354. Schlumberger 1892a:78, no. 4 and pp. 83–84, nos. 12–14 for further examples.

which originally ended in a phallus, and the inscription, "Heal from envy and do not cast the Evil Eye" (*UGENETE ZHLOU KAI MH BASKAINE*) and the further words, *TOIS BASKANOIS KATAPROKTO TRUPANON*, which Meisen has taken as "an obscene exclamation."[355] The Greek verb *trypaô* ("bore, pierce through") is used in an obscene sense in Theocritus *Idylls* 5.42 and *Anthologia Palatina* 4.243 (Antistius). The related noun, *to trypanon*, denotes a carpenter's tool, a borer or auger. Meisen does not venture a translation, but "a borer up the ass of Evil Eye possessors" might capture its sense.[356]

An apotropaic cavalier figure appears in a wall fresco of the Christian monastery of St. Apollo at Bawait, Upper Egypt (fourth to sixth century CE).[357] It depicts a cavalier, identified by Perdrizet as Saint Sisinnios the Parthian, martyred by emperor Maximian (286–305 CE). From horseback the cavalier saint spears a female figure on the ground (lower left). This female demon, named "Alabasdria" in the fresco, is linked by Perdrizet with the demoness *Gyllou*, kidnapper of children, alias *Baskosynê* ("Evil Eye"), slayer of children. Above the head of the female demon in this composite design is an Evil Eye pierced by three daggers from above and attacked from below by an ibis, two serpents and a scorpion. An owl and other beasts and demons in animal form (crocodile, centaur, hyenas) are also depicted. On the right of the horse and rider are a winged female creature/mermaid named as daughter of the demoness and a young centaur with harpoon (and phallus?).[358] The Bawait fresco as a whole provided the

Illus. 2.9
Fresco at the monastery of St. Apollo, Bawait, Egypt (fourth–sixth century CE) of St. Sisinnios the Parthian as cavalier spearing a prostrate infanticidal demoness named Alabasdria (alias Gylou), and, above the demoness, an Evil Eye attacked by three daggers from above, an ibis, two serpents, and a scorpion
(from Perdrizet 1922:14, fig. 6)

355. Meisen 1950:173.

356. Meisen (1950:173) includes in his list a badly damaged clay urn from Königshofen in Elsass (fourth century CE), on which the attacked Eye and circle of enemies is only recognizable through comparison with other similar monuments.

357. Now in Egypt's Cairo Museum.

358. Perdrizet 1922:13–15 and fig.6 (p. 14); Naveh and Shaked 1987:120, fig. 20; Dunbabin 1991:32–33; Foskolou 2005:256–57 and plate 21.6. On Christian cavalier figures of the Sisinnios type see Perdrizet 1926:5–27; Peterson 1926:96–109; Leclercq 1950; Robert 1981:33–34 (Sisinnios also with St. Michael); Fauth 1999.

monastery a potent safeguard against the Evil Eye with an assembly of anti-Evil Eye images that are also encountered elsewhere.

The figure of the demoness who kidnaps or slays children has a long pedigree reaching back to Mesopotamian incantations. The demoness was identified variously as Lilitu or Lamashtu (Mesopotamian), Lilith (Hebrew), Lilita or Malwita (Syriac), or Gyllou, Gello, Gilo (Greek),[359] A recent study on Syriac charms by Alexey Lyavdansky (2011) concludes that numerous texts demonstrate that

> the concept in question may have been born in Ancient Mesopotamia not later than [the] Old Babylonian period (1800–1600 B.CE). It was borrowed by adjacent Aramaic-speaking people in Syria, as attested by the text from Arslan Tash (ca. VII c. B.CE), and by the creators of Aramaic magic bowls in Sassanian Mesopotamia (V–VII c. CE). It is most natural to think that the 'strangling female demon' was inherited by the tradition of Syriac charms from the language of Aramaic magic bowls together with many other figures, motives and formulas, common to these two traditions. The borrowing of a concept from Byzantine magic is possible in principle, but less feasible in this particular case.[360]

In the course of this history, the figure, it is now evident, also was associated with the Evil Eye, whose personification as demoness was identified as *Baskosynê* ("Evil Eye").

In the medieval *Prayers* or *Legends of Saint Sisinnios*, the demoness Gylou is said to have taken away six infants of a certain woman named Meletine prior to a visit of St. Sisinnios who comes to aid her.[361] This demoness, who admits to twelve other names, is the figure that appears on many cavalier anti-Evil Eye amulets. In the late *Legend* (or *Prayer*) *of St. Michael*, in which the archangel Michael encounters an Evil Eye,[362] the demoness is called not Gylou but rather *Baskosynê*: "Fear, O Evil Eye, the great name of God" (*phobêthêti, Baskosynê, to mega onoma tou theou*)."[363] *Gylou* and *Baskosynê/Baskania* are both considered demonesses that take the lives of

---

359. On the demoness Gello/Gyllo etc. see Spier 1993:60–62; Johnston 1995; Hartnup 2004:4–6.

360. Lyavdansky 2011:15–21.

361. For the Greek text and French translation see Perdrizet 1922:16–18; on Gylou see Perdrizet 1922:19–25.

362. Text in Reitzenstein (*Poimandres* 1904:295–98), according to the fifteenth-century Paris ms 2316.

363. Reitzenstein 1904:297; Perdrizet 1922:24, 30; Meisen 1950:159; Robert 1981: 30.

new-borns, akin to the ancient Mesopotamian demoness Lamashtu and her Hebrew equivalent, Lilith.[364]

An amuletic two-sided bronze plaque (Syrian or Palestinian provenance) presents on the obverse a haloed cavalier spearing from horseback a prostrate demoness with lion below facing right and the inscription, "One God who conquers evil." On the reverse is an attacked Evil Eye pierced from above by a trident and spearhead (or nail) and attacked from below by five creatures (lion, ibis/stork, serpent, scorpion, and hyena or leopard), with the inscription, "Iaô, Sabaôth, Michael help." The amulet could be either Jewish or Christian.[365]

An amuletic two-sided medallion from Cyzicus in Phrygia, Asia Minor, depicts on the obverse an angel (Araaf) on the right facing a cavalier (Solomon) spearing from his horse a demoness lying on the ground. Above the horse, a star and a serpent move toward the demoness. The inscription reads: "Flee, Loathsome One, Solomon, along with the angel Araaf, is chasing you" (*pheuge memisimeni. Solomonos dioki se angelos Araaph*). The reverse shows busts of Sun and Moon with burning torches and between them a Trisagion. Beneath them is a lion with open mouth springing over a demoness lying on ground and attacking a large Evil Eye. The inscription reads: "Michael, Gabriel, Uriel, Raphael, protect the bearer [of this amulet]." The amulet could be either Jewish or Christian.[366]

There can be little doubt that for the wearers of these amulets, predominantly Christians, the main threat to be averted was that posed by the Evil Eye. Most of them "identified the demon who is pierced and trampled specifically with the power which works through the Evil Eye, *phthonos* or *baskania* or *baskosynê*."[367] The figure of the cavalier conquering evil underwent modification over the centuries from its Ptolemaic Egyptian origin to its Jewish adaptation to the figure of Solomon (third century CE) and then its Christian adaptation to Sisinnios and other saints and warrior figures (George, Theodore and, later, Demetrius). The chief point of the icon,

---

364. On Saint Sisinnios, the Archangel Michael and the Demoness Gylou see Greenfield 1989; Foskolou 2005:256–57; on Gello, Gylo, Gylou, Yello, see also Spier 1993; Lyavdansky 2011. On Lamashtu and Lilith see Gordon 1957; Wasserman 1995; van der Toorn 1999; Wiggermann 2000; Foskolou 2005 and, previously, Vol. 1, chap. 2 and Vol. 3, chap. 1.

365. Kelsy Museum of Archaeology, University of Michigan, no. 26115 = Bonner 1950, no. 299; Dunbabin 1991:33 and Plate 5e.

366. Perdrizet 1903:46–47 and figs. 1 and 2; Dunbabin 1991:33 and Plate 5, fig. d.

367. Dunbabin 1991:33.

however, remained constant": the rider receives from God the power to triumph over evil,"[368] especially over the deadly Evil Eye.

The Gesture of the Mano fica

A recurrent protective gesture on amulets is that of the *mano fica*. In one instance, this gesture forms one end of a Christian amulet shaped like a phallus and a fish; it illustrates the combining of apotropaic symbols on Christian anti-Evil Eye amulets.[369]

The Gesture of the Mano Cornuta

The fourth-century sarcophagus of Junius Bassus (died 359 CE), considered the most famous instance of early Christian relief sculpture, depicts a key figure in the story of Jesus Christ and his making the anti-Evil Eye gesture of a *mano cornuta*.[370] Among the several scenes carved on the sarcophagus, which is adorned with motifs of both pagan and Christian cultures, is a double scene in the top row of the front side depicting the trial of Jesus before Pontius Pilate. In the course of washing his hands, Pilate has raised his left hand to his chin; his right hand, resting on his left thigh, makes the gesture of a *mano cornuta*.[371] Speculating about why this gesture should be included in this scene, we might recall that the biblical account of the trial of Jesus before Pilate (Mark 15:1–15/Matt 27:1–26) states that Pilate perceived that "it was out of envy (*phthonon*) that the chief priests had delivered him [Jesus] up" (Mark 15:10; cf. Matt 27:18). The artist, aware of the conventional association of envy and the Evil Eye, likely portrayed Pilate as making this precautionary gesture against the Evil-Eyed envy of the Judean authorities.

---

368. Walter 1989–90:42.

369. See Dölger 1922 2:444; 3, plate 77.4, and above, p. 103. On the *mano fica* in Greek and Roman cultures see Vol. 2:162, 179, 180–83, 212–14, and passim.

370. This sarcophagus, made for the Christian burial of the recently converted Roman magistrate Junius Bassus, originally was placed under Old St. Peter's Basilica in Rome. It is now below the modern basilica in the Museo Storico del Tesoro della Basilica di San Pietro (Museum of Saint Peter's Basilica) in the Vatican.

371. Lowrie 1947:89.

Early Christianity (and Islam) through Late Antiquity 145

Illus. 2.10
Scene on sarcophagus of Junius Bassus (359 CE): Pontius Pilate about to wash his hands, making the sign of the *mano cornuta*

A stunning ceiling mosaic of the sixth-century church of San Vitale in Ravenna depicts a scene of an altar at which the biblical persons Abel (on the left) and Abraham or Melchizedek (on the right) are offering sacrifices. Frederick Thomas Elworthy and Siegfried Seligmann both include this sample of mosaic art in their classic works on the Evil Eye.[372] From heaven above, a right hand of God extends downward toward the altar and, according to Elworthy and Seligmann, is making the manual gesture of a *mano cornuta*.[373] There are other examples in this and other churches of Ravenna of a divine hand extended from heaven.[374] A seated figure of St. Luke also appears to be making the *mano cornuta* gesture with his right hand.[375] "In no other case known to the writer," Elworthy states, "does the *Dextera Dei* appear so unmistakably as a *mano cornuta*" as in the Abel-Abraham/Melchizedek mosaic.[376] The image, however, it must be conceded, is too indistinct to make a conclusive judgment and thus the significance of this gesture also is open to question.[377]

---

372. Elworthy 1895/1958:265–66 and fig. 113; Seligmann 1910 1:385, fig. 71; 2:137. On this mosaic see also Vol. 2:185, 187.

373. Elworthy 1958/1895:266; Seligmann 1910 2:137

374. Elworthy 1895/1958:268, fig. 116; 269, fig. 117.

375. Ibid., 266, fig. 114; also Seligmann 1910:2:137 and 1:389, fig. 72.

376. Elworthy 1895/1958:266.

377. Engemann (1980) insists that none of the ancient pictorial depictions of this gesture, either in content or context, can be shown to have had the aim of warding off evil or insult (1980:492, 498) and claims (1980:492) that the gesture of the *mano cornuta* does not appear on ancient amulets (in contrast to the frequent occurrence of the *mano fica*).

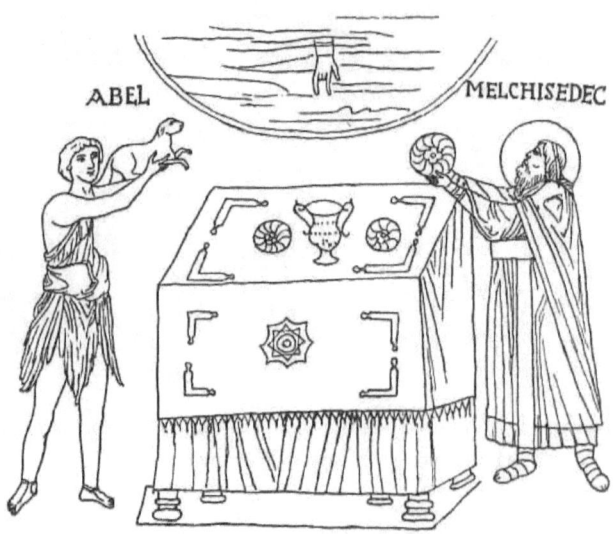

Illus. 2.11
Sketch of the ceiling mosaic, Basilica of San Vitale, Ravenna (sixth century CE)
(from Seligmann 1910, 1:385, fig. 71; also 389, fig. 72)

Various Other Apotropaic Figures and Objects

Figures of the anchor cross, the tau cross, dove, lamb, shepherd, and fish also appear together with other anti-Evil Eye symbols (Meisen 1950:164).

The figure of a *phallus* appears on a bas-relief from Beirut, Lebanon (Syria), regarded by Leclercq as Christian.[378] The accompanying inscription reads "Evil-Eyer, be slain" (*PATAXI BASKANOS*).[379]

The *owl*, a bird of ill omen in Roman culture, also is among these representations, symbolizing either an envious Evil Eye[380] or a power counteracting the Evil Eye, in accord with the principle of "like against like (*similia similibus*)."[381] Several Jewish-Christian amulets of Late Antiquity found in the vicinity of Tunis, North Africa, show on the face of the amulet an owl symbolizing envy and the devil,[382] and an inscription on the reverse com-

378. Leclercq 1924:1844.

379. Waddington 1870: nos. 2360, 2406; Perdrizet 1900:293. See also previously, Vol. 2.

380. So Perdrizet 1922:29; Meisen 1950:173, cf. also Meisen 1950:146, 153, 173–74 for the owl on Greek and apotropaics.

381. Meisen 1950:173–74, 153.

382. Merlin 1940:489.

bating *invidia*/envy. On these medallions and related monuments, *invidia*/envy was equated with an *oculus invidiosus*, i.e. an envious Evil Eye.[383] Similar owl amulets with the Latin inscription *Invidia invidiosa* ("envious Envy") were found in Carthage and the Tunisian cities of Kef and Haidra.[384]

A bronze disk amulet from Carthage shows an owl with six stars and the inscription, "The lion of the tribe of Judah [along with] Gabriel and Victory has conquered you" (*Bicit* [*t* in the form of a cross] *te leo de tribus Juda G[abriel] Vic[toria]*). On the reverse is inscribed, in part, "+ Envious Envy" with a reference to the "bird of the night sky."[385]

A bronze disk amulet from Carthage with an owl and six stars on the obverse has an inscription that reads, "The lion of the tribe of Judah [along with] Gabriel and Victory has conquered you" (*Bici[t in the form of a cross] te leo de tribus Juda G[abriel] Vic[toria]*). An inscription on the reverse names the amulet's bearer and reads:

> Envious envy, the bird of the night sky suffers envy; there is nothing for you to do against a soul that is pure and unstained, whose name is Istefania.
>
> + *Invidia invidiosa, invidia[m] patiatu[r] avis qui se noctu celum fecerit nihil tibi ad anima pura et munda, qu[ae] vocatur Istefania* +.[386]

A copper amulet with loop from Carthage shows an owl with spread wings and five stars, with the surrounding inscription, "The lion of the tribe of Judah and root of David has conquered" (*Vicit leo de tribus Juda radix David*). The inscription on the reverse appears above two palms and reads,

> Envious Envy, may nothing weary a pure and unstained soul.
>
> *Invidia invidiosa, nihil taedeat animam puram et [m]undam.*[387]

A copper amulet with a loop for wearing from Kef in Tunisia[388] has, on the obverse, an owl with a surrounding inscription reading in part, "the arm of God will bind you" (*Ligabit te brachium Dei . . .*).[389] The inscription of the

383. Merlin 1940:489 and n.4.

384. Ibid., 487–88; Meisen 1950:173–74.

385. + *Invidia Invidiosa. Invicta adstat, ur[get] avis*, or as a variant reading: *Inbicia dasiatur abis quis ne nontum collum fecerit. Istonfian;* in *Bulletin de Comité* (1914): clxxxvii–clxxxviii and *Bulletin de Comité* 1916:137–45; Meisen 1950:173–74.

386. *Bulletin du Comité* (1928):202–8; Meisen 1950:174.

387. A variant reading: *nihil timeat anima pura et muda, [M]ichael Rafael Uriel Gabriel. Victoria. Bulletin de Comité* (1916):136; Meisen 1950:174.

388. In the collection of medallions of the Queen of Holland in Den Haag.

389. *Ligabit te brachium Dei. Id non praevaleat infl[austum]. Quiriacdi, in Deo vivas.*

reverse reads in part, "Envious Envy, there is nothing for you to do against a soul that is pure and unstained . . . the arm of God and of Christ and the Seal of Solomon will bind you . . . peace to this house."[390]

A lead amulet from Haidra (ancient Ammaedura) in Tunisia likewise has on the obverse an owl and on the reverse the inscription, "Envious Envy, there is nothing for you to do against a soul that is pure and unstained" (*Invidia invidiosa n[i]hil tibi ad anima[m] pura[m] et munda[m]*).[391]

A Carthaginian Christian medallion amulet (c. sixth–seventh century CE) has an owl surrounded by six stars with an inscription from Rev 5:6: *bicit leo de tribu Iuda, radix David* ("the lion from the tribe of Judah, root of David, has conquered") and on the reverse,

> Envious Envy, there is nothing for you to do against a soul that is pure and unstained, Michael, Raphael, Uriel, Gabriel + Victoria.
>
> *Invidia invidiosa, nihil tibi ad anima pura et munda. Michael, Raphael, Uriel, Gabriel + Victoria.*[392]

The Bawait fresco from the same period, with Solomon as cavalier lancing an Evil Eye, also shows an owl over an Evil Eye under attack; see above, p. 141 and Illus. 2.9.

A copper medallion from Rome bears an owl, encircled with the word *Dominus* and seven stars. The whole is encircled with the inscription, "The lion from the tribe of Judah [and] root of David has conquered you" (*Bicit te leo de tribu Juda radix Davit*). The reverse has a conjuration inscription reading:

Illus. 2.12
Christian Carthaginian medallion amulet depicting an owl surrounded by six stars, with an inscription from Rev 5:6 (from Perdrizet 1922:30, fig. 10)

> Jesus Christ. The arm of God and Seal of Solomon will bind you. Nocturnal bird, may you have no power [to attack] a pure soul and [have authority] over [it], whoever you might be.

390. *Invidi[a] [i]nvidiosa. Nihil tibi ad anima pura et munda. Quiriacei, sata maligna non tibi p[ra]evalea[n]t. Ligabit te Dei brachium dei et Christi et signu[m] et sigillu[m] Solomo[nis]+ Paxcasa*; see Reuvens 1830:29–32; Merlin 1940:487–88; Meisen 1950:174.

391. Merlin 1940:486–93; Meisen 1950:174. For two other owl amulets from Carthage and Dougga see Merlin 1940:488, nos. 6 and 7.

392. ILCV 1.2388 A/B illustrated in Perdrizet 1922:30, fig. 10 and Opelt 1966: col. 899.

Iesus Christus. Ligabit te bratius dei [brachium Dei] et sigillus Salomonis. Abis notturna, non baleas [accedere] ad anima[m] pura[m] et supra [eam potestatem habere], quisvis sis.[393]

Among the apotropaic objects used by Christians to thwart the Evil Eye and other pernicious forces were, in addition to the amulets already mentioned, *bullae*, which like medallions, were worn as pendants, the image of the phallus or the fish, the Christian cross, engraved finger rings and Solomon's ring, bells and phylacteries.[394]

Small metal or leather containers (*bullae*) containing apotropaic texts were worn as neck pendants by children and women, identical to pagan practice and similar to the Jewish use of phylacteries.[395] The texts of the Christians, however, were of the Lord's Prayer and passages from the Gospels and other sacred writings deemed to be particularly powerful.[396] John Chrysostom attributed apotropaic power to such texts of the Gospels.[397] Such a capsule with a Gospel excerpt was sent by Gregory the Great to Queen Theolinde for her son Adulwaldus.[398] Medallions had loops or holes through which cords were passed to allow them also to be worn as apotropaics, as mentioned above.

The cross and making the sign of the cross were specifically Christian means for warding off evil and the Evil Eye.[399] This was explicitly encouraged by John Chrysostom.[400] Crosses affixed to door lintels of a house in Antioch, Syria, were accompanied by an inscription declaring the power of the cross to ward off the Evil Eye. It reads: "Of this house the Lord shall

393. De Rossi 1869:61–62; *Bulletin de Comité* (1916):139–40; Perdrizet 1922:29; Merlin 1940:487–88; Meisen 1950:174.

394. Dobschütz 1910:422–23, 425–28; Meisen 1950:157–77; Russell 1995:38–43.

395. See John Chrysostom, *Stat.* (PG 49.196); *Hom. Matt.* 72 (PG 58. 669); Isadore of Pelusiam, *Epistle* 2.150 (PG 78. 603–604); see Dölger 1932b for a child's *bulla* with *Chi Rho* and *Alpha* and *Omega*; on *bulla*, see further, Leclercq 1910.

396. See Dobschütz 1910:425; Meisen 1950:170. See also above "Passages from the Sacred Scriptures." For photographs of such containers from Anemurium, see Russell 1995: figs. 9 and 10.

397. John Chrysostom, *Hom. Jo.* 32.3 (PG 59.186-88); *Hom. 1 Cor. 43.4* (PG 61.372-74); *Stat., Hom. 19. 4* (PG 49.195-98).

398. Gregory the Great, *Epistle* 14.12 (PL 77.1316); Meisen 1950:170.

399. For this practice see also Dölger 1932a; cf. also above, pp. 97, 101–4, 107–9, 111, 122–24, 127–28, 130, 136, 139, 146, 148.

400. John Chrysostom, *Adv. Jud.* 8. 8 (PG 48.939-942; *Catech. illum.* 2 (PG 49. 240, 246); *Hom. Matt. 54.4* on Matt. 4 (PG 58:536-538); *Hom. Matt.* (*De adoratione pretiosae crucis*, PG 58:838); *Hom. 1 Cor.* 12.13 on 4:10 (PG 61.105-6); *Hom. Col.* 8.5 on 3:5-7 (PG 62.357-360). See also Cyril of Jerusalem, *Catech.* 13.36 (PG 33.816); Dobschütz 1910:426-27; Budge 1930:336-49, 359-53.

guard the entrance and the exit; for, the cross being set before, no malignant eye [= Evil Eye] shall prevail against it."[401]

An amulet could have the shape of a cross itself.[402] Crosses were also put on objects of adornment, especially rings, apparel and other articles of clothing, lamps, combs, sarcophaguses, and grave inscriptions. Cross amulets and coins with crosses have been found at various grave sites (Meisen 1950:165).[403]

A modern Greek Orthodox custom consists of attaching a small cloth Greek cross to one's clothing, for males on the inside of their coat jacket lapel, to ward off the Evil Eye. These apotropaic crosses are often given as gifts.[404]

Small bells (*tintinnabula*) were also found in number at Anemurium, Asia Minor.[405] Bells were employed by Christians, as by Israelites and pagans, to ward off the Evil Eye,[406] another practice known and condemned by John Chrysostom (*Hom. 1 Cor. 12.13* on 4:6, PG 61.105).

CHRISTIAN LITURGICAL AND ECCLESIASTICAL APOTROPAIC PRACTICE

Ancient fear of the Evil Eye and its identification by the Greek and Latin church fathers as a tool of the Devil left a lasting mark on Greek cultural history down to the present. Beside the evidence of Evil Eye belief and practice, however, in contemporary daily Greek culture,[407] this dread of the Evil

---

401. Downey 1962:133. See also Prentice 1906:141. For similar Christian formulas averting *phthonos* by name see IGLSyr 4.1909 and Grégoire 1922, no. 230.

402. See Meisen 1950:164, with reference to a sixth-century golden cross found in 1863, San Lorenzo, Rome, on the breast of the deceased. The cross was hollowed out in order to contain relics. On it was written in cruciform on both sides: "the cross is life for me; for you, Death, an enemy. God Immanuel is with us" (*crux est vita mihi, Mors, inimice, tibi* and *Emmanouêl nobiscum Deus*).

403. On the cross as apotropaic see also Dölger 1932a.

404. Personal communication of George Kotsovalis, a Greek Orthodox student at the University of San Francisco. On modern Greek customs see Arnaud 1911 (liturgical), 1912; Campbell 1964:324–38; Blum and Blum 1970:221. 310; Dionisopolos-Mass 1976; Papanikolas 2002; Apostolides 2008:52–55; Chryssanthopolou 2008; Roussou 2014.

405. Russell 1995:42–43 and fig. 11 (photograph of one of four bells).

406. Russell 1995:42–43. On the apotropaic function of bells against the Evil Eye see Espérandieu 1919; Trumpf-Lyritzaki 1981:172–75; Espérandieu et al. 1991; Trzcionka 2007:107; and previously, Vol. 2.

407. On Evil Eye belief and practice in modern Greece see Dodwell 1819 2:30–37; Arnaud 1912 (prayer for protection against the Evil Eye, p. 386); Lawson 1910:8–15; Schmidt 1913; Hardie 1923/1992; Gubbins 1946; Herter 1950; Georges 1962; Campbell

Eye appears in the official liturgy of the Greek Orthodox Church. A prayer for the deliverance of a child from the Evil Eye and the forces of evil, for example, in the *Mikron Evchologion of the Greek Orthodox Church*, asks for protection from, among other things, "every Satanic attack" and "the Evil eye of mischievous and wicked men":

> Remove, drive away and banish every diabolical activity (*diabolikin energeian*) every Satan attack (*satanikin ephodon*) and every plot, evil curiosity and injury, and the evil eye (*ophthalmon baskanian*) of mischievous and wicked men... where it was brought about by beauty or bravery, or happiness, or jealousy and envy (*phthonou*) or evil eye (*baskanias*) ... look down on this Thy creature and watch over him (her)and send him (her) an angel of peace, a mighty guardian of soul and body who will rebuke and banish from him (her) every wicked intention, every spell and evil eye (*baskanian*) of the envious [demons] and envious men...[408]

Given the association of the Evil Eye with the Devil, the exorcism of the one entailed an exorcism of the other.

A prayer for a woman after childbirth includes a request for her preservation from "every approach of invisible spirits; yea, O Lord, from sickness and infirmity, from jealousy and envy, and from the evil eye," and for mercy on her and the infant.[409] On the Liturgy of St. Mark and the prayer for deliverance from envy and Satan, see above, p. 96.

POPULAR REMEDIES OF EVIL EYE INJURIES

Beyond liturgical practices, popular remedies for healing children of suspected Evil Eye injury have been found to be widespread in modern Greek rural areas.[410] A Christian incantation from West Macedonia (Bogatsko) for the healing of a child with spittle and licking follows the recitation of forty "Our Fathers": "The cow gave birth to a calf; its mother, licking it, undid the

---

1964: 324–38; Blum and Blum, 1965; Dionisopoulos-Mass 1976; Herzfeld 1981, 1984, 1986; Storace 1997; Aquaro 2004.

408. Aquaro 2004:81, following the translation of Rev. Evagoras Constantinides, *Mikron Evchologionon i Agiasmatarion* 1989:194–15. On the prayer see Aquaro 2004: 80–86.

409. Aquaro 2004:85, citing Saint Tikhon's Monastery Research Library and Collection 1998:4. On the Evil Eye and the Greek Orthodox liturgy (including a prayer for the liberation of the ill from the Evil Eye), see also Arnaud 1911:78–80.

410. Hardie 1992/1923:114–22.

Evil Eye with her spittle. And I, the mother, have undone the evil spell by licking. May the child live and prosper and not suffer any harm!"[411]

Spittle used to heal injury from the Evil Eye continues a practice of ancient time[412] and recalls Paul's reference to prophylactic spitting in his letter to the Galatians.[413] In some Greek villages, a cross known as a *monokero* (carved by monks on Mt. Athos) is used to cure people attacked by the Evil Eye (Aquaro 2004:92). Regina Dionisopoulos-Mass (1976:44–51) describes further modern Greek practices involving religious formulas for warding off, or healing injury from, the Evil Eye. Roy Kotansky has reported on an ancient Christian gold lamella (second century CE) that was designed to relieve a severe headache brought on by the demon *Gorgôpa*.[414] The lamella reads: "Turn away, O Jesus, the Grim-Faced One (*Gorgôpa*) and on behalf of your maidservant her headache . . ."[415] The severed head of the Gorgon/Medusa (notorious caster of the Evil Eye) Kotansky plausibly regards as "an appropriate folkloric representation of the headache itself."[416] Far older Greek tradition thus lives on in new Christian appropriation.[417]

The Greek Orthodox legend of St. George, slayer of dragons/demons and reliever of illnesses, is an assimilation to the Jewish and Christian figure of Solomon as cavalier attacking the Evil Eye.[418] This assimilation is a further illustration of the cultural blending of Evil Eye traditions. Patron saint of England and honored around the world, George, the cavalier martyr and saint, is revered also in Islam.

EVIL EYE BELIEF AND PRACTICE IN ISLAM: A BRIEF NOTE

The belief has thrived in Islam since the emergence of Islam as a social and religious movement in sixth-century CE Arabia.[419] The subject deserves a

---

411. Hardie 1992/1923:116; Aquaro 2004:92. For an ancient Coptic amulet designed to heal from fever, the Evil Eye, and other problems see Heidelberg Kopt. 544 discussed by Kelsey 1994.

412. See Vol. 2:19–21, 28, 29, 174–78.

413. See Vol. 3:240–50.

414. Kotansky 2002:37–46.

415. Ibid., 37; cf. PGM XVIIIa.1–4.

416. Ibid., 42.

417. On the Gorgo/Medusa myth and her petrifying ocular gaze see Leclercq 1933; and Vol. 2:133–39, 159, 162, 210, and illustrations 3–6, 28, 53, 54.

418. Aquaro 2004:96–100.

419. On the Evil Eye in Islam see Thomson 1880; Einszler 1889; Garnett 1891; De

discussion that would take us beyond the limits of this study. But given the contemporaneity of Islam's beginnings with the final focus of our study—Jewish and Christian Evil Eye belief and practice in late Roman antiquity—a few brief comments are in order.

Alongside Israel and Christianity, this third "people of the book" also has displayed from the outset a firm belief in the noxious Evil Eye. The belief accompanied Islamic expansion from the Arabian peninsula, Morocco, and the eastern Mediterranean region to India, and was embraced by the various populations of these regions—Muslims, Jews, Christians, and Hindus. In ancient Islam, the Evil Eye (Arabic: *al-'ayn;* or *al-nazra* ["the look"] or *'ayn al-ḥasūd* ("eye of envy"'") or *'ayn ḥārrah* ("hot eye") and its associated practices are closely similar in their features to those of Jewish, Christian and Greco-Roman cultures of antiquity. The eye is conceived as active organ whose glance can injure and destroy. Ibn Khaldun explains the nature and effect of the Evil Eye and its association with envy. It is

> natural and innate. It cannot be left alone. It does not depend on the free choice of its possessor. It is not acquired by him. [It is] an influence exercised by the soul of the person who has the evil eye. A thing or situation appears pleasing to the eye of a person, and he likes it very much. This [circumstance] creates in him envy and the desire to take it away from its owner. Therefore he prefers to destroy him.[420]

The Evil Eye is linked with envy and is thought to be aroused by children, nursing mothers, prized farm animals, fruitful fields, abundant harvests, valuable possessions. Family members, friends, neighbors, passers-by, rivals, and opponents are all potential possessors of the Evil Eye. The malignant glance is said to be a cause of illness, accidents, the drying up of a mother's milk or that of cows and goats; the withering of crops, the failure of a business or the burning down of a home. Praise and admiration arouse an envious Evil Eye. Compliments and declarations of praise must therefore

---

Vaux 1910:457–61; Seligmann 1910 1:16–17, 340–341; 2:341–43, 361–62;Westermarck 1926, 1:417–78; Herber 1927 (Hand of Fatima); Djordjevic 1934; Probst-Biraben 1933, 1936; ed-Dairabī 1940; Koebert 1948; Marçais 1960; Kriss and Kriss-Heinrich 1962; Stillmann 1970:81–94; Spooner 1976; Teitelbaum 1976; Kovalenko 1979, 1981; Ibrahim 1987, 1991, 1994; Fahd 1989:129; Sheikh-Dilthey 1990; Donaldson 1992; Kanafani 1993: Madison and Savage-Smith 1997; Romdon 2000; Krawietz 2002; O'Connor 2004; Abu-Rabia. 2005; Kahl 2006 (Christian and Islam commonalities regarding the Evil Eye); Touhami 2007, 2014, 2014; Campo 2009b; Al-Saleh 2010; Touhami 2010. On Arab and Persian amulets, including those against the Evil Eye, with illustrations, see Budge 1930:33–81. On Arabic proverbs concerning the Evil Eye, see Quatremère 1838 5:233–43.

420. Ibn Khaldun 1967 3:170–71, cited by Fahd, 1989:129.

be accompanied by the expression "Mashallah" ("It is as God has willed"), which credits Allah for the beauty of the object admired and disclaims any envious intent.

A variety of amulets and protectives are employed to defend against the Evil Eye. Small pieces of parchments on which are written the sacred name of God or verses of the Quran are carried in amulets or written on the entrances of family residences and places of occupation. Suras 112, 113, and 114 of the Quran are considered especially potent against the Evil Eye. Protective spells and formulas also are uttered.[421] The beauty of children is concealed and denied by hiding it or calling it ugly. Male infants are left unwashed and called by unflattering names. A "Hand of Fatimah" (*hamsa*) is worn not only as a piece of jewelry and adornment but also as an anti-Evil Eye protective. *Hamsas* adorning household objects such as lampholders, and images of this hand on homes and public buildings serve the same prophylactic purpose.[422] For Muslims, the color blue represents both a dangerous color, and also a color that protects against the Evil Eye (on the principle of "like influences like").[423]

Illus. 2.13
Hand of Fatima (*Hamsa*) as part of a lamp-holder, with apotropaic bells, Morocco (from Seligmann 2:195, fig. 163)

All these features of Islamic Evil Eye belief and practice are closely aligned with, and generally replicate, the belief and practices of the Greco-Roman, Jewish, and Christian cultures of Late Antiquity, with minimal adaptation to specifically Islamic tradition and culture. The concept is disapproved of by orthodox Islam since it seems to deny or ignore the absolute divine power and decree of God. But Evil Eye belief and practice has proved as impossible to eradicate in Islam as in Jewish and Christian circles. It persists today in Islamic folklore and on the fringes of religion and medicine. This issue of

---

421. See Seligmann 1910 1:322–25 for Islamic spoken spells against hostile forces, including an "eye of the envious," "blue Eye," and "every Eye that harms, that is evil."

422. On the Hand of Fatima, a pendent to Israel's Hand of Miriam, see also above, p. 38. On the apotropaic hand see Roheim 1992:219 for this amulet in "North Africa and the Middle East" among Arabs and Jews, citing Westermarck 1926 1:446. On the hand in antiquity and modernity see Seligmann 1910 2:164–88 and figs. 145–64; on Jewish hand amulets, 2:170, 176, 177, 193 and fig. 162; on the hand amulet in Islam, 1:168–172, 199 and fig. 155; 195 and fig. 163, and for the manual gesture of an outstretched hand, 2:178.

423. See Westermarck 1926 1:459; Dundes 1992:284.

Early Christianity (and Islam) through Late Antiquity 155

Evil Eye belief in Islam requires a study of its own. We mention Islamic Evil Eye tradition here because of the emergence of Islam at the close of the period under discussion. Islam's adoption of the belief and its associated practices further illustrates the striking stability and continuity of elements of the Evil Eye belief complex across the cultures of the ancient Circum-Mediterranean world and beyond.

CONCLUSION TO CHAPTER TWO

In the post-biblical period (second–sixth centuries CE), Evil Eye belief and practice in the Circum-Mediterranean world and Middle Eastern world of Late Antiquity showed no signs of waning. The literary, material, and iconographic evidence attests a continued and widespread dread of the envious Evil Eye among Circum-Mediterranean populations, including Jewish, Christian, and Islamic cultures, down through Late Roman antiquity and into the Middle Ages.

The archaeological data is particularly valuable and instructive, James Russell emphasizes, because it "provides a more objective record of how ordinary people coped with the evil eye in their daily lives than the prejudiced testimony of most literary texts."[424] For Byzantine Christians, he concludes, "[t]he worship of Christ and his cross was certainly an essential part of their lives, but it is hard to escape the impression that the control of the unseen force of the evil eye by the time-honored instruments of their ancestors was of more immediate concern to them."[425]

In respect to the written sources, *Jewish* rabbinic tradition attributes an Evil Eye even to Jewish holy men and appeals to the potent figures of Joseph, Solomon, and Miriam for protection. *Christian* theologians trace the Evil Eye to the Devil's malice and seek safeguards in Trinitarian invocations, holy books, Christ monograms, the holy cross, among other apotropaics. *Muslims* deplore the envious Evil Eye as well and prize the prophylactic Hand of Fatimah. Most of the features of Jewish and Christian Evil Eye belief and the means employed for warding off the malignant Eye were indistinguishable from pagan belief and practice, except for the modifications drawn from identifiable Jewish and Christian traditions.[426]

424. Russell 1995:38.
425. Ibid., 50.
426. On apotropaics, including those against the Evil Eye, in the Christian Byzantine and Medieval periods see Scot 1584; Schlumberger 1892a, esp. 74–75 (Evil Eye attacked and *phthonos* in legend), 1895; Seligmann 1910; Laurant 1936; Meisen 1952; Grabar 1974; Loewenthal 1979; Russell 1982, 1987, 1995; Lauer 1983; Vikan 1984;

The most significant, influential, and long-lasting modification made in Christian circles was a tracing of the Evil Eye to the devil, the prince of demons. This directed attention away from the Evil Eye as a personal human flaw, as it appears in the biblical tradition, to its identification with an external demonic entity that attacks and tempts humans and uses them and their eyes as its pernicious tools. This development represents a return to the pagan notion of a demonic force, a *baskanos daimôn*, that is external to the human community but always attacking humans and using them as instruments of evil. Accordingly, the Evil Eye is viewed not only as a *human* phenomenon and cause of disaster, illness, and death. It is, even more importantly, seen as originating with the devil and hence opposed to God, Jesus Christ, and all things godly, to the Church, its well-being, its teachings, and its members.

Evil Eye accusation becomes a tool of ecclesiastical polemic and a weapon for dealing with doctrinal heresy, social non-conformity, and whatever could be branded as deviant and dangerous. Humans taken as fascinators, possessors of an Evil Eye, were regarded not simply as dangerous strangers but as agents of Satan, identifiable with witches, enemies of God, and fair game for heretic trials and witch hunts.

Complain as they might about old wives tales and credulous Christians fearing the Evil Eye, the Church fathers and intellectual elites of this period were incapable of mounting an effective argument or program against the belief and its associated practices. Iconographical evidence attests how, in the waning centuries of Late Antiquity, Evil Eye belief and practice showed no sign of scaling down. The lasting legacy of the Fathers was not putting this potent belief and practice to bed, but only demonizing it and portraying it as a tool of Satan for corrupting gullible human beings. In the subsequent centuries Evil Eye belief and practice continued unabated.

The material evidence from Late Antiquity, in tandem with the literary sources, shows an obvious persistence of concern over the Evil Eye among Circum-Mediterranean cultures down through Late Roman antiquity and into the Middle Ages.

G. H. R. Horsley, analyzing numerous Christian documents of the imperial period, finds that belief in the Evil Eye "is attested frequently in Christian contexts" and regards it an illustration of "the blending of superstition and orthodox faith."[427] Karl Meisen, at the conclusion of his 1950

Culianu 1987; Jolly 1989; Spier 1993, esp. 60–62; Maguire 1994, 1995; Mantantseva 1994; Salmon and Cabre 1998; Hartnup 2004; Hinterberger 2010; Macredes, ed. 2010; Engemann 1969, 1975, 1980, 1981; Engemann et al. 1991; Herdick 2001; Vida 2002; Hintenberger 2010, 2011; Lyavdansky 2011.

427. Horsley 1982 2:208.

study, observed that belief in the Evil Eye did not suddenly disappear with the advent of Christianity but rather continued in lively fashion. Christians fought the Evil Eye with the same means as used by other Circum-Mediterranean peoples, filling it, however, with Christian or Jewish-Christian content.[428]

There is a striking sharing of ideas and motifs associated with the Evil Eye, while at the same time the employment of symbols and motifs specific to Jewish, Jewish-Christian, Christian, and Islamic expressions of the belief. Our evidence demonstrates the remarkable cross-cultural and cross-generational consistency in the ideas and motifs associated with the Evil Eye and its aversion—from 3000 BCE to 600 CE.

Christian evidence, in particular, shows a theological demonization of the Evil Eye and its enlistment in the ecclesiastical polemic against heresy and non-conformity that accompanies and informs Evil Eye belief and practice in the ensuing centuries. As Jewish and Christian cultures spread beyond the Mediterranean basin, subsequently joined by the expansion of Islam and a Gallic westward migration, the belief and its accompanying practices gained a solid foothold in Europe, North Africa, the Byzantine world, and points eastward. Despite the censuring yet vacillating attempts of the church fathers to challenge Evil Eye belief and practice, popular dread of the Evil Eye and efforts to thwart it continued unabated into the Middle Ages and beyond. From the medieval period down to the modern era, the Evil Eye, in ever novel adaptations of a relatively stable complex of beliefs, has continued to arouse human anxieties and haunt humanity's dreams. Notwithstanding the scientific abandonment of the concept of the eye as an active organ projecting energy, and despite the scientific shift from extramission to intromission theory of vision since the 1700s, Evil Eye belief and practice has persisted in haunting the imagination and behavior of philosophers, theologians, social scientists poets, novelists, TV crime families, newspaper cartoons and comic strips and untold numbers of persons seeking to account for causes of misfortune, illness, loss, and death. The legacy of the Evil Eye belief and practice of the ancient world remains in this twenty-first century a persistent focus of fear, fancy, forbiddance, phylaxis, and fascination.

428. Meisen 1950:176–77.

3

EPILOGUE

WE HAVE ARRIVED AT the end of our multi-volume study of the Evil Eye in the Bible and the ancient world. This is hardly the end of the Evil Eye story, however. For this belief has continued down through the centuries to the present day as a persistent dynamo of fear and censure. For over 5,000 years, dread of the Evil Eye and efforts to thwart or avoid its noxious power have haunted the history of western civilization. Our four-volume study has traced the early phases of this history—from Mesopotamian incantations to Late Roman, Byzantine, early Christian, Jewish, and Islamic texts, material objects, and apotropaic words, designs and gestures (c. 3,000 BCE to 600 CE).

The noxious power of the ocular gaze, the hostile glance—of humans, gods, demons, and even animals such as the wolf[1] and an expired hare[2]—for millennia has remained a focus of distress and high anxiety. In this study, following an initial survey of Evil Eye belief and practice from antiquity to the present, the primary focus has been Evil Eye belief and practice in the ancient world from c. 3,000 BCE to c. 600 CE). We have traced this belief in diverse societies of the ancient Near Eastern and Circum-Mediterrean world from the marauding *igi ḫul* and *ini limuttum* decried in Sumerian and Akkadian incantations, the eye (*'nn*) dreaded in Ugaritic incantations, and from the Evil Eye lore of the Egyptians regarding the sky god Horus and the protection sought in the *udjat*, the apotropaic Eye of Horus, to the

---

1. Rakocsy 1996:13–17 ("Wolfsblick")

2. "The dead hare casts an Evil Eye upon me" (*ho lagôs me baskainei tethnikôs*), Pherecrates, Frag. 189.

ophthalmos ponêros and *baskania* of Greeks and the *oculus malus* and *fascinatio* of the Romans, to the biblical Evil Eye references of the Israelite sages, Jesus of Nazareth, and Paulus of Tarsus, to the Evil Eye lore and apotropaics of Israel's rabbinic authorities and Christianity's postbiblical authors and Church fathers. Along this journey, which has taken us also to archaeological digs, ancient sites, and diverse forms of material evidence, we have examined the key components of the Evil Eye complex as it developed over time. This has included features of Evil Eye belief and practice which the biblical communities shared with their neighboring cultures and those that distinguished biblical belief and practice.

The development over the centuries of a constellation of interrelated notions forming an Evil Eye belief complex has lent this concept and its associated practices plausibility and power:

- the notion of the eye as an *active*, not passive agent, which projects energy that can harm, injure, destroy or kill whatever is struck by the ocular glance;
- the Evil Eye as activated by, and a vehicle of, envy, miserliness, greed, and other negative emotions;
- its activation as either intentional or unintentional;
- among its victims, particularly children, birthing mothers, attractive youths, and those enjoying success in domestic life, the stadium, and the battlefield;
- among its possessors, especially widows, strangers, the physically impaired, and those with unusual ocular features;
- the possibility of defense through a wide variety of words, gestures, rituals, and amulets.
- use of the Evil Eye belief to account for sickness, misfortune, defeat in battle, property loss, and death

Over the centuries and across cultures these features of the Evil Eye belief complex have shown a remarkable continuity and consistency. Evil Eye belief and practice is still with us in the twenty-first century in numerous regions across the globe, from rural Turkey to modern Manhattan and from Cinecittá to Hollywood. Abandoned today by many as a fossil of ancient superstition, it is still feared by countless others as a potent cause of sickness, injury, loss and death.

Evil Eye belief attributes otherwise inexplicable causes of injury, physical damage, sickness, and death to noxious ocular rays of energy assumed to be projected either intentionally or inadvertently from the maleficent eye of humans, animals, demons, or gods. Evil-eyeing can be prompted by viewing something arousing *feelings of envy or hostility* in the viewer, with the wish that the object viewed be damaged or destroyed. On the one hand, malevolent feelings are aroused by the *act of looking and beholding*. Secondly, these malevolent feelings are thought to arouse toxic energy that is transmitted through the beholding eye and against the object that is beheld. The *ocular glare or gaze or stare* can signal displeasure, censure, envy, ill will, hostility, defiance, or an intent to intimidate, injure, destroy, or strike fear in the heart of the object viewed. The harmful rays of energy thought to emanate from an Evil Eye were believed to be activated either intentionally or unintentionally, in the latter case with no volition or malevolent intent on the part of the viewer. In this latter case, the focus shifts from the attribution of blame and punishment to procedures of curing and restoration.

Damage from an Evil Eye can be avoided or thwarted, it has been believed, by specific words, gestures, amulets, and other apotropaic objects, designs, and devices enlisted to protect individuals, families, livestock, domiciles and gardens, work places, sacred sites, and public thoroughfares. Over the centuries, a vast array of verbal expressions, physical gestures, amulets and other apotropaic devices have been employed to defend against and ward off the Evil Eye's noxious power. Specific rituals have been developed in various cultures to detect (and neutralize) the Evil Eye as a cause of harm or injury. These apotropaic means and rituals have manifested a remarkable consistency in their design and employment, thus matching the equally remarkable consistency in the features conventionally constituting the Evil Eye belief complex as described and documented in the preceding volumes and chapters.

Evil Eye belief and practice in antiquity was sustained by a generally prevailing extramission theory of vision which conceived of the *eye as an active agent* projecting particles of energy against vulnerable targets. When a modern introversion theory of vision gradually replaced the ancient extramission theory of vision from the 1700s onward, the eye then was understood to be a *receptive organ* receiving external stimuli *rather than an active organ* emitting rays of destructive energy. This scientific determination of the passive, rather than active, nature of the eye and a now prevailing intromission theory of vision have fatally undermined the credibility of a destructive Evil Eye as previously conceived. Nevertheless, repeated studies in recent years have shown the persistence of this belief in an active eye, even among educated populations.[3] The intense and disconcerting

3. See Radin 1997:28–30, 155–56 and further studies he lists on 313, nn. 25 and 34; see also Gross 1999 on the four main contemporary areas holding an extramission theory of vision and the active Evil Eye. For further psychological research see van de

subjective awareness of being starred at experienced by humans, matched by the displeasure manifested by other primates at being "eyeballed," are "gaze aversion" phenomena still calling for further scrutiny.[4] The experience of discomfort at being the object of another's intense staring or glaring or hostile gaze accords with, and has been used to support, the conception of an Evil Eye that projects harmful energy against vulnerable victims and objects. Contemporary investigations of the eye's possible projection of energy also continue unabated.[5] These scientific studies by no means substantiate all the features of the traditional Evil Eye belief complex. They do provide results, however, that require some explanation that is not supplied by the prevailing intromission theory of vision that has replaced the earlier dominant extramission theory of vision.

Wherever this course of research may lead in the future, the prevalence and influence *in antiquity* of an Evil Eye belief presuming an active eye—including Israel and Christianity, Synagogue and the Church—is incontestable. Whoever wishes to read and contextually understand the Bible and the ancient Jewish and Christian traditions associated with its interpretation must be aware of this belief complex and repeated references to the Evil Eye in Sacred Scripture and related texts. accompanied by the thousands of relevant amulets, objects of art, jewelry and other material remains of Circum-Mediterranean antiquity. Familiarity with ancient Evil Eye traditions and customs, in other words, is essential for comprehending the writings of the Bible as reflections of, and responses to, their ancient historical, economic, social and cultural contexts.

Traces of Evil Eye belief and behavior in the Bible become intelligible in the light of a broad range of cross-cultural evidence from Babylonian incantations to the amulets of Late Roman antiquity. Thriving in small-scale societies marked by fragile ecologies, unrationalized economies, ineffective laws and intense social competition, the notion of the malignant and socially injurious power of the Evil Eye is symptomatic of a general perception of the human condition and its vulnerability to hostile forces both human and demonic, the properties of human physiology and affections, the moral and immoral propensities of human behavior, and the social behavior necessary for communal stability.

In the biblical communities, the Evil Eye was linked with envy, miserliness, and greed, dispositions deemed incompatible with the will of God

---

Ven-Zeelenberg-Pieters 2010.

4. See Coss 1992; Schrodinger 2005a, 2005b.

5. For research on ocular emission and sense of being starred at see Winer and Cottrell 1996; Winer et al 2002, 2003; Sheldrake 2003; Ross 2010 (response by Mesner 2010); Ross 2011; Roussou 2014; Risen 2015; Risen and Nussbaum 2015.

and injurious to communal solidarity. The menace of the Evil Eye was considered omnipresent. From cradle to grave an arsenal of words, gestures, amulets, and actions were employed to protect persons and property from the bearers of its deadly power. Accusation of Evil Eye possession provided a means to discredit rivals, mobilize public censure, and marginalize social deviants. The concept of the malignant and menacing Eye has served as one among many beliefs employed to account for otherwise inexplicable causes of illness, calamity, loss, and death. The phenomenon of the Evil Eye also was used to identify and explain manifestations of personal envy and social hostility. It underlined and promoted the values of generosity and the sharing of resources. It reinforced with extraordinary sanction attitudes and actions fostering group cohesion and communal well-being. And it was employed to encourage patterns of social interaction and personal conduct underwritten by God or the gods.

The Evil Eye belief complex has served to explain manifestations of personal and social distress and, through protective words, gestures, and amulets, to provide a sense of safety in an otherwise unpredictable and threatening universe. *Cognitively*, Evil Eye belief has constituted a concept of evil as *personally* grounded and *personally* activated, as human or demonic malice, as human or demonic or divine envy, and as a potent cause of misfortune, loss, injury and death.

Psychologically, the concept of a harmful Evil Eye coheres with a sense of the vulnerability of living creatures to threatening forces of evil and loss, and the fear and dread felt at the experience of a menacing glare or hostile stare. The existence and menace of an Evil Eye provides a name and an explanation for the cause of this fear and dread. The wearing of amulets and employment of powerful words, gestures, symbols, and rituals provide a sense of security and protection from attacks of the Evil Eye and other agents of evil.

Physiologically, physically impaired or disabled persons—hunchbacks, pygmies, or individuals marked by unusual ocular features (strabismus, wandering eye, blindness, knitted eyebrows)—have been deemed possessors of the Evil Eye. Those vulnerable to the Evil Eye included birthing mothers, newborns, youths, and all potential targets of envy (those enjoying good fortune, bountiful harvests, good looks and robust health, victory in battle and public acclaim).

From a *social perspective,* the belief has been employed to affirm key traits of group identity and to demarcate natives from Evil-Eyed strangers and aliens. The belief is found in societies rife with economic and social disparities, where competition and conflict occur over prized objects considered to be in scarce and limited supply. The belief reinforces specific group values prompting specific modes of social interaction. Socially marginal persons (widows, the physically disabled, strangers, aliens) have been suspected of possessing and employing an Evil Eye, and hence of posing a danger to family, neighbors and community alike. Accusations of Evil Eye possession were wielded socially to stigmatize and publically discredit individuals, communities, and entire ethnic groups as physically and socially deviant and threats to health, success, and community well-being. The belief has served as a mechanism of social control, a marker of social deviance, and an enforcer of social boundaries. The belief has reinforced with extraordinary sanction attitudes and actions fostering group cohesion and communal well-being.

From an *ethical perspective,* the Evil Eye belief has served to monitor, censer, and constrain negative dispositions associated with the Evil Eye: stinginess, greed, ungenerosity, and especially envy, thereby contributing to the lessening of internal group tensions and the maintenance of civic and domestic concord. The belief has played a role in curtailing individual attempts to advance socially beyond one's equals, to stand out as extraordinary, and "show up" or "outshine" one's neighbors in the competition for limited resources and rewards. Positively, it has served to encourage attitudes of liberality and actions of generosity, especially toward the poor and the needy.

From a *religious perspective,* Evil Eye belief has encouraged values and patterns of social action and personal deportment underwritten by God or the gods. In the case of Jewish, Christian and Islamic tradition, the belief stigmatizes specified dispositions and acts deemed contrary to the will of God and dangerous to the common weal and therefore as taboo also on religious grounds. For Israelites and followers of Jesus, this involved taking God as a moral model and to practice the liberality and compassion attributed to God himself. In the case of Christianity in the post-biblical period, the Evil Eye was associated with the Devil, alias Satan, chief demon and enemy of God and God's people.

Continuing to thrive in modern time at the level of popular folk wisdom, the notion of the Evil Eye has remained a means to account for sudden and otherwise inexplicable causes of misfortune, just as its preventative amulets, gestures, and rituals demonstrate the continuing human attempt to control the unpredictable forces threatening everyday life. Today it persists under a variety of forms and conditions. Among Mediterranean and Mediterranean-based cultures such as those of Turkey, Greece, Italy, Spain, Mexico and Latin America, Evil Eye belief remains overt, and appears linked to conditions of economic and social inequality, minimally centralized and effective political control, and extensive systems of patronage[6] Among enclaves of emigrants from these societies in North America, belief and practice are likewise overt and linked to concerns about protecting infants and possessions, marking and preserving ethnic group identities, and neutralizing encroachment from "outsiders." On the other hand, in mainstream industrial communities with their ideals of democratic equality and the interiorization of cultural norms and values, anxiety about envy echoes but replaces a less sophisticated fear of the Evil Eye itself.[7]

The persistence of this belief in its various articulations and the scope of its cultural manifestations make it a subject worthy of cross-disciplinary investigation. For it raises questions concerning a prominent item of cross-cultural belief and behavior that can profitably be analyzed from a diversity of vantage points: from biology and psychology to the social sciences, from history to semiology, from the classics to the comic strips. Theology and exegesis, too, as this study has shown, can join this conversation. The four volumes presented here have focused on Evil Eye belief and practice in the Bible and the ancient Circum-Mediterranean cultures in the light of which the biblical material is best understood. This body of research could provide a basis and model for a continuation of investigation of Evil Eye belief and practice from the medieval period to the present.

From ancient time to the present, the Evil Eye, however manifest or latent its expression, remains a potent expression of malice and hostility. Evil Eye Fleegle and "The Sopranos" are but the most recent characters in an extended and colorful tale. Current research on the eye as a weapon, as well as a signal, of hostile intent persists unabated, assuring that the mystery of the Evil Eye remains for the foreseeable future a lively focus of fear and fascination.

---

6. Garrison and Arensberg 1976.
7. Schoeck 1966; Foster 1972.

BIBLIOGRAPHY 1

1. ANCIENT PRIMARY SOURCES

Acta Apostolorum Apocrypha. Edited by R. A. Lipsius and M. Bonnet. 2 vols. in 3 parts. Vol. 1 (1891); vol. 2.1 (1898); vol. 2.2 (1903). Leipzig: H. Mendelsohn, 1891–1903; reprinted, Darmstadt: Wissenschaftliche Buchgesellschaft, 1959.

"Acta Ioannis." In *Acta Apostolorum Apocrypha*, edited by R. A. Lipsius and M. Bonnet. 1898. Vol. 2.1:151–216

"Acta Pauli et Theclae." In *Acta Apostolorum Apocrypha*, edited by R. A. Lipsius and M. Bonnet, 1891. Vol. 1:235–72.

"Acta Thomae." In *Acta Apostolorum Apocrypha*, edited by R. A. Lipsius and M. Bonnet, 1903. Vol. 2.2:99–291.

"The Acts of John." By K. Schäferdiek. In *New Testament Apocrypha*. 2 vols. Edited by Edgar Hennecke, and Wilhelm Schneemelcher. Translated by R. McL Wilson. Philadelphia: Westminster Press, 1965. Vol. 2:188–259.

"The Acts of Paul and Thecla." In "The Acts of Paul." *By W. Schneemelcher.* In *New Testament Apocrypha*. 2 vols. Edited by Edgar Hennecke, and Wilhelm Schneemelcher. Translated by R. McL Wilson. Philadelphia: Westminster Press, 1965. Vol. 2:322–390, especially 353–64.

"The Acts of Thomas." By G. Bornkamm. In *New Testament Apocrypha*. 2 vols. Edited by Edgar Hennecke, and Wilhelm Schneemelcher. Translated by R. McL Wilson. Philadelphia: Westminster Press, 1965. Vol. 2: 425–531.

Ambrose. *De fide ad Gratianum Augustum (Exposition of the Christian Faith)*. Edited by O. Faller. CSEL 78. Vienna, 1962.

———. *Exposition of the Christian Faith*. 5 books. Translated by H. de Romestin, E. de Romestin and H. T. F. Duckworth. In *Nicene and Post-Nicene Fathers*. Second Series, Vol. 10. Edited by Philip Schaff and Henry Wace. Buffalo, NY: Christian Literature Publishing, 1896.

———. *In Epistolam Beati Pauli ad Galatas*. PL 17.357–94.

Ambrosiaster. *Commentaria in Epistolam ad Galatas*. PL 17.7.

Ante-Nicene Fathers. Vol. 6. *The Fathers of the Third Century*. Translated by S.D.F. Salmon. Edited by Alexander Roberts, James Donaldson, and A. Cleveland Coxe. Buffalo, NY: Christian Literature Publishing Co., 1886.

Antiochus Monachus, *Pandecta scripturae sacrae*. PG 89.1428–1849.

Bibliography 1

Apocalypse of Enoch. "2 (Slavonic) Apocalypse of Enoch." By F. I. Andersen. *OTP* 1 (1983) 91–213.
The Apocrypha and Pseudepigrapha of the Old Testament in English. 2 vols. Edited by R. H. Charles. Oxford: Clarendon, 1913.
The Apocryphal New Testament: A Collection of Apocryphal Christian Literature in an English Translation. Edited by J. K. Elliott. Oxford: Oxford University Press, 2005
The Apostolic Fathers: Greek Texts and English Translations. Edited and translated by Michael W. Holmes; after the earlier work of J. B. Lightfoot and J. R. Harmer. 3rd ed. Grand Rapids: Baker Academic, 2007.
The Apostolic Tradition: A Commentary. By Paul F. Bradshaw, et. al. Hermeneia; Minneapolis: Fortress, 2002.
Arnobius of Sicca. *Adversus Nationes.* Edited by Concetto Marchesi. Turin: Paravia et sociorum, 1953.
Artemidorus of Ephesus. *Artemidori Daldiani Onirocriticon Libri V.* Edited by Roger Ambrose Pack. Bibliotheca Scriptorum Graecorum Et Romanorum Teubneriana. Leipzig: Teubner 1963.
Augustine, Aurelius, of Hippo. In *Patrologia Latina*, vols. 31–47.
———. *Augustine. De civitate Dei.* 2 vols. Edited by Bernard Dombart and Alphonse Kalb. CCSL 47–48. Turnhout: Brepols, 1955.
———. *Concerning the City of God against the Pagans.* Translated by Henry Bettenson. New York: Penguin Books, 1972.
———.*Confessions.* Translated by R. S. Pine-Coffin. New York: Penguin, 1961.
———. *Confessionum, libri tredecim.* Edited by Lucas Verheijen. CCSL 27. Turnhout: Brepols, 1981.
———. *A Select Library of the Nicene and Post-Nicene Fathers of the Christian Church.* Series 1, Vol. 3. *St. Augustine on the Holy Trinity, Doctrinal Treatises, Moral Treatises.* Edited by Philip Schaff. Buffalo: Christian Literature Publishing, 1887.
Sermones. PL 38–39.
Ausgewälte koptische Zaubertexte. 3 vols. Edited Angelicus M. Kropp. Brussels: Fondation Égyptologie, 1930–32.
Basil of Caesarea. *Enarratio in prophetam Isaiam.* PG 30.116–668.
———. "Homily 11, Concerning Envy/*Peri phthonou*." PG 31. 372–86. ET by M. Monica Wagner in *Saint Basil: Ascetical Works. The Fathers of the Church. A New Translation.* Vol. 9:463–74. New York: Fathers of the Church, 1950.
———. *Basil: Letters and Select Works.* In *Nicene and Post-Nicene Fathers of the Christian Church.* Series 2. Vol. 8. Edited by Philip Schaff and Buffalo: Christian Literature, 1895. Reprinted, Grand Rapids: Eerdmans, 1968.
Bernand, Étienne, ed. 1969. *Inscriptions métriques de l'Égypte gréco-romaine. Recherches sur la poésie épigrammatique des Grecs en Égypte.* Annales littéraires de l'Université de Besançon, 98. Paris; Les Belles Lettres.
Clavis Patrum Graecorum. 5 Vols. Edited by M. Geerad. 5 vols. Turnhout: Brepols, 1974–1983.

Bibliography 1   167

Clement of Alexandria. *Clemens Alexandrinus*. Edited by Ludwig Früchtel. Berlin: Akademie-Verlag, 1970.

———. *Titi Flaui Clementis Alexandrini opera omnia*. 4 vols. Edited by Reinhold Koltz. Leipzig: Schwickerti, 1831.

Clement of Rome. *1 Clement*. In *The Apostolic Fathers*. Translated and edited by K. Lake. 2 vols. Cambridge: Harvard University Press, 1952.

Corpus Christianorum, Series Latina. Turnhout: Brepols, 1953/1954–. (CCSL)

Corpus Scriptorum Ecclesiasticorum Latinorum. Vienna: Verlag der Österreichischen Akademie der Wissenschaften/Universität Salzburg, 1866–. (CSEL)

Cyprian of Carthage. *De zelo et livore/On Envy and Rancor*. In *S. Thasci Caecili Cypriani Opera Omnia*. Edited by G. Hartel, 417–32. CSEL 3.1.1. Vienna: Verlag der Österreichischen Akademie der Wissenschaften/Universität Salzburg, 1868.

———. *De zelo et livore/On Envy and Rancor*. PL 4.637–652.

———. "Treatise 10. On Jealousy and Envy." In *Ante-Nicene Fathers*. Vol. 5: *Hippolytus, Cyprian, Caius, Novatian* by A. Cleveland Coxe. Appendix, edited by Alexander Roberts and James Donaldson. Revised and Chronologically arranged with brief prefaces and occasional notes by A. Cleveland Coxe. New York: Christian Literature Publishing, 1886.

Cyril of Alexandria. *St. Cyril of Alexandria. Commentary on the Twelve Prophets*. Volume 1. Translated by Robert C. Hill. The Fathers of the Church, A New Translation, Vol. 115. Washington, DC: The Catholic University of America Press 2007.

Cyril of Jerusalem. *Cyril of Jerusalem, Gregory Nazianzen*. In *Nicene and Post-Nicene Fathers of the Christian Church*. Series 2, Vol. 7. Edited by Philip Schaff and Henry Wace. Translated by Edwin Hamilton Gifford. Buffalo, NY: Christian Literature Co. 1893. Reprinted, Grand Rapids: Eerdmans, 1968.

Drower, E. S. 1937. "Šapta d-Pišra d-Ainia (Mandaic 'Scroll for the Exorcism of [Evil] Eyes')." *JRAS* 69:589–611.

———. 1938. "Šapta d-Pišra d-Ainia." *JRAS* 70: 1–20.

———. 1943. "A Mandaean Book of Black Magic." *JRAS* 75:149–81.

Duling, Dennis C. 1993. "Testament of Solomon." *The Old Testament Pseudepigraph*. Vol. 1. *Apocalyptic Literature and Testaments*. Edited by James H. Charlesworth, 935–87. Garden City, NY: Doubleday.

ed-Dairabī, A. 1940. *Kitābu muǧarrabāti*... [Arabic Book of Magic] Cairo, 1940.

Epictetus. *Discourses* and *Encheiridion*. 2 vols. Translated by W. A. Oldfather. LCL. Cambridge: Harvard University Press, 1966 (1925).

———. *Epicteti Dissertationes ab Arriani digestae*. Edited by H. Schenkl. Bibliotheca Teubneriana. Stuttgart: Teubner, 1965 (1916).

Epicurus: The Extant Fragments. Edited by Cyril Bailey. Oxford: Clarendon, 1926.

Epigrammata Graeca ex lapidibus conlecta. Edited by Georg Kaibel. Berlin: Reimer, 1878; reprinted 1965.

Epistolographi Graeci. Edited by Rudolf Hercher. Paris: Didot, 1873..

Eusebius. *Life of Constantine*. Edited and translated by Averil Cameron and Stuart Hall., Oxford: Clarendon, 1999.

Fragmenta Pseudepigraphorum quae supersunt graeca. Edited by A.- M. Denis. PsVTG 3. Leiden: Brill, 1970.

Gsell, Stephane, ed. 1922. *Inscriptions latines de l'Algérie*. Paris and Algiers: Champion.

Gignoux, P., ed. 1987. *Incantations magiques syriaques*. Collection de la Revue des Études Juives. Louvain: Peeters.

168   Bibliography 1

Gollancz, Hermann, ed. 1912. *The Book of Protection, being a Collection of Charms Now Edited for the First Time from Syriac MSS with Translation, Introduction and Notes, with 27 Illustrations*. London: Frowde. Reprinted, Cambridge: Cambridge University Press, 2011.

Gordon, C. H. 1934. "Aramaic Magical Bowls in the Istanbul and Baghdad Museums." *ArOr* 6: 324–26.

———. 1937. "Aramaic and Mandaic Magic Bowls."*ArOr* 9:84–106.

Grégoire, Henri, ed. 1922. *Recueil des inscriptions grècqes-chrétiennes d'Asie Mineure*. Vol. 1. Paris: Leroux.

Gregory Nazianzus. *Cyril of Jerusalem, Gregory Nazianzus*. In *Nicene and Post-Nicene Fathers of the Christian Church*. Series 2, Vol. 7. Edited by Philip Schaff and Henry Wace.Translated by Edwin Hamilton Gifford. Buffalo, NY: Christian Literature Publishing, 1893. Reprinted, Grand Rapids: Eerdmans, 1968.

———. *Gregory of Nazianzus*. By Brian Daley. The Early Church Fathers. London: Routledge, 2006.

———. *Poemata de se ipso 55* (PG 37.2.1052).

———. *St. Gregory of Nazianzus. Select Orations*. Translated by Martha Vinson. The Fathers of the Church. Washington, DC: Catholic University of America Press, 2003. [Oration 6, pp. 3–20.]

Gregory of Nyssa. *The Catechetical Oration*. Edited by J. H. Srawley. Cambridge Patristic Texts. Cambridge: Cambridge University Press, 1903.

———. *De Beatitudinibus 7* (PG 44.1288b)

———. *De Virginitate; De Beatitudinibus*. Edited and translated by F. Oehler. Vol. 4 of *Bibliothek der Kirchenväter*. Leipzig, 1859.

———. *Discours catéchétique (Oratio catechetica magna)*. Edited by M. Ekkehard Muhlenberg. Translated by M. Raymond Winling. SC 453. Paris: Cerf/Paillart, 2000. PG 45.11–105.

———. *Dogmatica minora, Pars II*. In *Gregorii Nysseni opera, Volumen III, Pars II*. Edited by W. Jaeger. H. Langerbeck, and H. Hörner, 65–97. Leiden: Brill, 1987.

———. *Encomium in xl martyres*. PG 46.760c.

———. *Gregory of Nyssa: Dogmatic Treatises; Select Writings and Letters*. In *Nicene and Post-Nicene Fathers*. Series 2, Vol. 5. Edited by Philip Schaff and Henry Wace. Translated by William Moore and Henry Austin Wilson. New York: Christian Publishing Literature, 1893.

———. *Gregory of Nyssa. Oratio funebris in Meletium episcopum, In Sermones, pars 1*. In *Gregorii Nysseni Opera*. Vol. 9.1. Edited by G. Heil, A. van Heck, E. Gebhardt, and A. Spira, 441–57. Leiden: Brill, 1992.

———. *La Vie de Moïse ou Traité de la perfection en matière de vertu*. Translated by Jean Daniélou. SC 1. Paris: Cerf, 1942.

———. "On Infants' Early Deaths." In *Nicene and Post-Nicene Fathers*. Series 2, Vol. 5: 372–81. Edited by Philip Schaff and Henry Wace. Translated by William Moore and Henry Austin Wilson. Buffalo, NY: Christian Literature Publishing, 1893.

———. *The Life of Moses*. Translation, introduction, and notes by Abraham J. Malherbe and Everett Ferguson. New York: Paulist, 1978.

Gregory Thaumaturgus. *Fragmentum in evangelium Matthaei*. PG 10.1189.

———. "On the Gospel according to Matthew (6:22–23)." In *Ante-Nicene Fathers*, Vol. 6.2:74. Edited by Alexander Roberts, James Donaldson, and A. Cleveland Coxe. Translated by S. D. F. Salmond. Buffalo, NY: Christian Literature Publishing, 1886.

Hennecke, Edgar, and Wilhelm Schneemelcher, eds. 1963, 1965. 2 vols. *New Testament Apocrypha*. Translated by R. McL. Wilson. Philadelphia: Westminster.

Herdick, Michael. 2001. "Mit Eisen gegen die Angst: Überlegungen zur Interpretation Vor -und Frühgeschichtlicher Mineralien-Amulette und Bemerkungen zu einer Gruppe Merowingerzeitlicher Kugelanhängervon." *Concilium medii aevi* 4:1–47.

Herrmann, Christian. 1994. *Ägyptische Amulette aus Palästina/Israel*. Orbis Biblicus et Orientalis 138. Göttingen: Vandenhoeck & Ruprecht.

———. 2002. *Ägyptische Amulette aus Palästina/Israel II*. Orbis Biblicus et Orientalis 184. Göttingen: Vandenhoeck & Ruprecht.

Inscriptiones Latinae Christianae Veteres. 3 vols. Edited by Ernst Diehl. Berlin: Weidmann, 1927–31. Vols. 1–3 reprinted 1961–67. Vol. 4, Supplement, edited by Jacques Moreau und Henri Irénée Marrou, Berlin: Weidmann. 1967.

Inscriptions Grecques et Latines de Syrie. 21 vols. Edited by L. Jalabert, R. Mouterde, and C. Mondésert. Vol. 4: *Laodicée et l'Apamène* (nos. 1243–1997). Bibliothèque archéologique et historique, 61. Paris: Geuthner, 1929–55.

Inscriptions latines de l'Algérie. 1922/1957. Edited by Stephane Gsell. Paris and Algiers: H. Champion.

Isbell, Charles D., ed. 1975. *Corpus of Aramaic Incantation Bowls*. SBLDS 17. Missoula, MT: Scholars.

Isidore of Seville. *Etymologiarum*. 2 vols. Edited by W. M. Lindsay. Oxford: Clarendon, 1911.

———. *Origines/Ethymologiae*. 2 vols. *The Etymologies of Isidore of Seville*. Translated by Stephen A. Barney, W. J. Lewis, J. A Beach, and Oliver Berghof. Cambridge: Cambridge University Press, 2006.

Jerome. *Commentariorum/Commentarius in epistulam ad Galatas. Libri tres*. PL 26. 307–438.

———. *Commentarii in epistulam Pauli apostoli ad Galatas*. Edited by Giacamo Raspanti. S. *Hieronymi Presbyteri Opera, Pars I. Opera Exegetica*, 6. CCSL 77A. Turnhout: Brepols, 2006.

———. *Commentarius in Matthaeum*. Edited by D. Hurst and M. Adriaen. CCSL 77. Turnholt: Brepols, 1969.

———. *Explicatio in epistulam ad Galatas*. PL 30.847–48 [= abbreviated version of PL 26.346–48].

———. *Jérome, Saint. Commentaire sur S. Matthieu*. 2 vols. Edited by Emile Bonnard. SC 242, 259. Paris: Cerf, 1977, 1979.

———. *St. Jerome. Commentary on Galatians*. Translated by Andrew Cain. The Fathers of the Church. A New Translation, vol. 121. Washington, DC: The Catholic University of America Press, 2010.

———. *St. Jerome's Commentaries on Galatians, Titus, and Philemon*. Edited and translated by Thomas P. Scheck. Notre Dame, IN: University of Notre Dame Press, 2010.

John Chrysostom. *Ad populum Antiochenum de statuis, Homiliae 1–21*. PG 49. 15–222.

———. *Adversos Judaeos* (*Orationes 1–8*). PG 48.843–942.

———. *Catecheses ad illuminandos*. PG 49.223–40.

———. *De futurae vitae deliciis*. PG 51.347–54.

———. *De sacerdotio. Sur Le Sacerdoce*. Edited by A.-M. Malingrey. Source Chrétiennes, 272. Paris: Cerf, 1980.

———. *Homiliae in Acta Apostolorum 1–55*. PG 60.13–384.

———. *Homiliae in epistulam ad Colossenses* 1–12. PG 62.299–392.
———. *Homiliae in epistulam ad Galatas commentarius*. PG 61.611–82.
———. *Homiliae in epistulam ad Ephesios* 1–24. PG 62.29–176.
———. *Homiliae in epistulam ad Hebraeos* 1–34. PG 63.113–236.
———. *Homiliae in epistulam ad Philippenses* 1–15. PG 62.29–176.
———. *Homiliae in epistulam ad Romanos* 1–32. PG 60.391–682.
———. *Homiliae in Genesim* 1–67. PG 53.21–385; 54.385-580. http://www2.iath.virginia.edu/anderson/commentaries/ChrGen.html.
———. *Homiliae in Iohannem* 1–88. PG 59.23–482.
———. *Homiliae in Matthaeum* 1–90. PG 57.13–58.794.
———. *Homiliae in primum epistulam ad Corinthios* 1–44. PG 61.9–382.
———. *Homilia in primum epistulam ad Corinthios 12.13* (on 1 Cor. 4:6). PG 61.105–106.
———. *Homiliae in secundam epistulam ad Corinthios*. PG 61. 381–610.
———. *Homiliae in primum epistulam ad Timotheum* 1–18. PG 62.501–600.
———. *Homily on Galatians 2:11*. PG 51.371–88.
———. *In paralyticum demissum per tectum* (PG 51. 47–54)
———. *Saint Chrysostom: Homilies on the Gospel of Saint Matthew*. In *Nicene and Post-Nicene Fathers of the Christian Church*. Series 1, Vol.10. Translated by M. B. Riddle. Edited by Philip Schaff and Henry Wace. Buffalo, NY: Christian Literature Publishing, 1886–1890; Reprinted, Grand Rapids: Eerdmans, 1956.
———. *Saint Chrysostom: Homilies on the Epistles of Paul to the Corinthians*. In *Nicene and Post-Nicene Fathers of the Christian Church*, Series 1, Vol. 12. Translated by Talbot W. Chambers. Edited by Philip Schaff. New York: Scribner's, 1886–1890; Reprinted, Grand Rapids: Eerdmans, 1956.
———. *Saint Chrysostom: Homilies on Galatians, Ephesians, Philippians, Colossians, Thessalonians, Timothy, Titus, and Philemon*. In *Nicene and Post-Nicene Fathers of the Christian Church*, Series 1, Vol. 13. Translated by Gross Alexander. Edited by Philip Schaff. New York: Scribner, 1886–1890; Reprinted, Grand Rapids: Eerdmans, 1956.
———. *Saint Chrysostom: Homilies on the Gospel of St. John and the Epistle to the Hebrews*. In *Nicene and Post-Nicene Fathers of the Christian Church*, Series 1, Vol. 14. Translated by Charles Marriott. Edited by Philip Schaff and Henry Wace. New York: Scribner's, 1886–1890; Reprinted, Grand Rapids: Eerdmans, 1956.
———. *Saint Chrysostom: Letters*. In *Nicene and Post-Nicene Fathers*, Series 2, Vol. 6. Translated by W. H. Fremantle, G. Lewis and W. G. Martley. Edited by Philip Schaff and Henry Wace. Buffalo, NY: Christian Literature Publishing, 1893.
———. *Saint Chrysostom: On the Priesthood, Ascetic Treatises, Select Homilies and Letters, Homilies on the Statues to the people of Antioch*. In *Nicene and Post-Nicene Fathers of the Christian Church*, Series 1, Vol. 9. Translated byW. R. W. Stephens. Edited by Philip Schaff. New York: Scribner, 1886–1890; reprinted, Grand Rapids: Eerdmans, 1956.
———. *Sancti Patris Johannis Chrysostomi archepiscopi Constantinopolitani. Homiliae in Matthaeum*, XV–XXIV. Edited by F. Field. Vol. 1:186–356. Cambridge: Officina academica, 1839.
———. *Sermones in Genesim* 1–9. PG 54.581–630.
———. *Sermons sur la Genèse*. Edited by L. Brottier. SC 433. Paris: Cerf, 1998.

———. *St. John Chrysostom: Eight Sermons on the Book of Genesis.* Translated by R. C. Hill. Brookline, MA: Holy Cross Orthodox Press, 2004.

John Chrysostom (Pseudo-). *Opus imperfectum in Mattheaeum*, edited by J. van Banning. CCSL 87B. Turnholt: Brepols, 1988.

John of Damascus. *Sacra parallela.* PG 96.9–442.

Joseph und Aseneth. By Uta Barbara Fink. Revision des griechischen Textes und Edition der zweiten lateinischen Übersetzung. Fontes et Subsidia ad Bibliam pertinentes 5. New York: de Gruyter, 2009.

Josephus. *Jewish Antiquities.* Translated by H. St. J. Thackeray, Ralph Marcus, Allen Wikgren and L. H. Feldman. LCL, vols. 4–10 of 10 vols. Cambridge: Harvard University Press, 1930–1965.

———. *The Jewish War.* Translated by H. St. J. Thackeray. LCL, vols. 2–3 of 10 vols.. Cambridge: Harvard University Press, 1927–1928.

———. *Josephus.* 10 vols. Translated by H. St. J. Thackery et al. LCL. Cambridge: Harvard University Press, 1926–1965.

———. *The Life; Against Apion.* Translated by H. St. J. Thackeray. LCL, vol. 1 of 10 vols. Cambridge: Harvard University Press, 1926.

Justinius. *Iustinii Historiae Philippicae.* Edited by Frederick Dübner. Leipzig: Teubner, 1831.

Kitab-Mugarrabat [Arabic book of magic]. See ed-Dairabī, A. *Kitābu muǧarrabāti . . .* [Arabic Book of Magic]. Cairo, 1940.

Lactantius. *De Opificio Dei.* In *The Minor Works.* Translated by Mary F. McDonald. *The Fathers of the Church*, vol. 54. Washington, DC: Catholic University of America Press, 2010.

———. *The Divine Institutes, Books 1-VII.* Translated by Mary F. McDonald. Washington, DC: Catholic University of America Press, 1964.

———. *L. Caeli Firmiani Lactanti Opera Omnia: Accedunt Carmina Eius Quae Feruntur Et L. Caecilii Qui Inscriptus Est De Mortibus Persecutorum Liber.* Edited by Samuel Brandt and Georg Laubmann. CSEL19 and 27. Vienna: Tempsky, 1890, 1893.

———. *L. Caelius Firmianus Lactantius. Divinarum institutionum libri septem.* Fasc. 1: Libri I et II. Edited by Eberhard Heck and Antonie Wlosok. Bibliotheca Teubneriana. Munich: Saur, 2005.

Levene. Dan, ed. 2003. *A Corpus of Magic Bowls: Incantation Texts in Jewish Aramaic from Late Antiquity.* London and New York Kegan Paul.

Libanius: Autobiography and Selected Letters. 2 vols. Edited by A. F. Norman. LCL. Cambridge: Harvard University Press, 1992.

Magische Texte aus der Kairoer Geniza. By P. Schäfer, P. and S. Shaked. I. Texte und Studien zum antkiken Judentum 42. Tübingen: Mohr/Siebeck, 1994.

Magische Texte aus der Kairoer Geniza. By P. Schäfer, P. and S. Shaked. II. Texte und Studien zum antiken Judentum, 64. Tübingen: Mohr/Siebeck, 1997.

Mark the Deacon, *The Life of Porphyry, Bishop of Gaza.* Translated by G. F. Hill. Oxford: Oxford University Press, 1913.

Midrash Bereshit Rabbah. Edited by J. Theodor and H. Albeck. Berlin: 1812–1931; reprinted, 2nd ed., Jerusalem 1962.

Midrash Rabbah. Vilna, Lithuania: Romm, 1884–1887. Reprinted, Jerusalem 1961. ET: *The Midrash Rabba.* Translated by H. Freedman and Maurice Simon. 5 vols. Reprinted, London, 1977.

Midrash Tanhuma. Edited by Salomon Buber. Vilna: Romm, 1885.

Mikron Evchologion ê Agiasmatarion. Edited by Fr. Evagoras Constantinides. Merriville, IN: Evagoras Constantinides, 1989.
Mishnah, The. Translated by Herbert Danby. Oxford: Clarendon, 1933.
Mishnah, The. Edited and translated by Jacob Neusner. New Haven: Yale University Press, 1988.
Morgan, Michael A. 1983. *Sepher Ha-Razim. The Book of Mysteries.* SBL Texts and Translations 25. Pseudepigrapha Series 11. Chico, CA: Scholars.
Naveh, Joseph and Shaul Shaked, eds. 1987. *Amulets and Magic Bowls. Aramaic Incantations of Late Antiquity.* 2nd. ed. Jerusalem: The Magnes Press. (1985). Reprinted, Varda, 2009.
———. 1993. *Magic Spells and Formulae: Aramaic Incantations of Late Antiquity.* Jerusalem: Magnes, 1993.
New Testament Apocrypha. 2 vols. Edited by Edgar Hennecke and Wilhelm Schneemelcher. Translated by R. McL Wilson. Philadelphia: Westminster, 1963, 1965.
"The Acts of John." Vol. 2. By K. Schäferdiek. Translated by R. McL Wilson, 2:188–259.
"The Acts of Paul. 3. The Acts of Paul and Thecla." By W. Schneemelcher. Translated by R. McL Wilson, 2:322–90, esp. 353–64.
"The Acts of Thomas." Vol. 2. By G. Bornkamm. Translated by R. McL Wilson, 2:425–531.
Nicene and Post-Nicene Fathers, Series 1, Vol. 9. *Saint Chrysostom: On the Priesthood, Ascetic Treatises, Select Homilies and Letters, Homilies on the Statutes.* Translated by W. R. W. Stephens. Edited by Philip Schaff. Buffalo, NY: Christian Literature Publishing, 1886. Reprinted, Grand Rapids: Eerdmans, 1956.
Nicene and Post-Nicene Fathers, Series 1, Vol. 10. *Saint Chrysostom: Homilies on the Gospel of St. Matthew.* Translated by M. B. Riddle. Edited by Philip Schaff and Henry Wace. Buffalo, NY: Christian Literature Publishing. Reprinted, Grand Rapids: Eerdmans, 1956.
Nicene and Post-Nicene Fathers, Series 1, Vol. 12. *Saint Chrysostom, Homilies on First and Second Corinthians.* Translated by Talbot W. Chambers. Edited by Philip Schaff. Buffalo, NY: Christian Literature Publishing, 1889. Reprinted, Grand Rapids: Eerdmans, 1956.
Nicene and Post-Nicene Fathers, Series 1, Vol. 13. *Saint. Chrysostom: Homilies on Galatians, Ephesians, Philippians, Colossians, Thessalonians, Timothy, Titus, and Philemon.* Buffalo, NY: Christian Literature Publishing, 1889. Reprinted, Grand Rapids: Eerdmans, 1956.
Nishmat Hayyim. Edited by R. Hayyim Abulafia. Salonica: Mordechai Nahman, 1806.
Noy, David, ed. 1993. *Jewish Inscriptions of Western Europe.* Cambridge: Cambridge University Press.
Noy, David and Hanswulf Bloedhorn, eds. 2004. *Inscriptiones Judaicae Orientis. III. Syria and Cyprus.* Texts and Studies in Ancient Judaism 102. Tübingen: Mohr/Siebeck.
The Old Testament Pseudepigrapha. 2 vols. Edited by James H. Charlesworth. Garden City, NY: Doubleday, 1983.
Origen. *Contra Celsum.* Edited by M. Borret, SC 132 (Books 1–2, 1967); 136 (Books 3–4, 1968), 147 (Books 5–6, 1969), 150 (Books 7–8, 1969). Paris: Cerf, 1942–.
———. *Origen: Contra Celsum.* Translated by H. Chadwick. Cambridge: Cambridge University Press, 1965.

Otsar Midrashim: A Library of Two Hundred Minor Midrashim. Edited by D. Eisenstein. 2 vols. New York: 1915; reprinted, 1969.
Papyri Osloenses. 3 vols. Vol. 1 edited by S. Eitrem; vols. 2 and 3 edited by S. Eitrem and Leiv Amundsen. Oslo: Det norske videnskaps-akademi, on commission by Jacob Dybwad, 1925–1936.
Papyrus Turner. *Papyri Greek and Egyptian.* Edited by P. J. Parsons et al. in Honor of Eric Gardner Turner. Graeco-Roman Memoirs 68. London: Egypt Exploration Scociety, 1981.
Patrologia Graeca. *Patrologiae cursus completus. Series graeca.* 176 vols. Edited by Jacques-Paul Migne. Paris: Garnier, 1857–1876.
Patrologia Latina. *Patrologiae Cursus completus, Series latina.* 221 vols. Edited by Jacques-Paul Migne. Paris: Garnier, 1844–1864.
Paulus Silentarius. *Ecphrasis of Hagia Sophia. Three Political Voices from the Age of Justinian: Agapetus Advice to the Emperor; Dialogue on Political Science; Paul the Silentiary Description of Hagia Sophia.* Translated by P. N. Bell. Liverpool: Liverpool University Press, 2009.
Pesiqta de-Rav Kahana. 1868. Edited by S. Buber. Lyck. Edited by B. Mandelbaum. New York, 1962.
Pesiqta Rabbati. Edited by M. Friedmann. Vienna, 1880.
Procopius of Caesarea Palestine. *The Secret History.* New York: Penguin Classics, 1982.
Qur'an. *The Qur'an: A New Translation.* By Tarif Khalidi. New York: Penguin Classics, 2008.
Sammelbuch griechischer Urkunden aus Ägypten. Edited by Friedrich Priesigke, Friedrich Bilabel, Emil Kiessling, and Hans-Albert Rupprecht. 1915–1993. 18 vols. Berlin: de Gruyter.
Sefer Hasidim. Edited by J. Wistinetski and J. Freiman. 2nd ed. Frankfurt: Vahrmann, 1924.
Sepher Ha-Razim. Edited by M. Margalioth. Jerusalem: Yediot Achronot, 1966.
Sepher Ha-Razim. The Book of Mysteries. Edited by Michael A. Morgan, SBL Texts and Translations 25. Pseudepigrapha Series 11. Chico, CA: Scholars, 1983.
Talmud, Babylonian. *The Babylonian Talmud.* Translated into English with Notes, Glossary and Indices under the editorship of Rabbi Dr. I. Epstein. 34 vols. in 6 parts. London: Soncino, 1935–1960.
Talmud, Babylonian. *Hebrew-English Edition of the Babylonian Talmud, Baba Mezi'a.* Edited by S. Daiches and H. Freedman. London: Soncino, 1962.
Talmud, Palestinian/Jerusalem. *The Jerusalem Talmud.* Translated by Heinrich Walter Guggenheimer. *First Order: Zeraim, Tractates Peah and Demay.* New York: de Gruyter, 2000.
Talmud, Palestinian. *Talmud Yerushalmi.* Krotoschin, 1866; Zitomir, 1860–1867; Vilnius, 1922.
Targumim
    T. Onkelos, T. Jonathan. Sperber, Alexander, ed. *The Bible in Aramaic based on old manuscripts and printed texts,* Second Impression. Volume I: *The Pentateuch according to Targum Onkelos* with a foreword by Robert P. Gordon. Volume II: *The Former Prophets according to Targum Jonathan.* Volume III: *The Latter Prophets according to Targum Jonathan,* Volume IV A: *The Hagiographa. Transition from translation to Midrash.* Volume IV B: *The Targum and the Hebrew Bible.* Leiden: Brill, 2012.

Targum Neofiti.
  Targum Neofiti 1: Genesis (The Aramaic Bible, Volume 1A) Edited by Martin McNamara. Collegeville, MN: Michael Glazier, 1992.
  Neophyti 1: Targum Palestinense MS de la Biblioteca Vaticana, Vol. 1: Genesis. Edited by Alejandro Díez Macho, Edición Príncipe, Introducción General y Versión Castellana (Madrid: Consejo Superior de Investigaciones Científicas, 1968).
T. Yerushalmi (Jerusalem Targum).
  The Targums of Onkelos and Jonathan Ben Uzziel on the Pentateuch, with the fragments of the Jerusalem Targum from the Chaldee, Edited by J. W. Etheridge. London: Longman, Green, Longman, and Roberts, 1862–1865.
Tatian, *Diatessaron.* "The Diatessaron of Tatian." In *Ante-Nicene Fathers.* Volume 9: *The Gospel of Peter, the Diatessaron of Tatian, the Apocalypse of Peter, the Vision of Paul, the Apocalypse of the Virgin and Sedrach, the Testament of Abraham, the Acts of Xanthippe and Polyxena, the Narrative of Zosimus, the Apology of Aristides, the Epistles of Clement* (complete text), *Origen's Commentary of John, Books 1–10, and Commentary on Matthew, Books 1, 2, and 10–14.* Translated by A. Cleveland Coxe. Edited by Alexander Roberts and James Donaldson. Revised and Chronologically arranged with brief prefaces and occasional notes by A. Cleveland Coxe. New York: Christian Literature Publishing, 1896–97.
Tertullian of Carthage. *Ad martyras, Ad Scapulam, De fuga in persecutione, De monogamia, De virginibus velandis, De pallio.* Edited by V. Bulhart. CSEL 76. Vienna, 1957.
———. *De praescriptione haereticorum, De cultu feminarum, Ad uxorem, De exhortatione castitatis, De corona, De carne Christi, Adversus Iudaeos.* Edited by E. Kroymann. CSEL 70. Vienna, 1942.
———. *De spectaculis, De idololatria, Ad nationes, De testimonio animae, Scorpiace, De oratione, De baptismo, De ieiunio, De anima, De pudicitia.* Edited by A. Reifferscheid, G. Wissowa. CSEL 20. Vienna, 1890.
———. *De virginibus velandis.* Translated and edited by V. Bulhardt. CSEL 76. Vienna, 1957.
———. *Tertullian: Treatises on Marriage and Remarriage. To His Wife, An Exhortation to Chastity, Monogamy.* Edited by William P. Le Saint. Ancient Christian Writers 13. New York: Newman, 1951.
Testament of Solomon.
  "Testament of Solomon." Edited by David M. Miller, and Ken M. Penner. Edition 1.0. No pages. In *The Online Critical Pseudepigrapha.* Edited by Ian W. Scott, Ken M. Penner, and David M. Miller. Atlanta: Society of Biblical Literature, 2006. Online: http://www.purl.org/net/ocp/testament-of-solomon.
  "Testament of Solomon. (First to Third Century A.D.) A New Translation and Introduction." By Dennis C. Dulling. In *Old Testament Pseudepigrapha*, Vol. 1, edited by James H. Charlesworth, 935–87. Garden City, NY: Doubleday, 1993.
  Testamentum Salomonis. PG 111.1316–58.
  "*Testamentum Salomonis.*" Edited by Ferdinand Florenz Fleck. In *Wissenschaftliche Reise durch das südliche Deutschland, Italien, Sicilien, und Frankreich* 2/3. Anedota maximam partem sacra, 113–40. Leipzig: Barth, 1837. [Ms. P, now

in Bibliotheque Nationale, Paris, and standard text until Ms D (published by Istrin, 1898)]

Testaments of the Twelve Patriarchs.

The Greek Versions of the Twelve Patriarchs. Edited by Robert Henry Charles. Oxford: Oxford University Press, 1908; Reprinted, Hildesheim: Georg Olms, 1962.

Testamenta XII Patriarcharum. Edited by Marius de Jonge. PsVTG 1. Leiden: Brill, 1970.

Theodoret.

Theodoret, Jerome, Gennadius, and Rufinus: Historical Writings. In *Nicene and Post-Nicene Fathers.* Series 2, Vol. 3. Edited by Philip Schaff and Henry Wace. Buffalo, NY: Christian Literature Publishing, 1893.

Eranistes. By G. H. Ettlinger. Oxford: Clarendon, 1975: 61–266.

Tosefta. Edited by Saul Lieberman. New York: Jewish Theological Seminary, 1955.

Victorinus, Marius. *Commentarii in Epistulas Pauli ad Ephesios, ad Galatas, ad Philippenses.* Edited by F. Gori. CSEL 83.2. Vienna: Verlag der Österreichischen Akademie der Wissenschaften/Universität Salzburg, 1986.

———. *In epistulam Pauli ad Galatas liber 1.* PL 8. 1145–98.

Vulgata. Biblia Sacra: Iuxta Vulgatam versionem. 2 vols. Edited by R. Weber, 2 vols. Stuttgart: Württembergische Bibelanstalt, 1969.

Waddington, W. H. 1870. *Inscriptions grecques et latines de Syrie.* 4. ed. Paris: Didot.

Wagner, M. Monica, trans. 1950. *The Fathers of the Church. A New Translation.* Vol. 9: 463–74. New York: Fathers of the Church. [ET of Basil, "Homily 11. Concerning Envy/*Peri phthonou*." PG 31.372–386].

2. SECONDARY STUDIES AND REFERENCE WORKS

Abu-Lughod, Lila. 1988. *Veiled Sentiments, Honor and Poetry in a Bedouin Society.* Berkeley: University of California Press, 1988.

Abu-Rabia, Aref. 2005. "The Evil Eye and Cultural Beliefs among the Bedouin Tribes of the Negev, Middle East." *Folklore* 116/3:241–54.

Al-Saleh, Yasmine. 2010. "Amulets and Talismans from the Islamic World." In *Heilbrunn Timeline of Art History.* New York: The Metropolitan Museum of Art, 2000–. http://www.metmuseum.org/toah/hd/tali/hd_tali.htm.

Anonymous. 1974. "Evil Eye." *Encyclopedic Dictionary of Judaica*, edited by Geoffrey Wigoder, 181. New York: Amiel.

Apostolides, Anastasia. 2008. "Western Ethnocentrism: A Comparison between African Witchcraft and the Greek Evil Eye from a Sociology of Religion Perspective." Masters thesis, Faculty of Theology, University of Pretoria, South Africa, 2008.

Arnaud, Louis. 1911. "Quelques superstitions liturgiques chez les Grecs. V. Le mauvais oeil." *Échos d'Orient* 14:75–80.

———. 1912. "La baskania ou le mauvais oeil chez les Grecs modernes." *Échos d'Orient* 15:385–94, 510–24.

Aschkenazi, S. 1984. "The Belief in the 'Evil Eye' as Reflected in Jewish Folklore." [in Hebrew] *Yes'a Am* 22:100–111.

Bagatti, B. 1971. "Altre medaglie di Salamone cavaliere e loro origine." *Revista di archeologia cristiana* 47:331–42.

———. 1972. "I Giudeo-Cristiani e l'anello di Salamone." *Recherches de science religieuse* 60:151–60.
Barakat, R. A. 1973 "Arabic Gestures." *Journal of Popular Culture* 6: 749–87.
Bar-Ilan, Meir. 1993. "Witches in the Bible and in the Talmud." In *Approaches to Ancient Judaism*, edited by Herbert W. Basser and Simcha Fishbane, 7–32. Atlanta: Scholars.
———. 2002. "Between Magic and Religion: Sympathetic Magic in the World of the Sages of the Mishnah and Talmud." *Review of Rabbinic Judaism* 5:383–99.
Barkay, Gabriel, Marilyn J. Lundberg, Andrew G.; Vaughn, and Bruce Zuckerman. 2004. "The Amulets from Ketef Hinnom: A New Edition and Evaluation." *BASOR* 333: 41–71.
Barkay, Gabriel. 2009. "The Riches of Ketef Hinnom." *BAR* 35/4–5:22–35, 122, 124, 126.
Bartelink, G. 1983. "BASKANOS, Désignation de Satan et des démons chez les auteurs chrétiens." *Orientalia Christiana Periodica* 49:390–406.
Bauer, P. V. C., M. Rostovtzeff et al., eds. 1929–69. *The Excavations at Dura-Europos conducted by Yale University and the French Academy of Inscriptions and Letters 1928 to 1937*. 9 vols. New Haven: Yale University Press.
Betz, Hans Dieter. 1997. "Jewish Magic in the Greek Magical Papyri *(PGM VII.* 260–71*)*." In *Envisioning Magic: A Princeton Seminar and Symposium*, edited by Peter Schaefer and Hans G. Kippenberg, 45–63. Studies in the History of Religions 75. Leiden: Brill.
Bille, Mikkel. 2010. "Seeking Providence through Things: The Word of God versus Black Cumin." In *An Anthropology of Absence: Materializations of Transcendence and Loss*, edited by Mikkel Bille, Frida Hastrup and Tim Flohr Sorensen, 167–84. New York: Springer, 2010.
Billerbeck, Paul. 1922–1961. [and Hermann L. Strack]. *Kommentar zum Neuen Testament aus Talmud und Midrasch*. 6 vols. 3rd ed. Munich: Beck, 1922–196l.
———. 1928. *Exkurse zu einzelnen Stellen des Neuen Testaments*. Vol. 4.1 in *Kommentar zum Neuen Testament aus Talmud und Midrasch*. 3rd ed. Munich: Beck.
Exkurs 21. "Zur altjüdischen Dämonologie" 4.1:501–535.
Exkurs 22. "Die altjüdische Privatwohltätigkeit." 4.1:536–558.
Exkurs 23. Die altjüdische Liebeswerke." 4.1:559–610.
Birnbaum, Philip. 1975. "Evil Eye." *A Book of Jewish Concepts*, 462–63. Rev. ed. New York: Hebrew Publishing.
Black, Stephen K. 2005. *Paideia, Power and Episcopacy: John Chrysostom and the Formation of the Late Antique Bishop*. PhD diss., Graduate Theological Union, Berkeley, California, 2005.
———. 2017. *Paideia, Power and Episcopacy: John Chrysostom and the Formation of the Late Antique Bishop*. Berkeley: University of California Press.
Blau, Ludwig. 1898. *Das altjüdische Zauberwesen*. Jahresbericht der Landes-Rabbinerschule in Budapest für das Schuljahr 1897-98. Budapest. 1898. Reprinted, Westmead, UK: Gregg, 1970.
———. 1907a. "Amulet." In *JE* 1:546–50.
Blau, Ludwig [and Kaufmann Kohler]. 1907b. "Evil Eye." In *JE* 5:280–81
Bohak, Gideon. 2008. *Ancient Jewish Magic: A History*. Cambridge: Cambridge University Press.

Bonneau, Danielle. 1982. "L'apotropaïque 'Abáskantos' en Égypte." *Revue de l'historie des religions* 99/1: 23–36.
Bonner, Campbell. 1950. *Studies in Magical Amulets Chiefly Graeco-Egyptian*. Ann Arbor: University of Michigan Press.
———. 1951. "Amulets Chiefly in the British Museum: A Supplementary Article." *Hesperia* 20: 301–45 and plates 96–100.
Brav, Aaron. 1908/1992. "The Evil Eye among the Hebrews." *Ophthalmology* 5 (1908): 427–35. Reprinted in *The Evil Eye: A Casebook*, edited by A. Dundes. 2nd expanded ed., 44–54. Madison: University of Wisconsin Press, 1992.
Brightman, F. E. 1896. *Liturgies Eastern and Western*. Vol. 1. Oxford: Clarendon.
Brown, Peter. 1970. "Sorcery, Demons and the Rise of Christianity: From Late Antiquity to the Middle Ages." In *Witchcraft Accusations and Confessions*, edited by Mary Douglas, 17–45. London: Tavistock.
———. 1972. *Religion and Society in the Age of Saint Augustine*. New York: Harper & Row.
———. 1992. *Power and Persuasion in Late Antiquity: Towards a Christian Empire*. The. Curti Lectures. Madison: University of Wisconsin Press.
Brox, Norbert. 1974. "Magie und Aberglaube an den Anfängen des Christentums." *Trierer Theologische Zeitschrift* 83: 157–80.
Budge, Ernest Alfred Wallis. 1978/1930. *Amulets and Superstitions*. New York: Dover, 1978; reprinted from Oxford: Oxford University Press, 1930.
Campbell, John. K. 1964. *Honour, Family and Patronage. A Study of Institutions and Moral Values in a Greek Mountain Community*. Oxford: Oxford University Press.
Campo, Juan Eduardo. 2009a. "Amulets and Talismans." In *Encyclopedia of Islam*, 40–41. Encyclopedia of World Religions. New York: Facts on File.
Campo, Juan Eduardo. 2009b. "Evil Eye." *Encyclopedia of Islam*, 220–21. Encyclopedia of World Religions. New York: Facts on Files.
Canaan, T. 1914. *Aberglaube und Volkmedizin in Lande der Bibel*. Abhandlungen des Hamburgischen Kolonialinstituts 20.Volkerkunde, Kulturgeschichte und Sprachen 12. Hamburg: Friederichsen.
Casanowicz, I. M. 1917a. "Two Jewish Amulets in the United States National Museum." *JAOS* 37:43–56.
———. 1917b. "Jewish Amulets in the United States National Museum." *JAOS* 37:154–67.
Cavassini, Maria Teresa. 1954. "Lettere cristiane nei papyri greci d'Egitto." *Aegyptus* 34:266–82.
Chryssanthopolou, Vassiliki. 2008. "The Evil Eye among the Greeks of Australia. Identity, Continuity, and Modernization." In *Greek Magic: Ancient, Medieval and Modern*, edited by J. C. B. Petropoulos, 106–18. London: Routledge.
Cohn, Yehudah B. 2008. *Tangled Up in Text: Tefillin and the Ancient World*. Brown Judaic Studies 351. Providence, RI: Brown Judaic Studies.
Cumont, Franz. 1926. *Fouilles de Doura-Europos 1922–23*. 2 vols. BAH 9. Paris.
Daremberg, Charles and Edmond Saglio, eds. *Dictionnaire des antiquités grecques et romaines*. 10 vols (5 double volumes). Paris: Hachette, 1877–1919.
Davis, Eli. and David A. Frenkel. 1995. *The Hebrew Amulet. Biblical-medical-general* [in Hebrew]. Jerusalem: Institute for Jewish Studies.
Delatte, A. and P. Derchain. 1964. *Les intailles magiques gréco-égyptiennes*. Cabinet de médailles, Bibliothèque nationale. Paris: Bibliothèque nationale.

de Rossi, J. B. 1869. *Bulletin d'archéologie chrétienne* 7:61–62.
De Vaux, Carra. 1910. "Charms and Amulets (Muhammadan)." In *HERE* 3:457–61.
De Wet, Chris Len. 2007. "The Homilies of John Chrysostom on 1 Corinthians 12: a Model of Antiochene Exegesis on the Charismata." M.A. thesis, Ancient Language and Culture Studies, Faculty of Humanities, University of Pretoria.
Dickie, Matthew W. 1995. "The Fathers of the Church and the Evil Eye." In *Byzantine Magic: Papers from Dumbarton Oaks Colloquium*, edited by H. Maguire, 9–34. Dumbarton Oaks Research Library and Collection.
———. 2001. *Magic and Magicians in the Greco-Roman World*. New York: Routledge.
Dictionnaire d'archéologie chrétienne et de liturgie. 15 vols. Edited by F. Cabrol and H. Leclercq. Paris: Letouzey & Ané, 1907–1953.
Dionisopoulos-Mass, Regina.1976. "The Evil Eye and Bewitchment in a Peasant Village." In *The Evil Eye*, edited by C. Maloney, 42–62. New York: Columbia University Press.
Dirven, Lucinda. 1999. *The Palmyrenes of Dura-Europos: A Study of Religious Interaction in Roman Syria*. Leiden: Brill.
DiTomasso, Lorenzo. 2012. "Pseudepigrapha Notes IV: 5. The Testament of Job. 6. The Testament of Solomon." *Journal for the Study of the Pseudepigrapha* 21:313–20.
Dobberahn, F. E. 1976. *Fünf Äthiopische Zauberrollen: Text, Übersetzung, Kommentar*. Beiträge zur Sprach- und Kulturgeschichte des Orients, 25. Walldorf-Hessen:Verlag für Orientkunde.
Dobschütz, Ernst von. 1910. "Charms and Amulets (Christian)." In *HERE* 3:413–30.
Dölger, Franz Joseph. 1922–27, 1943. *ICHTHYS: Der heilige Fisch in den antiken Religionen und im Christentum*. 5 vols. Münster: F. J. Dölger Institut/Aschendorff. Vol. 1 (1922; 2nd ed, 1928); 2 (1922); 3 (1922); 4 (1927); 5 (1943).
———. 1932a. "Das Anhängekreuzchen der hl. Makrina und ihr Ring mit dem Kreuzpartikel." *Antike und Christentum* 3:81–116.
———. 1932b. "Eine Knabenbulla mit Christus-Monogramm auf einer Bronze des Prov. -Museums zu Trier." *Antike und Christentum* 3:253–56 and Plate 13.
Downey, Glanville. 1962. *Antioch in the Age of Theodosius the Great*. Norman: University of Oklahoma Press.
Duling, Dennis C. 1975. "Solomon, Exorcism, and the Son of David." *HTR* 68:235–52.
———. 1984. "The Legend of Solomon the Magician in Antiquity: Problems and Perspectives." 1–23. *Proceedings: Eastern Great Lakes Biblical Society 4*. Westerville, OH: EGLBS.
———. 1985. "The Eleazar Miracle and Solomon's Magical Wisdom in Flavius Josephus's Antiquitates Judaicae 8.42–49." *HTR* 78:1–25.
———. 1988. "The Testament of Solomon: Retrospect and Prospect." *JSP* 2:93–95.
———. 1992. "Solomon, Testament of." In *ABD* 6:117–19.
———. 1993. "Testament of Solomon." In *Old Testament Pseudepigrapha*, Vol. 1, edited by James H. Charlesworth, 935–87. Garden City, NY: Doubleday.
Du Mesnil du Buisson, R. 1939. *Les peintures de la Synagogue de Doura-Europos, 245–256 après Jesus Christ*. Rome: Pontifical Biblical Institute.
Dunbabin, Katherine M. D. 1978. *The Mosaics of Roman North Africa*. Oxford: Oxford University Press
———. 1989. "*Baiarum Grata Voluptas*: Pleasure and Dangers of the Baths." *PBSR Papers of the British School at Rome* 57:33–46.

———. 1991. "*Inbide calco te. . .* Trampling upon the Envious." In *Tesserae: Festschrift für Joseph Engemann*, edited by Ernst Dassmann und Klaus Thraede, 26–35 and Plates 4 and 5. JAC Ergänzungsband 18. Münster: Aschendorff.

———. 1999. *Mosaics of the Greek and Roman World*. Cambridge: Cambridge University Press.

Dunbabin, Katherine M. D., and M. W. Dickie. 1983. "Invida rumpantur pectora: The Iconography of Phthonos/Invidia in Graeco-Roman Art." *JAC* 26:7–37 & Plates 1–8.

Dundes, Alan, ed. 1992. *The Evil Eye: A Casebook*. 2nd expanded edition. Madison: University of Wisconsin Press, 1992. (1st ed.: *The Evil Eye: A Folklore Casebook*, New York: Garland, 1981).

Dura Europos. *Crossroads of Antiquity*. 2011. Edited by L. R. Brody and G. L. Hoffman. Chestnut Hill, MA: McMullan Museum of Art, Boston College.

Échos d'Orient (Paris, 1897–1942) succeeded by *Revue des études Byzantines*.

Edwards, Dennis. 1971. "The Evil Eye and Middle East Culture." *Folklore Annual of the University Folklore Association* 3:33–41.

Einszler, Lydia. 1899. "Das böse Auge." *Zeitschrift des deutschen Palästinavereins* 12: 200–22.

Eitrem, Samson E., and L. Amundsen, eds. 1925–36. *Papyri Osloenses*. 3 vols. Oslo: Dybwad.

Eitrem. Samson E., and Anton Friderichsen. 1921. *Ein christliches Amulett auf Papyrus Videnskapsselskapets Forhandlinger for 1920*, 1. Kristiania (Oslo): Dybwad. Reprinted in Eitrem, ed. *Papyri Osloenses* 1 1925, no. 5, p. 21.

Elliott, John H. 1988. "The Fear of the Leer: The Evil Eye From the Bible to Li'l Abner." *Forum* 4/4:42–71.

———. 1991. "The Evil Eye in the First Testament: The Ecology and Culture of a Pervasive Belief." In *The Bible and the Politics of Exegesis: Essays in Honor of Norman K. Gottwald on His Sixty-Fifth Birthday*, edited by David Jobling et al., 147–59. Cleveland, OH: Pilgrim.

———. 1994. "The Evil Eye and the Sermon on the Mount: Contours of a Pervasive Belief in Social Scientific Perspective." *Biblical Interpretation* 2:51–84.

———. 2007. "Envy, Jealousy and Zeal in the Bible: Sorting Out the Social Differences and Theological Implications—No Envy for YHWH." In *To Break Every Yoke: Essays in Honor of Marvin C. Chaney*, edited by Robert Coote and Norman K. Gottwald, 344–63. Sheffield: Sheffield Phoenix Press.

———. 2008. "God—Zealous or Jealous but never Envious: The Theological Consequences of Linguistic and Social Distinctions." In *The Social Sciences and Biblical Translation*, edited by Dietmar Neufeld, 79–96. Symposium Series, 41. Atlanta: Society of Biblical Literature.

———. 2015a. *Beware the Evil Eye: The Evil Eye in the Bible and the Ancient World*. Volume 1. *Introduction, Mesopotamia, and Egypt*. Eugene, OR: Cascade Books.

———. 2015b. "Jesus, Paulus und der Böse Blick: Was die modernen Bibelversionen und Kommentare uns nicht sagen." In *Alte Texte in neuen Kontexten: Wo steht die sozialwissenschaftliche Bibelexegese?*, edited by Wolfgang Stegemann and Richard E. DeMaris, 85–104. Stuttgart: Kohlhammer.

———. 2016a. *Beware the Evil Eye: The Evil Eye in the Bible and the Ancient World*. Volume 2. *Greece and Rome*. Eugene, OR: Cascade Books.

———. 2016b. *Beware the Evil Eye: The Evil Eye in the Bible and the Ancient World*. Volume 3. *The Bible and Related Sources*. Eugene, OR: Cascade Books.

———. 2017a. "Envy." In *The Ancient Mediterranean Social World: A Sourcebook*. Edited by Zeba Crook. Grand Rapids: Eerdmans.

———. 2017b. "Evil Eye." In *The Ancient Mediterranean Social World: A Sourcebook*. Edited by Zeba Crook. Grand Rapids: Eerdmans.

Elworthy, Frederick Thomas. 1895/1958 *The Evil Eye. An Account of This Ancient and Widespread Superstition*. London: Murray, l895. Reprinted with an Introduction by Louis S. Barron, New York: Julian Press, 1958.

Enciclopedia dell'arte medioevale. 12 vols. Rome Istituto della Enciclopedia italiana, c. 1991–2002. Rome: Istituto dell'Enciclopedia Italiana fondato da Giovanni Treccani. Online: http://www.treccani.it/enciclopedia

Encyclopaedia Judaica (German). 10 vols. Edited by Jacob Klatzkin, Nahum Goldmann, and Ismar Elbogen. Berlin: Eschol, 1928–34.

Encyclopaedia Judaica (English). 14 vols. Cecil Roth and Geoffrey Wigoder, gen. eds. Jerusalem: Keter Books/New York: Macmillan, 1972. 2nd ed. Fred Skolnik, editor in chief. 22 vols. New York: Thomson Gale, 2006.

Encyclopædia of Islam, The: A Dictionary of the Geography, Ethnography and Biography of the Muhammadan Peoples, 4 vols. and Suppl. Edited by M. T. Houtsma, et al., Leiden: Brill and London: Luzac, 1913–38. 2nd ed. by P. J. Bearman, Th. Bianquis, C.E. Bosworth, E. van Donzel and W. P. Heinrichs et al. 12 vols. Leiden: Brill, 1960–2005.

Encyclopedia of Islam. 2nd ed. Edited by P. J. Bearman, T. Bianquis, C. E. Bosworth, E. van Donzel and W. P. Heinrichs. 12 vols. with indexes and etc., Leiden: Brill, 1960–2005. 3rd ed. Edited by Kate Fleet, Gudrun Krämer, Denis Matringe, John Nawas, and Everett Rowson 2007.

Encyclopedia of Islam. Edited by Juan E. Campo. Encyclopedia of World Religions. New York: Facts on Files, 2009.

Encyclopaedia of Islam, Shorter. [Abridgment of the 1st ed., 1913–1938]. Edited by H. A. R. Gibb and J. H. Kramers on behalf of the Royal Netherlands Academy. Leiden: Brill, 1953.

Encyclopaedia of Religion and Ethics. 13 vols. Edited by James Hastings et al. 13 vols. Edinburgh: T. and T. Clark, 1908–1926.

Engemann, Josef. 1969. "Fisch, Fischer, Fischfang." *RAC* 7:959–1097.

———. 1975. "Zur Verbreitung magischer Übelabwehr in der nichtchristlichen und Christlichen Spätantike." *JAC* 18:22–48 + 14 figures & Plates 8–16.

———. 1980. "Der 'Corna' Gestus—Ein antiker und frühchristlicher Abwehr- und Spottgestus?" *Pietas*. Bernhard Kötting FS. Edited by Ernst Dassmann and K. Suso Frank, 493–98. JAC Ergänzungsband 8. Münster: Aschendorff.

———. 1981. "Glyptik." In *RAC* 11:270–313.

Engemann, J., S. H. Fuglesang, G. Vikan, and M. Bernardini. 1991. "*Amuleto.*" [Introduction: Engemann; West: Englemann; North: Fuglesang; Byzantine: Vikan; Islam: Bernardini] *Enciclopedia dell' Arte Medievale*. Rome: Istituto della Enciclopedia Italiana.

Espérandieu, E. 1919. "Tintinnabulum (*kôdôn*)." In *Dictionnaire des antiquités grecques et romaines*, 5:341–44.

Fahd, Toufic. "Magic in Islam." 1989. In *Hidden Truths. Magic, Alchemy, and the Occult. Religion, History, and Culture,* edited by L. E. Sulliivan, 122–130. New York: Macmillan.

Faraone, C. A. 2009. "Stopping Evil, Pain, Anger, and Blood: The Ancient Greek Tradition of Protective Iambic Incantations." *Greek, Roman, and Byzantine Studies* 49/2: 227–55.

Fauth, Wolfgang. 1999. "Der christliche Reiterheilige des Sisinnios-typs im Kampf gegen eine vielnamige Dämonin." *Vigilliae Christianae* 53: 401–25.

Finneran, Niall. 2003. "Ethiopian evil eye belief and the magical symbolism of iron working." *Folklore* 114: 427–32.

Fitzgerald, F. Scott. 1915–16. "Evil Eye: A Musical Comedy in Two Acts." [Program] Presented by the Princeton University Triangle Club, Season of 1915–1916.

Ford, James Nathan. 1998. "'Ninety-Nine by the Evil Eye and One from Natural Causes': KTU² 1.96 in Its Near Eastern Context." *Ugarit-Forschungen* 30:201–78.

———. 2000. "Additions and Corrections to 'Ninety-Nine by the Evil Eye . . . '" *Ugarit-Forschungen* 32:711–15.

Foskolou, Vassiliki. 2005. "The Virgin, the Christ-child and the Evil Eye." In *Images of the Mother of God: Perceptions of the Theotokos in Byzantium,* edited by M. Vassilaki. 251–62 with 7 plates. Burlington, VT: Ashgate.

Frankel, Ellen, and Betsy Platkin Teutsh. 1992. *The Encyclopedia of Jewish Symbols.* Northvale, NJ: Aronson.

Furst, Rachel. 1998. "Red Strings: a Modern Case of Amulets and Charms." In *Jewish Legal Writings by Women,* edited by Micah D. Halpern and Chana Safrai, 259–77. Jerusalem: Urim.

Garnett, Lucy M. J. 1891. *The Women of Turkey and Their Folk-Lore: The Jewish and Moslem Women.* London: Nutt.

Gaster, Moses. 1910. "Charms and Amulets (Jewish)." In *HERE* 3: 451–55.

Gaster, Theodor H. 1962. "Demon, Demonology." In *IDB* 1:817–24.

———. 1969. *Myth, Legend and Custom in the Old Testament: A comparative study with chapters from Sir James G. Frazer's Folklore in the Old Testament.* 2 vols. New York: Harper.

———. 1989. "Amulets and Talismans." In *Encyclopedia of Religion,* edited by M. Eliade, New York: Macmillan, 1987. Reprinted in L. E. Sullivan, *Hidden Truths,* 1989:145–50.

Ghedini, G. 1923. *Lettere cristiane dai papiri greci del III e del IV seculo.* Supplement to Aegyptus 18.1. Milan: Giuseppe.

Gibson, E. P. 1975. "A unique Christian epitaph from the Upper Tembris Valley." *Bulletin of the American Society of Papyrologists* 12:151–57.

Ginsberg, Louis. 1961. *The Legends of the Jews.* 7 vols. Philadelphia: Jewish Publication Society of America.

Gitler, H. 1990. "Four Magical and Christian Amulets." *Liber Annus* 40:365–74 and Plates 61–62.

Goar, J. ed. 1730. *Euchologion sive rituale Graecorum.* Venice, 1730. Reprinted, Graz: Akademische Druck- & Verlagsanstalt, 1960.

Gollancz, Hermann. 1912. *The Book of Protection, being a Collection of Charms Now Edited for the First Time from Syriac MSS with Translation, Introduction and Notes, with 27 Illustrations.* London: Henry Frowde; reprinted Cambridge University

Press, 2011; Gorgias Press, 2012. [Codex A, §§1–54 (xxv–lx); Codex B, §§1–12 (lxi–lxxiii); Codex C, §§1–29 (lxxiii–lxxxvii)].
Goodenough, Erwin Ramsdell. 1953–68. *Jewish Symbols in the Greco-Roman Period.* 13 vols. Bollingen Series 37. New York: Pantheon.
Gordon, Benjamin Lee. 1937. "Oculus fascinus (Fascination, Evil Eye)." *Archives of Ophthalmology* 17:290–319. Reprinted as "The Evil Eye." *Hebrew Medical Journal* 34 (1961) 261–91.
Gordon, Cyrus H. 1934. "Aramaic Magical Bowls in the Istanbul and Baghdad Museums." *ArOr* 6:324–26.
———. 1937. "Aramaic and Mandaic Magic Bowls."*ArOr* 9:84–106.
———. 1957. "A World of Demons and Liliths." In *Adventures in the Ancient Near East*, 160–84. London: Phoenix.
Grabar, A. 1974. "Amulettes byzantines du moeyn âge." In *Melanges d'histoire des religions offerts à Henri Charles Puech*, 531–41. Paris: Presses Universitaires de France.
Greek Lexicon of the Roman and Byzantine Periods. 2 vols. Edited by E. A. Sophocles. New York: Scribners, 1900.
Greenfield, R.P.H. 1989. "Saint Sisinnios, the Archangel Michael and the Female Demon Gylou: the Typology of the Greek Literary Stories." *Byzantina* 15:83–142.
Gregg, Robert C. 2000. "Marking Religious and Ethnic Boundaries: Cases from the Ancient Golan Heights." *Church History* 69:519–57.
Gross, Charles G. 1999. "The Fire That Comes from the Eye." *The Neuroscientist* 5/4: 58–64.
Grünbaum, M. 1877. "Beiträge zur vergleichenden Mythologie aus der Hagada." *Zeitschrift der morgenländischen Gesellschaft* 31:183–359.
Gsell, Stéphane, Xavier Dupuis, and H.-G. Pflaum, eds. 1922. *Inscriptions latines de l'Algérie.* Paris: Champion.
Hachlili, Rachel. 1998. *Ancient Jewish Art and Archeology in the Diaspora. Handbook of Oriental Studies.* Erste Abteilung. Der Nahe und Mittlere Osten 35. Leiden: Brill.
Handwörterbuch des deutschen Aberglaubens. 10 vols. Edited by H. Bächtold-Stäubli and E. Hoffmann-Krayer. Berlin: de Gruyter, 1927–1942. Reprinted, 1987.
Hazard, Willis Hatfield. 1893. "A Syriac Charm." *JAOS* 15:284–96.
Heath, M. 2004. "John Chrysostom, Rhetoric and Galatians." *Biblical Interpretation* 12/4:369–400. http://eprints.whiterose.ac.uk/398/1/heathm14.pdf
Heller, B. 1972. "Amulett." In *Encyclopedia Judaica* 2:735–46.
Herber, J. 1927. "Le Main de Fathima." *Hesperis* 7:209–19.
Herrmann, Christian. 1994. *Ägyptische Amulette aus Palästina/Israel.* Orbis Biblicus et Orientalis 138. Göttingen: Vandenhoeck & Ruprecht.
———. 2002. *Ägyptische Amulette aus Palästina/Israel II.* Orbis Biblicus et Orientalis 184. Göttingen: Vandenhoeck & Ruprecht.
Herter, Hans. 1950. "Böse Dämonen im frühgriechischen Volksglauben." *Rheinisiches Jahrbuch für Volkskunde* 1:112–43.
Herzfeld, Michael. 1981. "Meaning and Morality: A Semiotic Approach to Evil Eye Accusations in a Greek Village." *American Ethnologist* 8:560–74.
———. 1984. "The Horns of the Mediterranean dilemma." *American Ethnologist* 11:439–54; discussion: 12 (1985) 369–71.
———. 1986. "Closure as Cure: Tropes in the Exploration of Bodily and Social Disorder." *Current Anthropology* 27:107–20.

Hinterberger, Martin. 2010. "Envy and Nemesis in the Vita Basilii and Leo the Deacon." In *History as Literature in Byzantium*, edited by Ruth Macredes, 187–206. Surrey, UKs: Ashgate.

———. 2013. *Phthonos: Missgunst, Neid und Eifersucht in der Byzantinischen Literatur.* Serta Graeca series 29. Wiesbaden: Reichert.

Hirsch, Emil G. 1892. "The Evil Eye." *The Folk-Lorist* 1:69–74.

Hodges, R., W. Bowden, and K. Lako, eds. 2004. *Byzantine Butrint: Excavations and Surveys 1994–99.* Oxford: Oxbow.

Hopkins, C. 1979. *The Discovery of Dura-Europos.* New Haven: Yale University Press.

Horsley, G. H. et al., eds. 1981—. *New Documents Illustrating Early Christianity.* 10 vols. North Ryde, New South Wales: The Ancient History Research Centre, Macquarie University.

Hübner, Ernst Emil. 1871. *Inscriptiones Hispaniae christianae.* Berlin: Reimer.

Ibn Khaldun. 1858. *Al-muqaddimah.* Edited by M. Quatremère. 3 vols. Paris: Duprat. Translated by Franz Rosenthal as *The Muqaddimah: An Introduction to History.* 2nd ed. 3 vols. Princeton: Princeton University Press, 1967.

Jastrow, Marcus. *Dictionary of the Targumim, the Talmud Babli and Yerushalmi, and the Midrashic Literature.* 2 vols. New York: Pardes, 1950.

Jeffers, A. 1996. *Magic and Divination in Ancient Palestine and Syria.* Leiden: Brill.

Jewish Encyclopedia, The. Isidor Singer, gen. ed. 12 vols. New York: Funk & Wagnalls. 1st ed., 1901–1907; 2nd ed., 1912; 3rd ed, 1927.

Jones, Brice C. 2016. *New Testament Texts on Greek Amulets from Late Antiquity.* Library of New Testament Studies 554. London: Bloomsbury T. & T. Clark.

Kahl, Thede. 2006. "Der Böse Blick: Ein gemeinsames Element im Volksglauben von Christen und Muslimen." In *Religion und Magie in Ostmitteleuropa: Spielräume theologischer Normierungsprozesse in Spätmittelalter und Früher Neuzeit*, edited by Thomas Wünsch, 321–35. Religions- und Kulturgeschichte in Ostmittel- und Südosteuropa 8. Münster: Lit-Verlag. https://www.academia.edu/12456713/Der_B%C3%B6se_Blick_-_Ein_gemeinsames_Element_im_Volksglauben_von_Christen_und_Muslimen._In_W%C3%BCnsch_Thomas_Hg._Religion_und_Magie_in_Ostmitteleuropa._Religions-_und_Kulturgeschichte_in_Ostmittel-_und_S%C3%BCdosteuropa_Bd._8_M%C3%BCnster_S._321–336.

Kalmin, Richard. 2012. "The Evil Eye in Rabbinic Literature of Late Antiquity." In *Judaea-Palaestina, Babylon and Rome: Jews in Antiquity.* Edited by Benjamin Isaac and Yuval Shahar, 111–38. Texts and Studies in Ancient Judaism 147. Tübingen: Mohr/Siebeck.

Kanafani, Aida S. 1993. "Rites of Hospitality and Aesthetics." In *Everyday Life in the Muslim Middle East*, edited by Donna Lee Bowen and Evelyn A. Early, 128–35. Indiana Series in Arab and Islamic Studies. Bloomington: Indiana University Press.

Kaufman, R. 1939. "Amulets." *Universal Jewish Encyclopedia* 1:288–91.

Kehl, A. 1974. "Antike Volksfrömmigkeit und das Christentum." In *Die Alte Kirche*, edited by H. Frohnes and U. W. Knorr, 1:313–43. Munich: Kaiser.

Kelsey, Neal. 1994. "Amulet to Heal Ahmed from Fever, Evil Eye, and Other Problems (Heidelberg Kopt. 544)." In *Ancient Christian Magic: Coptic Texts of Ritual Power*, edited by Marvin Meyer, Richard Smith, and Neal Kelsey, 101. San Francisco: HarperSanFrancisco.

Kennedy, A. R. S. 1910. "Charms and Amulets (Hebrew)." In *HERE* 3:439–41.

Kern-Ulmer, see Ulmer, Rivka Brigitte Kern
King, C. W. 1873. *Early Christian Numismatics and Other Antiquarian Tracts*. London: Bell & Daldy.
Kirschenblatt-Gimblett, Barabra and Harris Lenowitz. 1973. "The Evil Eye (The Good Eye) Einehore." *Alcheringa* 5:71–77.
Klutz, Todd, ed. 2003. *Magic in the Biblical World. From the Rod of Aaron to the Ring of Solomon*. JSNTS supplementary series 245. Sheffield: Sheffield Academic Press.
Kohler, Kaufmann and Blau, Ludwig. 1907. "Evil Eye." In *The Jewish Encyclopedia* 5:280–281.
Kosior, Wojciech. 2014. " 'It Will Not Let the Destroying [One] Enter.' The Mezuzah as an Apotropaic Device According to Biblical and Rabbinic Sources." *The Polish Journal of the Arts and Culture* 9/1:127–44.
Kotansky, Roy. 1991. "Incantations and Prayers for Salvation on Inscribed Greek Amulets." In *Magika Hiera*, edited by Christopher A. Faraone and Dirk Obbink, 107–37. New York: Oxford University Press.
———. 1994. *Greek Magical Amulets. I. The Inscribed Gold, Silver, Copper, and Bronze Lamellae. Part One. Published Texts of Known Provenance*. Papyrologica Coloniensia 22/1. Opladen: Westdeutscher Verlag.
———. 1995. "Greek Exorcistic Amulets." In *Ancient Magic and Ritual Power*, edited by Marvin Meyer and Paul Mirecki, 243–77. Religions in the Graeco-Roman World 129. Leiden: Brill.
———. 2002. "An Early Christian Gold Lamella for Headache." In *Magic and Ritual in the Ancient World*, edited by Paul Mirecki and Marvin Meyer, 37–46. Religions in the Graeco-Roman World 141. Leiden: Brill.
Kötting, Bernhard. 1950. *Peregrinatio religiosa: Wallfahrten in der Antike und das Pilgerwesen in der alten Kirche*. Forschungen zur Volkskunde 33–35. Münster: Regensberg.
———. 1954. "Böser Blick." In *RAC* 2:473–482.
———. 1978. "Geste und Gebärde." In *RAC* 10:895–902.
Koukoules, Phaidon. 1948. *Byzantinôn bios kai politismos. Vie et civilisation byzantine*. 6 vols. Collection de l'Institut francais d'Athenes. Athens: Institut francais d'Athenes, 1948. [1.1: 244–48 on the evil eye in Byzantium.]
Kovalenko, Anatoly. 1979. *Les concepts de magie (sihr) et de sciences occultes ('ilm al-gayb) en Islam*, Doctoral Thesis. Université de Strasbourg.
———. 1981. *Magie et Islam*. Geneva: Minute.
Kraeling, Carl Hermann. 1956. *The Excavations at Dura-Europos*. Final Report 8.1. *The Synagogue*. New Haven: Yale University Press.
Krawietz, Birgit. 2002. "Islamic conceptions of the evil eye." *Medicine and Law* 21/2: 339–55.
Kriss, Rudolf and Hubert Kriss-Heinrich. 1962. *Volksglaube im Bereich des Islam*. Vol. 2. *Amulette, Zauberformen und Beschwörungen*. Wiesbaden: Otto Harrassowitz, 1962
Lampe, G. W. H., ed. *A Patristic Greek Lexicon*. Oxford: Clarendon, 1961–68.
Lauer, H. H. 1983. "Böser Blick." *Lexikon des Mittelalters* 2:470–72.
Leclercq, Henri. 1910. "Bulla." In *DACL* 2.1: 1331–34.
———. 1924. "Amulettes." In *DACL* 1.2: 1784–860; cols. 1843–47 on "Le mauvais oeil."
———. 1933. "Méduse." In *DACL* 11.1:195–99.
———. 1936. "Oeil." In *DACL* 12.2: 1936–43, cols. 1936–41 on "Le mauvais oeil."

———. 1950. "Sisinnios." In *DACL* 15.1: 1497–98.
Levi, Doro. 1941. "The Evil Eye and the Lucky Hunchback." In *Antioch-on-the-Orontes. III. The Excavations 1937–1939*. 5 vols. Edited by Richard Stillwell. Publications of the Committee for the Excavation of Antioch and Its Vicinity. Princeton: Princeton University Press, 1934–72. Vol. 3 edited by Richard Stillwell, 1941, 220–32.
———. 1947 *Antioch Mosaic Pavements*. 2 vols. Princeton: Princeton University Press. Vol. 1: 28–34 & plates, esp. XL. Vol. 2, plate IVa-c., see figs. 12–14.
Lévy, Isaac Jack, and Rosemary Lévy Zumwalt. 1987. "The Evil Eye and the Power of Speech among the Sephardim." *International Folklore Review* 5:52–59.
———, eds. 2002. *Ritual Medical Lore of Sephardic Women. Sweetening the Spirits, Healing the Sick*. Urbana: University of Illinois Press.
Levy, Jacob. 1924. *Wörterbuch über die Talmudim und Midraschim*, including contributions by Heinrich Leberecht Fleischer. 2nd edition, with supplements und corrections by Lazarus Goldschmidt. Berlin: Harz, 1924. Reprinted, Darmstadt: Wissenschaftliche Buchgesellschaft, 1963.
Lexikon der byzantinischen Gräzitität, besonders des 9.–12. Jahrhunderts. Edited by E. Trapp et al. Vienna: Austrian Akademy of Science, 2001–2007.
Lexikon des Mittelalters. 9 vols. Edited by Bruno Mariacher. Munich: Artemis & Winkler (vols. 1–6); Munich: LexMA-Verlag (vols. 7–9), 1980–1998. Munich: DTV, 2002.
Leyerle, Blake. 1993. "John Chrysostom on the Gaze." *Journal of Early Christian Studies* 1:159–74.
Liddell, H. G., R. Scott, and H. S. Jones. 1968. *A Greek–English Lexicon*. Oxford: Clarendon.
Lilienthal, Regina. 1924. "Ayin hara (Eyin hore)" *Yiddische Filologye* 1: 245–71.
Limberis, Vasiliki. 1991. "The Eyes Infected by Evil: Basil of Caesarea's Homily, On Envy." *HTR* 84:163–84.
Löwinger, Adolf. 1926. "Der Böse Blick nach jüdischen Quellen." *Menorah* 4: 551–69.
Louth, Andrew. 1984. "Envy as the Chief Sin in Athanasius and Gregory of Nyssa." *Studia Patristica* 15: 458–60.
Lyavdansky, Alexey. 2011. "Syriac charms in Near Eastern context: Tracing the Origin of Formulas." In *Oral Charms in Structural and Comparative Light*. Edited by T.A. Mikhailova, J. Roper, A. L. Toporkov, and D. S. Nikolayev, 15–21. Proceedings of the Conference of the International Society for Folk Narrative Research's (ISFNR) Committee on Charms, Charmers and Charming, 27–29th October 2011, Moscow. Moscow: Probel.
Macredes, Ruth, ed. 2010. *History as Literature in Byzantium*. Surrey, UK: Ashgate.
Maddison, Francis and Emilie Savage-Smith. 1997. 2 vols. *Science, tools and magic*. Part One. *Body and spirit, mapping the universe*, Emilie Savage-Smith with contributions from Ralph Pinder-Wilson and Tim Stanley. Part Two. *Mundane worlds*. The Nasser D Khalili Collection of Islamic Art, vol. 12. London: The Nour Foundation in association with Azimuth Editions and Oxford University Press.
Maguire, Henry. 1990. "Garments pleasing to God: The Significance of Domestic Textile Designs in the Early Byzantine Period." *Dumbarton Oaks Papers* 44, 215–24.
———. 1994. "From the Evil Eye to the Eye of Justice: The Saints, Art, and Justice in Antium." In *Law and Society in Byzantium: Ninth-Twelfth Centuries*. Edited by A. E. Laiou and D. Simon, 217–39. Washington, DC: Dumbarton Oaks.

———. 1995. "Magic and the Christian Image." In *Byzantine Magic*, edited by Henry Maguire, 51–71. Washington, DC: Dumbarton Oaks Research Library and Collection, distributed by Harvard University Press.

———.1997. "Magic and Money in the Early Middle Ages," *Speculum* 72:1037–54.

———. ed. 1995. *Byzantine Magic*. Washington, DC: Dumbarton Oaks Research Library and Collection, distributed by Harvard University Press.

Maguire, E. D., H. P. Maguire, and M. J Duncan-Flowers, eds. 1989. *Art and Holy Powers in the Early Christian House*. Urbana: University of Illinois Press.

Maloney, Clarence, ed. 1976. *The Evil Eye*. New York: Columbia University Press.

Manganaro [Mancanaro], Giacomo. 1995. "Documenti magici della Sicilia dal III al VI sec. d. C." In *Hestiasis, Studi di tarda antichità offerti a Salvatore Calderone*, Studi Tardoantichi 6, 13–42. Messina: Sicania.

Mantantseva, T. 1994. "Les amulettes byzantines contre le mauvais oeil du Cabinet des Medailles." *JAC* 37: 110–21.

Marçais, Philippe H. 1986. "Ayn and the Evil Eye." *Encyclopedia of Islam*. 2nd edition. Edited by P. J. Bearman, Th. Bianquis, C. E. Bosworth, E. van Donzel, W. P. Heinrichs et al. 12 vols. Leiden: Brill, 1960–2005; Vol. 1 (1986):786.

Meisen, Karl. 1950. "Der böse Blick und anderer Schadenzauber in Glaube und Brauch der alten Völker und in frühchristlicher Zeit." *Rheinisches Jahrbuch für Volkskunde* 1:144–77.

———. 1952. "Der böse Blick, das böse Wort und der Schadenzauber durch Berührung im Mittelalter und in der neueren Zeit." *Rheinisches Jahrbuch für Volkskunde* 3 (1952) 169–225.

Menzel, H. 1955. "Ein christliches Amulett mit Reiterdarstellung." *Jahrbuch des Römisch-Germanischen Zentralmuseums Mainz* 2: 253–61.

Merkelbach, R. and H. C. Youtie. 1975. "Der griechische Wortschatz und die Christen." *ZPE* 18:101–54.

Merlin, A. 1940. "Amulettes contre l'invidia provenant de Tunisie." *Revue des Études Anciennes* 42:486–93.

Mesner, Douglas. 2010. "Letter to the Editor: A Dialogue Regarding Colin Ross' article 'The Electrophysiological Basis of Evil Eye Belief.'" *Anthropology of Consciousness* 21/2: 103–05.

Meyer, Marvin. 1994. "Greek Texts of Ritual Power from Christian Egypt." In *Ancient Christian Magic: Coptic Texts of Ritual Power*, edited by Marvin Meyer, Richard Smith, and Neal Kelsey, 49–50. San Francisco: HarperSanFrancisco

Meyer, Marvin, Richard Smith, and Neal Kelsey, eds. 1994. *Ancient Christian Magic: Coptic Texts of Ritual Power*. San Francisco: HarperSanFrancisco, 1994; reprinted in paperback edition, Princeton: Princeton University Press, 2000.

Michaelides, Demetres. 1994. "A Solomonic Pendant and Other Amulets from Cyprus." In *Tranquilitas*, V. Tran Tam Tink Festschrift, edited by M. Jentel et al., 403–12. Quebec: University of Laval.

Montgomery, James A. 1910–11. "Some Early Amulets from Palestine." *JAOS* 31: 272–81.

———. 1913. *Aramaic Incantation Texts from Nippur*. University of Pennsylvania, The Museum, Publications of the Babylonian Section, Vol. 3. Philadelphia: University Museum.

Moriggi, Marco, ed. 2014. *A Corpus of Syriac Incantation Bowls: Syriac Magical Texts from Late-Antique Mesopotamia*. Magical and Religious Literature of Late Antiquity 3. Leiden: Brill.
Moss, Leonard W., and Stephen C. Cappannari. 1976. "Mal'occhio, Ayin ha ra, Oculus Fascinus, Judenblick: The Evil Eye Hovers Above." In *The Evil Eye*, edited by C. Maloney, 1–15. New York: Columbia University Press.
Nador, George, ed. 1975. *An Incantation against the Evil Eye*. Academia Maimonideana. Documenta inedita: Nr. 2. Middlesex Northwood: Bina.
Naff, Alixa. 1965. "Belief in the Evil Eye among the Christian Syrian-Lebanese in America." *Journal of American Folklore* 78:46–51.
Naldini, Mario.1968. *Il Cristianesimo in Egitto. Lettere private nei papyri dei secoli II-IV*. Florence: Le Monnier, 1968. Nos 1–977; 2nd ed. Fiesole 1998.
Neis, Rachel. 2012. "Eyeing Idols: Rabbinic Viewing Practices in Late Antiquity." *JQR* 102:533–60.
———. 2013. *The Sense of Sight in Rabbinic Culture: Jewish Ways of Seeing in Late Antiquity*. Cambridge: Cambridge University Press.
Niehoff, Maren R. 1992. *The Figure of Joseph in Post-Biblical Jewish History*. Arbeiten zur Geschichte des antiken Judentums und des Urchristentums, 16. Leiden: Brill.
Nikolaou, Theodorus. 1969. *Der Neid bei Johannes Chrysostomus unter Berücksichtigung der griechischen Philosophie*. Abhandlungen zur Philologie und Pädagogik 56 Bonn: H. Bouvier.
Noy, David. 1971. "Evil Eye." In *Encyclopedia Judaica* 6:997–1000.
O'Connor, K. M. 2004. "Popular and Talismanic Uses of the Quran." In *Encyclopaedia of the Quran*, edited by Jane Dammen McAuliffe, 163–82. Leiden: Brill.
Olszewski, Marek-Titien. 2001. "Mauvais oeil et protection contre l'envie dans la mosaïque de Cheikh Zouède au Sinaï (IVe-Ve siècle) [The Evil Eye and Protection Against Envy in the Sheikh Zuweid Mosaic in Sinai (4th-5th century])." In D. Paunier and C. Schmidt, eds., *La mosaïque gréco-romaine VIII: actes du VIIIème Colloque international pour l'étude de la mosaïque antique et médiéval*. Lausanne (Switzerland): 6–11 octobre 1997, 276–301. Lausanne: Cahiers d'archéologie romane. *Phthonos* and *baskania*, pp. 282–87. https://www.academia.edu/2303463/ Mauvais_%C5%93il_et_protection_contre_lenvie_dans_la_mosa%C3%AFque_ de_Cheikh_Zou%C3%A8de_au_Sina%C3%AF_IV-Ve_si%C3%A8cle_The_ Evil_Eye_and_Protection_Against_Envy_in_the_Sheikh_Zuweid_Mosaic_in_ Sinai_4th-5th_century.
Patai, Raphael. 1983. "T'khelet-Blue." In *On Jewish Folklore*, 86–95. Detroit: Wayne State University Press.
Patristic Greek Lexicon, A. Edited by G. W. H. Lampe. Oxford: Clarendon, 1961–68.
Perdrizet, Paul. 1900. "Melanges Epigraphiques." *Bulletin de Correspondance Hellénique* 24: 285–323.
———. 1903. "Sphragis Solomonis." *Revue des études grecques* 16: 42–61.
———. 1922. *Negotium perambulans in tenebris*. Publications de la Faculté des Lettres de l'Université de Strasbourg 6, 5–38. Strasbourg: Istra.
Peringer von Lillieblad, Gustaf. 1685. *De amuletis Hebraeorum dissertatio*. Uppsala University. Holmiæ: Johann Georg Eberdt.
Peterson, Erik. 1926. *Eis Theos: Epigraphische, formgeschichte und religionsgeschichtliche Untersuchungen*. Forschungen zur Religion und Literatur des Alten und Neuen Testaments n.F. 24. Göttingen: Vandenhoeck & Ruprecht.

———. 1982. "Das Amulett von Acre." In *Frühkirche, Judentum, und Gnosis. Studien und Untersuchungen* by E. Peterson, 346–54. Darmstadt: Wissenschaftliche Buchgesellschaft.

Petropoulos, J. C. B., ed. 2008. *Greek Magic: Ancient, Medieval and Modern.* Routledge Monographs in Classical Studies. New York: Routledge.

Piccirillo, M. 1979. "Un braccialetto cristiano della regione de Betlem." *Liber Annus* 29:244–52.

Pilhofer, Peter and Ulrike Koenen, 1998. "Joseph I (Patriarch)." In *RAC* 18: 715–48.

Plassmann, O. 1960. *Das Almosen bei Johannes Chrysostomus,* Münster: Aschendorff

Posner, Raphael, Judith Baskin, Shalom Sabar, and Theordore Schrire. 1971. "Amulet." In *Encyclopedia Judaica* 1:906–15. Jerusalem: Keter.

Prentice, William K. 1906. "Magical Formulae on Lintels of the Christian Period in Syria." *American Journal of Archaeology* 10:137–50.

Probst-Biraben, J. H. 1933. "La Main de Fatima et ses Antécédents Symboliques." *Revue Anthropologique* 43:370–75.

———. 1936. "Les Talismans contre le Mauvais Oeil." *Revue Anthropologique* 46: 171–80.

Publications of the Princeton University Archaeological Expeditions to Syria in 1904–5 and 1909. Division II: Ancient Architecture in Syria, by H. C. Butler. Division III: Greek and Latin Inscriptions in Syria, by E. Littmann, D. Magie, D. R. Stuart. Section A.: Southern Syria. Part 2: Southern Haurân. Section B: Northern Syria. Part 2: II Anderîn, Kerrātîn, Marâtâ. Part 3: Djebel Rîha and Djebel Wastaneh, by W. K. Prentice. Leiden: Brill, 1909, 1910. Abbrev. PAES

Quatremère, Etienne Marc, trans. and ed. 1838. "Proverbes Arabes de Meidani." *Journal Asiatique,* 3. Séries. Vol. 4: 497–543; Vol. 5: 5–44. 209–58.

Radin, Dean. 1997. *The Conscious Universe. The Scientific Truth of Psychic Phenomena.* New York: HarperCollins.

Rakoczy, Thomas. 1996. *Böser Blick, Macht des Auges und Neid der Götter: Eine Untersuchung zur Kraft des Blickes in der griechischen Literatur.* Classica Monacensia 13. Tübingen: Narr.

Ramsey, William. 1897. *Cities and Bishoprics of Phrygia.* Vol. 1, Part 2. Oxford: Clarendon. Online: http://digi.ub.uni-heidelberg.de/diglit/ramsay1897bd2/0378

Reitzenstein, Richard. 1904. *Poimandres. Studien zur griechisch-ägyptischen und frühchristlichen Literatur.* Leipzig: B. G. Teubner.

Reminick, Ronald A. 1976. "The Evil Eye Belief among the Amhara of Ethiopia." *Ethnology* 13 (1974) 279–91. Reprinted in *The Evil Eye,* edited by C. Maloney, 85–101. New York: Columbia University Press, 1976.

Reuvens, J. C. 1830. *Lettres à M. Letronne sur les papyrus bilingues et grecs.* Leiden: Luchtmans, 1830.

Risen, Jane L. 2016. "Believing What We Do not Believe: Acquiescence to Superstitious Beliefs and Other Powerful Intuitions." *Psychological Review* 123:182–207. http://dx.doi.org/10.1037/rev0000017.

Risen, Jane L., and A. David Nussbaum 2015. "Believing What You Don't Believe.' *The New York Times Sunday Review* 11-1-2015, p. 9. Added 11-15-2015 for vol 1.1.

Robert, Louis. 1944. "Hellenica." *Revue de philologie, de literature et d'histoire anciennes* 18:41–42.

———. 1951. "Bulletin épigraphique." *REG* 64:119–216.

———. 1965. "Échec au mal." *Hellenica* 13:265–71.

———. 1981. "Amulettes Grecques." *Journal des Savants* 3–44.
Robert, Louis, and Jeanne Robert. 1956. "Bulletin épigraphique." *REG* 69:104–191.
———. 1965. "Bulletin épigraphique." *REG* 78:70–204.
———. 1966. "Bulletin épigraphique." *REG* 79:335–440.
Rodkinson, Michael Levi. 1893. *History of Amulets, Charms, and Talismans: A Historical Historical Investigation into Their Nature and Origin*. New York: New Talmud Publishing.
Romdon, M. A. 2000. *Kitab Mujarobat: Dunia Magi Orang Islam-Jawa*. Yogyakarta: Lazuardi.
Rosenzweig, A. 1892. *Das Auge in Bibel und Talmud*. Berlin: Mayer & Müller.
Ross, Barry. 1991. "Notes on Some Jewish Amulets: 'ayin ha-ra' and the Priestly Blessing." *Journal of the Association of Graduates in Near Eastern Studies* 2:34–40.
Ross, Colin Andrew. 2010. "Hypothesis: The Electrophysiological Basis of Evil Eye Belief." *Anthropology of Consciousness* 21/1:47–57.
———. 2011. "Creencias tradicionales y campos electromagnéticos." *AIBR: Revista de Antropologïa Iberoamericana* 6:269–88.
Roussou, Eugenia. 2014. "Believing in the Supernatural through the 'Evil Eye': Perception and Science in the Modern Greek Cosmos." *Journal of Contemporary Religion* 29:425–38.
Russell, James Burton. 1982. "The Evil Eye in Early Byzantine Society. Archaeological Evidence from Anemurium in Isauria." *Jahrbuch der Österreichischen Byzantinistik* 32/3. XVI. Internationaler Byzantinistenkongress, Vienna 1981. Akten II/3, 539–48. Vienna: Österreichische Akademie der Wissenschaften.
———. 1987. *The Mosaic Inscriptions of Anemurium*. ÖAW Philologische-Historische Klasse Denkschriften 190. Vienna: Österreichische Akademie der Wissenschaften.
———. 1995. "The Archaeological Context of Magic in the Early Byzantine Period." In *Byzantine Magic*, edited by H. Maguire, 35–50. Washington, DC: Dumbarton Oaks.
Saint Tikhon's Monastery Research Library and Collection, ed. 1998. *The Great Book of Needs*. Vol. 1. *The Holy Mysteries*. South Canaan, PA: St. Tikhon's Seminary Press, 1998.
Schäfer, P. 1990. "Jewish Magic Literature in Late Antiquity and Early Middle Ages." *Journal of Jewish Studies* 41:75–91.
Schienerl, Peter W. 1992. *Dämonenfurcht und böser Blick: Studien zum Amulettwesen*. Aachen: Alano/Herodot.
Sheldrake, Rupert. 2003. *The Sense of Being Starred at and Other Unexplained Powers of the Human Mind*. New York: Crown.
Schermann, Theodor, ed. 1904. *Die griechischen Kyprianosgebete: Oriens christianus* 3:303–23.
Schlumberger, Gustave. 1892a. "Ámulettes byzantins anciennes destinés à combattre les maléfices et maladies." *REG* 5:72–93; reprinted in Schlumberger, *Mélanges d'Archéologie Byzantine*. Paris: Leroux. 1895:118–40.
———.1892b. *Amulettes byzantins anciens destinés à combattre les maléfices et les maladies*. Paris: Leroux, 1892.
———. 1895. *Mélanges d'Archéologie Byzantine*. Paris: Leroux. 1895.
Schmid, Daniela. "Jüdische Amulette aus Osteuropa—Phänomene, Rituale, Formensprache." PhD diss., University of Vienna, 2012. [On Der böse Blick [The Evil Eye], 81–89, under "Magische Phänomene und Rituale"]

Schoeck, Helmut. 1987. *Envy: A Theory of Social Behaviour*. Indianapolis: Liberty Press, 1987. Reprint of New York: Harcourt, Brace & World, 1970. Originally published as *Der Neid, eine Theorie der Gesellschaft*. Freiburg: Alber, 1966.

Schoedel, William. 1985. *Ignatius of Antioch : A Commentary on the Letters of Ignatius of Antioch*. Hermeneia. Philadelphia: Fortress.

Schrire, T. 1982. *Hebrew Magic Amulets. Their Decipherment and Interpretation*. New York: Behrman House. Reprint of *Hebrew Amulets*. London: Routledge & Kegan Paul, l966.

Schrodinger, Erwin. 2005a. "The Sense of Being Stared at. Part 1. Is it Real or Illusory?" *Journal of Consciousness Studies* 12:10–31.

―――. 2005b. "The Sense of Being Stared at. Part 2. Its Implications for Theories of Vision." *Journal of Consciousness Studies* 12:32–49.

Schroer, Silva. 1984. "Zur Deutung der Hand unter der Grabinschrift von Chirbet el Qöm." *UF* 15:191–99.

Schroer, Silvia, and Thomas Staubli. 2001. *Body Symbolism in the Bible*. Translated by Linda M. Maloney. Collegeville: Liturgical Press/Michael Glazier.

Schürer, Emil. 1909/1970. *Geschichte des Jüdischen Volkes im Zeitalter Jesus Christi*. 3 vols. Leipzig: Hinrichs, 1901, 1907, 1909. Reprinted, Hildesheim: Olms, 1970. Vol. 3 §32. Palestinian-Jewish Literature: "VII. "Zauberformeln und Zauberbücher." Pp. 407–20. ET: *The History of the Jewish People in the Age of Jesus Christ (175 B.C.–A.D. 135)*. A New English Version Revised and edited by Geza Vermes and Fergus Millar, Matthew Black and Martin Goodman. 3 vols. Edinburgh: T. & T. Clalrk, 1973–1986. P. S. Alexander, trans., "Incantations and Books of Magic." 3/1 (1987) 342–79.

Seawright, Helen L. 1988. "The Symbolism of the Eye in Mesopotamia and Israel." MA thesis, Wilfried Laurier University. Online: http://scholars.wlu.ca/etd/94.

Seeliger, Hans Reinhard. 1989. "Die Verwendung des Christograms durch Konstantin im Jahre 312." *Zeitschrift für Kirchengeschichte* 100:49–68.

Segal J. B., and E. C. D. Hunter. 2000. *Catalogue of the Aramaic and Mandaic Incantation Bowls in the British Museum*. London: British Museum Press. 143 bowls

Seligmann, Siegfried. 1910. *Der Böse Blick und Verwandtes: Ein Beitrag zur Geschichte des Aberglaubens aller Zeiten und Völker*. 2 vols. Berlin: Barsdorf. Reprinted Hildesheim: Olms, 1985 (2 vols. in one).

―――. 1922. *Die Zauberkraft des Auges und das Berufen: Ein Kapitel aus der Geschichte des Aberglaubens*. Hamburg: Friederichsen , 1922. Reprinted, Den Haag: Couvreur, 1980.

―――. 1927a. *Die magischen Heil- und Schutzmittel aus der unbelebten Natur, mit besonderer Berücksichtigung der Mittel gegen den Bösen Blick. Eine Geschichte des Amulett-wesens*. Stuttgart: Strecker & Schroeder, 1927. Reprinted, 3 vols. Edited by Jürgen Zwernemann. Berlin: Reimer Verlag, 1996–.

―――. 1927b. "Auge." In *Handwörterbuch des deutschen Aberglaubens*, edited by H. Bächtold-Steubli and E. Hoffmann-Krayer. Vol. 1:679–701.

Shachar, I. 1981. *Jewish Tradition in Art: The Feuchtwanger Collection of Judaica*. Translated by R. Grafman. Jerusalem: Israel Museum.

Shrut, Samuel D. 1960. "Coping with the 'Evil Eye,' or Early Rabbinical Attempts at Psychotherapy." *American Imago: A Psychoanalytic Journal for the Arts and Sciences* 17:201–13.

Sinai, Turan (Tamas). 2008. "'Wherever the Sages Set Their Eyes, There Is Either Death or Poverty.' On the History, Terminology, and Imagery of the Talmudic Tradition about the Devastating Gaze of the Sages." *Sidra* 23:137–205. [Hebrew, with English summary, pp. viii-ix].
Snyder, Graydon. 1985. *Ante Pacem: Archaeological Evidence of Church Life before Constantine*. Macon, GA: Mercer University Press.
Soderlund, O. and H. 2013. "The Evil Eye in Cultural and Church History." Online: http://aslansplace.com/wp-content/uploads/2013/07/The_Evil_Eye_In_Cultural_and_Church_History-Soderlund.pdf
Spier, Jeffrey. 1993. "Medieval Byzantine Magical Amulets and Their Tradition." *Journal of the Warburg and Courtauld Institutes* 56:25–62 and six plates.
Spooner, Brian. 1976. "The Evil Eye in the Middle East." In *The Evil Eye*, edited by Clarence Maloney, 76–84. New York: Columbia University Press; reprinted from *Witchcraft Confessions and Accusations*, edited by Mary Douglas, 311–19. Association of Social Anthropologists of the Commonwealth Monographs 9. London: Tavistock, 1970.
Staude, Wilhelm. 1934. "Le mauvais oeil dans la peinture chrétienne d'Abyssinie." *Journal Asiatique* 225:231–57
———. 1954. "Die Profilregeln in der christlichen Malerei Äthiopiens und die Furcht von dem 'Bösen Blick.'" *Archiv für Völkerkunde* 9:116–61.
Stegemann, Viktor. 1934. *Die koptischen Zaubertexte der Sammlung Papyrus Erzherzog Rainer in Wien*. Sitzungsberichte der Heidelberger Akademie der Wissenschften, Philosophisch-historische Klasse .Jahrgang 1933/34. 1. Abhandlung 1. Heidelberg: Winters.
Stillmann, Yedida. 1970. "The Evil Eye in Morocco." In *Folklore Research Center Studies*. Vol. 1, edited by Dov Noy and Issachar Ben Ami, 81–94. Jerusalem: Magnes.
Storace, Patricia. 1997. *Dinner with Persephone*. New York: Vintage books (Random House).
Stratton, Kimberly B. 2007. *Naming the Witch: Magic, Ideology, and Stereotype in the Ancient World*. Gender, Theory, and Religion. New York: Columbia University Press.
Swartz, Michael D. 2010. "ReViews: Repelling the Evil Eye." *Biblical Archaeology Review* 36/5. Online: http://www.basarchive.org/sample/bswbBrowse.asp?PubID=BSBA&Volume=36&Issue=5&ArticleID=28.
Tarelko, Michael. 2000. "A Magical Scroll in the Drower Collection DC 21 Šapta d-pišra d-aina 'The Scroll of the Annihilation of the Eyes.'" *ARAM* 12: 249–52.
Teman, Elly. 2008. "The Red String: The Cultural History of a Jewish Folk Symbol." In *Jewishness: Expression, Identity, and Representation*, edited by Simon J. Bronner, 29–57. Jewish Cultural Studies 1. Portland, OR: Littman Library of Jewish Civilization.
Thomas Aquinas. 2010. *Catena aurea in Matthaeum*. Centre Traditio Litterarum Occidentalium. Turnhout: Brepols.
Thomson, William McClure. 1880. *The Land and the Book: Or, Biblical Illustrations Drawn from the Manners and Customs, the Scenes and Scenery of the Holy Land*. 3 vols. New York: Harper.
Tilford, Nicole. 2015a. "Evil Eye." In *Oxford Bibliographies*. Edited by Christopher Matthews. http://www.oxfordbibliographies.com/view/document/obo-9780195393361/obo-9780195393361-0112.xml.

Tilford, Nicole. 2015b. "The Affective Eye: Re-examining a Biblical Idiom." *Biblical Interpretation* 23:207-21.

Touhami, Slimane. 2007. "Contrer l'œil envieux. Croire et faire autour de l'*aïn* dans le Maghreb de France." PhD diss., l'Université de Toulouse, 2007.

———. 2010 *La Part de l'oeil. Une ethnologie du Maghreb de France*. Paris: Editions du Comité des travaux historiques et scientifiques.

———. 2014. "D'un oeil à l'autre.Parcours ethnologique et engagement autour de l'expérience culturelle des migrants. From One Eye to the Other: An Ethnological Trajectory and Commitment around the Cultural Experience of Migrants." *Journal des anthropologues* 138-139:355-73.

Trachtenberg, Joshua. 1970/1939. *Jewish Magic and Superstition: A Study in Folk Religion*. New York: Atheneum; a reprint of New York: Behrman, 1939.

Trzcionka, Silke. 2004. "Relating to the Supernatural: A Case Study of Fourth-Century Syria and Palestine." PhD diss., University of Adelaide.

———. 2007. *Magic and the Supernatural in Fourth Century Syria*. London: Routledge.

———. 2011. "A Syrian-Christian Perspective on the Supernatural." *American Foundation of Syriac Studies*, 1–10. http://www.syriacstudies.com/2013/07/30/a-syrian-christian-perspective-on-the-supernatural.

Ulmer, Rivka Brigitte Kern. [aka Kern-Ulmer] 1991. "The Power of the Evil Eye and the Good Eye in Midrashic Literature." *Judaism* 40:344-53.

———. 1992/93. "Zwischen ägyptischer Vorlage und talmudischer Rezeption: Josef und die Ägypterin." *Kairos* 24/25:75-90.

———. 1994. *The Evil Eye in the Bible and in Rabbinic Literature*. Hoboken, NJ: Ktav.

———. 1998. "Die Macht des Auges (der böse Blick) in der rabbinischen Literatur." In *Approaches to Ancient Judaism*, New Series vol.13. Edited by Jacob Neusner, 121-38. South Florida Studies in the History of Judaism 164. Atlanta: Scholars.

———. 2003. "The Divine Eye in Ancient Egypt and in the Midrashic Interpretation of Formative Judaism." *Journal of Religion and Society* 5:1-17.

The Universal Jewish Encyclopedia. Edited by Isaac Landman. 10 vols. + Index vol. New York: Universal Jewish Encyclopedia, 1939-1943.

Unnik, W. C. van. 1971. *APHTHONOS METADIDÔMI*. Brussels: Paleis der Academien.

———. 1973. "De *aphthonia* van God in de oudchristelijke literatuur." *Mededelingen der koninlijke Nederlandse Akademi van Wetenschappen*, Afd. Letterkunde n. r. 36/2:17-55. Amsterdam: Noord-Hollandsche Uitgevers Maatschapij.

van de Ven, N., M. Zeelenberg, and R. Pieters. 2010. "Warding off the Evil Eye: When the Fear of Being Envied Increases Prosocial Behavior." *Psychological Science* 21:1671-77.

van Haelst, Joseph. 1976. *Catalogue des papyrus littéraires juifs et chrétiens*.Université de Paris IV. Série Papyrologie 1. Paris: Publications de la Sorbonne.

Vecchiato, N. 1994. "Evil Eye, Health Beliefs and Social Tensions Among the Sidama." In *New Trends in Ethiopian Studies. Proceedings of the 12th International Conference of Ethiopian Studies*, edited by H. Marcus, 1033-43. Asmara, NJ: Red Sea Press.

Veikou, Christina. 1998. *Kakó matí: H koinonikê kataskeuê tês optikês epikoinônias*. Athens: Hellēnika Grammata.

———. 2008. "Ritual World and Symbolic Movement in Spells against the Evil Eye." In *Greek Magic: Ancient Medieval and Modern*, edited by J. C. B. Petropoulos, 95-105. Routledge Monographs in Classical Studies. New York: Routledge.

Veltri, Giuseppe.1996. "Jewish Traditions in Greek Amulets." *Bulletin of Judaeo-Greek Studies* 18:33–47.
Verheyden, Joseph, ed. 2012. *The Figure of Solomon in Jewish, Christian and Islamic Tradition: King, Sage and Architect*. Themes in Biblical Narrative: Jewish and Christian Traditions 16. Leiden: Brill.
Vida, Tivadar. 2002. "Heidnische und christliche Elemente der awarenzeitlichen Glaubenswelt, Amulette in der Awarenzeit." *Zalai Muzeum* 11:179–209.
Vikan, Gary. 1984. "Art, Medicine, and Magic in Early Byzantium." *Dumbarton Oaks Papers* 38:65–86.
Villiers, Elizabeth, and Anton Maximilian Pachinger. 1927. *Amulette und Talismane, und andere geheime Dinge. Eine volkstümliche Zusammenstellung von Glücksbringern, Sagen, Legenden und Aberglauben aus alter und neuer Zeit; Talismane aus aller Herren Länder; orientalische Volkssagen und Mysterien*. Berlin: Drei Masken.
Vukosavovic, Filip, ed. 2010. *Angels and Demons: Jewish Magic Through the Ages*. Jerusalem: Bible Lands Museum. [catalogue of a Bible Lands Museum exhibition in 2010 including amulets, objects, books, manuscripts and ephemera; photos and essays]
Walter, Christopher. 1989–1990. "The Intaglio of Solomon in the Benaki Museum and the Origins of the Iconography of Warrior Saints." (Δελτίον of the Friends of Christian Archaeology). *XAE* (Athens) 15/4:33–42.
Weitzmann, Kurt, ed. 1979. *Age of Spirituality. Late Antique and Early Christian Art. Third to Seventh Century*. Catalogue of the exhibition of the Metropolitan Museum of Art, Nov. 19, 1977—Feb. 12, 1978. New York: Metropolitan Museum of Art and Princeton University Press.
Westermarck, Edvard Alexander. 1926. *Ritual and Belief in Morocco*. 2 vols. London: Macmillan.
Wilken, Robert Louis. 1983. *John Chrysostom and the Jews: Rhetoric and Reality in the Late Fourth Century*. Berkeley: University of California Press.
Winer, Gerald A. and Jane E. Cottrell 1996. "Does Anything Leave the Eye When We See? Extramission Beliefs of Children and Adults." *Current Directions in Psychological Science* 5:137–42.
Winer, Gerald A., Jane E Cottrell, Virginia Gregg, Jody S. Fournier, and Lori A. Bica. 2002. "Fundamentally Misunderstanding Visual Perception: Adults' Belief in Visual Emission." *American Psychologist* 57:417–24.
Winer, Gerald A., Jane E. Cottrell, Virginia Gregg, Jody S. Fournier, and Lori A. Bica. 2003. "Do Adults Believe in Visual Emissions?" *American Psychologist* 58:495–96.
Winkler, H. A. 1931. *Salamo und die Karina: eine orientalische Legende von der Bezwingung einer Kindbettdämonin durch einen heiligen Helden*. Veröffentlichungen des Orientalischen Seminars der Universität Tübingen 4. Stuttgart.
Wyss, B. 1951. "Johannes Chrysostomus und der Aberglaube." In *Heimat und Humanität: Festschrift für K. Menli zum 60 Geburtstag*, 262–74. Schweizer Archiv für Volkskunde 47. Basel: Krebs.
Yardeni, Ada. 1991. "Remarks on the Priestly Blessing on Two Ancient Amulets from Jerusalem." *VT* 41:176–85.
Zellinger, Johann Baptist. 1933. *Augustin und die Volksfrömmigkeit. Blicke in den frühchristlichen Alltag*. Munich: Huebner.

Zoega Dana, Georg. 1810. *Catalogus codicum Copticorum manu scriptorum qui in Museo Borgiano Velitris adservantur* (opus posthumum); cum VII tabulis Aeneis. Rome: Sacrae Congregationis de propaganda fide.

Zumwalt, Rosemary Lévy. 1996. "Let it go to the garlic": Evil Eye and the Fertility of Women among the Sephardim. *Western Folklore* 55/4:61–80.

BIBLIOGRAPHY 2
Works Concerning the Evil Eye Supplementing the Bibliographies of Volumes 1–3

Agis, Derya F. 2010. "Beliefs of the American Sephardic Women Related to the Evil Eye." 1–21. Hadassah-Brandeis Institute, Brandeis University. http://www.brandeis.edu/hbi/publications/workingpapers/docs/agis.pdf

Aguirre, Luz. 2010. "Evil Eyes." [poem] *Voices: The Journal of New York Folklore* 36/3–4:17.

Almar, George. "The Evil Eye! A Melo-drama in Two Acts." Duncombe's British Theatre Nineteenth Century English Drama 77. London. Duncombe.

Anderson, Gary A. 2013. *Charity: The Place of the Poor in the Biblical Tradition*. New Haven: Yale University Press.

Annandale, David. 2012. "Evil Eye." [short story]. Canada: North Door Books.

Baer, R. D., S. C. Weller, J. C. González Faraco, and J. Feria Martin. 2006. "Las enfermedades populares en la cultura Española actual: un studio comparado sobre el mal de ojo." *Revista de Dialectoligia y Tradiciones Populares* 61/1:139–56.

Baldacchino, Jean-Paul. 2010. "The Evil Eye (ghajn) in Malta: Grappling with Skinner's Pigeons and Rehabilitating Lame Ducks." *Australian Journal of Anthropology* 21: 188–207.

Baldo, Michela. 2012. "Malocchio in Nino Ricci's *Lives of the Saints*." *Quaderni d'italianistica* 33/1:37.

Balikienė, Monika. 2010. "The Evil Eye of Origin and Conservation theory." *Folk Culture* 1/130:54–62.

———. 2012a. "Bloga akis šiuolaikinėje Lietuvoje." ["The evil eye in modern Lithuania"]. *Liaudies kultūra* 5/146: 54–59.

———. 2012b. "Tikėjimo Bloga Akimi Raiška Šiuolaikinėje Lietuvoje [Evil Eye Expression of Modern Lithuania]." PhD thesis. Kaunas: Vytautas Magnus University. Online: http://talpykla.elaba.lt/elaba-fedora/objects/elaba:2068452/datastreams/MAIN/content.

———. 2013. "Bloga akis: tradicijos raiška modernaus žmogaus gyvenime. ["Evil Eye: Representation of Tradition in the Life of Modern Man"]. *Res Humanitariae* 13: 57–73. Online: http://journals.ku.lt/index.php/RH/article/viewFile/736/751.

Balmain, Colette. 2002. "Mario Bava's The Evil Eye: Realism and the Italian Horror Film." *Post Script* 21/3:20.

Baumbach, Sibylle. 2010. "Medusa's Gaze and the Aesthetics of Fascination." *Anglia* 128/2:225–45. https://www.academia.edu/985623/_Medusa_s_Gaze_and_the_Aesthetics_of_Fascination.

Bava, Mario, director. *"The Evil Eye*; and *La Ragazza che sapeva troppo* ["*The Girl Who Knew Too Much*"] [film]. 1964.

Berger, Allan S. 2011. "The Evil Eye: A Cautious Look." *Journal of Religion and Health* 52:785–788

———. 2012. "The Evil Eye—An Ancient Superstition." *Journal of Religion and Health* 51:1098–103.

Blanco, Cecilia. 2008. *Mal de Ocho: Como Evitarlo y Como Curalo*. Absalon.

Bohigian, George M., and Norman B. Medow. 2000. "Many cultures have tried to thwart the effect of evil eye." *Ophthalmology Times* 25/12:12.

Boileau, Pierre, and Thomas Narcejac. 1959. *The evil eye*. [mystery novel]. London: L. Hutchinson. Spanish edition: *El Mal de Ojo*. Biblioteca Oro Terror 28. Plaza & Janés., 1982.

Borsje, Jacqueline. 2012. *The Celtic Evil Eye and Related Mythological Motifs in Medieval Ireland*. Studies in the History and Anthropology of Religion 2. Leuven: Peeters.

Borsje, Jacqueline, and Fergus Kelly. 2003. "The Evil Eye in Early Irish Literature and Law." *Celtica* 24: 1–39. http://www.celt.dias.ie/publications/celtica/c24/c24-1-39.pdf

Bower, B. M. 1921. "The Evil Eye of the Sawtooth." [short story]. *Sawtooth Ranch* 1/1/1921: 10.

Brisset, Joseph Mathurin. 1833. *Le mauvais Oeil*. Reprinted, Kessinger Legacy reprints. 2010.

Brooks, Michelle. 2004. "The Evil Eye" [poem]. *Anthology of New England Writers* 16: 23.

Buckland, Raymond. 2001. "Evil Eye." In R. Buckland, *The Witch Book: The Encyclopedia of Witchcraft, Wicca, and Neo-paganism*, 160. Canton, MI: Visible Ink Press.

Buckland, Raymond. 2001. "Fascination." In R. Buckland, *The Witch Book: The Encyclopedia of Witchcraft, Wicca, and Neo-paganism*, 171. Canton, MI: Visible Ink Press.

———. 2001. "Garlic." In R. Buckland, *The Witch Book: The Encyclopedia of Witchcraft, Wicca, and Neo-paganism*, 203. Canton, MI: Visible Ink Press.

Burriss, Eli Edward. 1972. *Taboo, Magic, Spirits*. Westport, Connecticut. Greenwood Press Publishers.

Cacciatore, Paola Volpe. 2012. " 'Cicalata sul fascino volgarmente detto jettatura.' Plutarch, *Quaestio convivalis* 5.7." In *Plutarch in the Religious and Philosophical Discourse of Late Antiquity*, edited by Laurato Roig Lanzillotta and Israel Muñoz Gallarte, 171–80. Ancient Mediterranean and Medieval Texts and Contexts 14. Leiden: Brill.

Cairns, D. 2011. "Looks of Love and Loathing: Models of Vision and Emotion in Ancient Greek Culture." *Metis* 9:37–50.

Cajun, André. 1946. " 'Ol' Evil Eye' Making Voodoo." African American Tales. New Orleans: Cajun Publishing Co.

Casabianca, Silvia. "*Curanderos* and '*mal de ojo*,' an every day reality in Latin America." *Saludify*, 1 Mar. 2013. http://saludify.com/curanderos-mal-de-ojo.

Chiaradonna, Michael, James T. Vance, and Heather Hummel. 2011. *Malocchio. The Evil Eye Murders.* [murder mystery novel] Evil Eye Murder Series 1. Charlottesville, VA: PathBinder.

Cohan, John Alan. 2010. "Envy and the Evil Eye." Chapter 9, pp. 114–126 in *The Primitive Mind and Modern Man.* Sharjah, UAE: Bentham Science.

Cohen, Maria Manzari. 1995. "The Mediterranean Evil Eye Charms." *Faces* 12/4: 10.

Dado, Natasha. 2015. "The 'Evil eye' and Turkish Coffee in Arab Culture." *Arab American News* 31/1529 (5/30/2015):7.

Daniel, Roland. 1942. *Evil Eyes.* London: Wright.

Davis, Basil S. 1999. "The Meaning of PROEGRAFH in the Context of Galatians 3.1." *New Testament Studies* 45:194–212.

DeCandido, GraceAnne A. 2014. " 'Amma' Continues to Ward Off Evil Eye as Rekha Turns 60." *News India Times* 345/42 (10/17/2014): 24.

de Ceglia, Francesco Paolo. 2014. "The Evil Eye." [review] *Diva 218* (August 2014):33.

DeForest, Mary. "Baseball and the Evil Eye." http://www.academia.edu/9551209/Baseball_and_the_Evil_Eye

Degen, Andreas. 2012. "Concepts of Fascination, from Democritus to Kant." *Journal of the History of Ideas* 73:371–93.

Deix, Manfred. 1989. *Mein böser Blick.* [graphics, cartoons]. Munich: Heyne.

De Ley, Herman. 1981. "Beware of blue eyes! A note on Hippocratic pangenesis (AER., ch. 14)." *L'Antiquité Classique* 50/1:192–97.

Delmonaco, Joseph P. 1984. "The Evil Eye in the Mediterranean." *Honors Projects Overview.* Paper 112. Anthropology Dept., Rhode Island College. http://digitalcommons.ric.edu/honors_projects/112.

de Santis, Agata, director. 2010. "Mal'occhio." [Canadian documentary film on the Evil Eye in the Italian community]. https://vimeo.com/ondemand/malocchio.

de Vidas, A. A. 2007. "The Symbolic and Ethnic aspects of Envy among a Teenek Community (Mexico)." *Journal of Anthropological Research* 63:215–37.

DeVidas-Kirchheimer, Gloria. 2000. *Goodbye, Evil Eye.* [Short stories, including "Goodbye, Evil Eye"] London: Holmes & Meier.

Diamond, Ann. 1994. *Evil Eye* [fiction]. Montréal: Véhicule.

Dickie, Matthew W. 1994. "An Epitaph from Stratonikeia in Caria." *Zeitschrift für Papyrologie und Epigraphik* 100:109–18.

Drudge, Matt. "Beware the Obama 'Evil Eye.'" *Drudge Report*, 6/30/2009.

D'Silva, Neil. 2015. *The Evil Eye and the Charm: Stories of the Indian Lemon-Chili Charm.*[Collection of three short stories based on the Indian nimboo-mirchi (lemon-chili) charm, which is supposed to ward off evil]. Amazon Kindle E-book.

Elworthy, Frederick Thomas. 2011. *Der Böse Blick: eine umfassende Darstellung von der antike bis Heute.* Leipzig: Bohmeier, 2011. German translation of Elworthy, Frederick Thomas. 1895. *The Evil Eye. An Account of This Ancient and Widespread Superstition.* London: Murray.

Engelbert of Admont, c. 1331. *Tractatus de fascinatione.*

"The Evil Eye or The Many Merry Mishaps of Nid and the Weird Wonderful Wanderings of Nod." 1899. [A musical that opened in New York City Jan 16, 1899 and played through Jan 23, 1899]. https://www.ibdb.com/Production/View/456540.

The Evil eye plucked out, or, A discourse proving that church-revenues cannot be alienated by any secular persons or powers: without a manifest violation of the known fundamental laws of this kingdom and of publick justice and common-honesty. 1670. London: Printed for Rob. Clavel and to be sold by H. Brome.

Farber, Walter. 2014. *Lamaštu: An Edition of the Canonical Series of Lamaštu Incantations and Rituals and Related Texts from the Second and First Millennia B.C.* Mesopotamian Civilizations 17. Winona Lake, IN: Eisenbrauns.

Farnol, Jeffrey. 1911. "In Which I Forswear Myself and Am Accused of Possessing The 'Evil Eye.'" Book One, Chapter XXX in *The Broad Highway* [fiction]. Boston: Little, Brown.

Friedenthal, Meelis. 2012. "Kuri silm: toimemehhanismid lähtuvalt antiiksetest ja keskaegsetest tajuteooriatest. [The Evil Eye: Descriptions of Operation According to Ancient and Medieval Theories of Perception]" *Mäetagused* 51:7–20.

Frobes-Cross, Nicholas, and Alan Dundes. 2002. "The Evil Eye: An Interview with Alan Dundes." *Cabinet Magazine* 5 (Winter 2002). http://cabinetmagazine.org/issues/5/frobes-cross.php.

Fulgum, Mary Margaret. 2001. "Coins Used as Amulets in Late Antiquity." In *Between Magic and Religion: Interdisciplinary Studies in Ancient Mediterranean Religion and Society*, edited by S. R. Asirvatham, C. O. Pache, and J. Watrous, 139–47. Lanham, MD: Rowman & Littlefield.

Gautier, Théophile, and Guy de Maupassant. 1892. *The Evil Eye* by T. Gautier and *The Scharenbach Inn* by Guy de Maupassant. Chicago: Homewood.

Ghilzai, Shazia Akbar, and Azma Kanwal. 2016. "Semiotic Analysis of Evil Eye Beliefs among Pakistani Cultures and their Predetermined Behavior." *Research Issues in Social Sciences* 1:47–67. https://www.researchgate.net/publication/303856156_Semiotic_Analysis_of_Evil_Eye_Beliefs_among_Pakistani_Cultures_and_their_Predetermined_Behavior

Gholamhosseinzadeh, Gholam Hossein and Afsoon Ghambari. 2011. "Belief in the Evil Eye among People of Antiquity and Divine Religions." *International Journal of the Humanities* 18:1–18.

Ghosh, A. 1983. "The Relations of Envy in an Egyptian Village." *Ethnology* 22:211–23.

Gilliespie, Alfred. 1966. "The Evil Eye." [short story] *Saturday Evening Post* 239/2 (1/15/1966):48.

Giuman, Marco. 2013. *Archeologia dello squardo: Fascinazione e baskania nel mondo classic.* Archeologica 173. Rome: Bretschneider.

G.L.S. 1999. "Armenians and the Evil Eye." *Faces* 16/1:39.

Godkin, Georgina Sarah. 1894. *Il Mal Occhio, Or, The Evil Eye.* Harry Houdini Collection, Library of Congress. London: Swan Sonnenschein.

Goev, Angel. 1992. *Urochasvaneto: bŭlgarski narodni viārvaniiā. [Casting the Evil Eye in the Bulgarian Folk Beliefs].* Volume 1 of *Bŭlgarska narodna magiiā.* Gabrovo: Tekhnosist.

Goodwin, Jason. 2011. *An Evil Eye.* [detective novel] New York: Farrer, Straus & Giroux.

Häegele, Hannelore. 2014. *The Eye and the Beholder: The Depiction of the Eye in Western Sculpture with Special Reference to the Period 1350–1700 and to Colour in Sculpture.* Newcastle: Cambridge Scholars.

Haid, Karen. 2012. "Curses, Cures and Charms Italian Style." *Italian America* 17/2:22

Halliday, William Reginald. 1963. *Greek and Roman Folklore.* New York: Cooper Square.

Hill, Douglas, and Paul Hamlyn. 1968. *Magic and Superstition.* London: Hamlyn.

Hinterberger, Martin. 2010. "Envy and Nemesis in the Vita Basilii and Leo the Deacon." In *History as Literature in Byzantium*, edited by Ruth Macredes, 187–206. Burlington, VT: Ashgate.

———. 2013. *Phthonos: Missgunst, Neid und Eifersucht in der Byzantinischen Literatur.* Serta Graeca Series 29. Wiesbaden: Reichert.

Howe, Maud. "The Evil Eye and Witches Night in Rome." *The Century Magazine* 1904.

Huenemann, Karyn. 2014. "Bye-Bye, Evil Eye." *Resource Links* 20/1:28.

Hyde, Walter Woodburn. 1936. *Greek Religion and Its Survivals.* New York: Cooper Square.

Kerbel, Deborah. 2014. *Bye Bye Evil Eye.* [juvenile fiction] Dancing Cat Books/Cormorant Books.

Khalil-Habib, Nejmeh. 2007. "Struck by an Evil Eye." [short story]. *Nebula* 4/2:287.

Kirchheimer, Gloria Devidis. 2000. *Goodbye, Evil Eye.* New York: Holmes & Meier.

Koç, Bozkurt, and Akın Temür. 2014. "The Superstitious Mystery Behind the Eye: The Symbol of Eye and the Way that the Evil Eye Bead Is Reflected in Turkish Society from the Ancient History to the Present." *Journal of History School* 7/18:11–50. https://www.academia.edu/22136547.

Kuhnke. Elizabeth . 2015. "The Eyes Have it." In *Body Language for Dummies,* 77–94. 3rd ed. Chichester, UK: Wiley.

Langton, Edward. 1949. *The Essentials of Demonology: A Study of Jewish and Christian Doctrine, Its Origin and Development.* London: Epworth.

Larraya, Fernando Pagés. 1998. *Tratado de la Fascinación.* Córdoba: Prospopis.

Lea, Henry Charles. 1821 "Evil Eye, or, Fascinum: Observations on an Antique Bas-relief, on which It Is Represented, Being the Only One of the Kind Discovered." Society of Antiquities of London. Henry Charles Lea Library, University of Pennsylvania. London: Society of Antiquities.

MacGabhann, F. 1995. "The Evil Eye Tradition in North East Ireland." *Sinsear: The Folklore Journal* 8:89–100.

Macquoid, Katharine Sarah. 1876. *The Evil Eye and Other Stories.* London: Chatto & Windus.

McGann, Oisin. 2009. *The Evil Eye.* Edinburgh: Barington Stoke.

Mendoza Forrest, Satnam K. 2011. "The Evil Eye, Corpse-Abusing Criminals, Demon Worshippers, and Friends." In S. K. Mendoza Forrest, *Witches, Whores, and Sorcerers: The Concept of Evil in Early Iran,* 83–112. Austin: University of Texas Press.

Miah, N. M. *My Evil Eye.* 2006. [fiction]. London: Valhalla.

Mishra, Archana. 2003. *Casting the Evil Eye: Witch Trials in Tribal India.* New Dehli: Roli.

Mitchell, A. G. 2013. "Disparate Bodies in Ancient Artefacts: the Function of Caricature and Pathological Grotesques among Roman Terracotta Figures." In *Disabilities in Roman Antiquity: Disparate Bodies, A Capite ad Calcem,* edited by Christian Laes, C. F. Goodey, and M. Lynn Rose, 275-98. Mnemosyne Supplements 356. Leiden: Brill.

Mitchell, Corey. 2006. *Evil Eyes.* [account of a serial killer, Coral Eugene Watts]. New York: Pinnacle Books/Kensington Books.

Mouse, Anon E. 2016. *The Evil Eye of Sani. A Bengali Folktale: Baba Indaba Children's Stories.* London: Abela.

Mughazy, Mustafa Abd-Elghafar. 2009. "Pragmatics of the Evil Eye in Egyptian Arabaic." *Studies in the Linguistic Sciences* 30/2:147–58. https://www.ideals.illinois.edu/handle/2142/9656.
Oates, Joyce Carol. 2013. *Evil Eye: Four Novellas of Love Gone Wrong*. New York: Mysterious Press (Grove/Atlantic).
O'Connor, K. M. 2004. "Popular and Talismanic Uses of the Quran." In *Encyclopaedia of the Quran*, edited by J. D. McAuliffe, 163–82. Leiden: Brill.
Ogilvie, Ruthe. 2012. *Cast an Evil Eye*. [fiction] Vol. 3 of the Stuart Trilogy. Bloomington, IN: Trafford.
Olmo Lete, Gregorio del. 2014. *Incantations and Anti-Witchcraft Texts from Ugarit*. Studies in Ancient Near Eastern Records 4. Berlin: de Gruyter.
Osterman, Helen Macie. 2012. *Emma Winberry and the Evil Eye: A Prequel*. [fiction]. Watseka, IL: Weaving Dreams.
Paine, Sheila. 2004. *Amulets: A World of Secret Powers, Charms and Magic*. London: Thames & Hudson.
Palimeris, Gerassimos. 2014. "The Evil Eye." *Annals of Ophthalmology* 24/4:301
Panofsky, Erwin. 1967. *Studies in Iconography: Humanistic Themes in the Art of the Renaissance*. Boulder, CO: Westview.
Parks, Wynn. 1996. "When Looks Can Kill." *World & I* 11/10:224.
Parks, Wynn. 2009. "Evil Eye." In *Taber's Cyclopedic Medical Dictionary*. 21st ed. 2 volumes. Vol. 1: 1396. Philadelphia: Davis.
Patterson, Jean and Arzu Aghayeva. 2000. "The Evil Eye. Staving Off Harm—With a Visit to the Open Market." *Azerbaijan International* 8/3:55–57. http://azer.com/aiweb/categories/magazine/83_folder/83_articles/83_evil.html.
Pavitt, William Thomas. 1970. *The Book of Talismans, Amulets, and Zodiacal Gems*. New York: Weiser.
Padayachee, Deena. 2014. "The Evil in the Eyes." [poem]. *Poet* 6/25/2014, p. 1.
Phillips, Matt. 2016. "Malocchio. The hidden economic lessons of the evil eye." http://qz.com/491696/the-hidden-economics-behind-the-evil-eye/.
Pilo, Chiara. 2013. "Appendice iconografica—elenco delle illustrazioni." In *Archeologia dello sguardo. Fascinazione e Baskania nel mondo classico*, edited by M. Giuman, 143–49, 181–85. Archeologica 173. Rome: Bretschneider.
Plagemann, Bentz. 1962. "They Think We Have the Evil Eye." [short story] *Saturday Evening Post* 235/8 (2/24/1962) 58.
Powers, Harrison. 1982. *Evil Eye Beagle*. Watermilll.
Primitif, Georges. 1957. *The Evil Eye—A Novel*. New York: Elite.
Radi, Saâdia. 2014. "Le mauvais oeil." Chapter I of *Surnaturel et Société: L'explication magique de la maladie et du malheur à Khénifa. Maroc*, edited by Matthias De Meyer, 19–39. Maktabat al-Maghreb: Centre Jacques-Berque.
Radt, Wolfgang. 1983. "Ein Altärchen aus Pergamum für die Erinyens Megaira." In *Beiträge zur Altertumskunde Kleinaseins: Festschrift für Karl Bittel*, edited by R. M. Boehmer and H. Hauptmann, 1:449–53. Mainz: von Zabern.
Regourd, Anne. 2013. "Divination by Dropping Shells (wadʿ) [Cowie shells] in Ṣanʿāʾ, Yemen." *Magic, Ritual & Witchcraft* 8/2:171.
Rhodes, Chloe. 2012. *Black Cats and Evil Eyes*. London: O'Mara.
Risen, Jane L. 2016. "Believing What We Do not Believe: Acquiescence to Superstitious Beliefs and Other Powerful Intuitions." *Psychological Review* 123:182–207. http://dx.doi.org/10.1037/rev0000017.

Risen, Jane L., and A. David Nussbaum 2015. "Believing What You Don't Believe.' *The New York Times Sunday Review* (11/1/2015) 9.
R., J. 2013. "An Eye for an Eye." *National Geographic* 223/4:21.
Robbins, Barney R. 1934. *A Dissertation on the Evil Eye*. New York: Privately printed.
Roig Lanzillotta, Lautaro and Israel Muñoz Gallarte, eds. 2012. *Plutarch in the Religious and Philosophical Discourse of Late Antiquity*. Studies in Platonism, Neoplatonism, and the Platonic Tradition 14. Leiden: Brill.
Rollis-Tmantfillou, Judith. 1994. "Healing [of Evil Eye injury] Ancient and Modern." *British Medical Journal* (International Edition) 309/6960:1023.
Ross, Colin Andrew. 2010. "Hypothesis: The Electrophysiological Basis of Evil Eye Belief." *Anthropology of Consciousness* 21:47–57. http://onlinelibrary.wiley.com/doi/10.1111/j.1556-3537.2010.01020.x/abstract.
———. 2011. "Creencias tradicionales y campos electromagéntcos." *AIBR: Revista de Antropologïa Iberoamericana* 6/3:269–88.
Roussou, Eugenia. 2005. "*To Kako Mati: ekfrazontas ton topiko politismo [The Evil Eye: Expressing the Local Culture]*." *Ditikomakedoniko Grammata* 17:373–83.
———. 2011. "Orthodoxy at the Crossroads: Popular Religion and Greek Identity in the Practice of the Evil Eye." *Journal of Mediterranean Studies* 20:85–106.
———. Eugenia. 2014. "Believing in the Supernatural through the 'Evil Eye': Perception and Science in the Modern Greek Cosmos." *Journal of Contemporary Religion* 29:425–38.
———. 2015. "The Material Culture of the Evil Eye: Merging Orthodoxy and NewAge Spirituality in Greece." http://materialreligions.blogspot.gr/2015/05/the-material-culture-of-evil-eye.html.
Rubin, Norman A. 2010. "The Evil Eye." *World & I* 25/11:5
Saeterbakken, Stig. 2001. *Det Onde Øye* [essays]. Oslo: Cappelen.
Sainsbury, Geoffrey and James Kirkup. 1959. *Le Mauvais Oeil. The Evil Eye. Comprising the Evil Eye and The Sleeping Beauty. Translations of "Le Mauvais Oeil" and "Au Bois Dormant."* London.
Schlesier, Renate. 1990. "Apopompe." *Handbuch religionswissenschaftlicher Grundbegriffe*, edited by H. Cancik, B. Gladigow, and Karl-Heinz Kohl, 2:38–51. Stuttgart: Kohlhammer.
———. 1990. "Apotropäisch." In *Handbuch religionswissenschaftlicher Grundbegriffe*, edited by H. Cancik, B. Gladigow & Karl-Heinz Kohl, 2:41–45. Stuttgart: Kohlhammer.
———. 1991. "Mythenwahrheit versus Aberglaube: Otto Jahn und der böse Blick." In *Otto Jahn: Ein Geisteswissenschaftler zwischen Klassizismus und Historismus*, edited by W. Calder III, H. Cancik, and B. Kytzler, 234–57. Stuttgart: Teubner.
———. 1994. "Zauber und Neid. Zum Problem des bösen Blicks in der antiken griechische Tradition." In *Tradition und Translation: Zum Problem der interkulturellen Übersetzbarkeit religiöser Phänomene. Festschrift für Carsten Colpe zum 65. Geburtstag*, edited by Christoph Elsas, 96–112. Berlin: de Gruyter.
Schroer, Silva. 1984. "Zur Deutung der Hand unter der Grabinschrift von Chirbet el Qöm." *Ugarit-Forschungen* 15:191–99.
Secunda, Shai. 2014. "The Fractious Eye: On the Evil Eye of Menstruants in Zoroastrian Tradition." *Numen* 61:83–108. https://www.academia.edu/5719015/The_Fractious_Eye_On_the_Evil_Eye_of_Menstruants_in_Zoroastrian_Tradition.

Bibliography 2

Sexton, Anne. 1999. "The Evil Eye." [poem]. *The Complete Poems: Anne Sexton.* Anne Sexton and Maxine Kumin. New York: Houghton Mifflin.
Shaw, John Balcom. 1911. "The Evil Eye." *The Expositor and Current Anecdotes* 13:660–61.
Shetty, Geema. 1997. *Nazar Lagna: Casting an Evil Eye.* Honors, Creative Writing, Brown University.
Silillas, Rafael. 1905. *La fascinación en España. Brujas, Brujerías—Ameletos.* Madrid: Arias.
Simkin, A. 1998. "Another Look at 'the Evil Eye.'" *Alternative Therapies in Health and Medicine* 4/4:16.
Slade, Michael. *Evil Eye and Hangman.* 2 vols. Bergenfield, NJ: Signet.
Soar, Katy. "From the Gorgon to the Gift Shop: A Brief Archaeology of the Evil Eye." *Folklore Thursday* July 2016. http://folklorethursday.com/material-culture/gorgon-gift-shop-brief-archaeology-evil-eye/#sthash.SADuqg5k.dpbs.
Spence, Sarah. 1996. "'Le cop mortal': The Evil Eye and the Origins of Courtly Love." *Romantic Review* 87:307–18.
Spiro, A. M. 2005. "Najar or Bhut—Evil Eye or Ghost Affliction: Gujarati Views about Illness Causation." *Anthropology and Medicine* 12:61–73.
Stallings, A. E. 2005. "Evil Eye." [poem] *Poetry* 186/1:14.
Steinhart, M. 1995. *Das Motiv des Auges in der griechischen Bildkunst.* Mainz: Philipp von Zabern.
Stewart, Natacha. 1972. *Evil Eye and Other Stories.* Boston: Houghton Mifflin.
Sütterlin, Christa. 2016. "Universals in Ritualized Genital Display of Apotropaic Female Figures." *Human Ethology Bulletin*—Proceedings of the V. ISHE Summer Institute (2016): 30–46.
Szpirglass, Jeff. 2012. *Evil Eye.* [fiction]. Toronto: Star Crossed.
Tadić, Novica. 1992. "Eye, Evil Eye." [poem, translated by Charles Simic]. In *Night Mail: Selected Poems,* 35. Oberlin, OH: Oberlin College Press.
Thomas, Cherylann. 2011. *Evil Eyes. A Daughter's Memoir.* Xlibris.
Townson, Hazel and David McKee. 1994. *Who's Afraid of the Evil Eye?* Andersen Young Readers Library. Red Fox Younger Fiction Series. London: Anderson.
Trout, Lawana. 1975. *The Evil Eye: A Collection of Superstitions and Strange Happenings.* New York: Scholastic Book Services.
Vanel, Louis. 2004. *Mal de ojo y envidia: amuletos y hechizos infalibles.* Buenos Aires: Libro Amigo.
Van Straten, Roelof. 1994. *An Introduction to Iconography.* Translated by Patricia de Man. Documenting the Image 1. Yverdon: Gordon & Breach.
Vassiliou, G. 1969. "The Evil Eye." *American Journal of Psychiatry* 126/2:270–71.
Villalba, Mariano. 2016a. "Esoterismo y poder en Castilla y Aragón. Enrique de Villena y su Tratado de la Fascinación (1425) y Tratado de Astrología (1438). [Master's thesis, Sociología de la Cultura y Análisis Cultural, Instituto de Altos Estudios Sociales de la Universidad Nacional General de San Martín, Argentina.]
———. 2016b. "Cábala y aojamiento en el Tratado de la Fascinación de Enrique de Villena." *Melancolia* 1:30–50. https://www.academia.edu/29725771/Cábala_y_aojamiento_en_el_Tratado_de_la_Fascinación_de_Enrique_de_Villena.
Volpe Cacciatore, Paola. 2012. "'Cicalata sul fascino volgarmente detto jettatura:' Plutarch, Quaestio convivalis 5.7." In *Plutarch in the Religious and Philosophical Discourse of Late Antiquity,* edited by Lautaro Roig Lanzillotta and Israel Muñoz

Gallarte, 171–79. Studies in Platonism, Neoplatonism, and the Platonic Tradition 14. Leiden: Brill.
Vulturescu, George. 2015. "The Evil Eye, the Good Eye." [poem] *Notre Dame Review* 39:126.
Wendt, Heidi. 2016. "Galatians 3:1 as an Allusion to Textual Prophecy." *Journal of Biblical Literature* 135:369–89.
Wilkinson, A. 1971. *Ancient Egyptian Jewelry.* London: Methuen.
Wilson, Carol Bakker. 2014. *For I Was Hungry and You Gave Me Food: Pragmatics of Food Access in the Gospel of Matthew.* Eugene, OR: Pickwick Publications.
Wünsch, Thomas et al. ed. 2006. *Religion und Magie in Ostmitteleuropa. Religions- und Kulturgeschichte in Ostmittel- und Südosteuropa.* Vol. 8. Berlin: Lit Verlag.
Wurmser, Leon and Heidrun Jarass, eds. 2007. *Jealousy and Envy: New Views about Two Powerful Feelings.* Psychoanalytic Inquiry Book Series 24. New York: Erlbaum.
Wynne, Anthony [Robert McNair Wilson]. 1925. *The Mystery of the Evil Eye: A Novel.* London: Hutchinson.
Zizzo, Daniel John. 2002. "Fear the Evil Eye." Department of Economics discussion paper series, University of Oxord 91. Oxford: Oxford University, Department of Economics.

INDEX

ANCIENT NEAR EASTERN SOURCES

KTU² 1.96	42
Nippur Aramaic Bowl Incantation Text 30.3–4	42
VAT 10018:3–4	110

OLD TESTAMENT (HEBREW, GREEK)

Genesis	83, 87
4:3–8	95
17:1	26
23:3–20	12
23:8–9	9
27:41–38:22	95
28:3	26
32:17	8, 12
32:13–21	8
32:13–14	8
32:17	8, 12
32:20	8
35:11	26
35:16–20	40
37:8	12
37:11	95
42:1–5	8
43:14	26
48:1–22	25
48:3	26
48:16	20, 26
49:22	8, 19, 20, 25, 34, 35
49:25	26
Exodus	
2:11–15	95
6:3	26
22:17	2
33:7–11	9
Numbers	
6:24–26	8, 18, 26
7:1	18
11:29	95
12:1–14	95
12:14	95
16:12–14	95
24:4	26
24:16	26
33:50–56	9
Deuteronomy	
6:4–9	28
7:15	8, 10
15:7–11	6, 7, 72
18:10–11	2
28:53–57	72
28:54–57	7
28:54	1, 6, 7, 79
28:56	1
32:8	26
Joshua	
17:15	9, 15

1 Samuel/1 Kingdoms
2:32 — 79
4:19–21 — 40
17:38 — 12
18:6–9 — 96
18:9 — 12, 69, 79, 96

1 Kings
4:29–34 — 133

2 Kings
19:3 — 40

Job
5:17 — 26
6:4 — 26
6:14 — 26
8:5 — 26

Psalms
3 — 26
18:14 — 26
67 — 27
68:15 — 26
91 — 26

Proverbs
22:9 — 7, 9
23:6–7 — 9
23:6 — 1. 6, 13, 22, 69, 79. 81
28:22 — 1. 9. 12, 13, 22. 79

Ecclesiastes
4:4 — 69
6:4–5 — 40

Isaiah
13:8 — 40

Jeremiah
13:21 — 40
22:23 — 40
30:6 — 40
49:24 — 40

Ezekiel
1:24 — 26
10:5 — 26

Zechariah
14:20 — 29, 33

APOCRYPHA

Epistle of Jeremiah
69/70 — 1

2 Maccabees
12:40 — 32

4 Maccabees
1:26 — 1
2:15 — 1

Sirach/Ecclesiasticus
14:3 — 1, 6, 72, 79
14:5 — 6, 79
14:6 — 1, 79
14:8 — 1, 6, 7. 79
14:9 — 1. 79
14:10 — 1, 6, 7, 13, 52, 59, 79
18:18 — 1, 6, 79, 80
31:12–13 — 13
31:13 — 1, 11, 59, 73
31:14 — 79
37:7 — 79
37:11 — 1, 95
37:12 — 79

Tobit
4:1–21 — 6
4:5–19 — 72
4:7 — 1. 6, 7, 52
4:16 — 1, 6, 7, 52

Wisdom
2:24 — 53, 54, 63
4:12 — 1. 22, 79, 80

PSEUDEPIGRAPHA

Testament of Solomon — 133
6:4–5 — 23
7:3 — 22
7:8 — 23
8:11 — 22
11:6 — 133
12:3 — 133
13:1–7 — 23, 134
13:1 — 23
13:3–4 — 23
13:5 — 23

Index   207

13:6	23
13:7	23
15:10–15	133
16:7	40
17:4–5	133
18:1–42	135
18:3	22
18:5–10	22
18:15	22
18:16	22
18:20	22
18:22–30	22
18:31	22
18:33	22
18:34	22
18:35	22
18:37	22
18:38	22
18:39	22, 135, 136
18:40	22

NEW TESTAMENT

Matthew
6:22–23	1, 5, 6, 7, 59, 72, 89
6:23	59, 79, 89
20:1–15/16	1, 7, 69
27:1–26	144
27:18	93

Mark
7:22	1, 59, 79
15:1–15	144
15:10	93, 144

Luke
2:36–38	57
11:34–35	5, 7
11:34	6, 59, 72, 79

Acts
7:9–15	19
7:9	12

Galatians
3:1	1, 51, 54, 57, 59. 79, 80, 81, 82, 88, 89, 90

FLAVIUS JOSEPHUS

Antiquities of the Jews 8.2.5	21, 133

RABBINIC WRITINGS

Mishnah

Pirke Avot
2:9	5
2:11	11
5	6
5:13	6
5:19	12

Berakoth
3:3	28

Gittin
4:6	28

Kelim
23:1	28, 32

Menaḥot
3:7	28
4:1	28

Mikwa'ot 10:2	28, 32
Moed Katan 3:4	28

Shabbat
6:1	29
6:2	28
8:3	32

Shevu'ot
3:8	28
3:11	28

Terumot
4:3	6, 7

Talmudim

Babylonian Talmud

Arakhin
16a	11

Bava Batra
2b	11, 18, 31
64b	6
71a	7

75a	4, 6, 13, 14	*Shabbat*	
118a–b	8, 15	33b	13, 14
118b	19, 20	34a	13, 14
141a	17, 18	53a	30
		57b	29
Bava Metzi'a		66b	15, 29
30a	16, 18	67a	30
59b	13, 14	78b	32
84a	8, 13, 18, 19, 20, 25, 26		
87a	4, 6, 9	*Sotah*	
107a	18	36b	19, 20, 26
107b	8, 10	38b	6
Berakhot		*Yevamot*	
20a	8, 18, 19, 20, 25	45a	14
54b	12	106a	14
55b	11, 19, 20, 25, 29, 30	Jerusalem/Palestinian Talmud	
Betsah		*Bava Batra*	
15b	14	4, 14d	6
Gittin		10	6
68a	22	64b	6
Hagigah		*Berakhot*	
5a–b	17	9	4
5b	13	13d	4
Kiddushin		*Ma'aser Sheni*	
82a	4, 11	5, 55d	30
Megillah		*Peah*	
15b	13	1, 15d	28
Mo'ed Qatan		*Sanhedrin*	
17b	13	10, 28a	10
		10, 29b	4, 6
Nedarim		*Shabbat* 14,14c	10
7b	10, 13		
38a	7		
50a	33		
54b	32		
Pesaḥim			
26b	16, 18		
50b	13, 16		
53a	29, 30, 33		
Sanhedrin		*Avot of Rabbi Nathan*	
68a	33	1.16, 31b	4, 5, 11
93a	11	1.40	6
100a	13, 14	*Derekh Eretez Zuta* 6	11
101a	30	*Midrash Aggadah*	
109a	12	II, 89	18

MIDRASHIM AND OTHER RABBINIC WORKS

Midrash Ha-Gadol
  Gen 48:15 — 8
  Gen 49:22 — 8

Midrash Tehillim 87:2 — 14

Netivot Olam 107d — 4

Nishmat Hayyim 3:27 — 4

Otsar Midrashim 60b — 13

Pesiqta Rabbati 5:10 — 8, 18, 26

Pesiqta de Rab Kahana
  18 — 13
  90b — 13
  136a–137a — 13
  136a–137b — 14

Pirqe Rabbi Eliezer
  32 — 12

Rabbah
  Genesis Rabbah
    45:5 — 10, 12
    53:13 — 10, 12
    56:11 — 15, 16
    58:7 — 9, 12
    61:3 — 4, 6, 10
    76:8 — 8 12.
    76:9 — 12, 15, 31
    78:10 — 21
    84:10 — 12
    91:2 — 8, 15, 17
    91.6 — 8
  Exodus Rabbah
    31 (91c) — 6
    31:7 — 7
    31.17 — 9, 12
  Leviticus Rabbah
    17:3 — 10
    26.7 — 18, 31
  Numbers Rabbah
    7:5 — 4, 7. 10
    12 — 8
    12:4 — 11, 32
    20:6–11 — 12
    21:15 — 7

Deuteronomy Rabbah
  1:25 — 12
  6:4 — 7, 10

Esther Rabbah
  2:1 — 4, 12
  7:12 — 13

Seder Eliyahu Zuta
  9 — 11

Sefer Hasidim (ed. J. Wistinetzki and J. Freiman, 1924²), 242 no. 981 — 4

Sifre Leviticus 25:23 — 6

Sifre Numbers 100 — 7

Tanhuma (ed. Buber)
  Emor 4, 36b — 4
  Emor 6, 43a (printed edition) — 4, 12
  Miqets 13, 99b — 17

Tosefta Ma'aser Sheni 5.13 (96) — 30

Tosefta Shabbat 4.5 (115.14) — 30

Yalqut Shimoni
  1. 845 — 11
  2. 73 — 4

Targumim
  Targum Yerushalmi I (=Targum Pseudo-Jonathan)
    Gen 42:5 — 8, 15
    Exod 33:7–11; — 9
    Exod 33:8 — 9
    Num 33:55 — 9
  Targum Canticle
    8:6 — 28

GREEK AND ROMAN WRITINGS

Aeschylus
  Agamemnon
    241 — 73
    468 — 73
  Persians 81–82 — 73

Anthologia Palatina 4.243   141
Aristides
  Orationes 50   127
Aristotle
  Rhetoric
  2.9   75
  2.10 1387b–1388a   75
Aristotle (Pseudo-)
  Problemata Physica 20.34 926 b21–31   81
Artemidorus of Ephesus
  Onirocriticon 1.26, line 68   60
Euripides
  Iphigenia in Taurus 1217–18   55
  Troades 768   81
Homer
  Odyssey 4.150   89
Libanius
  Epistle 127.1   89
Petronius
  Satires 131.4   88
Plato
  Phaedo 95b   78
Pliny the Elder
  Natural History
  18.86   29
  28. 35, 39   30
Plutarch, *Quaestiones Convivales* (*Convivial Questions/Symposium/ Table Talk*), Book 5, Question 7 (5.7.1–6), *Moralia* 680C–683B
  Mor. 681E   73
  Mor. 682A   34
  Mor. 682D   34
Procopius of Caesarea Palestine
  Secret History 9.26   95
Virgil
  Aeneid 3.405–407   55
  Eclogues 3.103   80

INSCRIPTIONS, EPIGRAPHA

CIG
  4.9065b   130
  4.9688   125
IG
  14.2413.18   57, 78
IGLS
  2. 424   125
  4. 1599.6–7   105
  4.1909   124, 150
ILCV
  1.2388 (pp. 462–63)   58, 148
I. Tyre
  1.160   125
Kaibel, *Epig. Gr.* (ed. 1878)
  no. 734   55
  512, no. 1140   130
SEG
  7.232   105
  35.1558   105
  36.1313–1318   105

PAPYRI

P.Abinnaeus
  30.23–24   99
  35.28–29   99
  37.4   99
PGM
  2, P 3   105
  2, P 9.10   105
  4.850–929   23
  XVIIIa.1–4   152
P.Mich.
  8 (1951) 519.3–7   99
P.Oxy.
  20. 2276   99
P.Ryl.
  4. 604.25–26   99

PSI
  7 (1925) 825.21–22   99
  8 (1927): 180–181 (= SB 10841)   99
P.Turner
  49.4   106

EARLY CHRISTIAN WRITINGS

Acts of John   62
  Chs. 1–57   62
  19   62
  20–21   62
  20   62
  22–23   62
  22   62
Acts of Thomas   60
  5.42–43   60
  5.44   60
  5.45–46   60
  9. 82–118   60
  9.88   60
  9.89–98   60
  9. 95   61
  9.96   61
  9.99   60, 61
  9.100   61
  9.101   60, 61
  9.102   60
  9.106   60, 61
  9.107   60
  9.114   60
  9.116   60
  9.117   60, 61
  10. 120   61
  10.123   60, 61
  10.127   61
  10.131   60
  11.134–138   61
  11.134   61
  11.135   60
  11.136   61
  11.138   60, 61
  13.152   60
  13.162   60
  13.163   60

Ambrose of Milan
  Exposition of the Christian Faith
    1.10.67   93
Ambrosiaster (Pseudo-Ambrosius)
  Commentarium in Epistolam beati
    Pauli ad Galatas (on Gal 3:1) (PL
    17.352)   82
Antiochus Monachus
  Pandecta scripturae sacrae
    Homily 3, line 9   59
Athanasius of Alexandria
  On the Incarnation 5.2–3   55
Augustine, Aurelius, of Hippo
  City of God
    4.11   94
    7.21   94
    7.24   94
  Confessions 1.7.12   93
  Epistle /Letter
    1.1   94
    245.2   84
  On Christian Doctrine 2.20   84, 94
Basil of Caesarea, Cappadocia
  Enarratio in prophetam Isaiam
    (PG 30.116–668)
    16.315.16   59
  Epistles 188.8   74
  Homily 11, Concerning Envy/
    Peri phthonou/De invidia (PG
    31.372–85)   54, 67
    372–373   74
    372.26–32   69
    372.24–27   74
    372.32–376.7   69
    372.45–50   69
    373   72
    373.43–74   73
    376–377   73
    376   75
    376.8–9   74
    376.8   69
    376.10–11   72

376.10	69	Council of Elvira	
376.13–377.30	69	Canon 49	66
376.23–27	69	Cyprian of Carthage	
377.31–44	69		
377.34–44	72	*De zelo et livore/On envy and*	
377.45–50	74	*rancor* (PL 4.637–652)	63, 70
377.51–53	69	1–2	63
379–380	57	1	63
380–381	72	2	63
380	71	3–5	63
380.1–15	69	3	63
380.10–14	70	4	63
380.17–19	70	5	63
380.19	74	6	63
380.20–21	74	7	64
380.20	70	8	64
380.23	74	9	64
380.24–35	71	10	64
380.35–36	71, 72. 74	11	63, 64
380.36–45	71. 74	12	64
380.46–49	72	13	64
380.46–48	69	14–15	64
380.49–381.26	73	16	63, 64
380.50–53	71	17	63, 64
380.53	73	18	64
380.57	73	Cyril of Alexandria	
384.1–5	72		
384.30	72	*Commentarius in Joel Prophe-*	
384.43–385.36	72	*tam/ Commentary on Joel* (PG	
385.2–19	72	71.197–245).	
385.20	72	Joel 3:1–3 (PG 71.38.235d)	65

Caesarius of Arles

    Sermon 279 (PL 39.2272) 84

Catena in Matthaeum

Page 161, line 27	59

1 Clement

3:1–6:4	54
4:1–13	95
4:1–7	95
4:8	95
4:9	95
4:10	95
4:11	95
4:12	95
4:13	96
6:4	54

Cyril of Jerusalem

    Catechetical Lectures/Homilies

13.36 (PG 33.816)	149

Eusebius of Alexandria

    De Neomeniis et Sabbatis et de non observandis avium vocibus

    Sermon 7 (PG 86.1.354–357) 58, 96

Eusebius of Caesarea

Ecclesiastical History

5.21.2	57
8.1.6	57
10.4.14.1	57
10.8.2.2	57

Index   213

Life of Constantine
1.45 — 57
1.49.2 — 57
2.73 — 57
3.1.1 — 57
3.2.1 — 57
3.59.1 — 57
4.41.1 — 57
4.41.2 — 57

Gregory of Nazianzus, Cappadocia 78

Carmina
1.1.7.66 (PG 37.441a) — 57
1.1.27.8 (PG 37.499a) — 57
1.347 (PG 37.1476a) — 57

Oration 6 (PG 35.721–752) — 65

Oration 8 (Funeral oration for his sister Gorgonia) (PG 35.789–817) — 93

Poemata de se ipso
55 (PG 37.2. 1052) — 78
55 (PG 37.2.1599) — 78

Gregory of Nyssa, Cappadocia

De beatitudinibus 7 (PG 44.1288b) — 71

Encomium in xl martyres (PG 46.760c) — 77

The Life of Moses (SC 1, 282–284) 2.256–259, esp. 2.256 — 77

On Infants' Early Deaths (*De infantibus praemature abreptis labellum*) (PG 46.161–92) — 78

Oratio funebris in Meletium (PG 46.856) = *Sermones, pars 1*, in *Gregorii Nysseni Opera* (ed. Heil van Heck et al. 1992) 9.447.4. — 78

Gregory Thamaturgus of Pontus

Fragmentum in evangelium Matthaei (PG 10.1189) — 59

Gregory the Great

Epistle 14.12 (PL 77.1316) — 149

Ignatius of Antioch

To the Romans
1:1–2 — 51
2:2 — 51
3:1 — 51
3:2–4:3 — 51
3:2–3 — 51
5:1–3 — 51
5:3 — 52
7:1–3 — 52
7:1 — 52, 53
7:2 — 51, 52

Irenaeus of Lyons

Adversus Haereses 5.24.4 — 54

Isidore of Pelusiam

Epistle 2.150 (PG 78.603–604) 149

Jerome

Commentariorum in Epistulam ad Galatas (PL 26.307–438)
346–48 — 79
346 — 80
347 — 80, 81
384 — 81
385 — 81

Commentariorum in Matthaeum
4.23.5 [on Matt 23.5] (CCSL 77.212; PL 26.168) — 92

Explicatio in epistulam ad Galatas (PL 30)
847 — 79

Letter (to Oceanus)
69 — 54
69.1 — 80
77.12 — 80

John Chrysostom of Antioch and Constantinople

Ad populum Antiochenum de statuis 1–21 (PG 49.15–222)
Hom. 19.4 — 149
PG 49.195–98 — 92, 149
PG 49.196 — 149

Adversos Judaeos (*Orationes* 1–8) (PG 48.843–942)

8.8 (PG 48.939–42) 92, 149

Catechesis ad illuminandos
2 (PG 49. 240) 84
2 (PG 49. 240.53–55) 84
2.5 (PG 49. 240) 131

De futurae vitae deliciis
2 (PG 51.348) 83, 84

Homiliae in Acta Apostolorum
1–55 (PG 60.13–384)
Hom. 5 [on Acts 2:14] (PG 60.50) 54, 85

Hom 25 [on Acts 11:23] (PG 60.195) 54

Homiliae in epistulam ad Colossenses 1–12 (PG 62. 299–392)
Hom. 8 (PG 62.358) 84
Hom. 8.5 [on 3:5–7] (PG 62. 357–60) 50, 92, 149
Hom. 8.5 [on 3:5–7] (PG 62.357–59) 54, 84
Hom. 8.5 [on 3:5–7] (PG 62.357–58) 88

Homiliae in epistulam ad Ephesios 1–24 (PG 62.9–176)
Hom 10 [on 4:5] (PG 62.76) 85

Homiliae in epistulam ad Galatas commentarius (PG 61.611–82)
Hom. Gal. [on 3:1] PG 61.648 54, 59, 88, 89

Homiliae in epistulam ad Philippenses 1–15 (PG 62.177–298)
Hom. Phil. 2 [on 1:8–11] PG 62.198 85
Hom. Phil. 2 [on 1:8–11] PG 62.214 85

Homiliae in epistulam ad Romanos 1–32 (PG 60.391–682)
PG 60.447–451 83

Homiliae in Genesim 1–67 (PG 53.21–385; 54.385–580)
Hom. Gen. 14.1 PG 53.111 83
Hom. Gen. PG 54.525–32 83

Homiliae in Johannem 1–88 (PG 59.23–482)

Hom. Jo. 3.6 (PG 59.46) 92
Hom. Jo. 4.4 (PG 59.52) 92
Hom. Jo. 32.3 (PG 59.186–88) 149

Hom. Jo. 48.1 (PG 59.269) 54
Hom. Jo. 57.2-3 (PG 59.314) 91

Hom. Jo. 64 [on John 11:41–42] (PG 59.353–58) 84–85
Hom. Jo.64.1 [on John 11:41–42] (PG 59.382) 85

Homiliae in Mattheum 1–90 (PG 57.13–472; 58.471–794)
Hom, Matt. [on Matt 12:4] (PG 57.207) 83, 84
Hom. Matt. 17.2 (PG 57.257) 91
Hom. Matt. 17.3 (PG 57.258) 91
Hom, Matt. 40 [on Matt 12:9–10] (PG 57.439–46) 65, 70, 83
Hom, Matt. 54.4 [on Matt 4] (PG 58.536–38) 92
Hom, Matt. 64.3–4 [on Matt 20:1–16] (PG 58.612–13) 85
Hom, Matt 72 (PG 58.669) 149
Hom. Matt. (*De adoratione pretiosae crucis*) PG 58:838 84

Homiliae in primum epistulam ad Corinthios 1–44 (PG 61.9–382)
Hom. 1 Cor.12:13 [on 1 Cor. 4:6–10] (PG 61.105–6) 54, 59, 65, 84, 87, 88, 92, 149, 150
Hom. 1 Cor. 31 [on 1 Cor. 12:13–25] (PG 61.262–64) 70, 83, 85
Hom. 1 Cor. 33 [on 1 Cor 13:4] (PG 61.262) 54
Hom. 1 Cor. 43.4 [on 1 Cor 16:2] (PG 61.372–374) 149

Homiliae in secundam epistulam ad Corinthios (PG 61. 381–610)
Hom. 2 Cor. (PG 61.568–70) 83
Hom. 2 Cor. (PG 61.586–90) 83

Homiliae in primum epistulam ad Timotheum 1–18 (PG 62.501–600)
Hom. 1 Tim. (PG 62.518–520) 83
Hom. 1 Tim. 10 (PG 62.552) 84

In paralyticum demissum per tectum (PG 51.47–54)
Paralyt. (PG 51.49)   83, 84

Sermones in Genesim 1–9
Serm. Gen. 1.4 (PG 54.586)   83

John of Damascus
Sacra parallela (PG 96.217.25)   59
Sacra parallela (PG 96.217.30)   59

Justin Martyr

Dialogue with Trypho the Jew
30   49
76   2
85   2

Monarchia
1 (PG 6.313A)   55
1 (PG 6.313B)   55

Justin Martyr, Pseudo-

Address to the Greeks
38 (PG 6.307–308B)   55

Marius Victorinus Afer

In epistulam Pauli ad Galatas liber
1 (PL 8.1166–67)   82

Mark the Deacon

The Life of Porphyry 19   95

Martyrdom of Polycarp   51, 52–54
17:1   53
17:2   53

Origen, *Against Celsus*
1.6 (GCS 2.59; SC 132.92)   101
6.39   101
6.40   101
7.33.17   59

Procopius of Caesarea Palestine

Secret History 9.26   95

Tertullian

De carne Christi
2.2 (PL 2.800)   57

De virginibus velandis (PL 2.959; Bulhart, ed., CSEL 76, 1957:100)
15   96
15.1–3   56

Theophilus of Antioch

Ad Autolycus
2.9   54–55

OTHER SOURCES

The Book of Protection (ed. Gollancz 1912)
Codex A   114
Codex A, §5   121
Codex A, §12, p. 20   116
Codex A, §23, p. 34   27, 113, 115, 119. 120, 122
Codex A, §24   117
Codex A, §26   117
Codex A, §27, p. 38   115, 116
Codex A, §29   118
Codex A, §35. p. 47   115, 116
Codex A, §39   27, 118
Codex A, p. 55   116, 117
Codex A, §54   27, 118
Codex B, §5   119
Codex B, §8   119. 121
Codex B, §9, pp. 69–70   27, 111, 120, 122
Codex B, §10   118
Codex B, §19   120
Codex C, p. 58a   115
Codex C,   120
Codex C, §1   27, 121
Codex C, §2   121
Codex C, §19   111, 122

Divine Liturgy of St. Mark   96

Mikron Evchologion ê Agiasmatarion (ed. E. Constantinides), 1989:194–95   151

Mikron Evchologion (Small Book of Prayers) of the Greek Orthodox Church   104

Prayer for the deliverance of a child from the Evil Eye   151

Prayer for the Woman after childbirth 151
Prayer for Protection from the Evil Eye of mischievous and wicked men 104
Qur'an, The Holy 154
   Suras 112, 113, 114 154

Šapta d-Pišra d-Ainia (Mandaic "Scroll for the Exorcism of [Evil] Eyes") 42, 110
   Drower 1937:592, lines 30–36 110, 112
   Drower 1938:2, lines 2–23 111

Made in United States
Troutdale, OR
11/14/2025